A NATION TRANSFORMED

A Nation Transformed is a major collection of essays by a mix of young and eminent scholars of early-modern English history, literature and political thought. The fruit of an intense inter-disciplinary two-day conference held at the Huntington Library, California, it asks whether and in what ways the culture and politics of early-modern England was transformed by the second half of the seventeenth century.

In sharp contrast to those who have emphasized continuity and the persistence of the ancien regime, the contributors argue that England in 1700 was profoundly different from what it had been in 1640 – so different in fact as to be deemed a modern-izing society. Essays in the volume deal with changes in natural philosophy, literature, religion, politics, political thought and political economy. The fresh insights offered here, based on new and innovative research, will interest scholars and students of early-modern history, Renaissance and Augustan literature and historians of political thought.

ALAN HOUSTON is Associate Professor of Political Science, University of California, San Diego.

STEVE PINCUS is Associate Professor of History, University of Chicago.

A NATION TRANSFORMED

England after the Restoration

EDITED BY

ALAN HOUSTON

AND

STEVE PINCUS

CAMBRIDGE
UNIVERSITY PRESS

PUBLISHED BY THE PRESS SYNDICATE OF THE UNIVERSITY OF CAMBRIDGE
The Pitt Building, Trumpington Street, Cambridge, United Kingdom

CAMBRIDGE UNIVERSITY PRESS
The Edinburgh Building, Cambridge CB2 2RU, UK
40 West 20th Street, New York NY 10011–4211, USA
10 Stamford Road, Oakleigh, VIC 3166, Australia
Ruiz de Alarcón 13, 28014 Madrid, Spain
Dock House, The Waterfront, Cape Town 8001, South Africa

http://www.cambridge.org

First published 2001

Printed in the United Kingdom at the University Press, Cambridge

Typeface Baskerville 11/12.5 pt   *System* 3b2   [CE]

A catalogue record for this book is available from the British Library

Library of Congress Cataloguing in Publication data

A nation transformed: England after the Restoration / edited by
Alan Houston and Steve Pincus.
p.   cm.
Based on papers presented during a conference held at the Huntington Library
in San Marino, Calif., Nov. 1996.
Includes bibliographical references and index.
ISBN 0 521 80252 0 hardback
1. Great Britain – History – Restoration, 1660–1688 – Congresses.
2. England – Civilization – 17th century – Congresses.
I. Houston, Alan Craig, 1957. II. Pincus, Steven C. A.
DA435.N37 2001
941.06′6–dc21   00-067468

ISBN 0 521 80252 0 hardback

Contents

v

Contents

Notes on the contributors

GARY S. DE KREY is Professor of History at St Olaf College. He is the author of *A Fractured Society: the Politics of London in the First Age of Party, 1688–1715*. He has published several articles about politics and religion in the Restoration and is writing a book about Restoration London.

TIM HARRIS is Professor of History at Brown University. He is the author of *London Crowds in the Reign of Charles II* and *Politics under the Later Stuarts*, and editor of *Popular Culture in England, c. 1500–1850*. He is currently writing a book on the British revolutions of the late seventeenth century.

ALAN HOUSTON is Associate Professor of Political Science at the University of California, San Diego. The author of *Algernon Sidney and the Republican Heritage in England and America*, he is currently writing a book on the Levellers.

PAULINA KEWES is Lecturer in English at the University of Wales, Aberystwyth. Her publications include *Authorship and Appropriation: Writing for the Stage in England, 1660–1710* and articles on seventeenth- and eighteenth-century drama, criticism, publishing history, Dryden, Rowe and Rochester. She is writing a book on representations of history on the early-modern stage.

MARK KNIGHTS is Senior Lecturer in British History at the University of East Anglia, Norwich. He is the author of *Politics and Opinion in Crisis 1678–1681* and is working on a book about political culture in later Stuart Britain.

STEVE PINCUS is Associate Professor of History at the University of Chicago. He is the author of *Protestantism and Patriotism*, and a number of articles on seventeenth-century English politics and culture. He is currently finishing a book on the Glorious Revolution.

JOSHUA SCODEL is Associate Professor of English and Comparative Literature at the University of Chicago. He is the author of *The English Poetic Epitaph: Commemoration and Conflict from Jonson to Wordsworth* and articles on Montaigne, Bacon, Donne, Milton, seventeenth-century lyric and neoclassical criticism. He has recently completed a book on moderation and excess in early-modern English literature.

BARBARA SHAPIRO is Professor in the Graduate School, Department of Rhetoric, University of California, Berkeley. She is the author of *Probability and Certainty in Seventeenth Century England, Beyond Reasonable Doubt and Probable Cause: Historical Studies in the Anglo-American Law of Evidence* and *A Culture of Fact: England 1550–1720.*

NICHOLAS VON MALTZAHN is Professor of English at the University of Ottawa. He is the author of *Milton's History of Britain: Republican Historiography in the English Revolution*, and a number of articles on Milton, his contemporaries and the reception of their works.

RACHEL WEIL is Associate Professor of History at Cornell University. She is the author of *Political Passions: Gender, the Family, and Political Argument in England, 1680–1714.*

BLAIR WORDEN is Professor of Early Modern History at the University of Sussex. His books include *The Rump Parliament 1648–53* and *The Sound of Virtue: Philip Sidney's 'Arcadia'.* He is currently British Academy Research Professor.

Acknowledgements

This book took shape at the Huntington Library in San Marino, CA. In November 1996 a group of scholars from North America and Great Britain met to discuss England after the Restoration. Our explicit purpose was to challenge the conventions of recent Stuart historiography, which have emphasized consensus and continuity over conflict and change. We thank the trustees of the Huntington for generously sponsoring this two-day gathering. We are especially grateful to Robert C. Ritchie, the Huntington's Director of Research. Roy responded warmly to our original conference proposal and provided vigorous intellectual and material support throughout. This volume would not have been possible without his efforts. We also thank Peter Lake, whose comments brought the conference to a close. Though not reproduced here, Peter's remarks lent vibrancy to our collective deliberations; their impact can be seen in many of this volume's individual essays. Finally, we thank our fellow contributors for the quality of their research, the timeliness of their submissions and the patience with which they have met our editorial requests.

In a less tangible sense, this book originated fifteen years ago at the Bodleian Library. Pincus the historian and Houston the political scientist met during a readers' tug-of-war over the manuscript of Edmund Ludlow's *Voyce from the Watchtower*. Pincus was researching the Anglo-Dutch wars; Houston was tracing the republican imagination. Each was guided in his investigations by Wallace MacCaffrey. For nearly two decades Wallace has provided each of us a model, as both teacher and scholar, for combining fine-grained historical research and questions of broad intellectual concern. We dedicate this volume to him.

ALAN HOUSTON   STEVE PINCUS
San Diego   *Chicago*

ix

Introduction. Modernity and later-seventeenth-century England

Alan Houston and Steve Pincus

Later-seventeenth-century English men and women were obsessed by modernity. Some celebrated what was new and what was modern, others denounced it, but almost everyone commented upon it. Awareness of change in politics, culture and society was widespread and profound.

In politics, James Harrington famously contrasted ancient prudence – 'whereby a civil society of men is instituted and preserved upon the foundation of common right or interest' – with modern prudence 'whereby some man, or some few men, subject a city or a nation, and rule it according to his or their private interest'.[1] Forty years later 'Ancient Loyalty' concurred, lamenting the fact that 'inglorious interest' has been raised 'in my room' by modern politics: 'Interest, that over all bears sovereign sway, / Makes the friend faithful, and the rogue betray, / The soldier hazard life, and the great man obey.'[2] David Lloyd, by contrast, celebrated George Monck as following 'the best patterns of modern policy'.[3] For Lloyd, modern policy was not to be universally condemned. Indeed, it was in Monck's area of specialty, war, that many contemporaries noted important innovations. Sir James Turner, for example, castigated Justus Lipsius for preferring 'the ancient art of war to the modern one, in all its dimensions'.[4] Turner was convinced that there was more to the military revolution than the recovery and revival of ancient techniques; he believed that there was a valuable and distinctly modern method of warfare.

---

[1] James Harrington, 'Commonwealth of Oceana', in J. G. A. Pocock (ed.), *The Commonwealth of Oceana and A System of Politics* (Cambridge, 1992), pp. 8–9.

[2] *Modern Religion and Ancient Loyalty: a Dialogue* (1699), p. 4.

[3] David Lloyd, *Modern Policy Compleated* (1660), sig. A3r. Oliver Cromwell was simultaneously vilified for having designed the Protectorate 'under the notion of modern policy'. J.G., *The Sage Senator Delineated* (1660), p. 216.

[4] Sir James Turner, *Military Essays* (1683), p. 353.

I

In the realms of culture and learning as well as in those of politics and statecraft, the English began to discuss the relative merits of the ancients and the moderns. By posing the question, no matter how they resolved it, they were marking something new – even if the innovation was merely an unrequited thirst for novelty! Sir William Temple famously called upon his readers 'to judge whether the ancients or the moderns can be probably thought to have made the greatest progress in the search and discoveries of the vast region of truth and nature'.[5] That Temple resoundingly resolved this question in the negative should not blind us to its significance. Advances were being claimed in the sciences and the arts by individuals and societies as various as the Royal Society and the Athenian Society. They did not always receive a warm welcome. The Cantabrigian Richard Marsh was infuriated by the whole school of modernists, whom he condemned for asserting that 'we live . . . in an inquisitive thinking age; and what passed for reason in former times, will not do so now. Men are not to be put off with mysteries, and other things, that can't be explained; you must break the shell, or else they'll believe there's nothing in it: the vulgar exposition, we are told, is less rational: there must be a consideration had of nature, reason, philosophy, and just decorum in the several parts of it.'[6] The anonymous author of *Country Conversations* condemned 'modern comedies' because they made the 'genius of immodesty' to 'seem the soul of the play'.[7] Others thought there was much to be gained by the new rationalism and by modern learning. Joseph Walker, for example, not only sought to satisfy 'the active mind of men' which is always 'inquisitive after new things', but proclaimed his own commitment to the modern by entitling his scientific work *Astronomy's Advancement*.[8] Similarly, Robert Morden justified his new geography, written, 'according to the more accurate observations and discoveries of modern authors', on the grounds that 'all former geographies diligently compared with the more accurate observations and discoveries of late years, are greatly defective, and strangely erroneous'.[9] Whether or not they approved of it or valued it, then, the later-seventeenth-century English were deeply aware of

---

[5] Sir William Temple, 'Of Ancient and Modern Learning', in *Works* (London, 1814), III, 446.
[6] Richard Marsh (Fellow of St John's College), *The Vanity and Danger of Modern Theories* (1699), p. 14.
[7] *Country Conversations* (1694), p. 17.
[8] Joseph Walker, *Astronomy's Advancement* (1684), sig. [A7r].
[9] Robert Morden, *Geography Rectified: Or, A Description of the World*, 2nd edn (1688), sig. [ar].

cultural innovation, of new works which claimed to be simultaneously more rational and more empirically grounded.

Not only were there widely known claims for modern innovations
in statecraft and culture, but there was also a sense in which
modernity consisted in the democratization of knowledge. Whereas
Temple had lamented that 'the invention of printing has not perhaps
multiplied books, but only the copies of them', others realized that
even this recent advance represented something completely novel
and significant.[10] Charles Gildon noted that despite all of the
advances made since 'the restoration of learning' the dissemination
of knowledge was extremely limited. But 'though the treasure of
knowledge increased so vastly', he noted,

> yet the possessors of this treasure did not grow much more numerous than
> of old; so that the benefit of it reached only to such, as could go the expense
> of studying at the chargeable places called universities (few else being the
> better for this new revolution in the empire of wisdom) most of the rest of
> mankind were an ignorant generation, that bore the form, the shape, the
> image of men, and had the use of their tongue to make known their
> thoughts, but it was only to discover how very little difference there was
> betwixt them and their brothers the brutes.

Knowledge was the purview of the privileged few, Gildon noted, 'till
now'.[11] While Gildon thought somewhat better of recent developments in learning than did Temple, both agreed that knowledge was
more widely available. For Gildon this was a real achievement, the
achievement in particular of the Athenian Society.

Whether one thought the new theories, ideas and practices were
exciting or lamentable, emancipating or debilitating, progressive or
retrogressive, there was no doubting their newness. While much of
William Wotton's defence of modernity elicited mounds of criticism,
few in the seventeenth century dissented from his claim that 'the
present state of the designs and studies of mankind is so very different
from what it was 150 years ago'.[12]

Recently, however, the modernity of the later seventeenth century
has not only been criticized – as it was at the time – but denied. The
developments in state and society, in politics and culture, which
contemporaries either celebrated or castigated, are minimized or
ignored in much recent scholarship. Where contemporaries saw

[10] Temple, 'Of Ancient and Modern Learning', in *Works*, III, 446.
[11] [Charles Gildon], *The History of the Athenian Society* (1691), p. 4.
[12] William Wotton, *Reflections upon Ancient and Modern Learning* (1694), p. 1.

change, revisionist scholars see continuity. Jonathan Clark has suggested, for example, that 'a major casualty of recent research has been the assumption that there exists somewhere in our past a watershed separating "modern times" from an ancien regime whose practical implications for us can be disregarded'.[13] 'The pattern of an ancien regime State could profitably be traced back to 1660', Clark elaborates, '1688 only preserves what 1660 was supposed to have re-established.' This ancien regime – which remained vital until at least 1828–32 – had 'three essential characteristics: it was Anglican, it was aristocratic, and it was monarchical'.[14] Jonathan Scott has insisted that the 'events, structures and issues' in the period after 1660 'are almost xerox copies of events, structures and issues of the early Stuart period',[15] and celebrated the historiographical 'recovery of pre-modernity' of early-modern England. England in our period was a 'conservative pre-industrial society' in which only 'radical belief' – by which he means radical religious beliefs – could generate change. Historians, Scott believes, have been too 'deeply influenced by Marx' in their scholarly assessments.[16] The editor of one of the most recent and scholarly collections of essays on later-seventeenth-century Britain, Lionel Glassey, has followed Scott in arguing that 'fear' and 'memory' rather than novelty and modernity were the organizing concepts of the period. Far from being the harbinger of a new age, Glassey has concluded that the Revolution of 1688–89 'has something of the character of a counter-revolution'.[17]

[13] Jonathan Clark, '1688: Glorious Revolution or Glorious Reaction?' in Paul Hoftijzer and C. C. Barfoot (eds.), *Fabrics and Fabrications: the Myth and Making of William and Mary* (Amsterdam, 1990), p. 14.

[14] J. C. D. Clark, *English Society, 1688–1832* (Cambridge, 1985), pp. 6–7.

[15] Jonathan Scott, *Algernon Sidney and the Restoration Crisis* (Cambridge, 1991), p. 6. Tim Harris has recently and very usefully glossed Scott's insistence that post-1660 events were xerox copies of pre-1640 ones: 'Of course they were not – things change over time – and Scott's own scholarship shows that he does not quite mean what he appears to say . . . What we need to do is not reach for one extreme (in order to score a debating point) or opt for a bland middle-of-the-road answer (which evinces not so much intellectual cowardice as a refusal to make an intellectual judgement) but rather analyse the ways in which the new interacted with the old and the extent to which new developments and problems came to be understood (or not) within pre-existing interpretative frameworks.' Tim Harris, 'What's New about the Restoration?', *Albion* 29 (Summer 1997), 203–4. This, we hope, is very much the spirit with which the collection of essays has been constructed.

[16] Jonathan Scott, 'England's Troubles, 1603–1702', in Malcolm Smuts (ed.), *The Stuart Court and Europe* (Cambridge, 1996), pp. 21, 34–5. Scott's book of the same name – *England's Troubles* (Cambridge, 2000) – appeared after this volume went to press.

[17] Lionel K. J. Glassey, 'Introduction', in Glassey (ed.), *The Reigns of Charles II and James VII & II* (New York, 1997), pp. 4, 7, 9. John Morrill similarly has observed that after the Restoration of the monarchy in 1660 there was 'an explicit, even obsessive concern to return to the past'.

The revisionists have built their critique of modernizing scholarship on two separate but complimentary strands.[18] First, they have insisted that later-seventeenth-century English society remained committed to a deeply religious worldview. The Glorious Revolution was 'not part of a secularizing enlightenment', according to Tony Claydon, but 'still enmeshed in the spiritual thoughts and concerns of an earlier period'. Far from being modernizing, the organizing principle of the Revolution of 1688–89 was 'a deeply Christian ideology which rested upon a set of Protestant and biblical idioms first developed during the Reformation of the middle of the sixteenth century'.[19] Jonathan Scott suggests that the Revolution of 1688–89 was glorious precisely because 'it restored and secured, after a century of troubles, what remained salvageable of the Elizabethan church and state'.[20] Second, a group of revisionists have argued that if there was a new political ideology, a new worldview, which entered Britain in the later seventeenth century, then it was backward-looking not modernizing.[21] This political ideology, whether called civic republican or neo-roman, was committed to classical virtue rather than to modern political economy. The republican citizen 'was so much of a political and so little of a social animal as to be ancient and not modern', John Pocock has trenchantly argued, 'ancient to the point of being archaic'.[22] Republicanism, according to Scott, was the antithesis of 'modern politics'.[23]

What then is modernity? This question vexed social scientists for much of the second half of the twentieth century. The mass of scholarship on the subject has certainly reached no consensus either about modernity's content or about the timing of its arrival.[24] What does seem clear is that modernity consists of socio-economic, political

John Morrill, 'Introduction', to John Morrill (ed.), *Revolution and Restoration: England in the 1650s* (London, 1992), p. 14.

[18] Steve Pincus has advanced this analysis at greater length in 'Reconceiving Seventeenth-Century Political Culture', *Journal of British Studies* 38 (January 1999), 98–111.

[19] Tony Claydon, *William III and the Godly Revolution* (Cambridge, 1996), p. 5.

[20] Scott, *Algernon Sidney and the Restoration Crisis*, p. 27.

[21] This seems to be the point of Quentin Skinner's recent claim that 'the neo-roman theory rose to prominence in the course of the English revolution of the mid-seventeenth century' only to be supplanted 'during the nineteenth century' by 'classical liberalism'. Quentin Skinner, *Liberty Before Liberalism* (Cambridge, 1998), pp. ix–x.

[22] John Pocock, *Virtue, Commerce, and History* (Cambridge, 1985), p. 48.

[23] Jonathan Scott, 'The English Republican Imagination', in John Morrill (ed.), *Revolution and Restoration: England in the 1650s* (London, 1992), pp. 37–9.

[24] Miles Ogborn, *Spaces of Modernity: London's Geographies 1680–1780* (London, 1998), pp. 2, 6.

and experiential elements. There are a number of characteristics of modernity that appear regularly in social scientific discussions. These are not minimal requirements or necessary conditions; all need not be present for a society to be considered 'modern'. Nonetheless, they provide important cues for scholars interested in early-modern Europe. Immanuel Wallerstein and Terence Hopkins, in their classic formulation of modernization theory, highlighted the following: 'increases in a society's effective scale, including increased size, population, density, territory, interdependence of groups, degree of urbanization'; 'a progressive centralization of political power in national-level agencies, in particular, a growth of national-level, bureaucratically-organized administrative agencies, and a parallel decline in the scope of local autonomy and the power of local authorities', 'increasing democratization in the sense of more and more people influencing policies, enactments, and actions of central authorities', and 'a shift in the scale of the economically most self-sufficient unit from the household-village (or town-hinterland) complex to a society-wide or national economy, with a parallel increase in the economic dependence of smaller-scale units'.[25] Robert Pippin offers an overlapping but not identical analysis of modernity. Not surprisingly, as a philosopher he places greater emphasis on the experiential. According to Pippin, modernity may include the following: 'the emergence of the "nation state", a political unit constituted by a common language and tradition, with an authority transcending local feudal fealty'; 'more and more ambitious claims for the supreme authority of "reason" in human affairs, contra the claims of tradition, the ancestors and, especially, the church'; the 'demystification of life, especially natural phenomena'; 'an insistence on the natural rights of all individuals'; 'the domination of social life by a free market economy, with its attendant phenomena of wage labor, urbanization, and the private ownership of the means of production'; 'a belief in, if not the perfectibility, then at least the improvability of mankind, and a commitment (at least within the official culture) to a variety of virtues that originate in Christian humanism: tolerance, sympathy, prudence, charity and so on'.[26]

---

[25] Terence H. Hopkins and Immanuel Wallerstein, 'The Comparative Study of National Societies', *Comparative Research* 5 (October 1967), 37–8.

[26] Robert Pippin, *Modernism as a Philosophical Problem* (Oxford, 1991), p. 4. We have found similar descriptions of modernity in Edward Shils, 'On the Comparative Study of the New States', in Clifford Geertz (ed.), *Old Societies and New States: the Quest for Modernity in Asia and Africa*

These general characteristics of modernity help to locate its origins in space and time. Most, though not all, who write about the beginnings of modernity place it in early-modern Europe, very often in early-modern Britain. 'Modernity', notes Anthony Giddens in one of his more recent contributions, 'refers to modes of social life or organization which emerged in Europe from about the seventeenth century onwards and which subsequently became more or less world-wide in their influence.'[27] This is similar to the earlier assessment of Wallerstein and Hopkins, who proclaimed that 'a necessary condition of a society's modernization is its incorporation into the historically unique network of societies that arose first in Western Europe in early-modern times and today encompasses enough of the globe's population for the world to be viewed as a single network of societies'.[28] Implicit in each of these claims is the belief that the defining characteristics of the first modern societies were unique. As a result, the logic of the first instance – the explanation for the emergence of 'modernity' – is and must be distinct from the logic used to explain all subsequent instances of 'modernization'. This insight gave special importance to the early-modern period.

In the 1970s and 1980s, at the exact high point of revisionist scholarship in early-modern English historiography, modernization theory came under fierce attack throughout the social sciences. Modernization was seen as an overly schematic, universalist, teleological and potentially imperialist schematization.[29] Modernity was shown to have significant costs as well as benefits. In the context of the Cold War these claims naturally assumed a powerful ideological charge. Modernization theorists were seen as imposing a particularly Western – and often peculiarly American – model of capitalist development on the rest of the world.

These charges were justly levelled at many theories (and theorists) of modernity. All too often modernization was presented as an

(New York, 1963), pp. 2, 21; David E. Apter, *The Politics of Modernization* (Chicago, 1965), 67; Daniel Lerner, *The Passing of Traditional Society: Modernizing the Middle East* (Glencoe, IL, 1958), pp. 45, 50–1, 55, 58; Stephen Holmes, 'Aristippus In and Out of Athens', *American Political Science Review* 73 (March 1979), 115. The wellspring for all of these characterizations of modernity is the writings of the classical social theorists Max Weber, Emile Durkheim and Georg Simmel.

[27] Anthony Giddens, *The Consequences of Modernity* (Stanford, 1990), p. 1.

[28] Hopkins and Wallerstein, 'The Comparative Study', p. 39.

[29] See for example Dean Tipps, 'Modernization Theory and the Comparative Study of Societies: a Critical Perspective', in *Comparative Studies in Society and History* 15: 2 (1973), 199–226.

evolutionary process in which mid-twentieth-century Europe and America represented the point of convergence.[30] But some early scholars of modernity offered a less tidy, less universal and less morally certain vision. Modernity is a specific and highly influential form of social life. It did not emerge evenly in either space or time. Change frequently occurred in specific urban settings, leaving the countryside and other parts of the same urban landscape behind. Just as frequently changes which we might identify as modernizing were followed by others which we might see as tending in the opposite direction. Modernization need not imply simultaneous and unidirectional development across all dimensions of a society; it does not take 'a linear evolutionary form in the countries where, over an historical period, such changes eventually occur'.[31] And modernity, whatever specific shape it takes, has substantial costs. As David Apter warned long ago, 'we ought not to ignore the negative side' of modernization. 'Old forms of belief and social practices endowed with sanctity are often dismissed with cruelty and carelessness by those in positions of power. A cheerful confrontation of the future may easily be replaced by deep-rooted despair. For many, modernization is like hurtling through a tunnel at frightening speed without knowing what waits at the other end . . . Hence it is not surprising that in modernizing societies the mood fluctuates between an exciting sense of new freedom and hope in the future and a fearful, cynical, or opportunistic view.'[32] The push to modernity is accompanied by serious social and intellectual dislocations.

While any discussion of modernity implies a contrast with traditional society, it does not necessitate a complete and clean break. In modernizing societies there will of necessity be a great degree of continuity. 'Obviously', Giddens notes, 'there are continuities between the traditional and the modern, and neither is cut of whole cloth.'[33] Even though 'we can isolate, as a set of abstractions, some qualities that are functionally critical for premodern systems and others that are functionally critical for modern ones', Apter contends, 'real systems rarely change by rejecting the one in favour of

---

[30] S. N. Eisenstadt, *Patterns of Modernity*, vol. 1 *The West* (London, 1987), pp. 2–3; Samuel Huntington, 'The Change to Change: Modernization, Development, and Politics', *Comparative Politics* 3 (1971), 288–90.

[31] Hopkins and Wallerstein, 'The Comparative Study', p. 38.

[32] Apter, *Politics of Modernization*, p. xiii.

[33] Giddens, *Consequences*, p. 4.

the other. This lack of a clear break supplies some of the most confusing data that we are obliged to consider.'[34] Indeed, it is precisely these continuities, these 'confusing data', that are responsible for the specific characteristics of a region or nation. The fact that the emergence of modernity is messy, uneven and hard to specify, however, does not render it unimportant. As Charles Larmore has persuasively argued, 'an eye for continuities should not keep us from also seeing the significant changes modernity expresses, even if they amount more to shifts in emphasis than absolute breaks'.[35]

The end of the Cold War, combined with a tempering of the more extreme predictions of modernization theorists, has convinced a wide variety of humanists and social scientists that the emergence of modernity is again worthy of study. Perhaps one should not be surprised that old modernization theorists, such as Lucien Pye, have reemerged to proclaim the value of 'the early modernization and political development theorists'.[36] More significant are scholars like Anthony Giddens who, having rejected modernization theory in 1970s and 1980s, now suggest that we revisit the terrain armed with new questions and a greater appreciation for the ambiguous qualities of modernity. In a powerful recent essay Jeffrey Alexander has suggested that the sentiments that once motivated the critics of modernization theory are 'anachronistic. Modernization theory . . . stipulated that the great civilizations of the world would converge towards the institutional and cultural configurations of Western society. Certainly we are witnessing something very much like this process today, and the enthusiasm it has generated is hardly imposed by Western domination.' New understandings of democracy, the rule of law, civil society and economic markets – sober, chastened, with a greater appreciation for the ambiguities of these social forms and a clearer understanding that they are neither 'historical inevitabilities' nor 'linear outcomes' of a grand evolutionary process – have taken centre stage.[37] In this context, the persistent refusal to allow

---

[34] Apter, *Politics of Modernization*, p. xi. This problem is powerfully explored in Reinhard Bendix, 'Tradition and Modernity Reconsidered', *Comparative Studies in Society and History* 9 (1966–7), 292–346.

[35] Charles Larmore, *The Morals of Modernity* (Cambridge, 1996), p. 2.

[36] Lucian Pye, 'Political Science and the Crisis of Authoritarianism', *American Political Science Review* 84 (March 1990), 7.

[37] Jeffrey C. Alexander, *Fin de Siècle Social Theory. Relativism, Reduction, and the Problem of Reason* (London, 1995), pp. 42, 46.

questions about the emergence of modernity has potentially conservative political implications.[38]

We believe that it is time to reconsider the 'modernity' of early-
modern England. We feel that the best way to do so is through
discrete case studies. The emergence of modernity was anything but
tidy. Continuity and change were intermixed. Making sense of
innovation, particularly at this point in time, requires careful attention to local and specific features of the historical landscape.

As historians we do not take a position as to whether modernity is
a good or a bad thing – merely that it is a thing which needs to be
identified and explained. A modern society is one in which many, but
not necessarily all, of the elements described in the social scientific
and philosophical literature are present. It will have experiential and
structural elements for, as Miles Ogborn as emphasized, 'neither
accounts for the shape of the modern alone'.[39] These elements need
not be present throughout the entire society, but they should be
sufficiently wide-spread for contemporaries to have a sense of
profound change. The emergence of modernity is accompanied by
the perception of large-scale transformations. These perceptions, of
course, necessitate that the changes be both large and fairly rapid.
That late-seventeenth-century Englishmen and women in so many
different fields of inquiry thought they were witnessing the advent of
the modern age should persuade scholars to take that perception
seriously. That many late-seventeenth- and early-eighteenth-century
writers – like Alexander Pope, Jonathan Swift and a range of
Jacobites – denounced modernity does not mean, as so many have
argued, that English culture remained traditional. Rather the ele-
gance, sophistication and urgency of their arguments should alert us
that a society which underwent two revolutions in less than a century
was indeed undergoing some very profound changes.

English society changed profoundly and rapidly in the period under
consideration. Between 1500 and 1700 England's population
doubled, from less than 2.5 million to just over 5 million. London

---

[38] This has been a particular concern of Jürgen Habermas: 'We cannot exclude from the
outset the possibility' that antimodernists – both postmodern and neoconservative – are, 'in
the name of a farewell to modernity . . . merely trying to revolt against it once again' (*The
Philosophical Discourse of Modernity*, trans. Frederick G. Lawrence (Cambridge, MA, 1987),
pp. 4–5). See also Alexander, *Fin de Siècle*, pp. 24–39.

[39] Ogborn, *Spaces of Modernity*, p. 12.

grew from a compact city of 60,000 to a sprawling metropolis of nearly 600,000. Bristol, Newcastle, Exeter and York emerged along-side Norwich as major urban centres, and the number of towns with over 5,000 inhabitants increased five-fold. 'Taking the country as a whole, the proportion of those living in towns rose from around 10–12 per cent . . . to 22–23 per cent.'[40] Increasing numbers were 'masterless men', men (and women) who either failed or refused to be integrated into traditional rural and urban networks of power and authority. Between 1500 and 1700 the dissolution of the monasteries and the repeated sale of crown lands led to a massive transfer of property from institutional to private hands. The middling and lesser gentry came to own 45–50 per cent of all cultivated land. Commercial farming and production for markets, negligible in 1500, grew to dominate. At the same time, agriculture lost its supremacy as the basis of the English economy as a whole. By 1700 agriculture may have accounted for no more than 40 per cent of the gross national product, while industry and commerce accounted for up to 33 per cent.[41] London emerged as a major centre for world trade, challenged only by Amsterdam. These gross measures of development – of increases in England's 'effective scale' – were widely seen and felt, though often only 'dimly understood'.[42] As Tim Harris notes in his contribution to this volume, these changes do not all correspond to the later Stuart period. But they provide an essential backdrop for understanding the increasingly modern character of England after the Restoration.

Transformations in the state were no less profound. Max Weber famously defined the state as 'a human community that (successfully) claims the *monopoly of the legitimate use of physical force* within a given territory'.[43] Under Weber's influence, modernization has been identified with the 'growth of national-level, bureaucratically-organized administrative agencies, and a parallel decline in the scope of local autonomy and the power of local authorities'.[44] Steven Pincus argues

---

[40] C. G. A. Clay, *Economic Expansion and Social Change: England 1500–1700* (Cambridge, 1984), I, 20.

[41] *Ibid.*, II, 102.

[42] David Underdown, *Revel, Riot and Rebellion* (Oxford, 1985), p. 18. 'English society in the late-seventeenth century was still in many respects what it had been in the reign of Elizabeth . . . but it was also a society which had been irreversibly altered' (Keith Wrightson, *English Society 1580–1680* (New Brunswick, 1982), p. 13).

[43] Weber, 'Politics as a Vocation', in *From Max Weber*, trans. and ed. H. H. Gerth and C. Wright Mills (New York, 1946), p. 78.

[44] Hopkins and Wallerstein, 'Comparative Study', p. 37.

in this volume that the growth of the English state was 'decisively' affected by events in the middle of the seventeenth century. Citing Michael Mann's recent work on English state finance – which shows that it was 'only after 1660' that 'the state's financial size increase[d] substantially in real terms' – Pincus identifies the growth of the English state with the prosecution of the Anglo-Dutch wars of the 1650s, 1660s and 1670s. Economic strength and independence became 'a central and publicly acknowledged object of the English state'. James Harrington's 1656 dictum that sovereignty rests on the 'balance' of land ownership seemed increasingly out-of-date.[45] Ancient prudence was no longer appropriate to England's needs; population, not land, held the keys to prosperity and independence in the modern age. In the words of David Hume, 'trade was . . . esteemed an affair of state'.[46]

Wars bring taxes, and taxes must be levied and collected. In so doing they create potential points of conflict between citizens and their government. One of the most striking features of English politics after 1640 is the relative lack of resistance to substantially increased tax burdens. This cannot be traced to the development of new instruments of enforcement; as Michael Braddick has recently argued, 'the seventeenth-century state grew more powerful in the absence of significant institutional change'. Central government depended on the cooperation of unpaid local officials. Existing institutions were made 'more effective or more active' through changes in the self-understanding of actors participating in a co-operative social and political order.[47] English men and women increasingly saw the state as an essential tool or resource for the fulfillment of their needs. The emerging language of 'interest' helped cement this change in perspective. In 1659 Marchamont Nedham proclaimed that 'interest will not lie', and increasingly the English came to describe themselves and their polity in terms of their 'interests'. This seemed a matter of necessity. As Slingsby Bethel intoned in 1671, 'the prosperity, or adversity, if not the life and death

---

[45] 'An army is a beast that hath a great belly and must be fed; wherefore this will come unto what pastures you have, and what pastures you have will come unto the balance of property, without which the public sword is but a name or mere spitfrog' (Harrington, *Oceana*, in *Works*, p. 165).

[46] David Hume, 'Of Civil Liberty', in *Essays, Moral, Political, and Literary*, ed. E. F. Miller (Indianapolis, 1985), p. 88.

[47] Michael Braddick, 'State Formation and Social Change in Early-modern England', *Social History* 16 (1991), 6, 4.

of a State, is bound up in the observing or neglecting of its Interest'.[48] According to Alan Houston, 'the language of interest' was valued because it 'cut through the confusing and hypocritical cant of political life'. Interests were thought to be 'objective facts about men and states, distinct from and not reducible to beliefs, values, or psychic dispositions'. The language of interest dissolved old maxims and permitted the formulation of new ones. It enabled the English to distinguish between the interest of the nation and the interest of a sovereign or dynasty. It helped disaggregate military, confessional and economic dimensions of foreign policy. It also captured the growing importance of trade to English life. 'After the Restoration English people of all ideological stripes publicly argued that commerce lay at the heart of the national interest.'

Growth in the English state was accompanied by the increasing differentiation of politics and religion. This can be seen in foreign affairs: 'in the early seventeenth century the English evaluated the Dutch based on their propensity to advance the cause of true religion, whereas in the later seventeenth century' they did so 'with respect to the national interest'. Protestant universalism was replaced by nation-centred political economy. It can also be seen in domestic affairs. In a fine-grained study of James II's declarations of indulgence, Mark Knights argues that the struggle over indulgences helped 'divide civil and religious authority' by providing 'a sharper definition of the boundaries of church and state'. These changes have sometimes been captured by the term 'secularization', where secularization is taken to mean a quantitative decrease in religious belief and action. Revisionist historians have pointed to the sheer volume and variety of religious activity after the Restoration to prove that England was not 'modern'.[49] But as Blair Worden argues, the key to understanding 'the question of secularization' is to assess religion in qualitative, and not simply quantitative, terms. The English were not less religious; they were, increasingly, religious in different ways. New ideas, like Socinianism and deism, emerged. Dormant older ideas, like epicureanism, were publicly embraced. Religious life itself was increasingly identified with right conduct and the cultivation of good manners. 'Much of what we are witnessing can be described not as a decline of religion but as a change in its character.'

---

[48] Nedham, *Interest will not Lie. Or, A View of England's True Interest* (1659), p. 3; [Slingsby Bethel], *The Present Interest of England Stated* [1671], sig. A2.

[49] J. C. D. Clark, *The Language of Liberty 1660–1832* (Cambridge, 1994).

At the heart of these changes lay the recognition that 'diversity of belief had come to stay'. Prior to 1640 it was widely held that unity was part of the purpose of Christianity, and that neither families nor states could survive without the support of religion.[50] But 'the civil wars irrevocably broke the unity of Protestantism'. By the 1680s, even those who clung to the ideal of Christian unity were forced to acknowledge that the attempt to enforce uniformity on Protestants had 'neither provided political peace nor been conducive to the honor or propagation of religion'.

Faced with this fact, the English demonstrated increasing skill at separating religious belief and action from other spheres of life. Religion was a part of an individual's identity, not its single defining characteristic. In the words of John Spurr, 'in the increasingly sophisticated worlds of the gentry, the mercantile elites, the provincial towns and the cities, religious duties, sermon-tasting and church-visiting took their place as leisure activities alongside coffee-houses, political clubs, self-improving societies, newspapers, plays and taverns'.[51] Gentlemen scientists sought to protect their research by studiously maintaining professional boundaries. According to Barbara Shapiro, the Royal Society 'explicitly excluded religious and political topics from discussion to enable participants with different views to work together and to minimize problems with religious and governmental authorities'. Politicians appealed to reason and interest, not faith and virtue. So too did publicists. Evidence of lasting changes in the 'religious basis of society' can be found in John Toland's decision to rewrite Edmund Ludlow's *Memoirs*. As Worden argues, Toland 'knew that to make Ludlow a persuasive role model he had to strip him of the religious garb of that earlier generation and to present a figure motivated by political rather than religious ends'. Nicholas von Maltzahn finds a similar process at work in the 'transformation' of Milton's treatment of the heroic sublime. Milton's 'godly poetics' was 'animated' by Platonism and apocalypticism. In book VI of *Paradise Lost* Milton challenged the ideal of military heroism by portraying the causes and consequences of angelic rebellion and the War in Heaven. But under the influence of Longinus, Milton's friends and admirers divorced his 'poetic technique from his theological or moral teaching'. The religious sublime was

---

[50] Conrad Russell, 'Arguments for Religious Unity in England, 1530–1660', *Journal of Ecclesiastical History* 18 (1967), 201–26.

[51] John Spurr, *The Restoration Church of England 1646–1689* (New Haven, 1991), p. 384.

made available for secular imitation, and by the turn of the eighteenth century poets saw in Miltonic verse 'a method for vivid narrative description' of wars and battles. In the context of the War for the Spanish Succession, it contributed to the construction of 'a triumphally nationalist poetry'. Heroic poetry celebrating Marlborough's triumphs in the continental campaigns of 1704 and 1706 represented the apogee of this process. Ironically, Milton's War in Heaven provided *materiel* for an imperial civil religion.

It is not surprising that arguments for religious toleration thrived in this context. By the later seventeenth century 'more worldly arguments had come to the fore'. Toleration was good for trade; both served the national interest. But it was royal action – the indulgence of 1685 – that 'broke the equation of dissent with disloyalty'. As recently as the exclusion crisis, polemicists like Roger L'Estrange had argued that religious dissent necessarily implied political dissent. James II 'dramatically altered this equation' by defining loyalty in purely political, not politico-religious, terms.

Diversity and toleration do not necessarily imply secularization. As Worden notes, 'a voluntary religion may be at least as vital as a compulsory one. But diversity inevitably brings relativism', and it is Worden's 'impression that the later seventeenth century sees a growing readiness to describe as "opinions" what would earlier have been called "beliefs" or "articles of faith"'. Religious life was increasingly identified with the reformation of manners. Faith, word and doctrine were supplanted by work, conduct and civility.

Occupying common ground with this ethos of politeness was the cultivation of 'diversions'. During the 1640s and 1650s the terms divert, divertise, diversion and divertisement all gained currency. According to Joshua Scodel, this reflected a growing sense that all social classes needed useful pleasures as outlets for unruly passions. Scodel traces the influence of Abraham Cowley's *Pindarique Odes*, created to provide 'a poetic vehicle for diverting his countrymen from rebellious, disruptive ambitions by celebrating heroic daring in nonpolitical spheres'. Cowley praised 'heroic passivity', and hoped that 'warlike sports' like the battle of the sexes might forever replace civil war. Under Cowley's influence, later-seventeenth-century authors glorified country retirement and literary pursuits. Even the merchant was taken up as a model 'pacific hero' – but, Scodel notes mournfully, such poetry failed 'to reach sublime crests'.

New conceptions of authors and authorship gave added nobility to

the literary life. According to Paulina Kewes, the idea that an
'author' was the 'owner' of 'intellectual property' – that, for example,
a playwright owned the plots, characters, wit and words he crafted –
originated during the Restoration. In 1660 Charles II created a
theatrical duopoly in London by granting exclusive charters to two
companies, the King's and the Duke's. Each company had exclusive
rights to its own repertory. This eliminated a major traditional
obstacle to printing the texts of plays, since it did not endanger the
company's income from performances. In so doing, it enhanced the
status of the author. The play contained the literary labours of the
author; and though his or her property was immaterial, it could not
be alienated by performance or publication. Suits for plagiarism –
now seen as 'an invasion of the original author's right and a violation
of his (or her) literary property' – grew dramatically.

Ideas about women, marriage and the family were changing as
well. During the crises of the late 1670s and early 1680s, Tories
appealed to the family as a powerful political metaphor. Chaos in the
family mirrored instability in the nation; disorder occurred whenever
children (subjects) disputed the authority of their fathers (rulers). The
publication of Sir Robert Filmer's *Patriarcha* in 1679 reinforced this
line of thought, and helped cement a connection with arguments
developed prior to the civil war. But as Rachel Weil argues,
polemicists like John Locke, Algernon Sidney and James Tyrrell
refused to treat the family as nothing more than a political metaphor.
To them the family was 'an institution in which children were
produced and cared for' and 'through which the transfer of property
between generations was organized'. The concerns of this cluster of
theorists varied from the responsibilities of parents to the proper
conduct of sexual intercourse. Common to all was an awareness of
the new political economy. Healthy families produced more children,
and population growth was essential to the production of wealth in a
nation increasingly defined by trade and commerce.

Ironically, as Tim Harris argues in his contribution to this volume,
it was often the government itself that reinvigorated political passions. One consequence of the civil wars was a widespread and
'profound fear of the same thing happening again'. Another was a
heightened sense among the English that they possessed 'certain
rights – whether inalienable birthrights, inviolable rights at law, or
even obligations owed to them by their social and political superiors'.
In the minds of many, the Restoration entailed the restoration of the

rule of law. But the pinch of taxes, the imposition of religious codes, and the violent methods used to police society all conspired to make ordinary men and women chafe at the government. Many turned to the streets: enough that a new term – 'the mob' – was coined in the 1680s to describe those who participated in political rallies and demonstrations. One of the most striking aspects of the Restoration, Harris argues, is the way members of the 'governing elite' – both inside and outside of the government – appealed to those 'out-of-doors, courting the crowd, encouraging demonstrations, mass petitions, and collective manifestations of support'.

In the case of London, popular action grew out of long-standing radical traditions. Recent scholarly attention has focused on the outbursts surrounding the popish plot and the exclusion crisis.[52] But according to Gary De Krey the 'libertarian attachment to civic and individual rights' evident during the crises of 1678–81 were not 'underground' nor were they unique to that period. They were 'instead a noisy, showy, and overt element of civic politics throughout the Restoration'. London radicals constituted a 'distinctive community of discourse' that reached back to the 1640s, and was transmitted through family experiences and commitments, business connections and membership in dissenting churches. They demonstrated widespread suspicion of magistracy, attachment to their civic rights and confidence in the capacities of independent Protestant believers. At key moments – as in the contested shrieval elections of the early 1680s – they aggressively defended the autonomy of the corporation and its electors, and threatened the authority of the crown and its representatives.

England was not a democracy, and the governing elite were by no means democrats; but more and more people were 'influencing the policies, enactments, and actions of central authorities'. This is nowhere more evident than in the growing power and authority of public opinion. James VI and I repeatedly blocked public assessment of his policies by appeal to the *arcana imperii* of politics. In 1621, for example, he remonstrated with Parliament, declaring that foreign affairs were unsuited for public discussion: 'these are unfit Things to be handled in Parliament, except your King should require it of you:

---

[52] Richard Ashcraft, *Revolutionary Politics and Locke's Two Treatises of Government* (Princeton, 1986); Scott, *Algernon Sidney and the Restoration Crisis*; Alan Craig Houston, *Algernon Sidney and the Republican Heritage in England and America* (Princeton, 1991); Melinda Zook, *Radical Whigs and Conspiratorial Politics in Late Stuart England* (University Park, PA, 1999).

for who can have Wisdom to judge of Things of that Nature, but such as are daily acquainted with the Knowledge of Secret Ways, Ends, and Intentions of Princes, in their several Negotiations'. After the Restoration, the crown came to recognize that it could ignore public opinion only at its own peril. It also learned that public opinion could not be cultivated or swayed in traditional ways. Tim Harris puts the point this way: 'Queen Elizabeth projected an image of majesty and splendour to her subjects in an attempt to impress and awe . . . It could never be that straightforward for Charles II . . . [He] had to negotiate with his subjects, appeal to their sensibilities, convince and persuade – in short, he had to solicit their support by showing that his policies were designed to protect their interests and welfare.' James II learned the hard way that 'Elizabethan-type techniques for the manipulation of public opinion' were no longer effective.

Opinions concerning the actions, personnel and structure of government thrived in a variety of social settings. Print and scribal sources of information – newspapers and pamphlets, newsletters and manuscripts – circulated widely, despite attempts to regulate them. They were read silently in private and loudly in public; some were even 'performed' on street corners. Alehouses and pubs provided traditional sites for political discussion, as did dissenting churches. So, too, did the civic traditions of London; every meeting of the wardmote, every precinct assembly, every guild dinner provided occasion for the face-to-face exchange of ideas and arguments. New sites for conversation emerged. The first coffee house opened in Oxford around 1650, and soon after coffee drinking became all the rage. Preferring the stimulant of coffee to the stupefaction of strong drink, men (and women) met in coffee houses to trade gossip, share ideas, and learn the latest news from the continent. Behind all these conversations was a growing acceptance of the legitimacy of public discussion of affairs of state. With the Restoration the English public sphere was born.[53]

A favourite topic of conversation in all these settings was England's immediate past. Histories of England's decline into civil war and revolution were written as contemporary history, by men and women who had lived through the events narrated. The very term 'Restora-

---

[53] Steve Pincus, ' "Coffee Politicians Does Create": Coffeehouses and Restoration Political Culture', *Journal of Modern History* 67 (1995), 806–34. Cf. Jürgen Habermas, *Strukturwandel der Öffentlichkeit* (Frankfurt, 1962).

tion' meant a return to a former state or position, and first entered the English language in 1660.[54] But what *did* that mean? What had happened? Why had it happened? And how might it be prevented from happening again? Around these questions fierce controversy reigned. Royalists drew parallels between the 1640s and 1650s, on the one hand, and the 1670s and 1680s, on the other, in an attempt to undermine resistance to the crown. Scorched historical memories served as moral and political arguments. As Charles II reminded his subjects in a 1681 declaration 'Touching the Causes and Reasons That Moved Him to Dissolve The Two last Parliaments', 'who cannot but remember, That Religion, Liberty, and Property were all Lost and gone, when the Monarchy was shaken off, and could never be revived till that was restored'.[55] To bring the message home, he encouraged the presentation of loyal addresses and demonstrations. All of this was published or reported in the *London Gazette*. Whigs sought to deflate these claims by identifying them as part of a rhetorical strategy designed to discredit opposition. 'This is the true reason of the mention of the late War', wrote Thomas Hunt in 1682, 'that we may forgo our Parliaments for fear of another.'[56] Lest the English forget their rights, Whig publishers printed compilations of the London city charters and grants, as well as digests of the law. What matters here is not the validity of these claims, but the simple fact that they were self-consciously asserted and debated. The sheer availability of the civil war and interregnum as rhetorical resources – as a distinct epoch in English history – testifies to the transformation of English life after the Restoration.

[54] *OED* 'Restoration'.
[55] Charles II, *His Majesties Declaration* (1681), pp. 9–10.
[56] Thomas Hunt, *Mr Hunt's Postscript* (1682), p. 54. 'When [Tories] can say nothing more, they turn us over to *Forty two* for a parallel' (*A Seasonable Warning* [1679]).

CHAPTER I

The question of secularization

Blair Worden

In his book *The Secularization of the European Mind in the Nineteenth Century*, Owen Chadwick looks back to 'the years between 1650 and 1750, the age of Sir Isaac Newton and Leibniz, of Fontenelle and Spinoza, of John Locke and David Hume, and finally of Diderot and Voltaire'. These, he remarks, 'were the seminal years of modern intellectual history. In these years the Middle Ages ended at last.'[1] Perhaps it would be conceded, even by a generation of historians as suspicious of teleology as that which has succeeded Chadwick's, that the process he describes took place and was monumental; that the terms customarily used to describe it – the Age of Reason, the Enlightenment – have at least a shorthand usefulness; and that the England of Newton and Locke – and, we might want to add, of Hobbes – played a critical part in it.

It might also be agreed that the process was, at least at some level, one of secularization: that it belongs to the process described by Max Weber as the 'disenchantment of the world'.[2] But secularization is a large and treacherous word, its meanings contested for more than a century by social scientists, who invented it. Historians tend to use it in a practical spirit, again as shorthand. 'Secular', for us, normally means 'nonreligious' or 'other than religious'.

Did England become a less religious country in the later seventeenth century? To attempt to answer that question is to confront three sets of problems at the outset. The first concerns

---

[1] Owen Chadwick, *The Secularization of the European Mind in the Nineteenth Century* (Cambridge, 1975), p. 5. The extent of the change described by Chadwick was charted in Paul Hazard, *The European Mind 1680–1715* (New York, 1953: a translation of Hazard's *La Crise de la conscience européenne*, Paris, 1935). Let me thank, for their comments on a draft of this essay, Nicholas von Maltzahn, John Spurr and David Wootton – who however bear no responsibility for the outcome.

[2] Quoted by Peter Burke, in Peter Burke (ed.), *The New Cambridge Modern History*, vol. xiii (Cambridge 1979), p. 293.

subject matter. However we approach the general issue of secularization, it is not enough to stay with Newton and Locke on the high intellectual path to the Enlightenment. As Chadwick puts it, 'Enlightenment is of the few. Secularization is of the many.'[3] Its subject cannot be ideas alone; it must be society; and the relationship of high thinking to social change can be elusive. As well as the secularization of ideas there may be secularization of power – a shift in the balance of church and state or a decline in the power or status of the clergy. There may be secularization of conduct – a decline of religious observance or affiliation. There may be secularization of mentality – a decline in the part played by religion in determining people's attitudes or decisions or their explanations of the world around them; or a shift in perception from the dominance of the eternal or the other-worldly to the temporal and the this-worldly.

The second set of problems concerns what might be termed representativeness. Which people or which groups speak for the mood or spirit of an age? First there is the issue of evidence: we can hear the articulate and the vocal of the later seventeenth century, but not the inarticulate and the silent. Secondly, if an age – which after all consists of a succession of overlapping generations – has an identifiable mood or spirit, it is a fair guess that a large proportion of its inhabitants will be against it, or at least be slower than the rest to accept it. Gordon Cragg's fine short book about the history of religious thinking in the later seventeenth century is called *From Puritanism to the Age of Reason*. To begin with Puritanism, as he does, is fair enough, for in the 1650s Puritans more or less controlled politics, patronage and the press, and opinion often follows power. Yet historians have become as aware as the Puritans were of the Puritans' failure to reach the roots of the nation's sympathies.[4] Were Puritans more representative of their age than the defiant Anglicans who opposed them? Again: if, at the end of the seventeenth century, we look across to France, we see at once the high-water mark of the Counter-Reformation – the age of Bossuet – and the widespread influence of sophisticated irreligion. Which movement is the more representative? Earlier, a single age produces Leonardo and Luther: the Renaissance, which celebrates man, and the Reformation, which

---

[3] Chadwick, *Secularization*, p. 9.
[4] See especially J. S. Morrill, 'The Church in England, 1642–9', in Morrill (ed.), *Reactions to the English Civil War* (London, 1982), pp. 89–114; and Derek Hirst, 'The Failure of Godly Rule in the English Republic', *Past and Present* 132 (1991), 33–66.

humbles him. Religious movements often thrive on a sense of the
irreligion around them. Without eighteenth-century inertia, could
there have been Methodism? Is the rise of Methodism the sign of a
religious age or of a secular one?

The third set of problems concerns time-scale. If there is secularization in the decades following the Puritan Revolution it surely
belongs to a longer process. This is a difficulty for us in two ways: first
because of what would happen after our period, secondly because of
what had happened before it. The spirit of an age tends to be
decided on by posterity, which has identified the winners. There is
nothing wrong in identifying the winners. It is the historian's right,
perhaps even duty, to do so. But if we want to recreate the mental
context of the later seventeenth century it is a mixed blessing to know
that Hume and Smith and Voltaire and Rousseau lie round the
corner. Then there is what had gone before. The eighteenth-century
Enlightenment itself belongs to a story which goes back well beyond
the middle of the seventeenth century: behind the Enlightenment
there stand the Renaissance and Reformation. The only book to
have taken the 'secularization of early-modern England' for its
theme, C. John Sommerville's valuable work of that title, defines its
subject as 'the change from a religious culture to a religious faith':[5] a
change, that is, from a communal and ritual religion, a religion of
social cohesion, to one of private individual belief. Sometimes, in
Sommerville's scheme, secularization is hard to distinguish from the
move from Catholicism to Protestantism. For to him, Protestantism,
a religion which takes its stand on intellectual propositions, is more
vulnerable to disproof than Catholicism and thus more likely to
foster secular thinking.[6] At all events there is no theme that arises in
Sommerville's account of the later seventeenth century that does not
draw him back at least as far as the earlier sixteenth. From his
viewpoint the Reformation is the beginning of secularization. Yet
there is an alternative perspective too, which likewise requires us to
think back well beyond the later seventeenth century. Chadwick,
inverting Weber, calls the Reformation a 'baptism of the secular
world', which 'made all secular life into a vocation of God'.[7] From

[5] C. John Sommerville, *The Secularization of Early Modern England. From Religious Culture to Religious Faith* (Oxford, 1992), p. 3.
[6] *Ibid.*, esp. p. 10.
[7] Chadwick, *Secularization*, p. 8.

that perspective the Enlightenment shed not only its medieval inheritance but its Protestant one.

Sommerville is largely concerned with shifts of mentality: the decline of magic, for example, or what he calls the secularization of time. It would be hard to identify distinctive contributions made by the later seventeenth century to such processes. Equally the loss of secular power and social status by the clergy in relation to the laity, a process which begins with the Reformation if not before it, would not be a subject usefully confined to a few decades, or at least to the decades covered by this volume. Even if we take what may seem a more manageable theme, one closer to the prevalent concerns of this volume, the secularization of politics, the constraints of our allotted period may distort our perspective. Any political landscape left behind by an event such as the Puritan Revolution may be bound to look more secular. Yet that revolution, and the Puritanizing of politics that lay behind it, can be regarded as an aberration. Sometimes the later seventeenth century looks closer to the world before 1640 than to that of the mid century; or at least closer to the world before the 1620s, when the Thirty Years War and the crises both of church and of state at home brought doctrinal strife to the centre of politics.[8]

What happened in England after 1660 may thus have been, as far as politics is concerned, the resumption of a more normal service. Steven Pincus, in his remarkable book *Protestantism and Patriotism*, writes of the 'secularizing trend in political ideology' discernible from the later 1650s.[9] He is describing a move from a foreign policy based on apocalyptic zeal to one based on the calculation of national interest, and from the identification of popery with Antichrist to a concentration on the material aims of Catholic powers. Yet the language of the later seventeenth century which he persuasively quotes, and which can be so distant from that produced by the high millenarian excitement of the early 1650s, looks much less remote from the hard-headed vocabulary with which evangelical Protestants in the middle of Elizabeth's reign had sized up the perils from Rome and Madrid and demanded an energetic response to them.[10] Or again: historians now recognize, in the last years of Elizabeth's reign

---

[8] Cf. H. R. Trevor-Roper, *Religion: the Reformation and Social Change* (London, 1967), ch. 4.
[9] Steven A. Pincus, *Protestantism and Patriotism: Ideologies and the Making of English Foreign Policy, 1650–1668* (Cambridge, 1996), p. 447.
[10] See my *The Sound of Virtue. Philip Sidney's 'Arcadia' and Elizabethan Politics* (New Haven and London, 1996).

and the early years of James I's, the influence of the perspective brought to politics from the study of Roman history and especially of two guides to the subject, Tacitus and Machiavelli. In their insistence on the moral autonomy of politics, Tacitus and Machiavelli are secular guides. If, as can easily be imagined, Elizabeth had died a little earlier and the unresolved succession had plunged England into civil war, the ensuing polemic might have breathed a more secular language than that which would be voiced in 1642, even perhaps than that which would have been voiced had civil war broken out during the time of the popish plot and exclusion crisis.[11]

And yet, when every doubt and qualification have been expressed, the sense that something about the religious basis of society changed lastingly in the later seventeenth century will not go away. Cragg puts the point succinctly. 'Intensity of religious feeling', he finds, 'was steadily subsiding throughout the Restoration period. Earlier in the century every problem had had a religious aspect, and theological issues had been closely related to political developments.' Now 'a much more secular temper was beginning to prevail'.[12] My own sense of the change registered by Cragg was formed by archival experience. It emerged when I edited a portion of a manuscript written by the civil-war regicide Edmund Ludlow. In 1698–9 there were published the *Memoirs* of Ludlow, who had died six years earlier. For nearly three centuries the *Memoirs* were taken to be an authentic reproduction of what Ludlow had written, and were one of the best-known and most-used sources for the history of the civil wars. Then there came to light, and was acquired by the Bodleian Library, a substantial part of the manuscript by Ludlow on which the *Memoirs* were based, a document written mostly in the 1660s, early in our period, when he was in exile in Switzerland. It turned out that Ludlow's editor of 1698–9 had profoundly altered Ludlow's text. Above all he had virtually extinguished Ludlow's religious preoccupations. Ludlow's enormous manuscript, which carries the title not 'Memoirs' but 'A Voyce from the Watch Tower', is a hymn to providentialism and a work of rampant spiritual intensity and sectarian millenarianism, in which the civil wars are a microcosm of the struggle between Christ and Antichrist. None of that survives in the printed version, where Ludlow is a polite, stoical, incorruptible

---

[11] *Ibid.*, ch. 14.
[12] Gordon Cragg, *From Puritanism to the Age of Reason* (Cambridge, 1966), p. 209; cf. p. 35.

country gentleman, more concerned, in his political life, with the welfare of his country than with God. He is the equivalent of, indeed a role model for, the backbench MPs of the late 1690s who were troubled by the threat posed by the swelling of the state during William III's wars to the independence of the legislature.[13] As a nineteenth-century reader of the *Memoirs* wrote, the Ludlow who emerges from them is 'a man of Roman rather than Christian virtue'.[14]

One example will illustrate the contrast: the accounts given in Ludlow's manuscript, and the corresponding ones in the *Memoirs*, of the executions at the Restoration of regicides who, unlike Ludlow, had fallen into the government's hands: of what his manuscript calls 'the destruction and butchery of the faithfull witnesses'. In the *Memoirs*, the regicides die like Romans: in the manuscript 'those poor innocent lambs of Christ' meet their deaths like Christian martyrs. The contrast registers a shift not only of thought but of language. Describing the execution of the regicide Miles Corbet, Ludlow looks back to the trial of Charles I in 1649, where Corbet had signed the royal death-warrant. Corbet, the manuscript recalls, 'forebore to appear' in the regicide court until

the day the sentence was pronounced, at which tyme that word in Revelation 21.8, viz. the fearfull and unbeleeving shall have their part in the lake that burnes with fire and brimstone, did so worke upon him and powerfully prevayle with him that he durst not any longer absent himselfe, but made haste to come and sit amongst them, least the threatened punishment of the fearfull should be his portion.

In the published *Memoirs*, the passage becomes:

he appeared not among the judges by reason of some scruples he had entertained, till the day that sentence was pronounced. But upon more mature deliberation finding them to be of no weight, he durst no longer absent himself, coming early on that day into the court, that he might give a publick testimony of his satisfaction and concurrence with their proceedings.

Or there is the execution of the regicide John Barkstead. In the manuscript we read:

When the Lord called him forth to witness the justice of that act for which

---

[13] Edmund Ludlow, *A Voyce from the Watch Tower*, ed. A. B. Worden (London, 1978), Introduction.
[14] *Ibid.*, p. 5.

he suffered, he did it with much cheerefulness and satisfaction, declaring himselfe ready and willing to be offred up, as being very cleare in his conscience that what he was accused of and condemned for was done by him in obedience to the call of God, and the authority of the nation; and was often heard to say, and particularly the day before his execution to an emynent minister, that his great burthen then was that he ever lifted up a finger against any of the people of God who were of a contrary opinion to him; and desired them to love the image of Jesus Christ wheresoever they found it.

In the *Memoirs* the passage becomes:

When he was brought forth to confirm with the testimony of his blood that cause for which he had fought, he performed that part with chearfulness and courage, no way derogating from the character of a soldier and a true Englishman.[15]

The two voices of Ludlow, his own of the 1660s and that of his editor of the late 1690s, represent extremes. The ageing exile Ludlow, born in or around 1617, stoking, in impotent exile, the fires of his own indignation, seems a parody of Puritan millenarianism. The editor was, it seems, the young John Toland, the deist, who was born in 1670. No two religious positions were further apart in later-seventeenth-century England than those of Toland and Ludlow. But though Toland, in rewriting Ludlow, brought Ludlow's religious position much closer to his own, that was not his purpose, or at least not his principal purpose, in editing the *Memoirs*. He edited them for opportunist political reasons. He wanted to convert backbench MPs and public opinion to the radical Whig position to which he himself subscribed. He knew that to make Ludlow a persuasive role model he had to strip him of the religious garb of that earlier generation and to present a figure motivated by political rather than religious ends. Ludlow's manuscript could not have been published in the 1660s because it would have been seditious. It would have seemed seditious in the 1690s too, but less threateningly so – indeed almost comically so. There would have been a market for it (or at least for some portion of it) in the 1660s, no market for it in the 1690s. The rewriting of Ludlow registers a change in public taste.

Does it also register a decline of religious appetite? Contemporaries thought they were living in an age of declining religion. 'The influence which Christianity once obtain'd on men's minds',

15 *Ibid.*, pp. 6–7.

observed Thomas Sprat in 1677, 'is now prodigiously decay'd.'[16] This was, thought Anthony Wood, 'an age given to brutish pleasure and atheism'.[17] Many other people said similar things. A sense of religious decline, of course, was not new in the late seventeenth century or peculiar to it. Yet in that period the sentiment had a particular sharpness.

There were, perhaps, three reasons for this. The first was the burden of memory. The sense that the civil wars had been an affront to God, that society bore the guilt of it, that men's sinfulness had diverted Christian history from its proper course, crossed the boundaries of political and religious party. Secondly, there were the iconoclastic conduct and blasphemous language of wits and rakes and courtiers, together with the cynical social observation and the sexual explicitness of the Restoration stage. That spirit could be as offensive to Cavalier Puritans, to men of the stamp of John Evelyn, as to Roundhead ones. Thirdly, and for our purposes perhaps most significantly, there was the challenge posed by what was variously called epicureanism, Socinianism, deism, atheism.

That challenge was a theological one. But behind it, divines – the ruling Puritan divines of the 1650s, the ruling Anglican divines of the Restoration – saw a challenge to theology itself. Socinianism (a form of anti-trinitarianism) was a theological position. So was deism. But to their enemies those positions were postures concealing a contempt for the principle upon which Protestantism had been built, the primacy of faith. That was a fair inference. The English translation of that major work of European Socinianism, *Dissertatio de Pace*, published in 1654, had as its subtitle: 'wherein is elegantly and acutely argued, that not so much a bad opinion, as a bad life, excludes a Christian out of the kingdom of Heaven; and that the things necessary for salvation are very few and easy'. John Owen, who had been Cromwell's chaplain under the protectorate, maintained after the Restoration that Socinianism was responsible for the 'flood' of 'scepticism, libertinism and atheism' which had 'broken upon the world', and which had advanced until 'nothing certain be left, nothing unshaken'. 'The liberty of men's rational faculties having got the great vogue in the world', men were deciding 'that religion consists solely in moral honesty, and fancied

---

[16] Quoted by Sommerville, *Secularization*, p. 185.
[17] Quoted by John Spurr, *The Restoration Church of England 1646–1689* (New Haven and London, 1991), p. 221.

internal piety of mind towards the deity'.[18] Even a sympathetic
account of later-seventeenth-century religion would have to record
the developments which Owen, and his Anglican successors, recorded so unsympathetically.

The question is not whether the shift to which Owen was referring
occurred, for it surely did, even if we wonder whether it was as
extensive as he feared. The difficulty is to decide whether the process
was a secularizing one. For much of what we are witnessing can be
described not as a decline of religion but as a change in its
character.[19] From some standpoints, admittedly, that change may
seem one to a less religious kind of religion: to a religion altogether
less respectful of the clergy and altogether less sympathetic to
doctrinal systems or to religious uniformity; and to a religion which
humanizes God and thus makes him less divine. We nonetheless need
to distinguish, as Puritan and Anglican propaganda omitted to do,
between a drift, if it occurred, towards religious indifference or
unbelief and the wish to establish Protestantism on a new base. The
second was not a refutation of religion but an impulse to rescue it
from clericalism, from 'priestcraft', from dogmatism, from superstition and fanaticism. If Socinianism and deism can be seen as
destructive forces, which corroded Christian orthodoxy (or paved the
way for liberation from it), there is also a sense in which they were
meant to be a second Reformation.

At all events, generalizations about the secularization of later-
seventeenth-century England are less easy to advance than they
would have been a generation of historical scholarship ago. The
second half of this essay, which will draw heavily on the work of
others, will survey, in general and introductory terms, areas where
claims for secularization might be tested or substantiated.

One such area, the large one of politics, which figures in other
contributions to this volume, will for that reason be treated very
briefly in this one. The work of Mark Goldie, Tim Harris and others
has emphasized the continuing centrality of religious issues in the
political conduct and political thought of the Restoration.[20] The

---

[18] Blair Worden, 'Toleration and the Cromwellian Protectorate', *Studies in Church History* 21
(1984), 204–5.

[19] Cf. Mark Goldie, 'Priestcraft and the Birth of Whiggism', in Nicholas Phillipson and
Quentin Skinner (eds.), *Political Discourse in Early-Modern Britain* (Cambridge, 1993), p. 209.

[20] See especially Tim Harris, Paul Seaward and Mark Goldie (eds.), *The Politics of Religion in
Restoration England* (Oxford, 1990).

readiness of Whigs, or of critics of royal absolutism, to support the claim of the royal prerogative to issue declarations of indulgence is now seen as evidence not, or not only, of political inconsistency but of the primacy of a commitment to the toleration of dissent. And when William III and James II confronted each other in 1688, were not both men as confident that they represented God's cause as Charles I and Cromwell had been four decades earlier? The popish plot, the debate over occasional conformity, the Sacheverell trial, the Atterbury plot show the continuing power of religion to convulse politics in and beyond the later seventeenth century. The question is whether the language and preoccupations of those disputes repeat, or depart from, those which characterized the political convulsions wrought by religion earlier in the century. Was the Puritan Revolution a mental break with the past? For example, can we say that the regicide of 1649 – and the restoration of a sceptical king in 1660 – desacralized monarchy? Or did the martyrdom of Charles give new life to the divinity of kingship?

A second area is the influence of the printing press. When, two hundred years later, in the third quarter of the nineteenth century, people agreed that the tone of public life was becoming more secular, the evidence they most frequently cited was the power and content of the newspapers. It was said that the press brought the secular perspectives of politics, sport and fashion to a huge audience, which thus learned to savour the ephemeral instead of the eternal.[21] Whether the newsbooks of the seventeenth century can be credited with a comparable role it is hard to say. But from around 1641 the impact of popular print, the phenomenon to which the rise of the newsbooks belonged, brought a new dimension to politics. The press was not always and not necessarily a force against religion. Far from it. Sommerville calculates that of the books published between 1660 and 1700 which went into six or more editions, a half were on religious subjects, and that of those which went into twelve or more editions at least two-thirds were. Religion, as Sommerville remarks, was plainly the primary interest of the reading public. One of the top best-sellers of all was Richard Allestree's *The Causes of the Decay of Christian Piety*, a work first published in 1657 and reaching at least fourteen editions by the century's end.[22] Its popularity may show the

---

[21] Chadwick, *Secularization*, pp. 37–8.
[22] C. John Sommerville, *Popular Religion in Restoration England* (Gainesville, FL, 1977), pp. 30, 39; Sommerville, *Secularization*, p. 165.

extent to which Christian piety was believed to be in decay; but it
might equally well be regarded as evidence of piety's resilience, at
least among the thousands who bought the book. The Bible, and
sermons, seem to have sold in the Restoration as never before. 'Every
book-seller's stall groans under the burden of sermons, sermons',
remarked Edmund Hickeringill in 1680. Yet Hickeringill's following
words offer a different perspective. 'Sermons', he declared, were 'as
common' in bookshops 'as ballads', 'and as commonly cried about
the streets'.[23] Print proliferated in opposing ideological or intellectual
directions. If there were more religious books to read there were also
more nonreligious ones. Among the most frequently published
authors of late-seventeenth-century England, Lucretius is not far
behind Allestree.[24]

Thirdly, there is the legacy of the Puritan Revolution, a legacy so
distant from any intended by its participants. Here as elsewhere we
should hesitate to explain the intellectual developments of later-
seventeenth-century England solely in English or British terms.
Developments parallel to those in England took place on the
continent, whose mid-century civil wars were not religious ones. But
in England the civil wars irrevocably broke the unity of Protestantism. Diversity of belief had come to stay; as Locke wrote, 'the
diversity of opinions we know cannot be avoided'.[25] High-church
clergy made the last attempt in English history to impose religious
uniformity,[26] but they found little lay support. The Clarendon Code
was not, by itself, intended to convert anyone: it implicitly acknowledged the inconvertibility of those at whom it was aimed.

God, wrote Locke, 'could have none but voluntary subjects'.[27] The
movement for religious toleration did not necessarily betoken secularization, and the achievement of it – a partial achievement – in
1689 did not necessarily bring secularization. A voluntary religion

---

[23] Quoted by Spurr, *Restoration Church*, pp. 229–30.

[24] Sommerville, *Secularization*, p. 162.

[25] John Locke, *A Letter concerning Toleration* (Buffalo, NY, 1990 edn), p. 71.

[26] For that impetus see Mark Goldie, 'The Theory of Religious Intolerance in Restoration
England', in Ole Grell, Jonathan I. Israel and Nicholas Tyacke (eds.), *From Persecution to
Toleration: the Glorious Revolution in England* (Oxford, 1991), pp. 331–68. Cf. Goldie, 'John
Locke and Anglican Royalism', *Political Studies* 31 (1983), 61–85; Goldie, 'The Political
Thought of the Anglican Revolution', in Robert Beddard (ed.), *The Revolutions of 1688*
(Oxford, 1991), pp. 102–36.

[27] Richard Ashcraft, 'Anticlericalism and Authority in Lockean Political Thought', in Roger D.
Lund (ed.), *The Margins of Orthodoxy. Heterodox Writing and Cultural Response 1660–1750*
(Cambridge, 1995), p. 78.

may be at least as vital as a compulsory one. But diversity inevitably brings relativism. It is my impression that the later seventeenth century sees a growing readiness to describe as 'opinions' what would earlier have been called 'beliefs' or 'articles of faith'. Locke taught men what, after the collisions of certainties during the Puritan Revolution, they were perhaps ready to learn: that there are few things we can be certain about.[28] The word 'opinion', though it can be used pejoratively, also acquires a respectful usage. 'Sincerity', a word increasingly used with something like its modern meaning, can be as important as truth, even indistinguishable from it[29] (though that view, like most later-seventeenth-century perspectives which remind us of twentieth-century ones, provoked its own reaction[30]). Alongside the respect for 'opinion' we find the respectful use of the adjective 'internal' to describe the religion which a man keeps to himself. We catch the mood in Edmund Ludlow's *Memoirs* of 1698–9, where Ludlow's own long account of the spiritual exclamations with which the regicides John Jones and Adrian Scrope prepared themselves for death in 1660 is reduced to the remark that 'the gravity and gracefull meen of these ancient gentlemen' was 'accompanied with visible marks of fortitude and internal satisfaction'.[31] Puritans had emphasized inner religious experience, which was intense: their successors gave weight to inner religious reflection, which was philosophical. The new sentiment begins not with God's characteristics but with man's. In the earlier and mid-seventeenth century, religious nonconformists who invoked their consciences to defend their nonconformity were told that the conscience could err. By the later seventeenth century that charge was harder to sustain. My conscience becomes less a property leased to me by God, on his terms, more a property of my own.

The civil wars left behind them a profound reaction against what was called 'enthusiasm': indeed against all forms of religious expression which strained the nervous system. The marquis of Halifax warned his daughter not to emulate those 'who have an aguish devotion, hot and cold fits, long intermissions, and violent raptures. This unevenness is by all means to be avoided.' Severity and gloom

---

[28] Cf. Cragg, *From Puritanism to the Age of Reason*, p. 230.
[29] Cf. Locke, *Letter concerning Toleration*, p. 41; John Locke, *The Reasonableness of Christianity*, ed. I. T. Ramsey (London, 1958), p. 67.
[30] Cf. Goldie, 'Theory of Religious Intolerance', p. 346.
[31] Ludlow, *Voyce*, p. 7.

went out of fashion too, at least in some quarters. 'Devotion', Halifax thought, was of 'very little efficacy' when it was not a 'pleasure', for while religious 'duties are joys it is evidence of their being sincere; but when they are a penance it is a sign that your nature maketh some resistance'. 'Religion is a cheerful thing,' he remarked, 'so far from being always at cuffs with good humour that it is inseparably united to it. Nothing unpleasant belongs to it, though the spiritual cooks have done their unskilful part to give an ill relish to it.'[32] There is a new recognition of the proper place in religion of decorum, politeness, courtesy. True religion, explained the preacher Isaac Barrow, revealed itself in 'real courtesy, gentleness and affability', not in 'a sour and peevish humour'.[33]

We find, in the later seventeenth century, a growing sense that religion should be what civilizes us; that it should have less to say about salvation and more about integrity in our dealings with ourselves and others; that the test of a doctrine is not its truth but its usefulness to that human end. That outlook was not new. It characterizes, for example, Ben Jonson and his friends early in the century. In Jonson's poem 'To Penshurst', the children of the lord and lady of the house 'are and have been taught religion; thence / Their gentler spirits have sucked innocence'. What matters is the ethical and social efficacy of Penshurst's religion, not its content. But by the later seventeenth and early eighteenth centuries such perspectives can be found not only among the laity but among the clergy. The 'confident' assertion of dogma, thought the Restoration divine Joseph Glanvill, signifies 'ill manners'.[34] Among the laity the social priorities of religion became ever more marked. For *The Spectator*, the virtues of church-going have more to do with social cohesion than with worship. Church-going also becomes a function of fashion. John Spurr, the historian of the Restoration church, explains how 'in the increasingly sophisticated worlds of the gentry, the mercantile elites, the provincial towns and the cities, religious duties, sermon-tasting and church-visiting took their place as leisure activities alongside coffee-houses, political clubs, self-improving societies, newspapers, plays and taverns'.[35]

Alongside social change there was intellectual change. Religion

---

[32] Halifax, *Complete Works*, ed. J. Kenyon (Harmondsworth, 1969), pp. 274-5.
[33] C. H. Sisson ed., *The English Sermon*, vol. II *1650–1750* (Cheadle, Cheshire, 1976), pp. 72–3.
[34] Cragg, *From Puritanism to the Age of Reason*, p. 224.
[35] Spurr, *Restoration Church*, p. 384.

became the friend of reason and rationality. Reason, which in mid century had been suspected as the rival of faith, was now held to be its harmonious partner. Toleration, wrote Locke, was 'agreeable to the gospel of Christ, and to the genuine reason of mankind'; it was what 'the gospel enjoins' and 'reason directs'; 'we have from [Christ] a full and sufficient rule for our direction, and conformable to that of reason'.[36] Reason could mean many things, but it tended to mean two things above all: first, the process of ratiocination (which is the modern meaning); second, a divine light, or 'the very voice of God',[37] placed in our souls by him to awaken us to virtue and reverence. Over the later seventeenth century the first meaning advances, the second retreats.[38] Many clergy, Anglican and Puritan, were horrified by the appeal of what they had long been accustomed to call 'carnal reason': it would lead, they thought, to the 'natural religion' of the deists, 'which men might know, and should be obliged unto, by the mere principles of reason . . . without the help of revelation'.[39] Reason could seem the enemy not only of revelation but of mystery; or at least, those who commended the application of reason to religion were increasingly disposed to argue that where religion was mysterious its mysteries were best left to God. Here too the reaction against the Puritan Revolution – this time, against its murkiness and exaltation of language – played its part, fostering a growing mistrust of metaphor, producing pleas for a plain, lucid, explicit, unambiguous prose, and encouraging a reaction against the flights – often the spiritual flights – of metaphysical poetry and a preference for the measured control of the heroic or rhymed couplet.

Reason had another enemy too: the uncritical acceptance of authority. The sanctions of time and custom and inherited wisdom, those foundations of the church of England, were under threat, not least from Lockean political thought, which repudiated appeals from what has been to what ought to be. If Christianity took its stand on reason it might be destroyed by it. In 1672 Sir Charles Wolseley, who in his twenties had served on Oliver Cromwell's council, provided a 'rational justification' of the Christian religion called *The Reasonableness of Scripture-Belief*. Two decades later there followed John

---

[36] Locke, *Letter concerning Toleration*, pp. 17, 27; Locke, *Reasonableness*, p. 63.
[37] Cragg, *From Puritanism to the Age of Reason*, p. 42 (quoting Benjamin Whichcote).
[38] Isabel Rivers, *Reason, Grace and Sentiment: a Study of the Language of Religion and Ethics in England 1660–1780*, vol. I: *Whichcote to Wesley* (Cambridge, 1991), p. 63.
[39] Spurr, *Restoration Church*, p. 251 (quoting John Wilkins).

Locke's *The Reasonableness of Christianity* and John Toland's *Christianity not Mysterious*. Once people have come to think that Christianity is reasonable and not mysterious, it may not be long before they decide that there are still more reasonable and still less mysterious positions than Christianity to adopt. Wolseley unwittingly gave a hostage to the future by offering to abandon his claims for 'the reasonableness of scripture-belief' if anyone could 'palpably disprove any one matter of fact in the history of the Bible'.[40]

Yet when Locke wrote *The Reasonableness of Christianity* his purpose, of course, was to fortify Christianity, not to undermine it. It had been the mischief of the priests, he thought, to 'exclude reason from having anything to do in religion'.[41] Like others he wanted to rescue religion from irrationality. It had become necessary, explained Bishop Burnet, 'to make all people feel the reasonableness of the truths, as well as of the precepts of the Christian religion'.[42] 'There is nothing so intrinsically rational', concurred Benjamin Whichcote, 'as religion is.'[43] If spokesmen for reason saw themselves as the allies of Christianity, so did another group whom again, with the long term in mind, we may regard as friends to secularity, the new scientists. To recall their priorities we need think only of Robert Boyle, whose 'main design', in his 'enquiries into nature', 'was to raise in himself and others, vaster thoughts of the greatness and glory, and of the wisdom and goodness of God'; and who in his will provided for eight annual sermons 'for proving the Christian religion against notorious infidels', and expressed the wish that the members of the Royal Society might have 'a happy success in their laudable attempts to discover the true nature of the works of God';[44] or of Isaac Newton, who 'had an eye upon such principles as might work with considering men for the belief in the deity'.[45] The telescope and microscope enhanced people's wonder at the beauty and design of God's work.[46]

Even so, when Joseph Glanvill explained that the activities of the Royal Society were the allies, not the enemies, of Christian faith, he was conscious of the body of opinion or prejudice that supposed otherwise.[47] The new science called for intellectual adjustment

---

[40] Worden, 'Toleration', p. 232.   [41] Locke *Reasonableness*, p. 57.
[42] Cragg, *From Puritanism to the Age of Reason*, p. 81.
[43] Rivers, *Reason, Grace and Sentiment*, p. 65.
[44] Cragg, *From Puritanism to the Age of Reason*, pp. 100, 107, 109.
[45] Frederick Nussbaum, *The Triumph of Science and Reason 1660–1685* (New York, 1962), p. 3.
[46] Marjorie Nicolson, *Science and Imagination* (Ithaca, NY, 1956), pp. 223ff.
[47] Cragg, *Puritanism and Liberty*, pp. 94–5.

amongst believers. First, much preaching and clerical publication remained rooted in the old cosmology. Though the new science made some inroads among the clergy and in the universities, for most divines the earth remained the centre of the universe, situated beneath heaven and above hell.[48] Secondly, while the scientists represented science as the ally of religion, they followed Bacon in wanting to keep the two logically separate. If God is the first cause and men study second causes, God's place in intellectual discussion will be diminished. Thirdly, the new science discredited the supernatural. If the universe operates like clockwork, or if God's majesty is to be deduced from the regularities rather than the irregularities of nature,[49] what room was there for the special providences, the interventions in daily life, traditionally ascribed to God? And what of the prodigies, earthquakes, storms, comets, and so on which Protestants had always taken as evidence of divine anger or admonition, and which it was ever easier, and seemed ever more sensible, to explain as natural phenomena? In Ludlow's manuscript those divine prodigies are ubiquitous: in his published *Memoirs* they have no place.[50] Equally, the parochialism betrayed by the supposition that God would condescend to decide the result of a battle, or to express a preference for the rule of one king rather than another, a parochialism derided by Pierre Bayle,[51] began to have its English critics too. There was mounting criticism also of the presumptuousness of detections of special providences. 'Take heed', Halifax advised his daughter, 'of running into that common error of applying God's judgements upon particular occasions. Our weights and measures are not competent to make the distribution either of his mercy or his justice; he hath thrown a veil over these things, which makes it not only an impertinence but a kind of sacrilege for us to give sentence in them without his commission.'[52] Halifax's voice may be no more representative of his time than those which expressed the 'common error' he scorned. Yet the assurance behind his scepticism heralds a new age.

A God who does not intervene in the events of this world is a more distant God. He is also a less frightening one. Our period sees a movement towards a gentler, kinder God. Commentators on God's

[48] *Ibid.*, p. 5.   [49] Sommerville, *Secularization*, p. 155.
[50] Ludlow, *Voyce*, p. 10.
[51] Hazard, *European Mind*, pp. 188–9.
[52] Halifax, *Complete Works*, p. 276.

providence say less about its omnipotence, more about its benevolence.[53] Sermons and works of theology (it seems) cite the Old Testament less, the New Testament more, though the change is more conspicuous among Anglicans than dissenters.[54] The world became less a vale of tears, more a place where a happiness approved by God might be secured. In the hands of Tillotson the Old Testament text 'Righteousness exalteth a nation', which in the previous generation had been an injunction to the English to behave as a chosen nation, was paraphrased as: 'religion and virtue are the great causes of public happiness and prosperity'.[55] The afterlife, too, assumed a more cheerful prospect. The doctrine of Hell, of the eternity of damnation, lost much of its force in the later seventeenth century, as D. P. Walker showed;[56] so did the more strident forms of millenarianism.[57] There was less talk of the devil. The persecution of witches declined, along with demonology.[58] 'We conceive the God of the Christians', wrote Burnet, 'to be a wise and good deity, not cruel or hostile to human nature.'[59] From an old-fashioned Puritan perspective, even from an old-fashioned Anglican one, God was getting soft. A Puritan MP had complained in 1650 that Socinians 'suppose him to be a good easy and indulgent God, content with anything'.[60] By the late seventeenth century the same MP would have found a much wider spectrum of opinion at which to direct that complaint. As God came to seem gentler and kinder, so did man. Witchcraft prosecutions and the use of torture in judicial proceedings declined.[61] Less was said about man's natural sinfulness, more about his natural sociability.[62] Human nature was becoming more a cause for self-satisfaction, less one for shame. The judge Matthew Hale believed that 'as the *credenda*', the required beliefs, of Christianity 'are but few and plain, so the *facienda*, or things to be done, are such as do truly ennoble and advance the humane nature'.[63] The ennoblement and

---

[53] Sommerville, *Secularization*, p. 186; Sommerville, *Popular Religion*, pp. 69, 75ff.
[54] Sommerville, *Popular Religion*, p. 65.
[55] Sisson, *English Sermon*, p. 192.
[56] D. Walker, *The Decline of Hell* (London, 1964).
[57] Cf. William Lamont, *Godly Rule* (London, 1969), ch. 5; Goldie, 'Priestcraft', p. 214.
[58] Sommerville, *Popular Religion*, p. 74.
[59] Quoted by Walker, *Decline of Hell*, p. 165.
[60] Quoted by Worden, 'Toleration', p. 204.
[61] Christopher Hill, 'Freethinking and Libertinism: the Legacy of the English Revolution', in Lund, *Margins of Orthodoxy*, p. 59.
[62] Rivers, *Reason, Grace and Sentiment*, p. 77.
[63] Worden, 'Toleration', p. 231.

advancement of 'the humane nature' had not seemed a legitimate or attainable goal to Calvinists. By the eighteenth century the revolution seemed complete. 'It is . . . quite unfashionable', lamented John Wesley, 'to say anything to the disparagement of human nature.'[64]

The gap between the world and the spirit was narrowing, the tension between this world and the next relaxing. Earlier in the century, piety and devotion had pulled in the opposite direction to interest. In our period that changed. 'Surely', observed Tillotson in 1675, 'nothing is more likely to prevail with wise and considerate men to become religious, than to be thoroughly convinced that religion and happiness, our duty and our interest, are really but one and the same thing.' 'Every man', he thought, 'is led by interest', and religion is 'the greatest friend to our temporal interests'. John Wilkins made the same point: 'when and where the true religion is publickly professed . . . the profession of religion will be so far from hindring, that it will rather promote a man's secular advantage'.[65]

A parallel shift is visible in the framing of arguments for religious toleration. Before the later seventeenth century, arguments for liberty of conscience had been couched almost exclusively in theological terms. Persecution, which its supporters claimed would save souls from eternal perdition, was held by its opponents to imperil it.[66] By the later seventeenth century more worldly arguments had come to the fore. Not least there was the argument, which in mid century had been voiced, if at all, only as an aside, that toleration would be good for trade,[67] a plea that gained momentum after the Clarendon Code had driven so many dissenters out of public life or the universities and into trade. Liberty of conscience, proclaimed Slingsby Bethel, was 'absolutely and indispensably necessary, for . . . advancing the trade and wealth of the kingdom': persecution, he said, was a 'philosophy of poverty'.[68] John Owen, who would have been horrified by such an argument in the 1650s, advanced it after the Restoration. Owen shifted his ground on another front too. In the Puritan Revolution he

---

[64] Rivers, *Reason, Grace and Sentiment*, p. 229.

[65] *Ibid.*, pp. 25, 84, 85. The advance of 'interest' is related by J. A. W. Gunn, *Politics and the Public Interest in the Seventeenth Century* (London, 1969).

[66] Worden, 'Toleration'.

[67] A. A. Seaton, *The Theory of Toleration under the Later Stuarts* (Cambridge, 1911), *q.v.* 'Toleration, economic arguments in favour of'; Cragg, *Puritanism*, p. 223.

[68] Mark Goldie, 'The Huguenot Experience and the Problem of Toleration in Restoration England', in C. E. J. Caldicott, H. Gough and J. Pitton (eds.), *The Huguenots and Ireland* (Glendale, IL, 1987), p. 182.

had taken liberty of conscience to be a right owing not to man but to God. Now he anticipated Locke's plea that 'liberty of conscience is every man's natural right', appealing to a Lockean argument about the origins of society and claiming, in Lockean terms, that it is a law of nature to permit divergencies from uniformity.[69]

But if there is one religious change above all characterized by the later seventeenth century, it is the retreat of theology, and the concomitant shift of Protestantism from a religion of faith towards a religion of works. This is a long-term trend, though, like many long-term trends, it may have been dependent on local short-term circumstances: how different the history of England might have been had Charles II been a king interested in theological controversy. But the great age of theological controversy was past. The epic quarrel between Calvinists and Arminians was dead. To the young, explains Spurr, its 'old-fashioned' preoccupations were 'fast becoming incomprehensible'.[70] In England, as in the Netherlands and in the Huguenot communities of France, Arminianism, of a watered-down kind, won out. Most Anglicans and most dissenters settled for an innocuous middle way.[71] With regard to doctrine, John Owen acknowledged to Stillingfleet, 'the sober Protestant people of England [are] of one mind'[72] – a striking statement, coming as it did from that embattled champion of Calvinism against Arminianism a generation earlier. From the 1650s, both on the Puritan side, where Richard Baxter took the lead, and on the Anglican one, where Henry Hammond took it, there was ever more emphasis on practical Christianity.[73] 'When men confine religion to speculation', observed Sir Charles Wolesley, 'they turn divinity into metaphysics, where they dispute without end: to reduce it to practice, is to pursue its proper tendency, and to make it (as indeed it is) the great principle of union and peace.' To attain salvation, he wrote, we need only 'live a sober, righteous, religious life here, such as is rationally best for ourselves, and others, and be gradually preparing for those eternal fruitions

---

[69] Cragg, *From Puritanism*, pp. 223–4; Goldie, 'Priestcraft', pp. 230–1; Locke, *Letter concerning Toleration*, p. 65. There is telling material on this question, as on others raised in this essay, in an unpublished paper by John Spurr, 'Conscience, Oaths and Toleration in Seventeenth-Century England'.

[70] Spurr, *Restoration Church*, pp. 316–17.

[71] Cragg, *From Puritanism*, pp. 26, 30; Spurr, *Restoration Church*, pp. 314ff.; Rivers, *Reason, Grace and Sentiment*, 24.

[72] Cragg, *Puritanism and Reason*, p. 20.

[73] On the Anglican side see Rivers, *Reason, Grace and Sentiment*, pp. 18ff. See too Spurr, *Restoration Church*, pp. 316–17.

that are to come'.[74] The test of Christianity became good conduct, not right belief.

That shift is not evidence, at least among those who articulated it, of religious indifference. It reflects the sense, across the doctrinal and ecclesiological spectrum, that the theological disputes of the inter-regnum had discredited religion, and that, if religion were to be saved, moral reformation must take the place of doctrinal conflict. Locke implied that men's morals were more important than 'doc-trines'. 'True religion', he said, is 'instituted . . . to the regulating of men's lives according to the rules of virtue and piety'; 'such a complete rule of life' as that of the apostles, 'as the wisest men must acknowledge, tends entirely to the good of mankind', and 'all would be happy, if all would practise it'.[75] Such views did not advance without opposition. From the 1650s to the 1690s there is a recurrent chorus of protest against the religion of, in the common term of the time, 'mere morality'; but that was how the tide was running. The word 'grace' changed its meaning, or at least its resonances. In a process so well described by Isabel Rivers, it became almost synon-ymous with virtue.[76] It had been the failing of priests, observed Locke, 'that religion was every where distinguished from, and preferred to virtue'.[77] That was a bridge which John Owen would not cross: the distinction between grace and virtue, he insisted in 1669, was 'the known and avowed religion of Christianity';[78] but in that as in so much else, Owen felt himself to be rowing against the current.

If we see the later seventeenth century through Owen's eyes, it will seem a time of religious loss. Many modern writers see it as one. The Restoration is portrayed as an era of diminished spiritual vision and achievement.[79] Here, for once, history has been written on behalf more of the losers than of the winners. We are more likely to think about the rising religious trends, Socinianism and deism, in terms of what their adherents did not believe than of what they did. We suspect those adherents of believing even less than they said they believed. We are conscious, rightly so, of the constraints within which people spoke and published; of the readiness of writers to convey

---

[74] Worden, 'Toleration', p. 231.
[75] Locke, *Toleration*, pp. 13, 16; Locke, *Reasonableness*, p. 67.
[76] Rivers, *Reason, Grace and Sentiment*, pp. 74–5, 76–7; cf. pp. 26, 37.
[77] Locke, *Reasonableness*, p. 60.
[78] Rivers, *Reason, Grace and Sentiment*, pp. 140–1.
[79] See e.g. Cragg, *From Puritanism*, p. 10; Sommerville, *Popular Religion*, p. 73; cf. Sisson, *English Sermon*, pp. 13–16, 19.

between rather than in the lines opinions which might provoke
punishment or censorship or disfavour or which they thought should
be confined to an esoteric audience and hidden from an exoteric one.
So in religious unorthodoxy we look for signs of atheism. Yet few
historians now contend that the later seventeenth century produced
much atheism in the sense in which we understand the term.[80]

What it did produce were religious perspectives far distant from
those supported by authority. It produced the 'natural religion' of
Charles Blount and the deists. And it produced the philosophy which
has been opened up by Mark Goldie and Justin Champion: the 'civil
religion' of the republican James Harrington, who wrote at the outset
of our period, and of his successors Walter Moyle and John Toland
and Robert Molesworth, who wrote at and after the end of it.[81]
When, in 1659, we find Harrington's friend and fellow-republican
Henry Neville getting into trouble in parliament for having allegedly
declared that he would sooner read Cicero than the Bible,[82] our
initial response may be to suspect him of atheism or frivolity or both.
Yet the civil religion of the ancient Romans held a powerful appeal to
the seventeenth century.[83] Religion and citizenship, maintained
republicans, were properly inseparable. It was the clergy, and the
dogma and superstition of priestcraft, that had separated them.

The test of a civil religion is not whether it is true but whether it is
useful: citizenship is the real divinity of man, and a man should be
encouraged to hold whatever apprehension of the deity makes him a
good citizen. What doctrinal beliefs the republicans themselves held it
is hard to be sure. But their perspective is only an extreme form of the
transforming tendency evident within orthodox Christianity across the
post-Restoration period: the shift of emphasis from faith to conduct.[84]

---

[80] The complexities of that subject are explored in Michael Hunter and David Wootton (eds.),
    Atheism from the Reformation to the Enlightenment (Oxford, 1992). See too Goldie, 'Priestcraft',
    p. 211; Lund, *Margins of Orthodoxy*, 'Introduction', p. 6; and, for a different perspective, David
    Berman, *A History of British Atheism from Hobbes to Russell* (London, 1988).
[81] Goldie, 'Priestcraft'; Goldie, 'The Civil Religion of James Harrington', in Anthony Pagden
    (ed.), *The Languages of Political Theory in Early-Modern Europe* (Cambridge, 1987); Justin
    Champion, *The Pillars of Priestcraft Shaken: the Church of England and its Enemies* (Cambridge,
    1992). Cf. Blair Worden, 'English Republicanism', in J. H. Burns (ed.), *The Cambridge History
    of Political Thought 1450–1700* (Cambridge, 1991), pp. 473–4; Worden, Part 1 of David
    Wootton (ed.), *Republicanism. Liberty and Commercial Society 1649–1776* (Stanford and
    Cambridge, 1994), pp. 105, 112, 190–1.
[82] Caroline Robbins (ed.), *Two English Republican Tracts* (Cambridge, 1969), p. 9n.
[83] Cf. Goldie, 'Priestcraft', p. 211; and see Peter N. Miller, *Defining the Common Good: Empire,
    Religion and Philosophy in Eighteenth-Century Britain* (Cambridge, 1994), pp. 91, 267.
[83] Tony Claydon's *William III and the Godly Revolution* (Cambridge, 1996) points at this transition.

CHAPTER 2

'Meer religion' and the 'church–state' of Restoration England: the impact and ideology of James II's declarations of indulgence[1]

Mark Knights

I

Religion was one of the key rallying cries of the Revolution, but what did contemporaries think it was and was their definition changed by the reign of the Catholic James II? This chapter will attempt to show how James's indulgences marked a turning point in discussions about religious truth. It will suggest that, while the abandonment of the enforcement of the penal laws was only part of a separation of church and state, a process that was to take many more years, the indulgences did help to divide civil and religious authority. Part of that shift hinged on a sharper definition of the boundaries of church and state. This fostered a more secular rhetoric about religion but, I shall argue, this had also been inherent in the way in which the penal laws were justified.

As a result of the legislation passed between 1661 and 1665 church and state were yoked back together after the mid-century crisis had split them apart.[2] The Restoration therefore heralded the reassertion of the political role of the church and the role of the king-in-parliament as defender of the faith. Yet the resulting 'church–state', as some dissenters called it,[3] acted not as the arbiter between

---

[1] I am grateful to the Huntington Library conference participants, as well as to David Wykes and Justin Champion, for their helpful comments on this chapter.

[2] For the best detailed discussion of the restored church, which nevertheless stresses some of its perceived weaknesses, see J. Spurr, *The Restoration Church of England 1646–1689* (London, 1991). Many of its themes are summarized in his 'Religion in Restoration England', in L. Glassey (ed.), *The Reigns of Charles II and James VII & II* (London, 1997). For the political context of the restoration settlement see P. Seaward, *The Cavalier Parliament and the Reconstruction of the Old Regime 1661–7* (Cambridge, 1989).

[3] The term was used by John Owen (cited in G. De Krey, 'Rethinking the Restoration: Dissenting Cases for Conscience 1667–1672', *Historical Journal* 38 (1995), 53–83, 54) and John Bunyan (C. Hill, *A Turbulent, Seditious and Factious People* (Oxford, 1989), pp. 329–30).

competing religious groups but as the enforcer of religious uniformity.[4] One of the fundamental questions facing Restoration society
was, therefore, to what extent civil authority could and should be
exercised over religious conscience.[5] I shall examine how men
viewed that relationship immediately prior to the Revolution of 1688
and in particular focus on the changing attitudes of churchmen.

For change there was. The 1662 Act of Uniformity asserted that
'nothing conduceth more to the settling of the peace of this nation
. . . or to the honour of our religion and the propagation thereof than
a universal agreement in the public worship of God Almighty'. But
by the late 1680s, whilst unity was still an ideal, it was recognized that
the attempt at enforcement of uniformity on Protestants had neither
provided political peace nor been conducive to the honour or
propagation of religion. As one pamphleteer remarked in 1687, with
only a small degree of exaggeration, there was not 'any party now in
England who holds it as a principle of their religion that it is lawful to
persecute or to make or execute laws for the inflicting of pains or
penalties for any matters of meer religion'.[6] It is worth exploring
what brought that change about and when it occurred.

Many calls had been made before the 1680s for a division between
private conscience and the state's coercive powers. My argument will
consequently not be about the *novelty* of such ideas but about shifts in
the way they were publicly discussed. The events of the late 1680s
shaped the ways in which it was possible for churchmen and
dissenters to talk about persecution. These changes were not the
culmination of a steady and linear progress of pluralistic attitudes
over the course of the century, though clearly men built on, or drew
inspiration from, earlier ideas. The pattern of the seventeenth
century seems instead to be one of oscillations and reactions, with
close alliances of clerical and civil authority on the one hand and
attempts to separate them on the other. The Restoration settlement
was a reaction to the perceived licence of toleration in the 1650s; and
the persecution of the early 1680s a response to the perceived

---

[4] For the pattern of persecution see A. Fletcher, 'The Enforcement of the Conventicle Acts
1664–1679', in W. J. Shiels (ed.), *Persecution and Toleration*, Studies in Church History 21
(Oxford, 1984).
[5] For an excellent discussion for what he calls the 'first restoration crisis' see De Krey,
'Rethinking the Restoration'.
[6] *A Letter from a Gentleman in the City to a Gentleman in the Country about the Odiousness of Persecution*
(1687), p. 15.

resurgence of dissent after the popish plot. Both movements produced backlashes against the identification of church with state, though that of the later 1680s was to prove the more enduring because it was subject to less revision.

The concept of change is nevertheless a contentious one, since much of the revisionism of the Restoration period, and beyond, has centred on the reassertion of the value of a politics of religion and the continuing primacy of religious conflict in political developments.[7] It is emphatically not my purpose to denigrate the excellent and long-called-for work that this line of argument has produced, since some corrective of earlier views, which often unduly ignored the religious perspective, was necessary; rather it is to raise queries about how far the reinterpretation has or can be taken, to question some of its implications and assumptions and, above all, to reassert the politics in the politics of religion. It is nevertheless important to state at the outset that this is not an argument that religion became unimportant. Religious issues were, and continued to be, a core element in shaping political allegiances; but, as I have suggested elsewhere, religion was one of several factors which help explain actions and that in different contexts these other identities could and did prevail.[8] It is thus necessary to examine the context of disputes very closely before labelling them 'religious' ones.

I shall first of all outline the nature of the 'church–state' by looking at the restoration religious settlement in order to stress its political dimensions. I shall argue that contemporaries themselves regarded the debate about toleration as a political and secular problem as much as a religious one and that it needs to be placed or replaced in that context. I shall stress that Cavalier ideology placed religious dissent within a political framework onto which a religious argument for intolerance was overlaid, increasingly in the 1670s but most clearly in the 1680s. We shall then be in a position to examine how James II's reign forced a reconsideration of the resulting alliance of church and state.[9] I shall argue that the 1680s was the decade in which politics and religion seemed most intertwined but that para-

---

[7] The concept provides the title for *The Politics of Religion in Restoration England*, ed. T. Harris, M. Goldie and P. Seaward (Oxford, 1990).

[8] 'A City Revolution: The Remodelling of the London Livery Companies in the 1680s', *English Historical Review* 112 (November 1997), 1141–78.

[9] The declarations have been discussed in Richard Boyer's *English Declarations of Indulgence 1687 and 1688* (The Hague, 1968), but this work is primarily interested in their context rather than their impact.

doxically there were inherent pressures, revealed in James's reign,
that were redefining more tightly the legitimate boundaries of the
civil power in a religious sphere as well as the more obvious political
one. The declarations of indulgence issued by James in 1687 and
1688 were central to this revision and the rhetoric on all sides was
about separating faith from authority. I shall suggest that by 1688 all
the major religious groups – the king, the Catholics, the church (both
high and low) and the dissenters – had come, or been forced, to
recognize the need for the suspension of persecution and with it
some re-evaluation of the role of the civil magistrate in ecclesiastical
affairs. I shall also try to show that this process promoted a reformation of manners – which thus preceded the Revolution rather than
being a product of it. The 1680s was a decade in which religion was
indeed at the forefront of politics; yet, ironically, religious tensions
pushed in a secularizing way. James's reign thus forced a re-
examination of what men meant by 'religion', helping to redefine it
as personal faith or what pamphleteers called 'positive' or 'true'
religion, or even 'mere' religion.[10]

Secularization is a slippery term which will be used here not to
mean religious indifference, nor a state in which the magistrate had a
purely secular role, nor to imply that religious differences ceased to
provoke heated political dispute, but to denote a process in which the
equation of church with state was reformulated so that the state had
ties rather than bonds to the church.[11] Since this chapter is primarily
concerned with how religion was conceived and whether it was
rightly subject to civil coercion, one other term that requires
comment is 'toleration'. Although the 1689 Act did not have the
word in its title, contemporaries did use it and it is to be found in
James's Scottish indulgences. To tolerate can mean to allow something positively, that is to say, without repugnance, and negatively,
that is, with forbearance for something of which one disapproves. It
is that essential ambiguity that makes the term so useful, for the
nuances of its meaning mirror contemporary attitudes.

---

[10] *A Discourse for taking off the Tests and Penal Laws* (1687), p. 3; *An Expedient for Peace* (1688), p. 1.
'Mere' meant 'pure' as well as 'only'. For the broad outline of the argument of a shift
towards personal faith see C. John Sommerville, *The Secularization of Early Modern England*
(Oxford, 1992) and, in a French context, M. de Certeau. *The Writing of History*, ch. 4,
translated by T. Conley (Chichester, 1988).

[11] Sommerville, *Secularization*, passim.

II

The return of the king in 1660 meant the return of the established church. The Cavaliers blamed dissent for the wars and toleration for anarchy. It was thus the political effects of toleration that were often most worrying to them. As a result, the Restoration religious settlement seemed more concerned about order than it was about 'true' religion.[12] Although the churchmen in Parliament who made the settlement were no doubt sincere in their adherence to their religious beliefs, the legislation was based on the maxim that 'it is impossible for a Dissenter not to be a REBEL'.[13] Again and again the legislation reveals a concern not so much with doctrinal uniformity as political quiescence. As one tract of 1688 exclaimed, 'is there any one law made against our later Nonconformists whose preamble does not run upon this topick, the breach of the peace and the undermining the very foundations of the government . . .?'[14]

A textual analysis of the legislation is enough to prove this. In addition to its sacramental test, the Corporation Act of 1661 required oaths against 'the traiterous position of taking arms' against the king, and against the Solemn League and Covenant as well as the oaths of allegiance and supremacy. The Act of Uniformity of 1662 again extracted the declaration against taking up arms and (until 1682) against the Solemn League and Covenant, though it was clear that this was designed to prevent any minister from endeavouring the 'change or alteration of government either in Church or State'. Moreover, and perhaps most importantly, it was primarily an act for the uniformity of the *clergy* not the *laity*. This slant was partly corrected by legislation against the Quakers in 1662 and conventiclers in general in 1664 and 1670, but it was clear that these later Acts were necessary for political reasons. The 1670 Act thus talked about 'the growing and dangerous practices of seditious sectaries and other disloyal persons, who under pretence of tender consciences have or may at their meetings contrive insurrections (as late experience hath shown)'. No mention was made of a religious justification. Moreover, both the 1664 and 1670 Acts specifically provided for private religious dissent. A conventicle was defined as an assembly of 'five persons or more assembled together over and besides those of the same house-

---

[12] This conclusion is also reached by Sommerville, *Secularization*, p. 126.
[13] *The Works of George Savile, Marquess of Halifax*, ed. W. Raleigh (Oxford, 1912), p. 139.
[14] *The Examination of the Bishops* (1688), p. 12.

hold if it be in a house where there is a family inhabiting'. This important provision was later made much of by apologists for the church who insisted that the law persecuted political assemblies which met under the colour of religion and did not infringe private conscience, which could be exercised in a limited fashion in a private household with up to four other people.[15] Defences of the penal laws duly stressed that they were 'purely political and not spiritual', and that dissenters were prosecuted simply 'because they have been guilty of the most horrible crimes of rebellion'.[16] Indeed the lack of anything positive in the settlement that enforced conformity on the laity in matters of religion was apparent in the fact that many religious prosecutions, especially in the 1680s, were for riots or routs. Moreover, the pattern of Restoration persecution suggests that, for all but a minority of zealots, the gentry in the localities chiefly enforced the laws when directed to do so from above and that such prompting came at times of political crisis.[17] In other words, for many laymen the penal laws were useful tools in times of crisis but could be rested at most other times and thus were primarily secular laws. The settlement was based on the association of religious with political dissent and religious tests were used for political ends.

The tenor of the religious political settlement was reflected in Cavalier ideology. The Cavalier political theory of intolerance was most cogently put forward by Roger L'Estrange in his *Toleration Discuss'd*, a tract first published in 1663 but revised and enlarged in 1670 and which went through two further editions.[18] The key to his philosophy lay in correctly defining the extent of human power in religious matters, for L'Estrange argued that in order to prevent chaos there must be a judge of faith as much as one of civil matters, even if that judge was fallible. The word of God was in itself insufficient as a judge because of the innumerable interpretations that could be placed on it. Nor could individual conscience offer peace, for 'nothing has embroyl'd us more then the mistaken rights of individuals'. It was therefore the magistrate who must be the judge of

---

[15] R. L'Estrange, *Toleration Discuss'd* (1670), p. 168.

[16] *A Short Answer to his Grace the D. of Buckingham's Paper* (1685), pp. 20–2.

[17] Fletcher, 'Enforcement of the Conventicle Acts'. One respondent to the 'three questions' of 1687–8 argued that he had 'never pressed ye execution of ym unless expressly reqrd by ye late kg or yt ye manifest necessity of ye publick peace requir'd it' (Bodleian Library, Tanner MS 29, memorandum in Sancroft's hand, f. 20).

[18] I hope to produce a more extensive analysis of L'Estrange's political and religious ideology elsewhere.

religion, otherwise 'the validity of a divine and unchangeable ordinance is subjected to the mutable judgement and construction of the people'. The conformist therefore saw the Christian and subject as having separate duties. A man was to follow 'truth with his soul and authority with his body'. Membership of a society did not remove freedom of conscience but man was no longer free in action, since that part of his duty was subject to the king. Scripture was thus 'the rule of our faith, not of our outward actions and practice'.[19]

L'Estrange's theory, which clearly echoes some Hobbesian sentiments, was fundamentally secular, and became even more avowedly so in the 1670 revision. L'Estrange argued that whereas the non-conformist made the question one of '*conscience* and *religion*', religious liberty was really a consideration of state, for 'private consciences weigh little in the scale against political societies'. The issue was one of politics not religion: 'The question is not, in matter of *religion*, whether to favour *sound faith* or *heresie*; but in *reason of state*, whether it is more *advisable* to *tolerate* the exercise of quite a *different religion*, or a separation from the *church-order establisht*.' L'Estrange recognized that liberty of conscience was a civil right in a society based on natural rights; it was therefore necessary to deny that such rights existed, since the alternative was unstable popular government in which the only law was 'the dictate of the Rabble'. Hence 'the state that allowes the people a freedom to choose their religion is reasonably to expect that they will take a freedom likewise to choose their government'. Moreover, they were likely to choose anarchy, L'Estrange argued, for men did not naturally love government and would judge it in their interests to remove it. The cavalier theory of intolerance therefore saw religion and politics as inseparably linked not because religion was the primary factor but because religious liberty was intimately tied up with political authority.[20]

L'Estrange's views were echoed in many sermons of the period.[21] But, as Mark Goldie has convincingly argued, a religious justification of persecution increasingly came to be heard in the 1670s and 1680s.[22] Churchmen began to reinforce persecution as part of the

---

[19] *Toleration Discuss'd* (1663), pp. 65–6, 82–3, 86–7, 89–90, 93; 2nd edn (1670), 206.

[20] *Toleration Discuss'd* (1663), p. 102; 2nd edn (1670), pp. 28–9, 37, 81, 106, 141.

[21] See, for example, Edward Pelling, *A Sermon* (1682) and R. Perrinchief, *Discourse of Toleration* (1668).

[22] M. Goldie, 'The Theory of Religious Intolerance in Restoration England', in O. Grell, J. Israel and N. Tyacke (eds.), *From Persecution to Toleration* (Oxford, 1991), pp. 332–68.

identity of the church–state. A theological argument was put forward
that coercion was an effective instrument of education and persuasion for misinformed and misguided consciences. This was not
incompatible with L'Estrange's views; indeed, part of their effective-
ness derived from an engraftment onto the core political values he
expressed. The turbulence of 1678–81 served to align more emphatically than ever before the political view of dissenters with the
religious one, an alignment that explains much of the vigour of the
1681–5 Tory reaction. Church and state had to stand together, it was
argued; indeed, they could only stand together if the one supported
the other. As the high-church parson of Great Yarmouth, Luke
Milbourne, told his flock in 1683 'the power of the civil magistrate is
the defence of the church'.[23]

The rise of the high churchmen in politics had important consequences for the church itself. The church hierarchy assumed a high
profile in the persecution of dissent – in 1683, for example, the bishop
of Exeter issued a letter against nonconformists which offered a
reward for the seizure of preachers[24] – and clamped down on clerics
who put forward arguments against persecution, as Samuel Bold,
Daniel Whitby, Edward Pearse and Edward Fowler all discovered.[25]
The group within the church most associated with advocacy of
conscience even appeared to be laying increasing stress on conformity to civil law, hence the outcry over Stillingfleet's and Tillotson's
sermons in the spring of 1680 in which they either attacked conscience unsupported by divine revelation or allowed it only a
theoretical, not a practical, liberty.[26] In their desire to condemn
misguided conscience churchmen of many different hues therefore
came near to denying the agency of conscience. *The Vanity of all
Pretences for Tolleration* (1685), for example, suggested that it was
difficult to distinguish conscience from sedition.[27] All this produced a
religion that appeared both to those outside it and to some inside it
to be persecuting and formalist in its nature. Dissenters referred to

---

[23] *The Originals of Rebellion* (1683), p. 29.
[24] *The Plea of the Harmless Oppress'd* (n.d.), pp. 13–17. Cf *An Answer to the Letter to a Dissenter* (1687),
p. 5.
[25] For a useful discussion of their cases see M. Goldie and J. Spurr, 'Politics and the Restoration
Parish: Edward Fowler and the Struggle for St Giles Cripplegate', *English Historical Review*
189 (1994), 572–96. In *The Conformist's Plea for the Nonconformist* (1682) Pearse suggested 'there
is a great noise and sound of religion, but little life and soul', pp. 7–9, 56.
[26] M. Knights, *Politics and Opinion in Crisis* (Cambridge, 1994), pp. 262–3.
[27] *The Vanity*, p. 4.

the 'persecuting clergy', and claimed 'that the penal laws must be the very essential part of the church of England'.[28] It was alleged that the church 'is afraid of Popery because of its violence, and yet uses force to compel' men to adhere to itself.[29] The Catholics ironically agreed that the reformed church had been 'founded in persecution, subsists by persecution and hath brought persecution into the very heart of her cannons'.[30] By 1685 therefore, the role of conscience had been played down, and the role of the church–state magnified (and its power perhaps exaggerated in the process), though the apparent triumph of a politics of religion had been achieved as a result of political imperatives and the promotion of a temporal religion of obedience to the state. The reign of James II was, however, to smash the assumptions on which the church–state was founded.

III

The debate about liberty of conscience began as soon as James succeeded to the throne. The duke of Buckingham's *Short Discourse upon the Reasonableness of Men's Having a Religion* (1685), which at least one critic thought influenced by William Penn,[31] initiated an exchange about the merits and disadvantages of indulgence.[32] Yet, as is well known, it was only after the failure of James's alliance with the church in 1685, a year which witnessed the severest level of persecution of the period, that the king embraced the idea of a general toleration. In what must be seen as a deliberate attempt to wipe the slate clean and usher in a new restoration on a proper footing, James II issued a new indulgence, twenty-seven years to the day after his brother's declaration at Breda had promised liberty of conscience. The terms of the indulgence are important and illuminating. James not only declared that religious persecution since the Reformation had failed to achieve its aims, but the central feature of his indulgence was the admission that it had been the king's 'constant

---

[28] *An Answer to a Letter to a Dissenter* (1687), pp. 2, 10.
[29] *A Letter from a Gentleman in the Country to his Friends in London upon the Subject of the Penal Laws* (1687), p. 5. Cf. Penn, *Good Advice* (1687), p. 10.
[30] *A Letter in Answer to Two Main Questions* (1687), p. 23.
[31] *A Short Answer to his Grace the D. of Buckingham's Paper* (1685), p. 12.
[32] *A Defence of the duke of Buckingham* (1685), p. 4. For a discussion of the controversy see Bruce Yardley, 'George Villiers, Second Duke of Buckingham and the Politics of Toleration', *Huntington Library Quarterly* 55: 2 (1992), 317–37. See also *The Vanity of all Pretences for Tolleration* (1685); Bodleian Library, Tanner MS 31, f. 19, bishop of Peterborough to Sancroft, 7 Apr. 1685; BL, Stowe 2753, ff. 1–17, 'The Misleading of the Common People', f. 16.

sense and opinion . . . that conscience ought not to be constrained,
nor people forced in matters of meer religion'. James thus announced
that the persecution of conscience was wrong in theory as well as in
practice.

The sincerity of the king's announcement that he had always
believed in liberty of conscience was, of course, questioned by many
contemporaries.[33] Historians have been as bemused by James's claim
to have always believed in liberty of conscience as contemporaries
evidently were.[34] But the ambiguities are perhaps testament to the
fact that James had always been concerned with the political
implications of religious belief. His credibility was, of course, to
become one of the main issues over the next eighteen months, but it
is important to be clear about the significance of his language in the
declaration. The most important and novel feature of his indulgence,
on which addresses of thanks focused,[35] was the principle that
conscience ought not to be constrained. The king may have had
political motives for doing so but he espoused a rhetoric which
tended to divide civil and religious authority, since he announced
that persecution by the state on grounds of religion was wrong. If
conscience *ought* not to be constrained it was because the civil
magistrate had no power or right to do so. James therefore broke the
equation of dissent with disloyalty and declared a reversal in royal
and Catholic policy.[36] This meant a rethinking of church–state
relations, especially when, in May 1688, James ordered the clergy to
read the reissued declaration from the pulpit of every church. One
government-licensed tract argued that the debate now centred on
the church's relations with the state 'and the matters being meerly
political, must be determined by the maxims of our states-men and
so no subject to be decided by the school-men and divines'.[37] The

---

[33] 'Ten Seasonable Queries', in G. Duckett, *Penal Laws and the Test Act* (1883), pp. 199–201; *A Letter to a Dissenter from his Friend at the Hague* (1688), pp. 2–3; Robert Ferguson, *A Representation of the Threatning Dangers* (1688), pp. 6–9, 16. 21; BL, Add. 34,729 (West papers), ff. 260–1, observations on Scottish declaration of indulgence.

[34] For discussions see R. Gwynn, 'James II in the Light of his Treatment of Huguenot Refugees in England 1685–6', *English Historical Review* 92 (1977), 820–33; J. Miller, 'James II and Toleration', in E. Cruickshanks (ed.), *By Force or By Default* (1989), pp. 8–27; D. N. Marshall, 'Protestant Dissent in England in the Reign of James II' (University of Hull PhD, 1976), esp. pp. 102–22, 213–20.

[35] The addresses were printed in the *London Gazette*.

[36] *A Letter in Answer to Two Main Questions* (1687), p. 3.

[37] *Parliamentum Pacificum* (1688), p. 50.

question was how the dissenters and the established church would react to these challenges.

IV

Analysing the response to the indulgences is not easy for a number of reasons. Most obviously, we are forced to rely on printed works and private correspondence at a time of recently renewed censorship, a court propaganda campaign and private nervousness about what to commit to paper. We cannot take the number of propagandist pamphlets advocating liberty of conscience to be representative of public opinion; or deduce that the few replies by members of the established church meant that the king's arguments had simply been accepted. This poses real problems, but they are not overwhelming ones. Some of the anti-governmental literature achieved a wide circulation and because the established church was still a legal licenser of printed material its voice was not entirely strangled. Halifax's *Letter to a Dissenter*, as its critics admitted, was widely dispersed, even 'among the unthinking and easie people' and James's dissenting ally Henry Care thought 'some crape gowns appeared so fond of promoting it, as if they had a mind to play the interlopers on the hawkers'.[38] Halifax's piece went through several editions, in- cluding one as 'a single sheet for conveniency of postage, [so] that no corner of the land' was spared. Some measure of its impact can be gauged from the fact that it provoked at least sixteen replies.[39] What hostile propagandists lacked in terms of number of titles, they made up for in numbers of copies distributed both in London and outside the capital. Moreover, even if people did not read the tracts they seem to have known what was in them. William Denton, for example, reported the contents of pamphlets attacking the indul- gences even though he admitted never having seen a copy of them; they were, he said, 'much desired by all People'.[40] James was so anxious about the spread of the adverse propaganda that he told his electoral agents to set up a counter-propaganda network of corre- spondents in the boroughs who could distribute tracts. According to one report, the court distributed 'above a hundred thousand of their

---

[38] *A Letter in Answer to Two Main Questions* (1687), p. 1; *Two Plain Words to the Clergy* (1688), p. 5.
[39] H. Care, *Animadversions on a Late Paper entituled A Letter to a Dissenter* (1687), p. 7; BL, Add. 34,515 (Mackintosh transcripts), p. 41, [James Johnston] to—, 8 Dec. 1687.
[40] BL, Verney papers M/636(42), William Denton to Sir Ralph Verney, 24 Aug. 1687.

papers' in May 1688 alone.[41] The printed exchanges were therefore recognized as important statements of positions at the time.

Part of the controversy was caused by the paradoxical nature of the declarations. The text of the indulgence issued in Scotland over a month before the English one and printed in the *London Gazette* pointed to the political limits of toleration when it railed against the Presbyterian field conventicles, calling them 'Rendezvous of Rebellion', for which there was to be continued persecution not liberty.[42] In the face of fierce criticism, James was forced to reissue the Scottish proclamation on 28 June in order to extend the indulgence more widely.

The fact that the indulgences were problematical helps explain how men could, initially at least, disagree about their responses, for the first reaction of both dissenter and churchman was one of confusion and division about how to proceed.[43] But the ideological lines did soon begin to be drawn, and the vigour of the dispute meant that positions rapidly became clear and obvious. I shall start with the dissenting response, in order to show that, like the king, the vast majority of nonconformists argued for liberty of conscience on the grounds that the civil magistrate ought not to persecute peaceable private religious opinion and that they employed a similarly secularizing rhetoric. I shall also argue that while some dissenters did place purely religious considerations above all else, a very large section of dissenting opinion increasingly placed civil concerns at the top of their agenda.

Gary De Krey has shown that most nonconformists had made the resulting distinction between the private and public well before James's reign.[44] A clear line of dissenting argument in favour of the indulgence was thus made on the basis of dividing church and state. Penn, of course, was the most ardent and perhaps most eloquent on this theme. He asserted that Christ 'laid not his religion in worldly empire, nor used the methods of worldly princes to propagate it'.

---

[41] BL, Add. 34,515, p. 64, [Johnston] to—, 23 May 1688.

[42] *London Gazette* no. 2221, 28 Feb.–3 Mar. 1687. Boyer suggests that at the time of issuing the Scottish proclamation, James had not decided to ally with the dissenters in England (*English Declarations*, p. 69). Certainly the decision to issue an English indulgence appears to have postdated the Scottish policy.

[43] *A Second Letter from a Gentleman in the Country to his Friends in London* (1687), licensed 11 April, p. 13 noted the mixed reaction of churchmen. I have considered the reaction of dissenters and the impact of the indulgence on the trading community of London in 'A City Revolution'.

[44] De Krey, 'Rethinking the Restoration', esp. p. 58.

Penn therefore urged a magna charta for liberty of conscience to 'have civil property secur'd out of the question of religion'.[45] He even went so far as to argue that the state should not interfere in religion, 'no, not to uphold it'.[46] But while few other dissenters agreed with this extreme view, he was by no means alone in championing a separation of church and state. Civil government, it was alleged by one pamphleteer, was 'a thing entire within itself and of distinct consideration from religion', aiming at the maintenance of peace among men not between man and God. There was thus 'a clear difference between civil government and positive religion'. Violation of the latter required spiritual not temporal punishment. Government and religion were 'two distinct things' and 'liberty and property are too sacred to be invaded for the sake of an opinion that no way hurts' civil authority.[47] As the Presbyterian Richard Burthogge put it

Christian religion and civil government are things so different, as in their originals, so in their natures; and ordained for ends so different . . . that in themselves and absolutely taken, they are nothing akin and of no relation one to another. Wherefore civil government (as such) cannot be oblig'd to concern itself in the business of religion.[48]

Henry Care referred to liberty of conscience as being 'part of the constitution of this kingdom, the natural birthright of every English man'. Indeed, he declared that religion, when interwoven with the interest of the state, declined and that 'by the Gospel, no man is to be abridged of any of his civil rights'.[49] In other words, politics and conscience had to be separated in order to preserve true religion and, rather than civil rights existing to promote godliness, it was God's word that acted as a safeguard for property.

It is also worth emphasizing that the most common arguments used by dissenters in favour of liberty of conscience pushed in a secularizing direction. Toleration was justified on grounds of property rights and trade. Liberty would, nonconformists argued, enlarge trade by encouraging immigration and by freeing the industrious

---

[45] Penn, *Good Advice* (1687), pp. 2, 45.
[46] *Ibid.*, p. 18.
[47] *A Discourse for taking off the Tests and Penal Laws* (1687), pp. 2–5.
[48] *Prudential Reasons for Repealing the Penal Laws* (1687), p. 1. For the authorship see the annotation on BL, printed books T.763. For his career see M. Goldie, 'John Locke's Circle and James II', *Historical Journal* 35 (1992), 579–84.
[49] Care, *Animadversions*, pp. 37, 39.

part of the nation.[50] The penal laws, they asserted, had also invaded property rights, contrary to magna charta, and impoverished many.[51] Penn claimed that as many as 15,000 families had been ruined since the Restoration 'for matters of meer conscience to God'.[52] Persecution thus did not make economic sense. Assuming a dissenting population of 100,000, Henry Care calculated that 'at least five hundred thousand other meaner people' depended on them for their employment.[53]

Since their arguments separated the civil and the religious, most dissenters were keen to distinguish between their desire to take advantage of toleration and political support for a Catholic king. Some dissenters did seek revenge on their former persecutors and important divines such as Vincent Alsop and Stephen Lobb did lend the king their support. But they were the exception rather than the rule, for most were aware of the political significance of their actions.[54] Thus the Quaker William Mead was prepared to preach before a dissenting lord mayor of London,[55] but not to become an alderman, saying he would be 'toole for noe man'.[56] 'I know of no Dissenter', wrote one apologist, who 'is shaking hands or entering into any engagement with [Catholics], more than what is natural to all men to desire and endeavour a free and undisturbed exercise of their religion according to the conviction of their consciences.'[57] Indeed, the number of dissenters who were uneasy about James's policies has often been understated. Especially after the winter of 1687–8 James found it increasingly difficult to find nonconformist support.

Evidence about dissenters' growing dislike of James's programme

---

[50] *The Examination of the Bishops* (1688), p. 21; *Indulgence to Tender Consciences Shewn to be Most Reasonable and Christian* (1687), p. 1; Burthogge, *Prudential Reasons*, pp. 9–10; *Considerations moving to a Toleration* (1685), pp. 4–5; *A Letter from Holland touching Liberty of Conscience* (1688), pp. 2–4.

[51] *A Letter from a Gentleman in the Country to Friends in London*, p. 5; *An Answer to the Letter to a Dissenter*, p. 6; *The Examination of the Bishops*, p. 22; *A Discourse for taking off the Tests and Penal Laws*, p. 10; Care, *Animadversions*, p. 3.

[52] *Good Advice* (1687), p. 57. [G. Larkin?], *An Address of Thanks on behalf of the church of England* (1687), verso, put the figure at 'three-score thousand' families.

[53] *Draconica* (1687), p. 26. Interestingly, his estimate is roughly the same as that produced by the Compton Census of 1676, which suggested a figure of almost 109,000.

[54] *An Apology for the church of England* [1688], p. 2. Cf. Ferguson, *A Representation of the Threatning Dangers*, p. 9.

[55] BL, M/636(42), John Verney to [Sir Ralph Verney], 16 Nov. 1687.

[56] *Ibid.*, Dr Paman to Sir Ralph Verney, 17 Aug. 1687.

[57] *An Answer to a Letter to a Dissenter* (1687), p. 2. Cf. Care, *Animadversions*, p. 14.

comes from a variety of sources. Roger Morrice's diary shows that by October 1687 he had abandoned his initial enthusiasm for the indulgence as he and his friends grew to see it as part of the king's designs to introduce popery.[58] James Johnston, who was providing William with first-class information about events in England and who was himself an ardent Presbyterian, reported the shift in nonconformist attitudes. In November 1687 he wrote that 'the Presbyterians and Independents are coming off from the fondness they had at first for the Toleration'.[59] By May 1688 Johnston could report that the dissenters had

> behaved themselves with honour . . . they hear that in the debates among the clergy, for reading or not reading [the declaration], the most plausible argument for reading was that if they did it not, it would offend the dissenters. Upon this some went and others sent to several of the clergy and told them that they must not judge of them by the tattle of a handfull of men, who being corrupted by the court have assumed to themselves the name of dissenters, that they might assure themselves that instead of being alienated from them for not reading, that they would be the more united to them.[60]

'The truth is,' Johnston reported, 'the people of the Presbyterian perswasion have told their ministers that if they tamper any more, they will give their leave and neither hear them nor pay them.'[61] The nonconformist divines had to listen to their flocks in what could be seen as the triumph of lay over clerical reasoning. Advice to the king suggested that the church's arguments about the collective danger to Protestantism won over many dissenters who were reduced to 'an indifference at le[a]st, if not an absolute reluctancy' about supporting James's policies.[62]

As David Marshall has argued, many dissenters' initial welcome of the indulgence gave way to hostility.[63] For most dissenters religious freedom had to become part of a political settlement. The Baptist author of an attack on Penn pointed out that religious liberty had to be part of a raft of other liberties: 'The name of liberty signifies nothing without the substance and the continuance, certainty and

[58] D[r] W[illiams] L[ibrary], MS 31.Q, f.179, 22 Oct. 1687.
[59] BL, Add. 34,515, p. 31, [Johnston] to—, 17 Nov. 1687.
[60] *Ibid.*, p. 65, [Johnston] to—, 23 May 1688.
[61] *Ibid.*, p. 79, [Johnston] to—, n.d. (c. June 1688). Cf. Bodleian Library, MS Tanner 29, f. 42, Sir Jonathan Trelawny to Sancroft, 1 July 1687.
[62] BL Add. 32095, f.247, advice to the king, n.d. (1688).
[63] Marshall, 'Protestant Dissent'.

security of it', he argued. 'Let us endeavour to secure our substantial liberties, our English liberties we have and ought to have, rather than to get the names of new ones which may fatally bring us into greater bondage in the end.'[64] Ironically conscience had to be separated from the sphere of the civil magistrate, but liberty of conscience could only be secure if the civil magistrate observed the law. Religion was no part of political authority, but it was part of politics. Liberty of conscience was desirable for the religious freedom it gave, but it was also a civil right carrying with it political implications. Religious liberty was seen as part of a broader package of freedoms, rather than as a single issue. Religion was thus a constituent part of a subject's identity and rights, rather than the single defining characteristic. Toleration was a political matter.

V

The focus of the church's fire was directed against the doctrine and practice of Catholicism;[65] but there was also a significant response to the indulgences. A consideration of the church's position in terms of its relationship with the civil power was an inevitable result both of the political reality and of theological introspection. Nearly all the public statements emanating from churchmen after the issue of the indulgence disavowed persecution. The church fell back on constitutional arguments that the Protestant religion was founded in law and therefore relied on observance of the law for its survival. Moreover, although the political situation pushed consideration of schemes for comprehension, much of the rhetoric coming from the church was about the abandonment of persecution for some form of liberty of conscience. Indeed, the public rhetoric of the church appeared to be moving in a direction that brought it close to the terms of the toleration as it was enacted in 1689.

The king's implicit disavowal that the dissenters posed a political threat removed the justification that lay at the heart of the Cavalier political theory of intolerance. Of course, churchmen did not simply relinquish long-held distrust of the dissenters simply because the king told them to; indeed, the fact that a Catholic king was urging alliance with the dissenters was highly suspicious. But the church did under-

---

[64] *Three Considerations Propos'd to Mr William Penn* (n.d. c.1688), pp. 1–4.
[65] For a listing of many of the exchanges see *A Catalogue of the Collection of Tracts for and against Popery*, ed. T. Jones (Chetham Society, vol. I, 1859; vol. II, 1865).

take a public revision of attitudes about persecution. Concern about the high-church agenda had, of course, been voiced in the 1670s and early 1680s by churchmen sympathetic to the plight of dissenters. Halifax's 'trimmer' had thus sought a form of religious liberty looking 'rather like a kind omission to enquire more strictly than an allowed toleration of that which is against the rule established'.[66] The call for moderation had been drowned out by the din of persecution in the early 1680s, but by 1687 the prevailing rhetoric was tolerationist.

One of the most remarkable responses to the infamous 'three questions' posed by the king to office-holders in the winter of 1687–8 came in answer to an enquiry about whether men would 'support the king's Declaration for liberty of conscience, by living friendly with those of all persuasions as subjects of the same prince and good Christians ought to do'.[67] Hardly any of those interviewed replied in the negative, irrespective of whether the answer to the first two questions (about the parliamentary repeal of the penal laws and tests) was positive, negative or noncommittal. We might expect moderate churchmen to have agreed; but it is remarkable that men of all stripes, including MPs who had sat in the loyalist 1685 Parliament, returned promises to support liberty of conscience in their neighbourhoods. Walter Chetwynd, MP for Stafford, had been described as 'orthodox' to the government and 'vile' by the earl of Shaftesbury, yet he declared in 1687 that he 'was never a friend to penall lawes, much lesse to tests'; and Sir Hugh Cholmley, MP, had spoken twice against exclusion in 1679 but in 1687 said he thought 'meanly of any one [who] should either slacken his kindness or other friendly office, meerly on account of religion or opinion'.[68] Perhaps Chetwynd's Catholic neighbour Lord Aston and Cholmeley's Catholic kinsman Lord Belasyse had influenced their views;[69] but what are we to make of Sir David Foulis, described as 'very well principled' by a courtier during the succession crisis, who said he had 'ever judged divers of the penall laws very severe'? or of George Gounter, Chichester's MP

[66] *Complete Works of . . . Halifax*, p. 77. See also *The Conformist's Plea for the Nonconformists* (1683), esp. pp. 57–9.
[67] The replies are printed in Duckett, *Penal Laws*. For exceptions to the tolerationist response see the replies of Sir Dennis Hampson, MP for High Wycombe (*ibid.*, II, 148) and Thomas Waite (II, 74).
[68] Duckett, *Penal Laws*, I, 55; II, 196.
[69] B. D. Henning, *The History of Parliament: The House of Commons 1660–1690* (1983), II, 48, 63.

in 1685, who had benefited from the Tory remodelling there but who insisted that he 'not only will but have and doe live neighbourly and friendly with my neighbours of a contrary persuasion'? or of Sir Thomas Slingsby, whom Shaftesbury thought a 'vile' courtier but who yet said he had 'alwayes been inclined to live peaceably and in charity with all people'?[70] It is possible that such men were insincere, had different interpretations to the king of what 'friends' were or were ultra-loyalists telling the government what they wanted to hear, not what they believed, in order to try to retain their seats. For some, it is true, there had undoubtedly been a very recent conversion.[71] Collectively, however, these examples suggest that even some strong 'Tories' disliked or grew to dislike persecution on purely religious grounds or, as important, were prepared to declare as much by 1688.

Once again, the pressure of lay opinion over the clerics is evident. Propagandists pointed to the tolerant nature of the nation 'which abhors cruelty and hath always a compassion for those who are under persecution'.[72] The severity of the persecution of 1681–5 thus heightened these feelings. Even critics of toleration and doctrinaire churchmen admitted that persecution was unpopular. One argued that 'all punishment is odious to the people and neither law nor reason nor necessity can perfectly reconcile them to it', while another stated that even if men were persecuted for sedition they pretended that they suffered for religion 'and this is often sufficient to create pity towards themselves and incense men against the church'.[73] To some degree such sympathy, and the accompanying dislike of informers, stemmed from the English preoccupation with property, as a story told in one tract reveals: in about 1669

> one Thomas Peard . . . of West Dean near Barnstaple, who kept many poor people at work in the cloathing trade, was prosecuted upon the Act for twenty pounds a month, so many months for not coming to church, that he was forced to quit his habitation and imployment. Upon this the poor people of many parishes go a begging and the numbers presently were so great that the justices were fain to meet and consulting together, conclude

---

[70] Duckett, *Penal Laws*, I, 93–5, 96, 177.
[71] See, for example, the response of Robert Pulleyn of Huntingdonshire in Duckett, *Penal Laws*, II, 72.
[72] *A Letter from a Gentleman in the City to a Gentleman in the Country about the Odiousness of Persecution*, p. 26. Cf. *A Discourse for taking of the Tests and Penal Laws* (1687), preface; Burthogge, *Prudential Reasons*, p. 4.
[73] *The Antithelemite* (1685), p. 2; W. Stanley, *The Faith and Practice of a Church of England Man* (1688), p. 186.

upon it to get the man's fines to be discharged. This being done, Peard returns to his business, takes the poor off their hands and finds them again the same living.[74]

Economics therefore encouraged pluralism. Religious forbearance thus combined with civil prudence.

It is not my intention to suggest that intolerant churchmen became ideologically convinced of the wisdom of liberty of conscience overnight, or that Tories became Whigs. But there does seem to have been a rethinking about the place of persecution on religious grounds or at least a striking silence about the need and legitimacy of such persecution. Political pragmatism was thus predominant. The author of a tract published early in 1689 asserted that 'the prevailing opinion now in England is Latitudinarian: Most men are so far improv'd in their judgements as to believe that heaven is not entail'd upon any particular opinion'.[75] Sir John Reresby observed that many saw in the 1687 indulgence a design to weaken the church, 'though many were of opinion that such a toleration was not of prejudice upon a politique account'. By 1688, Reresby believed, 'most men were now convinced that liberty of conscience was a thing of advantage to the nation', so long as it did not infringe the rights and privileges of the church.[76] An answer to Halifax's *Letter to a Dissenter* admitted that many gentlemen of the laity of the church were in favour of ease for dissenters and although a few of the clergy continued 'their old pulpit railings', the church had to follow influential lay opinion.[77] This irony was not lost on one writer who noted: 'Time was when there was nothing more abominable, more hainous, or more cry'd down by the gowned clergy of England than vox populi; now vox populi is the only suprema lex that guides them; they have no other fears than of the condemnations and censures of vox populi.'[78] Persecution was out of step with greater lay toleration. Archbishop Sancroft admitted as much when he wrote that the nonenforcement of the penal laws was lawful when the king and people consented and that such a situation prevailed in 1688.[79]

---

[74] *Considerations Moving to a Toleration* (1685), p. 4.

[75] *Some Remarks Upon Government* (1689), pp. 3–4.

[76] *Ibid.*, pp. 450, 497.

[77] *An Answer to the Letter to a Dissenter*, pp. 9, 11.

[78] *An Answer to a Letter from a Clergyman in the City* (1688), p. 11. Cf. *A Letter from a Clergy-Man in the Country* (1688), p. 19.

[79] Bodleian Library, MS Tanner 460, f. 29v 'Animadversions upon ye Vindication of ye Eccl[esiastic]all Com[mission]ers'.

The renunciation of persecution by the laity was mirrored in
Anglican apologetics, such as Halifax's hugely influential *Letter to a
Dissenter*, which suggested that nonconformists no longer had to deal
with 'rigid Prelates, who made it a matter of conscience to give you
the least indulgence' but that 'the common danger hath so laid open
that mistake, that all the former haughtiness towards you is for ever
extinguished and that it hath turned the spirit of persecution into a
spirit of peace, charity and condescension'. It all amounted, Halifax
believed, to a 'happy change'.[80] Reconciliation between churchmen
and dissenters, as is well known, accelerated after the declarations.[81]

The sincerity of the church's shift of emphasis was questioned by
some dissenters, especially as there were still clergymen who clung to
a defence of the penal laws.[82] But churchmen's desire to retain the
penal laws on the statute book did not necessarily mean a desire to
return to persecution. It was argued that their wholesale repeal
would remove the legislation outlining the Protestant religion's
doctrine. Nonenforcement of the laws, along the lines eventually
translated into law, was thus for some a preferable option. Two tracts
published in 1688 thus prefigured the terms of the Toleration Act by
arguing for the retention of the laws but new legislation for peaceable
dissenters.[83] Parliament was to settle 'the case for the profession of
their faith in matters meerly supernatural or the outward expression
of their worship so as both terminate only in God and neither wrong
nor hurt any man on Earth, in body, goods, and good name, but their
own souls only if they be mistaken therein'.[84] In other words,
toleration would now be tolerated, even if it was not enthusiastically
endorsed and the punishment for spiritual error was the personal risk
of losing salvation.

That shift had come about partly through the church's rediscovery
of conscience as a justification for passive resistance to civil authority.

---

[80] *Complete Works of Halifax*, p. 136. Cf. *A Plain Account of the Persecution* (1688), pp. 1–4; *Three
   Queries* [1688], p. 3; *An Answer from the Country to a Letter to a Dissenter* (1687), p. 5; G. Every, *The
   High Church Party 1688–1718* (London, 1956), pp. 22–3; *An Apology for the church of England*
   [1688], p. 5; BL, Add. 47,126, ff. 81–3, 'Against takeing off the penal laws and tests'.
[81] For an outline of the talks and their context see R. Thomas, 'Comprehension and
   Indulgence', in G. Nuttall and O. Chadwick (eds.), *From Uniformity to Unity 1662–1962* (1962).
[82] Care, *Animadversions*, pp. 10, 33; *A Letter from a Gentleman in the City to a Gentleman in the Country
   about the Odiousness of Persecution*, pp. 3–4; William Stanley's *The Faith and Practice of a Church of
   England Man* (1688), pp. 18–19, p. 185.
[83] *Free Thoughts of the Penal Laws, Tests and some late Printed Papers* [1688], *A Memorial from the
   English Protestants*.
[84] *A Memorial*, pp. 4, 9, 28.

Once the government had renounced the penal laws, the church was the body that could be labelled disloyal for refusing to obey the government and it therefore had to fall back on the claim that it was acting out of conscience. Reading the declaration was repeatedly and insistently announced to be against the conscience of the clergy.[85] 'Conscience is the common answer on the account of which the nobility and gentry do not consent' to repealing the penal laws and tests, concluded one hostile pamphleteer. Another remarked how the church pleaded conscience in the matter of reading the declaration when they had previously labelled this plea 'a meer pretence'.[86] 'It would make a man smile to see how the world turns round', remarked one nonconformist propagandist.[87] The church was accused of 'shameful inconsistency' for having previously disallowed private judgement[88] and for now making their will the law.[89] Conscience, the church now recognized, was something to be acted on, not just a theoretical liberty to hold an opinion.

Yet interestingly the clergy grounded their conscientious objection on a defence of secular law. They refused to read the declaration because it was illegal.[90] Sancroft told the king that the seven bishops in 1688 acted 'to preserve the laws of the land' and told the court that the declaration 'shook the force of all our laws and the very foundation of the reformed church of England . . . that it seemed to alter the whole frame of the government and introduce a new constitution'.[91] According to one government propagandist, the 'rumour ran of nothing else but *all* the laws to be lay'd aside, though only *some* penal laws were suspended'.[92] Just as the dissenters had concluded that religious liberty had to be based on security of the civil law, so the church opposed the declaration because it was based on a dispensing power which threatened to overturn all law. 'The

---

[85] *A Letter from a Clergy-Man in the City to his Friend in the Country* [1688], p. 2; *A Letter from a Clergy-Man in the Country to the Clergyman in the City* (1688), p. 26; Gutch, *Collecteana Curiosa* (1781), I, 339; Lonsdale, *Memoirs*, p. 465. Conscience was also the justification for Bishop Sprat's resignation from the Ecclesiastical Commission (Bodleian Library, MS Tanner 460, f.70v) and of the disobedience of the dons of Magdalen College (Bodleian Library, MS Tanner 29, f.112, R.W. to Henry Wharton, 17 Nov. 1687).

[86] *The Minister's Reasons for His Not Reading the king's Declaration Friendly Debated* (1688), p. 12.

[87] *Some Necessary Disquisitions and close Expostulations with the Clergy* (1688), pp. 17–18.

[88] *The Countrey-Ministers Reflections on the City Ministers Letter* (1688), p. 3.

[89] *A Letter from a Clergy-Man in the Country*, pp. 26, 38.

[90] They faced the civil charge of seditious libel.

[91] Gutch, *Collecteana Curiosa*, I, 346, 364–5, 378.

[92] *Parliamentum Pacificum*, p. 24.

church by law established' was one of the church's most commonly repeated mantras but now it acquired new significance. The reassertion of the constitutionalism of the national religion shifted the focus of debate back onto civil ground. Paradoxically, 'the former magnifiers of prerogative swagger[ed] for magna charta'.[93]

The shift of loyalty from king to church may appear to mark the triumph of religious allegiance over secular obedience, but it could not be achieved without dividing the church–state into its constituent parts and slimming down the recognized powers of the king over the church. A tract among Sancroft's papers which defended the seven bishops argued that the law of the land, not the word of the prince, was the rule of obedience and that 'such men as resigne themselves to an absolute obedience of any prince, without regard to the municipal laws of the countrey, must needs have extinguish'd their consciences which are the lights God has given us to walk by'.[94] The church's rhetoric pushed towards a personal faith unreliant on the coercive powers of the magistrate.

VI

The Cavalier theory of intolerance was based on the idea that there was such a thing as 'false religion' which could be persecuted.[95] Yet between 1685 and 1688 the Catholics argued more vigorously and more freely than ever before that theirs was the true faith, justifying their claims by the infallibility of the Catholic church. Infallibility and certainty therefore became major preoccupations of the period and lay at the heart of the debate about liberty of conscience. As Penn remarked, 'a Church that denies infallibility cannot force, because she cannot be certain'.[96] The church's refutations of infallibility led to a re-emphasis of the role of individual consciences and the ability of every man to judge for himself, and hence further towards a personal faith that lay outside the scope of the civil magistrate.

In 1686 the high-church William Sherlock published an important refutation of the Catholic position, in which he argued that the

---

[93] Care, *Animadversions*, p. 18.
[94] Bodleian Library, MS Tanner 460, ff. 167–8, 'Considerations on the Bp of Hereford's Discourse'.
[95] *The Vanity of all Pretences for Tolleration* (1685), p. 21.
[96] *Good Advice*, p. 20.

papists ran down Protestant certainty in order to trumpet Rome's infallibility. Sherlock's answer was that a Protestant could be certain because his certainty lay in reason. When the papists asked 'are you not sensible what a fallible thing Human Understanding is?', Sherlock replied that understanding was capable of distinguishing between truth and error, because of reason. Right reason led to right religion. But although he denied that reason was merely sense or feeling, he suggested that 'the very highest certainty of all is nothing else but an intuitive knowledge, or the minds seeing and discerning that natural evidence which is in things . . . a kind of natural sense and instinct, without reasoning about them'. Thus the more something required reasoning, the less certain one could be about it. Natural certainty was thus 'resolved into an intuitive knowledge'.[97] In refuting papal claims about infallibility, Sherlock was therefore admitting a large role for what dissenters preferred to call conscience. Richard Kidder, in a sermon licensed by the archbishop of Canterbury's chaplain and published in the same week as the indulgence in 1687, called this 'the judgement of private discretion'. He asserted that every man of an ordinary capacity was able to judge of what is true and false in matters of faith.[98] As one pamphleteer remarked, 'what's the plain English of all this but Liberty of conscience?'[99]

Kidder was not alone. The author of *The Protestant Resolv'd* (1688) attacked Catholics' claim to infallibility because it demanded 'a total submission of my own judgement and conscience . . . to their determination', whereas Protestantism allowed men to use their reason and judgement to discern between truth and falsehood.[100] The church was thus a guide; but ultimate responsibility lay with the individual and the conscience had to be free to act. The debate thus revolved around who was competent to judge matters of faith, and the answer given was not the state but the individual guided by the church. People had to exercise their free will and, through God's grace and reason, choose virtue.

The redefinition of religion as something private not public forced a reassessment of the strength of personal piety and placed emphasis

---

[97] Sherlock, *A Discourse concerning a Judge of Controversies in Matters of Religion* (1686), preface, p. 16.
[98] Kidder, *The Judgment of Private Discretion* (1687).
[99] *A Letter in Answer to a City Friend Shewing How Agreable Liberty of Conscience is to the church of England* (1687), p. 4.
[100] *The Protestant Resolv'd*, pp. 5, 35, 45–9.

on an active religiosity. It has been argued by some that it was William's invasion that ushered in a 'godly revolution';[101] but there is evidence that the climate for a spiritual revival predated the post-revolution movement for the reformation of manners.

By the early 1680s the dominant high churchmen laid most stress on conformity rather than on inculcating piety. Critics duly argued that coercion of the conscience destroyed conscientious religion – 'at best it maketh men religious by rote, which is no religion, or conformable for fear and interest, which is ir-religion and base hypocrisy'.[102] The dissenters' argument was that persecution destroyed godly men and 'open'd a door to let in debauchery and prophaneness . . . were ever men's lives so full of unrighteousness and ungodliness and all wickedness whatsoever as they are now?'[103] Profanity, it was alleged, was even rife among churchmen.[104]

Between 1685 and 1688, however, the scene changed. It was generally believed that the new monarch would 'chastise the late insolency of vice and by his own example bring morality into reputation'.[105] There was speculation at his accession 'that atheism, bawdery, blasphemy, drunkenness, swearing and other notorious immoralities will be more discountenanced than ever'.[106] According to James's own testimony, Protestant failure to control carnal appetites had helped turn him towards Rome in the first place.[107] Perhaps Robert Ferguson was right when he claimed that much of the king's fervour derived from a sense of guilt about, and desire to atone for, his own lusts.[108] James finally sent his mistress, Catherine Sedley, packing in 1686 and thereafter appears to have made greater efforts at marital fidelity. He also looked to those immediately about him. 'Never was any prince's court freer from debauchery and more orderly in the disposal of all officers in it', claimed one supporter; 'the diligent, virtuous, sober, ingenious and loyal are received without

---

[101] Tony Claydon, *William III and the Godly Revolution* (Cambridge, 1996); Dudley Bahlman, *The Moral Revolution of 1688* (Yale, 1968).

[102] *A Letter from a Gentleman in the City to a Gentleman in the Country about the Odiousness of Persecution* (1687), p. 31; *The Reasonableness of Toleration* (1687), p. 29.

[103] *The Present Interest of England in Matters of Religion* (1688), pp. 11, 19.

[104] *Some Necessary Disquisitions and close Expostulations with the Clergy* (1688), pp. 25–26. Cf. Burnet, *A Supplement to Burnet's History of My Own Time*, ed. H. C. Foxcroft (Oxford, 1902), p. 101.

[105] BL, RP 1028, Sir Robert Southwell to Sir Richard Bulstrode, 21 Feb. 1685.

[106] *HMC Egmont*, II, 148.

[107] *Lettres et Mémoires de Marie Reine d'Angleterre*, ed. Countess M. Van Bentinck (The Hague, 1880), p. 7.

[108] *A Representation of the Threatning Dangers* (1688), p. 8.

censure of their religion; the sloathful, turbulent, factious, debauched and irreligious are as much discouraged, as is most manifest by his severe charges against swearing and drunkenness'.[109]

But even if the example of a Catholic king might be dubious as a model to follow, the logic of the indulgence also promoted a revival of godliness. The dissenters were free to advocate piety. 'Press virtue, punish vice', urged William Penn,[110] and tract after tract supporting liberty of conscience stressed the importance of a pious life. As one pamphleteer put it, 'No man is a schismatick but he that departs from a good life, that fears not God nor loves his neighbour.'[111] Moreover, the indulgence itself stimulated the debate, since it granted a general toleration, for Christian and non-Christian alike, and it was therefore attacked for opening the way to superstition and atheism.[112] John Verney, who found the people of Wasing, in Berkshire, to be 'heathenish' believed that 'now there's a toleration, the[ir] irreligion will be intollerable, soe that they'll differ from beasts only in speech and not in sense and understanding'.[113] Thus those who lamented widespread irreligion saw the unlimited toleration as only likely to increase the paganism of the people. There was some justification for this in that ecclesiastical presentments for offences of a moral nature fell off as soon as prosecutions for nonattendance became impossible.[114] At the trial of the seven bishops, Sancroft argued that the indulgence 'let loose the reins to the most extravagent sects and licentious practices'.[115] It was therefore vital that James and his supporters counteract that argument. On 29 June 1688 the king issued a proclamation against debauchery, drunkenness and swearing,[116] and defenders of the indulgence were careful to point out that it did not give liberty to fornication, adultery, incest or blasphemy.[117]

But the indulgence also challenged the established church. To survive in the market place of faith in the post-toleration era the

---

[109] *How the Members of the church of England ought to behave* (1687), pp. 194–5.
[110] *Good Advice*, p. 18.
[111] *An Expedient for Peace* (1688), p. 9.
[112] *The Vanity of all Pretences for Tolleration* (1685), p. 5; *To the king's Most Excellent Majesty the Humble Address of the Atheists or the Sect of Epicureans* (1687).
[113] BL, M/636(41), John Verney to Edmund Verney, 2 Apr. 1687.
[114] G. V. Bennet, 'Conflict in the Church', p. 159, in *Britain after the Glorious Revolution*, ed. G. Holmes (Oxford, 1969).
[115] Gutch, *Collecteana Curiosa*, 1, 378.
[116] *A Bibliography of Royal Proclamations of the Tudor and Stuart Sovereigns*, ed. R. Steele (1967), 1, 468.
[117] *An Answer to a Letter from a Clergyman in the City* (1688), part 2, p. 9. Cf. *A Letter from a Clergy-Man in the Country*, p. 14.

church would be dependent on its 'own vertue and ability to preach'.[118] The Anglican voluntary societies grew more vigorous under the challenge of James's reign, deliberately establishing daily prayers to clash with the mass at the chapel royal.[119] One officially licensed tract, *Vertue's Triumph*, which was avowedly prompted by James's anti-vice proclamation but nevertheless attacked 'our adversaries the Romanists', argued for the unity of Protestants against the mass of profanity and debauchery which was 'the great plague of the nation at present'.[120] Such attitudes had official sanction. Sancroft sent articles to bishops on 16 July 1688 to insist that their clergy should be diligent in catechising and explaining the grounds of Christianity, offer daily services even in villages and urge frequent communion. This was the type of practical programme that had long been desired and it would be wrong to suggest that the indulgences suddenly put it on the agenda; nevertheless they did give it an important impetus. Ministers were to 'take all occasions to convince our own flock, that tis not enough for them to be members of an excellent church, rightly and duly reformed, both in faith and worship, unless they do reform and amend their own lives'.[121] In the summer of 1688, therefore, Catholic, dissenter and churchman strove to outdo each other's personal spirituality. The attempts to revive individual faith were a sign of how successful the separation of public religion and true religion, and of civil and religious authority had been. The greater separation of church and state, which can be labelled a secularizing process, had as part of its aim the rejuvenation of personal faith. William disdained the title of defender of *the* faith but he and his wife were ardent defenders of faith.[122]

VII

In December 1687 the shrewd and well-informed Johnston discerned a heightened awareness that the wholesale repeal of the penal laws would leave Protestantism vulnerable, 'so that now men make a

---

[118] *A Letter from a Gentleman in the Country to Friends in London* (1687), p. 7.

[119] E. Duffy, 'Primitive Christianity Revived: Religious Renewal in Augustan England', in D. Baker (ed.), *Renaissance and Renewal in Christian History*, Studies in Church History 14 (Oxford, 1977), pp. 287–300; Garnet V. Portus, *Caritas Anglicana* (1912), pp. 13–14.

[120] *Vertue's Triumph* (1688), pp. 5–10.

[121] *A Collection of Papers Relating to the Present Juncture of Affairs in England* (1688), p. 13.

[122] BL, Add 45,731, f. 118, Peter Wyche to Edmund Poley, 26 Feb. 1689. For the difference in the oaths taken by William and Mary to those taken previously see *The Eighteenth Century Constitution*, ed. E. N. Williams (Cambridge, 1965), doc.13.

distinction between taking these all away and making a new law, to exempt some men's persons and estates from punishment in matters of mere religion and conscience'.[123] In other words, the ideology behind the 1689 Toleration Act – the retention of the laws but exemption from their penalties – emerged shortly after James's issue of an indulgence and was not suddenly spawned by the events of the revolution.[124] A politics of toleration has also emerged. L'Estrange had allowed for the possibility that the Cavalier might agree to toleration if he 'could but hit upon such a measure as agrees with *piety* and *political convenience*'.[125] These conditions were met in James's reign. A limited toleration, a revival of personal piety and a common danger which necessitated Protestant unity for common security fitted the bill.[126] The civility of religion was stressed and, in its most extreme form, religion became part of a man's civil rights, part of his property. Burnet thus argued that Protestantism could be considered 'not as it is a religion, but as it is become one of the principal rights of the subjects to believe and profess it'.[127] Moreover, the secularization of the debate had also been apparent in the pressure exerted by both the dissenting and conformist laity on their spiritual leaders, whose naive pursuit of purely religious aims was tempered, and often overridden, by the political. Popery was also reaffirmed in a political light. While some pro-court dissenters were prepared to separate Catholicism from its bugbear of arbitrary government and allow its toleration as a faith and on grounds of conscience, for most observers it was precisely because popery could not be divorced from arbitrary government that it could not be tolerated.

There were essential paradoxes in James's reign. Churchmen put their religion above loyalty to their prince, seemingly placing religion over politics, and yet in order to safeguard the church they were forced to separate it from the powers of the state and reduce the authority of the prince in spiritual matters. They were also forced to employ a constitutionalist rhetoric and in order to preserve true

---

[123] BL, Add. 34,515, p. 36, [Johnston] to—, 8 Dec. 1687. Silius Titus, MP, was cited as an example of someone who held this view.

[124] The scheme being hammered out between the hierarchy and dissenters in July 1688 contained many provisions resembling those of the 1689 Act (Every, *The High Church Party 1688–1718*, pp. 22–3).

[125] *Toleration Discuss'd* (1663), p. 11.

[126] *A Letter to a Person of Quality occasion'd by the News of the Ensuing Parliament* (c.1688), pp. 7–8.

[127] *An Enquiry into the Measures of Submission to the Supreme Authority, forming part of A Second Collection of Papers* (1688), p. 6.

religion the definition of religion had to be narrowed. The extent of
civil authority had to be reduced, too, so that it did not dictate what
was religious truth. True religion could only be put first if it remained
a private concern. Moreover, to justify opposition to the king's
wishes, clerics rediscovered the role of conscience, the issue on which
they had been so at odds with the dissenters. The dissenters, for their
part, turned away in increasing numbers from policies designed to
woo them from the court, and they too employed arguments that
divided church from state.

The shifts of attitude and public rhetoric in James's reign should
not be seen out of context or exaggerated. Penn pointed out that the
church did have a tradition, of which even Charles I was a part, of
deploring the use of force against religion;[128] and developments in
the 1640s and 1650s had been important. It would also be foolish to
suggest that attitudes changed overnight or that the abandonment of
persecution meant embracing dissenters after the immediate crisis of
rampant popery had passed. Indeed, hatred of dissenters was in
many quarters undiminished by the events of James's reign and may
have increased in some places where churchmen found themselves
removed from office to make way for nonconformists. Religion
continued to provide a fertile ground for dispute, and the problem of
the persecution of non- or even anti-religious conscience had not
been sufficiently debated. Clergymen continued to involve themselves in politics; hence the continued assault on priestcraft. The
tendency towards a separation of church and state did not yet
encompass the removal of religion as a test for office, which had been
another important strand of James's campaign and the sore of the
Corporation Act therefore continued to fester after the Revolution.
Ironically, indeed, the greater separation of church and state advocated by dissenters undermined their argument that they should be
allowed to hold political office since it was very difficult to insist that
such service had nothing to do with the magistrate. Thus Sir
Bartholomew Shower, the brother of a prominent dissenting minister
but himself a prominent Tory who had been recorder of London in
James's reign, espoused liberty of conscience 'in matters merely
religious' but despised occasional conformists who subordinated
their conscience to their desire for office.[129] But the removal of

---

[128] *Good Advice*, pp. 33–6.
[129] *Calendar of State Papers Domestic 1698*, p. 378. I hope to develop this theme elsewhere.

religious tests for officeholders, though linked to the concept of liberty of conscience, was an essentially different idea: liberty of conscience was about limiting the scope of politics in religion, but the abolition of tests about limiting the scope of religion in politics.

I have not argued that religion ceased to be a dividing issue in later Stuart Britain or that 1687 ushered in a secular society. The separation of church and state was not completed in 1687, 1688 or 1689. But an important turning point in the process had been reached. The crown recognized that as a matter of principle the magistrate ought not to persecute religious conscience – that God was the 'sole monarchy over conscience'[130] – and the church admitted, no matter how reluctantly, that persecution could no longer be part of its armoury. Persecution was worse than error. Accordingly the church's rhetoric had changed. The church had found a confidence that it was a true religion; but it was less certain that it was the only true religion, since that claim would rest on an alien, popish concept of infallibility. The nonconformist argument, that it was 'not the having several parties in religion under a state, that is itself dangerous, but tis the persecuting of them that makes them so', was tacitly admitted.[131] This was the foundation of a pluralistic society: difference of opinion per se was not a cause for repression but seditious opinion was, defining sedition in purely civil terms. Faction could only be distinguished from conscience if the latter had liberty; once separated in this way, faction could be punished by the civil state. Sedition could be defined not as subversion of the church but as undermining the state. Sedition was thus secularised, just as the prosecution of immoral behaviour was also secularised after the Revolution through the societies for the reformation of manners.[132]

As one of James's propagandists observed, 'there are but two things in the world dear to all mankind: religion and property'.[133] The security of the latter could only be ensured by freedom in the former from state coercion. The removal of state coercion meant redefining relations between religious and civil power and acknowl-

---

[130] Address from the Dissenters of Southampton district, *London Gazette*, 25–9 Apr. 1687.
[131] *Reasons Humbly Offered* (1682), p. 3.
[132] T. Isaacs, 'The Anglican Hierarchy and the Reformation of Manners 1688–1738', *Journal of Ecclesiastical History* 33 (1982), 391–411.
[133] *An Address to the church of England* (1688), p. 1. The view echoes that stated by the duke of Buckingham in Parliament in 1675 (Yardley, 'Buckingham', p. 327).

edging that men's priorities had shifted from the pursuit and imposition of religious truth *over and above* property to the pursuit of religious
truth *and* property, from an emphasis on religious rites to one on
religious and civil rights. Civil and religious liberty became inseparable; but they were to be achieved through a greater separation of
church and state and a secular logic.

All these factors helped undermine a religious polity. Hooker had
been able to argue that all Englishmen were churchmen; Penn,
however, argued that a man could be a good Englishman but an
indifferent churchman.[134] The danger with the term 'politics of
religion' is that it implies a godly politics. Whigs and Tories were
indeed names with religious connotations but they represented
religion associated with, and perverted by, secular wrong-doing: theft
in the case of the Catholic Tories and rebellion in the case of the
Presbyterian Whigs.

[134] Russell Smith, *Religious Liberty* (Cambridge, 1911), pp. 33, 41.

CHAPTER 3

Radicals, reformers, and republicans: academic language and political discourse in Restoration London

Gary S. De Krey

I ACADEMIC LANGUAGE

Can we speak about radicals in seventeenth-century England? We certainly know of individuals and groups whose ideas and behaviour defied convention and propelled them towards resistance, rebellion and enthusiasm. But the language that many historians have employed to name and to characterize these groups and individuals has become increasingly controversial. One after another the conceptual shibboleths of the 'English Revolution' and of England's 'century of revolution' have come under question. The employment of the word radical to designate early-modern critics of the monarchical state and of hierarchical social and ecclesiastical organization is one of these.

In his revisionist manifesto of 1986, for instance, J. C. D. Clark rejected almost all previous analyses of pre-1820s' radicals or radicalism. For Clark, radicalism is a concept borrowed from nineteenth-century politics: it is inappropriate in writing about early-modern experiences. As a category, it has been most frequently used and misused – according to him – by Whiggish, liberal and Marxist historians seeking to find early-modern anticipations of modern critiques of state and society. Yet Clark himself discusses both radicals and radicalism from the 1770s forwards, employing these labels as deliberate anachronisms in order 'to indicate the form which a nineteenth-century genre took in an earlier period'. One principal point that he seeks to make in using this academic 'shorthand' is that historians have read *secular* nineteenth-century Radical meanings into the very different 'radicalism' of the eighteenth century.[1]

[1] This conceptual elimination of most usages of radical is critical in Clark's broader historiographical agenda of establishing a radical-free Hanoverian 'confessional state' as England's 'ancien regime' (1660–1832). J. C. D. Clark, *Revolution and Rebellion: State and Society in England in the Seventeenth and Eighteenth Centuries* (Cambridge, 1986), esp. pp. 6–9, 97–111;

With even greater asperity, Conal Condren has recalled scholars of seventeenth-century English political experience from the quest for a usable past to the pursuit of seventeenth-century language and its contemporary meanings. For Condren, the scholarly 'de-coding' or 'unpacking' of seventeenth-century language and practice frequently serves only to re-encode or repackage seventeenth-century ideas in more comfortable categories. The name radical serves as a prime example, according to him, of the academic habit of imposing twentieth-century scholarly conventions upon the 'relatively alien' vocabulary of seventeenth-century political debate. Drawing upon linguistic field theory, he sharply separates the political domain of the seventeenth century and its language from the political domain of the twentieth-century historian. For him, scholars who impose such modern, secular dispositional subfields as radical, moderate and conservative or left, centre and right upon the exceptionally fluid political language of seventeenth-century England have collapsed the past into the present. Like Clark, Condren believes that a careful consideration of the connections between seventeenth-century political language and the religious and legal debate of the same era is the best antidote to such domestications of the past.[2]

Forceful revisionist warnings have thus been offered, but many Restoration scholars persist in employing the radical category in their professional work and shoptalk. Despite the tenacity with which they cling to this usage, the entrance of the name radical into the field of Restoration studies is fairly recent. The classic Whig historians, who knew their nineteenth-century Radicals, did not use the word radical in their work about the seventeenth century.[3] In

---

J. C. D. Clark, *English Society 1688–1832: Ideology, Social Structure and Political Practice during the Ancien Regime* (Cambridge, 1986), Introduction and ch. 5, esp. pp. 277, 348. Also see, Alastair MacLachlan, *The Rise and Fall of Revolutionary England: an Essay on the Fabrication of Seventeenth-Century History* (New York, 1996).

[2] Conal Condren, 'Radicals, Conservatives and Moderates in Early Modern Political Thought: a Case of Sandwich Islands Syndrome?', *History of Political Thought* 10 (Autumn 1989), 525–42 with quotation at p. 527; Conal Condren, *The Language of Politics in Seventeenth-Century England* (New York, 1994), Introduction, esp. pp. 1–9; ch. 2, esp. pp. 33–43; and ch. 5, esp. pp. 140–4.

[3] Condren points to the exception of G. P. Gooch, for whom, see *English Democratic Ideas in the Seventeenth Century*, 2nd edn, with H. J. Laski (Cambridge, 1927; first published 1898), pp. 126–32, 277; Condren, *Language of Politics*, pp. 200–1. Although some Restoration historians of the first half of the twentieth century were interested in outspoken sectarians and plotters, they did not refer to them as radicals. See, for instance: Wilbur Cortez Abbott, 'English Conspiracy and Dissent, 1660–1674', *American Historical Review* 14 (April–July, 1909), 503–28, 696–722; and Iris Morley, *A Thousand Lives: An Account of the English Revolutionary Movement, 1660–1685* (London, 1954).

1961, J. R. Jones apparently became the first academic historian deliberately to use the name radical for the extreme wing of the Whig party, in London and elsewhere, in 1678–81.[4] For Jones, the radicals were the remnants of 'the levellers and the republicans' who had gone 'underground' in 1660 only to reappear in the politics of exclusion.[5] The name gained further respectability in Restoration studies when J. H. Plumb argued, in his Ford Lectures of 1965, that the Restoration Whigs had endorsed 'radical constitutional principles that stretch back to 1641'. Plumb also provided urban radicalism with a social base in London's lower middle class.[6]

Two examples will suffice to show how discussions of ideas and individuals designated as radical have been central in some of the most noted recent scholarship about the Restoration. Richard Ashcraft's study of John Locke and his times and Jonathan Scott's examination of Algernon Sidney have each provoked considerable discussion. Ashcraft provided us with a John Locke who moved in the ideological world of 'radical' London and country Whigs. According to him, echoes of the Leveller past can be detected in Locke's *Second Treatise* and in Whig ideology. Locke and the radical Whigs were also, according to Ashcraft, the advocates of enterprise and the carriers of capitalism. They were enemies of the hierarchy, privilege and monopoly that still obstructed the ambitious and innovative economic agendas of London merchants and their improving country cousins.[7]

For Jonathan Scott the revolutionary connection between the

---

[4] The name radical was not generally used by the broader cohort of Restoration specialists who dominated the scholarship of the 1960s and early 1970s. K. H. D. Haley used radical sparingly, as a synonym for extreme, in reference to some London Whigs: *The First Earl of Shaftesbury* (Oxford, 1968), pp. 600, 620. Maurice Ashley made the same limited use: *The Glorious Revolution of 1688* (London, 1966), p. 185. J. R. Western restricted the name radical to the interregnum: *Monarchy and Revolution: the English State in the 1680s* (London, 1972), p. 7. John Miller wrote about 'radical sects' in 1973 but used radical more broadly in the 1980s: *Popery & Politics in England, 1660–1689* (Cambridge, 1973); *The Glorious Revolution* (London, 1983), pp. viii, 21; *Restoration England: the Reign of Charles II* (London, 1985), pp. 3, 76.

[5] J. R. Jones, *The First Whigs: The Politics of the exclusion crisis, 1678–1683*, revised edition (London, 1970), pp. 14–16; *The Revolution of 1688 in England* (London, 1972), p. 306. Yet Jones denied that much potential for 'a revolutionary movement' or for a 'popular radicalism' could be found in Restoration England or its burgeoning urban capital.

[6] J. H. Plumb, *The Growth of Political Stability in England 1675–1725* (Harmondsworth, 1969), pp. 36–7, 138, 184–5.

[7] Richard Ashcraft, *Revolutionary Politics and Locke's 'Two Treatises of Government'* (Princeton, 1986), esp. chs. 4–7; Richard Ashcraft, 'The Radical Dimensions of Locke's Political Thought: a Dialogic Essay on Some Problems of Interpretation', *History of Political Thought* 13 (Winter 1992), 703–72. Ashcraft's treatment of Locke should now be read in conjunction with John Marshall, *John Locke: Resistance, Religion and Responsibility* (Cambridge, 1994).

Restoration and the interregnum is really republicanism rather than radicalism. Where Jones and Plumb found radicals in 1678–81, Scott finds republicans as well. The urban friends of Algernon Sidney turned the city of London into a 'republican bastion', according to Scott, just as Sidney and his parliamentary associates presided over an 'English republican renaissance'. But Scott nevertheless construes republicans as radicals. For him, republicanism is one of several late-seventeenth-century radical languages.[8]

Revisionist strictures about the early-modern employment of the name radical and some of the most important recent work about Restoration politics have, therefore, been pulling us in opposite directions. My own view is that the name radical retains its utility for Restoration studies. But we need to be more careful with our definitions, paying particular attention to how and when we employ such names as radical, republican and reformer. My arguments will be based upon evidence from the city of London, which is of unique importance for this topic. Jones and Plumb were responding to London evidence in their initial assertions about Restoration radicals. The Restoration city provides the firmest ground for Ashcraft's more recent anchorage of radicals in the urban social landscape of commerce, competition and initiative. London is also the most significant local centre of Scott's 'republican renaissance'. Finally, revisionist efforts to ban radicals from the seventeenth century have largely ignored the case of London.

2 POLITICAL DISCOURSE

Why have historians writing since the 1960s so frequently turned to the name radical to interpret the late-seventeenth-century political history of London?

Political discourse in the Stuart capital showed a consistent attachment by many electors, dissenters and Whigs to the privileges of citizenship, to chartered liberties, to historic birthrights and to the

---

[8] Jonathan Scott, *Algernon Sidney and the Restoration Crisis, 1677–1683* (Cambridge, 1991), pp. 107, 115, 117, 125, 126–7, 138–44, 162–73, 179–83; 'Restoration Process', *Albion* 25 (Winter 1993), 626–7. Also see, Jonathan Scott, *Algernon Sidney and the English Republic, 1623–1677* (Cambridge, 1988). Scott's treatment of Sidney should be read in conjunction with that of Alan Craig Houston, *Algernon Sidney and the Republican Heritage in England and America* (Princeton, 1991). Other recent historians of the Restoration who have employed the radical label in their work include Richard Greaves, Mark Goldie, J. G. A. Pocock, Lois Schwoerer and W. A. Speck. Also see *Biographical Dictionary of Seventeenth Century British Radicals*, ed. Richard L. Greaves and Robert Zaller, 3 vols. (Brighton, 1982–4).

'ancient constitution'. Moreover, the outspoken language in which these commitments were expressed reflected departures from prevailing conventions about obedience, divine right monarchy, and the hierarchical and prescriptive trappings of authority in church and state.

I will survey some evidence pointing to this canon of civic language about rights and liberties before turning to a definition of the name radical that is appropriate for the Restoration.[9] I will then develop arguments about the origins, meaning and transmission of radical language in the city. My point in surveying this evidence is to suggest that, contrary to Jones, the body of Restoration civic discourse that some scholars have characterized as radical was not an underground tradition that became detectable again only in the 1678–81 politics of exclusion. This libertarian attachment to civic and individual rights was instead a noisy and overt element of civic politics throughout the Restoration. Episodically expressed in the politics of the Corporation, it was nevertheless always at hand, always available for use by those unhappy with the direction of local and national affairs.

Vigorous expressions of this tradition figured in the 1659–60 revolt of London apprentices and citizens against the restored Rump and the New Model Army. In these urban episodes a revolution devoured itself. The libertarian language employed in the late 1640s by the Levellers and the sects against a Presbyterian-dominated parliament was now directed instead against sectarians and commonwealthmen who clung to power after overturning the more traditional parliamentary forms of the Cromwells.

An urban manifesto of August 1659, offered at the time of Sir George Booth's rising, for instance, denied the legitimacy of the Rump because the 'Authority of the People in Parliament' was 'usurped and abused' by so unrepresentative a body.[10] Six months later, as General George Monck approached his critical rendezvous

---

[9] I have previously explored some of this evidence in Gary S. De Krey, 'The London Whigs and the exclusion reconsidered', in A. L. Beier, David Cannadine and James M. Rosenheim (eds.), *The First Modern Society: Essays in English History in Honour of Lawrence Stone* (Cambridge, 1989), pp. 457–82; 'London Radicals and Revolutionary Politics, 1675–1683', in Tim Harris, Paul Seaward and Mark Goldie (eds.), *The Politics of Religion in Restoration England* (Oxford, 1990), pp. 133–62; 'Revolution *redivivus*: 1688–89 and the Radical Tradition in Seventeenth-Century London Politics', in Lois G. Schwoerer (ed.), *The Revolution of 1688–89: Changing Perspectives* (Cambridge, 1992), pp. 198–217.

[10] *An Express from the Knights and Gentlemen now engaged with Sir George Booth; To the City and Citizens of London* (1659); Austin Woolrych, 'Introduction', *Complete Prose Works of John Milton*, 8 vols. (New Haven and London, 1953–82), VII, 108–9.

with the Rump, he was addressed by 'elected' delegates of the 'apprentices and young men' of London. They informed him that 'our Civil Interest . . . consists in the Priviledges and Liberties to which we were born, . . . among which the grand and Essential Priviledge[,] which discriminates free men from slaves, is the interest which every man hath in the legislative power of the Nation'. A few days later the common council of London, lately returned to 'Presbyterian' domination, repudiated the authority of the Rump as leaving them in 'perpetual slavery'. The common councilmen demanded their 'undoubted Birthright' to be taxed only by a '*Full and Free Parliament*' made up of the 'rightfull Representatives of the people, by whom every individual doth consent'.[11]

Those Londoners who spoke against the Rump and who resisted the republic in 1659–60 have conventionally been described as royalists. Such a characterization clearly obscures more about them and their political discourse than it captures. Their demands for a free and representative parliament, and for political institutions that reflected their birthrights, were not arguments for monarchy per se but rather the same arguments that had been made against arbitrary rule in the 1640s. These ideas would be heard again and again in the Restoration city.

Many of the citizens who cheered the arrival of Charles II in the capital in May 1660 came quickly to the conclusion that the royalist settlement had no more secured their 'Priviledges and Liberties' than the abortive republican settlement that preceded it. London Presbyterians found themselves after 1662 in the same dissenting wilderness as sectarians. By the late 1660s, they were ready to join with other dissenters in confronting a church that coerced their consciences and a persecuting state that incarcerated their bodies, claimed their property in fines and abridged their civil liberties. Their initial target was not the king but rather the Cavalier Parliament, a body which, in their perceptions, was as inclined to arbitrary government as the Rump.

The years from 1669 to 1672 saw the eruption of a great contest about liberty of conscience in London that coincided with parlia-

---

[11] *To his Excellency the Lord General Monck. The Unanimous Representation of the Apprentices* (1659[60]); *To the Right Honourable the Lord Maior, Aldermen, and Commons of the City of London . . . The Humble Petition of divers Well-Affected Householders and Freemen* [1660]; *A Free Parliament Proposed by the City to the Nation* [1660]; *Londons Diurnal*, no. 1, 1–8 Feb. 1660, pp. 2–3; *Calendar of State Papers Domestic 1659–60* (hereafter *CSPD*), pp. 344–5, p. 359.

mentary adoption of a more severe act against conventicles. This controversy engulfed the press and embroiled the Corporation, where dissenters returned to office in significant numbers and where commonwealth spectres arose from their political graves. Baptist William Kiffin was chosen Sheriff of London and Middlesex. Onetime Leveller-sympathizer Henry Brandreth and onetime republican merchant Slingsby Bethel were returned as aldermen.[12] The London contest about coercion provoked street battles between the urban militia and crowds of Protestant conventiclers. It spilled into the courts, where Quaker defendants William Penn and William Mead turned their prosecution under the new Conventicle Act into public theatre reminiscent of the trials of John Lilburne. Penn argued that the Conventicle Act, which took away 'the LIBERTY and PROPERTY' of defendants, deprived freeborn Englishmen of 'natural Rights' and broke the 'Law of *nature*'. 'Where Liberty and Property are destroyed', he continued, 'there must alwayes be a state of force and war, which . . . will be esteemed intolerable by the *Invaded*, who will no longer remain subject.' Penn's warning that the state might collapse as persecuted subjects withdrew their loyalty was echoed by more 'churchly' dissenters like John Owen and John Humfrey. Owen argued that 'magistrates who coerce conscience must irresistibly extinguish the community itself' by preventing individuals from finding security 'in the good of the whole'.[13]

London dissenters chosen for common council in the midst of this contest about coercion were accused of undermining magistracy. This accusation was repeated in 1675 when dissenting common councilmen claimed a right of election to a minor Corporation judicial place. They charged Anglican Lord Mayor Sir Robert Vyner, who insisted upon a prerogative of appointment to the place, with attempting 'to subvert . . . the liberties of the city'. Vyner responded by claiming that the common councilmen intended 'to take the sole power of government into the hands of the commons'.[14]

The following year, civic and parliamentary opposition was con-

---

[12] Kiffin declined election, and the Court of Aldermen vetoed the wardmote elections of Brandreth and Bethel. Gary S. De Krey, 'The First Restoration Crisis: Conscience and Coercion in London, 1667–73', *Albion* 25 (Winter 1993), 565–80.

[13] [Thomas Rudyard], *The Peoples Antient and Just Liberties Asserted* (1670), pp. 47–8, 58–9; John Owen, *A Peace-Offering in an Apology* (1667) in *The Works of John Owen*, ed. W. H. Goold, 16 vols. (London and Edinburgh, 1852), XIII, 556–7.

[14] British Library, M/863/11: Coventry MSS. (Bath Papers), XVI, 9–11, 21–2; Corporation of London Records Office, Journal 48, fos. 128, 143, 147; *CSPD 1668–69*, p. 616.

joined in an effort launched in common hall, the electoral assembly of the city's liverymen, to promote a petition for a new parliamentary election. Francis Jenks, who initiated this manoeuvre, was acting as city agent for the troublesome duke of Buckingham. The son-in-law of Leveller theoretician William Walwyn, Jenks argued on behalf of the right of parliamentary electors to petition the crown. More importantly, he elevated the authority of the London parliamentary electorate of some eight thousand liverymen over the lord mayor, aldermen and common councilmen: 'The chief binding acts in our city government have always been made by the Common Hall, and the acts of the lord mayor, aldermen, and Common Council have been, and may be, nulled by the acts of the Common Hall.'[15]

In effect, Jenks had suggested that the city's elected officers were agents and representatives of its citizens and that London citizens could overturn decisions made on their behalf. A short step separated his argument from that made for popular authority in 1682 by dissenting Sheriff Thomas Pilkington. Pilkington then employed the power of his office against court-inspired attempts to impose Tory sheriffs on the Corporation for the following year. He publicly defended the proposition that the common hall electorate was 'the supreme authority in London', using these words to the very face of a monarch who also claimed that supreme authority. Much, of course, had happened in the Corporation of London in the intervening period. These were the years of the great crisis of the Restoration, a crisis that threatened repeatedly to explode the settlement of 1660–4. Thousands of Londoners signed petitions against popery and arbitrary government and in favour of parliament and Protestantism, a phenomenon dubbed 'Lilburneisme' by one apprehensive lord mayor. Popular language about popery and arbitrary government reflected a perception that this was a crisis not only about the constitution but also about reformation, and specifically about liberty of conscience.[16]

---

[15] Guildhall Library, MS 3589, fos. 6–7; Public Record Office Prob. 11 North 365, qu. 13 (will of William Walwyn); *An Account of the Proceedings at Guild-hall, London, at the Folke-moote* (1676); *CSPD 1676–77*, pp. 180, 253–6, 193–4.

[16] Folger Shakespeare Library, Newdigate Newsletter Lc. 732 (16 Jan. 1679); *CSPD 1682*, p. 417; Mark Knights, 'London Petitions and Parliamentary Politics in 1679', *Parliamentary History* 12: 1 (1993), 29–46 and esp. p. 31; 'London's "Monster" Petition of 1680', *Historical Journal*, 36, 1 (1993), pp. 39–67; *Politics and Opinion in Crisis, 1678–81* (Cambridge, 1994); Gary S. De Krey, 'Reformation in the Restoration Crisis, 1679–1682', in *Religion, Literature, and Politics in Post-Reformation England, 1540–1688* (Cambridge, 1996), pp. 231–52; Mark Goldie, 'Danby, the Bishops and the Whigs', in Tim Harris, Paul Seaward and Mark Goldie (eds.), *The Politics of Religion in Restoration England* (Oxford, 1990), pp. 75–105.

These issues convulsed the city in 1682. Ministerial efforts to recapture the London magistracy from the Whigs and to secure a legal ruling against the city's charter brought the crisis of the Restoration to a London climax that was rhetorically and physically violent. During the shrieval election of 1682, which took three months to complete, Whig electors appeared at meetings of common hall 'armed as if they had been goeing to a Battall', and they threatened at one point to 'pull' the lord mayor 'to pieces'. Algernon Sidney was present near Guildhall on one occasion, witnessing some of these scenes and hearing outraged electors complain about 'the most notorious violation of the ancient and known rights and privileges of this city that has ever been committed'. In the wake of this election, John Locke completed the *Two Treatises of Government*, critical chapters of which employ language reminiscent of the rhetorical slogans current in the London streets. Many London Whigs regarded the imposition of Tory sheriffs as the triumph of 'a military government' over the will of the electorate. Some of them would convert their political anger into plotting against the regime.[17]

This evidence about the language of politics in Restoration London suggests that we can speak about widespread suspiciousness of magistracy, attachment to the rights of citizenship, and confidence in the autonomy of individual Protestant believers. Under the right circumstances, these ideas could generate rhetorical and physical opposition, violence and even resistance. But nobody in the Restoration referred to those who expressed these ideas as radicals. This evidence does not, therefore, without further definition and interpretation, answer the objections of those who would drive the name radical from seventeenth-century English history.

3 CONSCIENCE

Can we, then, develop a definition of the word radical that would make it appropriate for many Restoration London Whigs and dissenters, despite its anachronistic character?

That many London dissenters and Whigs engaged in extreme

[17] Library of Congress: London Newsletters, VIII: 20, 22, 27 April; 24, 27, 29 June; 6, 8 July; 21, 28, 30 Sept. 1682; *CSPD 1682*, p. 431; John Locke, *Second Treatise of Government*, ed. Peter Laslett, in *Two Treatises of Government*, 2nd edn (Cambridge, 1967), chs. 18–19; Scott, *Restoration Crisis*, pp. 272–3; Marshall, *John Locke*, ch. 6; De Krey, 'London Radicals and Revolutionary Politics', pp. 146–55.

action is beyond doubt. Even so stringent a wordsmith as Condren acknowledges that the 'meaning of radical as extreme action' might be useful, if the word were not so laden with other intellectual baggage.[18] But in seeking to tame the city of London in 1682–3, Charles II engaged in extreme action, as did Cavalier MPs who imposed the divisive church settlement of 1662. A loose identification of radical with extreme action solves few problems.

Many London dissenters and Whigs could also be described as radical according to the seventeenth-century definition of radicality as a 'getting to the roots'. Intellectually, they got to the roots of what was at stake in the erection of a persecuting state. Indeed, I will argue that how they got to the roots of that matter was distinctive, innovative and laden with historical significance. Condren would reject such a proposition out of hand, however. According to him, if we look carefully at those in the 'whole late medieval and early-modern period' who have been misidentified as the 'carriers of history', we always find that they protest on behalf of traditions threatened by somebody else's innovations.[19] In Restoration England, popery and arbitrary government were innovative and challenging to tradition. Dissenters and Whigs, in Condren's construction, reacted to protect the *old* Protestant reformation and the *ancient* constitution. They were guardians of tradition, not radicals.

Let me therefore suggest a third definition. I would define political radicals as those who reject, challenge, or undermine the established political norms or conventions of their day, the intellectual rationales that legitimate those norms or conventions, and the structures of authority that maintain them.[20] What was radical about the discourse and the actions of London dissenters and Whigs was not only that they rejected some principal elements of the Restoration settlement of 1660–4. They also sought to pull up that settlement by the roots and to replace it with something different – with something more tolerant, more anchored in the 'birthrights' of Englishmen, and more in keeping with the personal sense of ownership that they already felt for their religious lives. In their political discourse and

---

[18] Condren, 'Radicals, Conservatives and Moderates', p. 541; Condren, *Language of Politics*, pp. 149, 160.

[19] Condren, 'Radicals, Conservatives and Moderates', pp. 533, 535–9; Condren, *Language of Politics*, pp. 153, 165–7, 158–9, 160–2.

[20] For a different definition, see J. C. Davis, 'Radicalism in a Traditional Society: the Evaluation of Radical Thought in the English Commonwealth 1649–1660', *History of Political Thought* 3 (Summer, 1982), 193–213.

behaviour, spokesmen for London dissenters and Whigs undermined Restoration conventions; and they devised resettlements of the Restoration church and state on new foundations.

Understandings of conscience and consent, in particular, lie at the heart of radical language and radical actions in Restoration London.

Whether articulated by Restoration sectarians or by more 'churchly' nonconformists, arguments for conscience became a wedge that loosened or uncoupled the nexus between prince and priest, and between magistrate and minister, that had been fundamental to English Protestantism since the 1530s. This was manifestly so among Baptists and Quakers, who rejected the ecclesiastical authority of the crown. But this was also so among independents and Presbyterians. They accepted the ecclesiastical authority of the prince to varying degrees, but they nevertheless now abandoned historic assumptions about the necessity of religious uniformity and about the legitimacy of religious coercion. Before 1660, ideas about liberty for conscience had fragmented English reformed Protestantism; but after 1660, and under persecution, ideas about liberty for conscience were mainstreamed by Presbyterians and independents who placed them at the heart of English reformed thought. Dissenting teachers and their London hearers and readers largely came to agree that Protestantism could better flourish through the persuasion of heart and mind than through the punishment of the body.

What did London teachers and citizens mean by conscience? Dissenting spokesmen whose works circulated in London defined conscience as a critical, moral and rational faculty that enables each individual to respond to God's command of obedience to divine will. Individuals are expected by God to employ this faculty to discern God's intentions for their behaviour and devotion. Indeed, every person must be free to exercise conscience in order to be truly human. As Sir Charles Wolseley, the onetime Cromwellian councillor and Restoration friend of Shaftesbury and Buckingham, put it: 'To say a man is not to judge for himself [in religious matters], is to . . . change him from a rational Creature to a Bruit.' Presbyterian spokesmen like John Humfrey and Richard Baxter agreed that any surrender of the free exercise of conscience to prince or priest is a sinful betrayal of personal accountability to God.[21]

[21] [Sir Charles Wolseley], *Liberty of Conscience upon its true and proper Grounds* (1668), pp. 5–6, 44; [John Humfrey], *A Case of Conscience* (1669), p. 5; J[ohn] H[umfrey], *The Obligation of Human Laws Discussed* (1671), pp. 77, 83; J[ohn] H[umphrey], *The Authority of the Magistrate, about*

Fundamental to the political theory of Restoration dissent was a division between a public sphere of life, for the governance of which the prince was responsible to God, and a personal sphere of faith, for the governance of which the individual was responsible to God. The personal sphere of faith was not an invisible sphere, however, but rather a sphere that extended into life in this world, one that encompassed outward conduct and worship. In separating these spheres, nonconformist writers employed the especially significant concept of vicegerency. If the magistrate was God's vicegerent in the public regime, then the conscience was God's vicegerent within the personal regime of faith and religious conduct. Any violation by church or by state of the vicegerency of conscience was an indefensible violation of the sovereignty of God, as that sovereignty was exercised in and through the individual conscience. As John Owen wrote, 'to take away . . . liberty of conscience, in things of its proper cognizance and duty . . . is to put God's great vicegerent out of his place and throne'. Or as John Humfrey put it, 'if the Magistrate command a thing against my Conscience, that Command (at least to me) is void, and without power. Gods Vicegerent within me, my Conscience, makes his external Voice to cease.'[22]

What is important here is the conversion of the concept of vicegerency from a rationale for the prince's authority into a rationale for maintaining a strong personal boundary against any inappropriate exercise of that authority. This construction of conscience was largely a Restoration achievement, for few writers on behalf of liberty of conscience before 1660 employed the concept of vicegerency in this manner.[23] And again, this understanding of

---

Religion, Discussed (1672), p. 72; Richard Baxter, *The Second Part of the Nonconformists Plea for Peace* (1680), p. 45; Gary S. De Krey, 'Rethinking the Restoration: Dissenting Cases for Conscience, 1667–1672', *Historical Journal* 38: 1 (1995), 53–83; Ashcraft, *Revolutionary Politics*, ch. 2.

[22] Owen, *Indulgence and Toleration Considered* (1667) in *Works*, XIII, 528; Humfrey, *Case of Conscience*, pp. 29–30. Also see, Humfrey, *Authority of the Magistrate*, p. 43; Philip Nye, *The Lawfulness of the Oath of Supremacy, and Power of the king in Ecclesiastical Affairs* (1683, but written earlier), pp. 20–1; Wolseley, *Liberty of Conscience upon its true and proper Grounds*, pp. 42–3; [Vincent Alsop], *Melius Inquirendum. Or, a Sober Inquiry*, 3rd edn (1681), pp. 364–5.

[23] The concept of the vicegerency of conscience does occur in William Walwyn, but it is neither central to Walwyn's thought nor well developed: [William Walwyn], *The Vanitie of the Present Churches* (1649), pp. 47, 50 in *The Writings of William Walwyn*, ed. Jack M. McMichael and Barbara Taft (Athens, GA, 1989), pp. 332–3. Colin Davis has explored the paradox of Christian liberty and bondage in pre-1660 arguments about liberty for conscience: J. C. Davis, 'Religion and the Struggle for Freedom in the English Revolution', *Historical Journal* 35: 3 (1992), esp. pp. 507–30.

conscience, which checked all temporal intrusions upon a personal sphere of faith and devotion, was articulated as strongly by Presbyterians like Humfrey as it was by sectarians. Moreover, dissenting authors maintained that if the exercise of conscience is a God-given liberty, then it is also a part of the natural created order to which the state itself must conform in order to exercise its authority legitimately. Mixing arguments from history and nature, William Penn defended 'liberty of conscience . . . as our undoubted right by the law of God, of nature, and of our own country'. John Owen argued that liberty of conscience 'naturally belong[s] unto all . . . men' and has been 'provided for' in 'the fundamental law' of all properly constituted states.[24] To root this argument in nature, to drive it to a foundation within the created order, was again to defend nonconformity itself in the most radical manner possible.

And if liberty for conscience was a natural right, then Restoration arguments for religious uniformity – and for coercion as a method of obtaining uniformity – were baseless despite their historic pedigrees. Whether arguing primarily for diversity of practice within the church or primarily for diversity of practice outside the church, Restoration dissenters therefore departed from a fundamental norm of classical Protestant and medieval Catholic statecraft. Major dissenting authors of the Restoration repeatedly treated diversity in the forms of Protestant expression as desirable and as sanctioned by God. 'Uniformity in Religion is beautiful and amiable', admitted Presbyterian John Corbet, but 'there is no constraining of all minds to one perswasion without imbasing their judgements to perfect slavery'. John Owen stressed that 'religion . . . is the choice of men, and he that chooseth not his religion hath none'. The author of a Protestant utopian piece of 1681 noted that 'as long as there is any variety to be found in nature, it will be discernable in the difference of thoughts and opinions of men'.[25]

Restoration dissenters, then, wished to uproot the Anglican estab-

---

[24] William Penn, *The Great Case of Liberty of Conscience* (1671) in *The Select Works of William Penn*, 3 vols. (London, 1825), p. 160; John Owen, *Truth and Innocence Vindicated* (1669), in *Works*, XIII, 491. Also see John Owen, *A Peace-Offering*, in *Works*, XIII, 558 and *Indulgence and Toleration*, p. 526.

[25] John Corbet, *The Second Part of the Interest of England* (1660), pp. 60, 76; Owen, *Indulgence and Toleration*, p. 532; *A Conference between a Bensalian Bishop and an English Doctor* (1681), p. 5. Also see John Humfrey, *A Defence of the Proposition* (1668), pp. 20–1; Alsop, *Melius Inquirendum*, pp. 19–20; Edward Bagshaw, *The Great Question concerning Things Indifferent in Religious Worship*, 3rd edn (1660), pp. 13–14; Baxter, *The Second Part of the Nonconformists Plea*, p. 181.

lishment maintained through coercive penalties and to replace the Anglican goal of uniformity with a Protestant order, variously defined, in which the gospel took root and flourished because individuals were persuaded of its truth. For them, Christian ministry was 'not to be compulsive, but perswasive'. Where Anglican bishops and apologists saw church and state as the hierarchical guardians of truths which must be imposed in order to be safeguarded, dissenters insisted upon the right of individual believers to 'Exercise . . . their own reason, or judgement', to 'search the Scriptures', and to 'try the Doctrines delivered'. Dissenters maintained that prescriptive policies on behalf of the gospel only left 'a people nuzled in ignorance and superstition'. They preferred a relatively open intellectual universe in which religious truth, like the truth of 'other Sciences', progressively developed through its free enlargement 'into [a] variety of Thoughts and Principles'.[26] Anglican spokesmen were not really exaggerating when they claimed that dissenting demands were 'utterly destructive' to the order that had recently been recreated. Indeed, the dissenting authors from whom I have quoted frequently expressed their hostility to coercion in rhetoric that was distinctly reminiscent of Leveller spokesmen like William Walwyn and Richard Overton.

The church structures proposed by Restoration dissenters were innovative, therefore; and so were their arguments against coercion.[27] The acceptance of Protestant diversity on the grounds that faithful believers might employ their consciences to come to different conclusions overturned assumptions of the English church–state in operation since the Elizabethan Act of Uniformity. That God might lead Christians in different directions within the same state and society was an idea that accorded with recent English experience but not with time-hallowed episcopal practice. And arguments that pitted the governance of conscience against the governance of the king also point the historian of intellectual change towards the 'enlightened' ideas of the future, as do arguments that employ reason and nature to shatter conventional practice.

[26] Henry Adis, *A Fannaticks Mite Cast into the kings Treasury* (1660), p. 12; Corbet, *Second Part of the Interest*, p. 61; [John Corbet], *A Discourse of the Religion of England* (1667), p. 20; [Sir Charles Wolseley], *Liberty of Conscience, the Magistrates Interest* (1668), p. 8.

[27] Although dissenting visions of a broad and flexible Protestant establishment with indulgence for those outside of it drew upon Cromwellian ecclesiastical structures, the Cromwellian church lacked a clear philosophical rationale. Blair Worden, 'Toleration and the Cromwellian Protectorate', in W. Shiels (ed.), *Persecution and Toleration*, Studies in Church History 21 (Oxford, 1984), pp. 199–233.

To point this out is not the same thing as suggesting that one pattern of ideas 'anticipated' a succeeding pattern. But it is to suggest that these arguments and their authors displayed a sophistication that is obscured by the revisionist claim that 'rhetorical mishap' or linguistic confusion are the chief attributes of those who have been misnamed as radicals.[28] And, to set aside momentarily the strong Protestant motifs that persisted in these dissenting proposals, we must acknowledge that the reformed order for church and state envisioned by some dissenters was, structurally speaking, closer to what was created in 1828 than what came about in the 'mere toleration' of 1689.[29] Indeed, the arguments made by dissenting authors and citizens on behalf of liberty for conscience contribute to our understanding of the Restoration decades as transitional, in their intellectual character, between the preceding century of Reformation and the century of Enlightenment that followed.

To suggest that the Restoration dissenting apologies that I have considered are all encoded in the agenda of reformation is perfectly true. And to suggest that the name reformer, in its Protestant sense, is as appropriate for many of the people I have discussed as the name radical is also true. Presbyterians and independents developed their visions of a new Protestant order with some traditional reformed conceptions about magistracy and ministry and about providence and personal responsibility. However, I am not comfortable with the revisionist claim that the concept of reformation was employed almost exclusively in the interests of tradition and of its conservation. That suggestion imposes pre-1640 language and definitions on the fluid intellectual world of the late seventeenth century, a world in which arguments about liberty for conscience were altering reformed Protestant modes and meanings. Restoration reformers hoped to improve on the work of the 'first reformers', and their idealization of the primitive church did not prevent them from rethinking and overturning earlier Protestant conventions. For them, 'reformation'

[28] Quentin Skinner, 'Meaning and Understanding in the History of Ideas', in James Tully (ed.), *Meaning and Context: Quentin Skinner and his Critics* (Princeton, NJ, 1988), p. 35; Condren, *Language of Politics*, p. 162.

[29] Humfrey was prepared to extend toleration but not full civil rights to Roman Catholics: *Defence of the Proposition*, p. 63. Dissenting writers like Wolseley and Penn were grappling with a redefinition of magistracy and kingship that even more fundamentally severed the nexus between civil authority and religious profession. De Krey, 'Rethinking the Restoration', pp. 63–5.

was a proactive agenda still to be accomplished rather than a reactive defence of old achievements.[30]

And they practised what they preached. In the name of 'fundamental' laws and privileges that provided liberty of conscience, dissenters in London and elsewhere frequently defied human laws that supported coercion.[31] They challenged the practice of coercion in their chapels, in the streets and in the courts, hoping to stop the engines of persecution in their tracks. Some dissenting spokesmen also explicitly sanctioned resistance in certain situations, despite their frequent warnings against the taking up of arms in most circumstances. Humfrey, for instance, frequently wrote about the exceptional conditions under which resistance might be legitimate. Penn and Wolseley warned of the political consequences of any unnatural 'invasion' of the sphere of conscience by the state. Hundreds of dissenting clergy left the church in 1662, motivated in part by their inability to take an oath forswearing resistance in all situations. And, in deploying contractarianism, or constitutional models of mixed government, or distinctions between obedience and submission, dissenting political argument could also take on tones that were as offensive to the Anglican mind as the idea of resistance.[32]

Condren's suggestion that 'resistance rhetoric was not prominent' in the Restoration is therefore misleading.[33] Moved by this whole body of discourse, London dissenters and electors were encouraged in political behaviour that ranged from opposition to conspiracy to rebellion. To employ the name radical for them, when they engaged in such behaviour and articulated such ideas most forcefully, strikes me as entirely appropriate.

---

[30] Gary S. De Krey, 'Reformation in the Restoration Crisis, 1679–1682', in *Religion, Literature, and Politics in Post-Reformation England, 1540–1688* (Cambridge, 1996), pp. 231–52; Condren, *Language of Politics*, pp. 157–8, p. 160.

[31] See, for instance, *The Englishman, or a Letter from a Universal Friend* (1670), pp. 9–11; Penn, *Great Case*, pp. 144, 147.

[32] *A Short Surveigh of the Grand Case of the present Ministry* (1663), p. 21; Humfrey, *Authority of the Magistrate*, pp. 29–35, 52–3, 75; Humfrey, *Obligation of Human Laws*, pp. 46–7; [John Humfrey], *Comprehension Promoted* [1673]; [John Humfrey], *The Peaceable Design* (1675), pp. 34–48; [John Humfrey], *An Answer to Dr. Stillingfleet's Sermon* (1680), pp. 18–23; Alsop, *Mischief of Impositions*, Epistle Dedicatory, C2; Richard Baxter, *The Nonconformists Plea for Peace* (1679), p. 32; Richard Baxter, *Second Part of the Nonconformists Plea*, p. 56; Penn, as found in Rudyard, *The Peoples Ancient and Just Liberties*, pp. 47–8; Penn, *Great Case*, p. 147–8; Wolseley, *Liberty of Conscience, the Magistrates Interest*, p. 6; Wolseley, *Liberty of Conscience upon its true and proper Grounds*, p. 29. Also see: [Anthony Ashley Cooper, earl of Shaftesbury and John Locke?], *A Letter from a Person of Quality* (1675), p. 16.

[33] Condren, *Language of Politics*, p. 120.

The name republican would also be appropriate for some radical Restoration Londoners – for Sheriff Slingsby Bethel, probably, or for some Whig readers influenced by mid-century commonwealth writers. The application of the names radical, reformer and republican should often not be done to the exclusion of each other. What Lawrence Stone suggested, some time ago, about the importance of multiple categorization remains as true for the usage of political and religious names in the Restoration as it does for the discussion of pre-1640 categories.[34] Yet, I believe that these cases for conscience were more important than republican writing in shaping the political perspectives of London dissenters and Whigs. A republican writer like Algernon Sidney, who published very little in his lifetime, certainly shared both language and perspectives with the dissenting authors whom I have reviewed.[35] Yet the dissenting attack upon coercion and persecution employs different language from the republican attack upon priestcraft and Restoration kingship. Where many Restoration Presbyterians hoped still to reclaim Charles II as a godly prince, republicans like Sidney abandoned him as a classical tyrant. Dissenters and commonwealthmen could make common cause, but they also understood their causes in different terms; and the readership for dissenting publications was far broader than that for republican tracts.

4 CONSENT

Examination of the civic discourse of London Whigs in 1679–82 also supports a characterization of some of their ideas and behaviour as radical. In defending their understanding of civic rights against 'arbitrary government', many London Whigs articulated consensual assumptions about government that challenged and undermined the political conventions of the Restoration. Fearing the 'subversion' of parliaments and the historic Corporation by the crown and the ministry, they were driven back to the roots of their understanding of legitimate government. They anchored their arguments for the autonomy of the Corporation in the rights of an active citizenry who

---

[34] Lawrence Stone, *The Causes of the English Revolution 1529–1642* (New York, 1972), pp. 33–5.

[35] Sidney was as strong a defender of conscience as any of the authors whom I have considered and often used similar arguments. See, for instance, Algernon Sidney, *Court Maxims* (c.1664–5), ed. Hans W. Blom, Eco H. Mulier and Ronald Janse, Cambridge Texts in the History of Political Thought (Cambridge, 1996), p. 95; Scott, 'Restoration Process', p. 625.

consented to the laws, authorities and practices that made up their government. And they derived these civic rights and privileges from the 'immemorial usage', the 'uninterrupted Custom', and the 'Common Law right' of the ancient constitution.[36]

Nevertheless, Restoration London Whigs who relied upon political language about a mythic Anglo-Saxon past were not necessarily conservators of political and rhetorical tradition. Instead, the grounding of political authority in the Corporation in the consent of the 'commons' by some Whigs points to them again as 'carriers of history'. They may well have idealized the past, but they also conceived and utilized the past in a way that transformed the political present. They employed language about the ancient constitution to limit and to reconceive the exercise of magisterial, ministerial and royal authority over the freemen of London.[37] They did not understand authority as rooted in hereditary, apostolic, or corporate successions. They neither understood monarchy as a form of government resting upon divine privilege, nor did they understand Charles II primarily as God's anointed. They certainly did not understand the civic constitution as one in which magistrates ruled as the king's urban commissioners, presiding over a prescriptive civic order that reflected a natural hierarchy of king, lords and commons.

Instead, spokesmen for the London Whigs understood the Corporation to be a political association created by freemen and accepted by a succession of princes and parliaments. They understood civic magistrates as 'stewards' and 'servants' of the 'commons' who exercised authority on their behalf and who might be removed or punished for violations of the 'trust' conferred upon them. They saw the lord mayor not as the personification of the king's authority within the Corporation but rather as a political 'Creature made by the pleasure of the Citizens'. They saw the parliamentary electorate assembled in common hall as the modern embodiment of the ancient folkmoot. Common hall was, therefore, the 'Supream Power of the Citizens of *London*'. And when the liverymen acted in their electoral capacity, they were understood by Whig spokesmen to be acting not

---

[36] *A Modest Enquiry concerning the Election of the Sheriffs* (1682), p. 25; Thomas Hunt, *A Defence of the Charter, and Municipal Rights of the City of London* (1683), p. 39; *The Priviledg and Right of the Freemen of London* (1682), pp. 1–2, 8; Tim Harris, *London Crowds in the Reign of Charles II: Propaganda and Politics from the Restoration until the exclusion crisis* (Cambridge, 1987), pp. 131–44.

[37] In this respect the Whigs of the 1680s apparently differed from the Levellers, as interpreted by Glenn Burgess, *The Politics of the Ancient Constitution: an Introduction to English Political Thought, 1603–1642* (University Park, PA, 1992), pp. 224–31.

only for themselves but also on behalf of the entire body of some twenty thousand rate-paying urban householders, some of whom would eventually join the liveried electorate themselves.

The freemen, and especially the liverymen, then, were the 'people' upon whose agreement the authority of the magistrates rested. Indeed, according to the Whigs, the common hall electors could annul acts of the common councilmen and aldermen that violated rights preserved in the charter; and they could assemble on their own authority. In sum, civic Whig propagandists understood the Corporation as a local government that rested upon the consent of the people rather than as one that rested upon the grants of a restored monarch. Citizenship was scarcely 'subsumed under subjection' for them.[38]

For much of the Restoration, the contradictions between these civic assumptions (some of which had enjoyed civil war articulations) and royal 'fictions of authority' were politely ignored. But when Tory magistrates claimed the king's authority in overturning the wishes of the electorate in the choice of sheriffs for 1682–3, many Whigs argued that 'if the *King* shall Commissionate any to do that which is against Law, that Commission is void'. Indeed, the Whig shrieval candidates, who continued to claim election after the declaration of their Tory rivals, actually appeared in public as the duly chosen agents of the electorate. The crown's continuing action against the city's charter was widely seen as an ominous effort to replace self-government with arbitrary government. According to one writer, the crown's suit presaged the 'Destruction and Death' of a 'great . . . Body Politick', and Thomas Hunt implied that the royal effort to 'change the Government' of corporations like London could only be the act of 'a Wicked and Miserable Tyrant'.[39]

Under these circumstances, Sheriff Thomas Pilkington reportedly asserted before the king himself the people's right to 'fortify' themselves in defence of their 'lives, liberty, and religion'. Reflecting upon these same civic experiences, John Locke asked what could more 'cut

---

[38] *The Nature of a Common-Hall Briefly Stated* (1682); *The Rights of the City Farther unfolded* (1682), pp. 2–3; *The Lord Mayor of London's Vindication* (1682), pp. 2, 5; *The Citizens of London, by their Charter* [1680]; *Matters of Fact in the present Election of Sheriffs* (1682), p. 1; *The Case between the Ld. Mayor & commons of London* (1682), pp. 6–7; *Modest Enquiry*, p. 43; *Priviledg and Right*, pp. 6, 8; Hunt, *Defence of the Charter*, pp. 35–6; Condren, *Language of Politics*, p. 91.

[39] Library of Congress, London Newsletters, VIII: 28, 30 Sept. and 5 Oct. 1682; *The Case of the Sheriffs for the Year 1682* (1682), p. 13; *Rights Farther Unfolded*, p. 2; *The Citizens Loss, when the Charter of London is Forfeited* (1683), p. 4; Hunt, *Defence of the Charter*, pp. 6, 8–9; Condren, *Language of Politics*, pp. 110–11.

up the Government by the Roots', than magisterial attempts to 'regulate Candidates and *Electors*, and new model the ways of *Election*'. The political discourse of many London Whigs had brought them to the brink of resistance to a government that had, they believed, violated their rights and overturned the principle of consent. In their thoughts and deeds, these active London citizens were no passive subjects.[40]

The crown's assault upon the London charter was also an assault upon perspectives that were strongly rooted in the city's institutional life. The principle of consent reflected the experience of participation, which was deeply embedded in civic culture. Householders were habituated to participation through the annual calendar of wardmoots and precinct meetings and through their rotation in the offices and responsibilities of ward and parish. The sense of citizenship was strong in the Corporation. Many householders expected to exercise the rights and privileges of property-owners, knowing that their payment of rates and assessments sustained government at every level from the parish to the realm. Sidney and Beatrice Webb once employed the early-nineteenth-century Radical slogan, 'a rate-payers' democracy' to describe this participatory civic polity, as it continued to operate through the 1830s.[41] The Webbs' characterization of London political culture raises yet another question. Should many London Whigs also be considered radical because they subscribed to *democratic* political assumptions?

We need to proceed with even more caution in answering this question than in considering the radical label. Even the most extreme and conceptually sophisticated London Whigs failed to describe themselves as democrats; but that is scarcely surprising, given that the word democratic was still largely a term of abuse. Most London Whigs maintained that they were loyal to monarchy, as they understood it. They believed that consent and representation were derived from an ancient constitution that also sanctioned 'English monarchy', which was quite different from its arbitrary and degenerate continental counterpart.[42] Primarily concerned about the

---

[40] London Newsletters, VIII: 21 Sept. 1682; Locke, *Second Treatise*, no. 222, p. 431; Condren, *Language of Politics*, pp. 92, 111.

[41] Sidney and Beatrice Webb, *English Local Government from the Revolution to the Municipal Corporations Act: The Manor and the Borough*, part two (London: Longmans Green, 1908), pp. 685–8.

[42] Corporation of London Records Office (hereafter CLRO) Journal 49, fo. 206; *Humble Petition and Address of the Right Honourable the Lord Mayor* (1681).

rights of those who were enfranchised through their possession of property and the city's freedom, London Whig spokesmen largely ignored the 'un-free'. Nevertheless, as they operated in the fluid and transitional intellectual world at the juncture of Reformation discourse and the language of Enlightenment, many London Whigs followed the Levellers in employing some categories from which a consciously democratic political theory *could* have been constructed.[43] That the London Whigs did not make this construction themselves should not lessen our surprise at how extensively they rethought and rejected the premises of Restoration monarchy, as applied to the Corporation.

Whig publishers, for instance, printed compilations of the city's charters and grants as if they were a written constitution, just as John Lilburne had done in the 1640s. According to the subtitle of one of these publications, the chartered rights of the city were '*every Free-Man's Privilege*'. Lest this egalitarian point be lost, an introduction explained that 'the *Great Ones*' had often sought to keep these privileges 'to themselves' leaving 'the *Little* ones' in 'the *Dark*'. The printing of the documents, however, would ensure 'that every One, both *Rich* and *Poor*, may have the same benefit'. Another publicist printed a digest of laws supporting Whig constitutional premises so that every '*Free-born Subject's Inheritance*' would be clear. And yet another spokesman argued that rights 'that . . . belong . . . to *Every Body* by vertue of the *Constitution*, . . . cannot be taken away from *Any*'.[44]

Not surprisingly, given this broad understanding of the rights of citizenship, London Whigs also understood legislators and magistrates as 'representatives' of the electors who had chosen them. The accountability of such representatives was assumed in the instructions that London Whig electors presented to their newly elected MPs for the Oxford Parliament. Influenced by an understanding of authority as a trust, some Whigs moved from claiming a right to cashier representatives who betrayed the people's trust to claiming a right to cashier a king who behaved in the same manner. London Whigs and

---

[43] David Wootton, 'The Levellers', in John Dunn (ed.), *Democracy: the Unfinished Journey, 508 BC to AD 1993* (Oxford, 1992), pp. 71–89.

[44] *The Abridgement of the Charter of the City of London; Being every Free-Man's Privilege* (1680), also reprinted as *The Priviledges of the Citizens of London: Contained in the Charters* (1682), 'To the Reader'; John Lilburne, *The Charters of London* (1646); *The Case of the Sheriffs for the Year 1682* (1682), p. 24; [Henry Care], *English Liberties: Or, the Free-Born Subject's Inheritance* (1682), pp. 1–5.

dissenters also assumed the equality of citizens before the law in their championship of the rights of freemen to trial by jury and of the rights of juries before judges.[45]

These arguments appealed to a far broader spectrum of the London citizenry than that attracted by the Levellers a generation earlier. The London Whigs had mainstreamed many pre-1660 political arguments once associated with Levellers and common-wealthmen, just as Restoration Presbyterians and independents had mainstreamed sectarian arguments about conscience. Consensual Whig arguments about the civic constitution were also reinforced by the dissenting principles already examined. The vicegerency of conscience intrinsically levelled all rank and status. In dissenting thought, each individual stood before God equally responsible for discerning divine expectations, just as in Whig thought, each freeman was entitled to equal protection in law for his possession of appropriate rights.[46]

As some loyalists believed, then, London was something of a democratic rhinestone among the Stuart crown jewels.[47] For this very reason, republican authors like Algernon Sidney were fascinated with the politics of the Corporation. But the Whig following in the Corporation was not, to reiterate, primarily or essentially a republican following. The devotion of the London Whigs to an ancient constitution and their championship of the rights of a guild-based electorate owed more to history and to experience than to the civic *virtu* of Machiavellian tradition. Ideas articulated by republican writers did circulate in the city, but most London Whigs responded to republican ideas from the perspective of their own concerns about consent and liberty for conscience. These concerns made London Whigs and dissenters an audience for republican writings and perspectives. But they were an audience of independently minded individuals quite capable of mixing ideas and language, and of merging history and reason, in hybrid ways that can mislead the historian and defy precise categorization.

Having argued that conscience and consent sustained radical ideas

---

[45] Care, *English Liberties*, pp. 21–5; *The Case of Edward Bushel, John Hammond, Charles Milson and John Baily* [1671]; *A True Narrative of the Proceedings at Guild-Hall* (1681).

[46] Dissenting authors and teachers with London followings argued for the principle of consent in ecclesiastical affairs just as consistently as Whig authors did in civic affairs. See, for instance: Richard Baxter, *The Nonconformists Plea for Peace* (1679), pp. 25–6; Vincent Alsop, *The Mischief of Impositions* (1680), p. 28.

[47] *The Lord Mayor's Right of Electing a Sheriff Asserted* (1682), p. 2.

in Restoration London, I would nevertheless like to offer some additional qualifications to the argument. We need to be wary about the depth of some historical actors' comprehension of the ideas they read or voiced, about the consistency over time in other actors' expression of those ideas, and about ascribing too much coherence to language produced for immediate and changing political circumstances. Our growing respect for the creativity of early-modern readers also suggests the likelihood of multiple contemporary readings of the works that have been cited here.

We cannot, therefore, assert that all the authors and civic figures whom I have mentioned were radical all the time or even most of the time. They were responding to the specific ecclesiastical and political circumstances of the Restoration that contradicted their understandings of conscience and consent. Their political anger and some of their discourse were contingent upon what were, to them, the frightening episodes through which they lived. Sometimes these dissenting and Whig spokesmen preferred accommodation to confrontation, and the radical edge largely came off their thinking under the very different political circumstances that prevailed after 1689. Living in a transitional age, they engaged in radical thoughts and actions that were also – in many cases – transitional or occasional.

Reflecting upon such problems, Colin Davis has suggested that we might speak with more accuracy about the 'radical moments' of particular individuals than about radical individuals per se.[48] I agree, and I also think that some individuals experienced longer radical intervals. But we do need to employ the name radical as an occasional category, just as we sometimes need to employ multiple categorization in applying the names radical, reformer, and republican. Occasional categorization enables us to grasp the sometimes radical insights of a Baxter and the more frequent radical outbursts of a Pilkington without suggesting that the restrained Baxter or the wealthy Pilkington were consistently or systematically radical in their thinking.[49]

Furthermore, I have argued for radical people and for radical ideas, but I have not argued for 'radicalism'. Those London authors

---

[48] J. C. Davis, 'Radical Lives', *Political Science* 37 (1985), 172.
[49] Similarly, Richard Ashcraft argued that Shaftesbury and Locke *became* radical in the political circumstances that prevailed after 1675, not that they were moved by radical principles at all times. Richard Ashcraft, 'Simple Objections and Complex Reality: Theorizing Political Radicalism in Seventeenth-Century England', *Political Studies* 40 (1992), 101–2.

and citizens about whom I have written did not subscribe to a coherent, systematic political creed or programme. Like many historical figures, London Whig and dissenting spokesmen did not always see the full implications of what they were saying or of what they were doing. Although they did undermine and repudiate existing structures, they had not fully sorted out or agreed upon the future that they desired. Thinkers like William Penn and John Humfrey obviously disagreed about much. If the intellectual historian must generally be concerned, therefore, about 'the efforts and confusions which ordinarily mark the activity of thinking',[50] the early-modern historian who uses the anachronistic name radical must seek to capture the ambiguous nature of the language and behaviour to which the category leads.

5 COMMUNITY

A final question to address is how the language and perspectives of individuals and groups deemed radical by some civil war and interregnum historians were transmitted to Restoration authors and actors? Can we speak of a radical tradition in seventeenth-century London, even if we accept that radical expressions were products of particular moments or intervals?

Building on the work of Ashcraft and Scott, I would propose that Restoration London Whigs and dissenters formed a distinctive community of discourse with civil war origins.[51] Radical, republican, and reformed Protestant language circulated, to varying extents, within this community. Encompassing all the dissenting persuasions that flourished in London, this community of discourse employed language about historical and natural rights, about reason and an ancient constitution, about conscience and consent, and about the menace of popery and arbitrary government that had gained rhetorical currency in the 1640s. These concepts could be developed and refracted in different and even in contradictory ways by Londoners responding to the different circumstances of the Restoration.

---

[50] Skinner, 'Meaning and Understanding', p. 49.

[51] This broad-stroke approach is not intended to overlook the important theological and ecclesiastical differences that had fragmented Puritanism and produced the sects. This community of discourse also extended into the established church, which included both clergy and laity of old Puritan stock. My language is influenced by Robert Wuthnow, *Communities of Discourse: Ideology and Social Structure in the Reformation, the Enlightenment, and European Socialism* (Princeton, 1989).

By this definition, the community of discourse of Restoration London Whigs and dissenters was neither a 'republican community' nor a radical community. But the language articulated amongst these people was language that set them apart from the very different language of Anglican loyalism. More than anything else, this was a community defined by a particular understanding of Protestant reformation, an understanding that had implications for the state as well as for the church. In time, the first London Whigs emerged as a political party that spoke for the community.

Several structures and facilities bound this community together and sustained the circulation of radical, reformed and republican language within it. Family experiences and commitments were of particular importance. Sometimes one family head active before the Restoration carried pre-1660 patterns of thought and perception forward for decades. John Wildman, who first came to public notice as a Leveller, and who became a city alderman after the Glorious Revolution, is a good example of this pattern, as is Sheriff Bethel. But by the Restoration decades, language and perceptions had often been communicated from one generation to the next. Francis Jenks was surely influenced by his Leveller father-in-law William Walwyn. Samuel Shute, who served as Thomas Pilkington's shrieval colleague in 1681–2, must have been influenced both by his elder kinsman Richard Shute, active in the civic upheavals of the 1640s, and by his father-in-law, independent divine Joseph Caryl.[52]

Often the inclusion of a young man within the household of an older master could reinforce perspectives that may already have formed in a family of origin. Thomas Pilkington, for instance, had been apprenticed in 1645 to Thomas Barnardiston, a prominent Puritan Levant merchant. Pilkington must also, in time, have become familiar with Barnardiston's younger kinsman, Sir Samuel Barnardiston. Sir Samuel was foreman of the jury that threw out the government's 1681 treason case against Shaftesbury. Similarly, Thomas Papillon, one of the disappointed Whig shrieval candidates of 1682, had been apprenticed in 1646 to merchant and kinsman Thomas Chamberlain. In November 1659, Chamberlain had reportedly suggested in common council that the London citizenry should 'take up armes for their own preservation' against the arbitrary,

[52] A. G. Matthews, *Calamy Revised* (Oxford, 1934), p. 104; Robert Brenner, *Merchants and Revolution: Commercial Change, Political Conflict, and London's Overseas Traders, 1550–1653* (Princeton, NJ, 1993), *passim*.

military rule of the Rump. Papillon's apprenticeship under Chamberlain had coincided with that of Michael Godfrey, who married Chamberlain's daughter. Both Papillon and Godfrey joined Sir Samuel Barnardiston on Shaftesbury's jury, which was impanelled by Pilkington.[53]

Such thick connections of business and blood were bred and reinforced amongst families whose spiritual life was focused upon the ministry of particular dissenting teachers. The shared experience of dissenting worship under persecution was a powerful forger of community amongst those from whom London's Whigs would emerge. Anglicans charged that dissenting conventicles were nurseries of sedition. They were, at the least, nurseries for the formation of dissenting identity – schools of conscience in which history and experience shaped discourse about rights and liberties into new Protestant agendas. One wonders, for instance, about Sheriff Shute's conversation with Charles Fleetwood, who had in 1659 been a leading member of the Committee of Safety. After 1673, Shute and Fleetwood were members of the same gathered church. A decade later, when Sheriff Shute sought to thwart the crown's capture of the 1682 shrieval election, another member of this church served on the London jury for the doomed Stephen College, and a fourth member apparently disrupted a critical aldermanic meeting.[54]

This London community of discourse naturally reflected the importance of conversation in a densely populated urban society accustomed to conducting its major business in a face-to-face manner. Every transaction at the Exchange, every meeting of wardmote and precinct assemblies, every guild dinner, and every conventicle and parish service provided opportunities for conversation, argument and discussion. But the facilities for exchange of ideas about rights and liberties and about Protestantism and parliamentary government were not limited to those that sustained conversation.

[53] Bodleian Library Clarendon MS 66, fo. 253; J. R. Woodhead, *The Rulers of London 1660–1689* (London, 1967), pp. 44, 77, 125, 130; Brenner, *Merchants and Revolution*, pp. 377, 421; Basil Duke Henning, *The House of Commons 1660–1690*, 3 vols. (London, 1983), I, 596–7, III, 202, 245.

[54] Shute was a member of Joseph Caryl's church, which merged with that of John Owen, of which Fleetwood was a member, in 1673. Caleb Hooke, another former member of Joseph Caryl's church, served on the College jury. Deacon William Pickard may have been the liveryman of that name who led protestors into an aldermanic court. CLRO MS 40/30; Dr Williams's Library: Congregational Library MS 52.a.38, Register . . . of the church of . . . Duke's Place; BL Egerton MS. 2543, fo. 251; *The Two Associations* (1681); *CSPD 1682*, pp. 430–1; Woodhead, *Rulers of London*, p. 149.

The bookstalls clustered around St Paul's provided further opportunities for the circulation of the political and religious language that defined this community of discourse. The city of London was the reading and printing capital of Protestant Europe, and the Stuart regime's efforts to control the press through licensing did not seriously impede the printed circulation of radical, reformed or republican ideas.

Moreover, echoes and creative adaptations of old printed language about reformation, about the commonwealth and about the rights of citizens also abounded within this Restoration community of discourse. The republication of the late Leveller work *London's Liberties* (1651) in 1682 is the best-known example of the revival in print of old radical arguments. But other examples could be provided. An opposition publishing campaign, for instance, coincided with Francis Jenks's efforts to arouse the liverymen in their 1676 common hall. Central to this effort was an intended reprint of Nathaniel Bacon's *Historicall Discourse* (1647), a classic of ancient constitutionalism, the arguments of which lent themselves to a variety of purposes.[55]

Collections of books, both old and new, may also have provided intellectual fare and political acculturation for networks of readers within this community. We know much about the Rotterdam library of the Quaker Benjamin Furley, which was used by English exiles abroad. May we suppose that smaller surviving collections of books from the 1640s and the 1650s retained the interest of their London owners or of the families and friends of their owners? Did Francis Jenks, for instance, have access to his father-in-law's library, which had once served a broader circle of interested readers? And to what extent did the earliest dissenting schoolmasters employ the reformed, radical and republican language of the 1640s and the 1650s in their reflections upon Restoration happenings? Curiously, all thirty students from the dissenting academy in Newington appeared at one London common hall in 1682 because they had learned, from their teacher or otherwise, that 'their lives liberties and fortunes lay at stake' there.[56]

---

[55] HMC no. 25, *Le Fleming*, pp. 128–32; Richard Greaves, *Enemies under his Feet* (Stanford, 1990), p. 234; Burgess, *Politics of the Ancient Constitution*, pp. 96–8. About publishing, see Harris, *London Crowds*, ch. 5; Knights, *Politics and Opinion*, ch. 6; Richard Greaves, *Deliver us from Evil* (New York, 1986), ch. 7; Greaves, *Enemies under his Feet*, ch. 5; Greaves, *Secrets of the Kingdom* (Stanford, 1992), pp. 15–20, 40–9, 302–5.

[56] *CSPD 1678*, p. 313; *CSPD 1682*, p. 286; Ashcraft, *Revolutionary Politics*, pp. 536–7; Scott, *Sidney and the English Republic*, pp. 172–3, 216–17; *Writings of Walwyn*, p. 2.

The London community of discourse that sustained radical language and actions was also arguably the formative community in the development of Europe's most sophisticated pre-Enlightenment reading public. Similarly, it was the critical community in the fashioning of Europe's most sophisticated preindustrial commercial economy. One observer of the East India Company in 1666 could find 'none but Presbiters' amongst its chief men, for instance; and the signal role of London dissenters in England's Financial Revolution, after 1689, has been established.[57] Dissenters and Whigs could be found among all London social and economic stations, of course. Yet the language and behaviour of wealthy merchants like Pilkington and of middling retailers like Jenks point to the convergence of reformed Protestantism and commercial enterprise in the distinctive discursive community from which radical ideas emanated.

Family and fortune, interest and intellect, education and experience, then, all bound this London community of discourse together. The articulation and the implementation of radical ideas, whether in particular moments or in lengthier intervals, were expressions of the concerns of a broader, Protestant community devoted to the principles of conscience and consent. Ideas and actions that undermined the structures, authorities and conventions of the Restoration establishment frequently emerged from the interplay of conversation, political rhetoric and creative reading in this community. That the political discourse of London Whigs and dissenters softened after 1689 is no argument against the radical moments and radical intervals that characterized many lives before 1689. The Glorious Revolution brought the very security for Protestantism and property that many Londoners had searched for in vain since 1662.

At the same time, we must acknowledge that the radical label can be as ambivalent, tricky and anachronistic as its revisionist critics have charged. But if we treat the name radical as a contingent category that must be discarded as soon as it leads us to a verbally alien seventeenth century, then the 'world we have lost' has truly been lost again. What is modern in the early-modern world is rendered less intelligible. The revisionist approach to the name radical freezes the past in its own language: indeed, it uncouples

---

[57] BL Add. MS 40,712, fo. 8; Steven C. A. Pincus, *Protestantism and Patriotism: Ideologies and the Making of English Foreign Policy, 1650–1668* (Cambridge, 1996), pp. 327–8; Gary S. De Krey, *A Fractured Society: The Politics of London in the First Age of Party, 1688–1715* (Oxford, 1985), pp. 99–112.

centuries and whole epochs in ways that sever connections and disable the investigator of change. Mystery has replaced history when the academic doors are locked with new-patterned keys cut in a subfield of another discipline known to few. The proposed banishment of the name radical would make more difficult the exchange of conclusions among scholars who work with different assumptions, with different evidence, and with different questions. Worse, it would deprive us of a useful category in reopening the seventeenth-century English past to broader audiences who have turned away from much contemporary academic language.

CHAPTER 4

The family in the exclusion crisis: Locke versus Filmer revisited

Rachel Weil

What impact the late-seventeenth-century revolution in political theory had upon ideas about women, marriage and the family has been a matter of controversy among scholars. Some (Mary Shanley, Lawrence Stone, Gordon Schochet, Melissa Butler) have argued that political contract theory challenged patriarchal authority in the family.[1] Others (most famously, Carole Pateman) contend that contract theory was no better for women, and perhaps worse than the patriarchalist political thought which preceded and rivalled it.[2] Almost all participants in the debate, however, have focused their analyses upon the paired figures of Robert Filmer (representing 'patriarchalism') and John Locke (representing liberalism or contract theory). While it is conventional in the history of political thought to imagine representative figures 'debating' across time, the practice unfortunately encourages some dubious assumptions and closes down fruitful avenues of inquiry.

First, to allow Locke and Filmer to represent not only patriarchalism and liberalism but the gender politics of those ideologies (that is, their effect upon relations of power between men and women) is

---

[1] Mary Shanley, 'Marriage Contract and Social Contract in Seventeenth-Century English Political Thought', *Western Political Quarterly* 32 (1979), 79–91; Gordon Schochet, 'The Significant Sounds of Silence: the Absence of Women from the Political Thought of Sir Robert Filmer and John Locke', in Hilda Smith (ed.), *Women Writers and the Early Modern British Political Tradition* (Cambridge, 1998), pp. 220–42; Lawrence Stone, *The Family, Sex and Marriage in England 1500–1800* (New York, 1977), especially pp. 239–44, 265–6; Melissa Butler, 'Early Liberal Roots of Feminism: John Locke and the Attack on Patriarchy', *American Political Science Review* 22 (1978), 135–50.

[2] Carole Pateman, *The Sexual Contract Aspects of Patriarchal Liberalism* (Stanford, 1988). Other feminist critiques of contract theory include Lorenne M. G. Clarke, 'Who Owns the Apples in the Garden of Eden?' in L. M. G. Clark and Lydia Lange (eds.), *The Sexism of Social and Political Theory: Women and Reproduction from Plato to Nietzsche* (Toronto, 1979); Ruth Perry, 'Mary Astell and the Feminist Critique of Possessive Individualism', *Eighteenth Century Studies* 23 (1990), 444–57; Carole Pateman and Teresa Brennan, ' "Mere auxiliaries to the commonwealth": Women and the Origins of Liberalism', *Political Studies* 27 (1979), 183–200.

to assume, rather than demonstrate, that each political theory carries with it a single, coherent set of ideas about gender. It is possible that not all political contractarians (or, conversely, not all patriarchalists) thought alike about women, marriage and the family. Even if it is legitimate to speak of a Whig view of gender, it cannot be assumed to be identical with John Locke's.

Second, it is misleading to think of Filmer and Locke 'debating', since they wrote at least thirty and as many as sixty years apart.[3] Moreover, Locke read Filmer through lenses coloured by time, ideology and polemical necessity. The interesting differences between Filmer and Locke's *version* of Filmer, it will be argued here, are indicative of what Michel Foucault would call an 'epistemic shift' over time.[4]

This essay will examine the differences between Locke and Filmer, between the Whigs and Filmer, and between what Filmer actually said about the family and what his Whig critics presented him as saying. This will make it possible to address two larger questions. First, in what sense, and at what level, were views of politics connected to views of gender; even if all Whigs did not share a common view of the family, was there nonetheless something they had in common that would allow us to refer to a 'whig ideology of gender'? Second, what do the differences between Filmer on the one hand and the Whigs as a group on the other indicate about the differences between the earlier and later parts of the seventeenth century?

A MAP OF MISREADINGS

As is well known, *Patriarcha* was published during the exclusion crisis as part of Charles II's propaganda campaign to defend his use of royal prerogative and prevent Parliament from altering the succession to the throne. Filmer was deemed relevant because he had attacked the same beliefs about the origin of political authority that Charles II and his Tory allies believed lay behind the exclusionist movement. He undertook to refute what he perceived to be the common and dangerous opinion that 'mankind is naturally endowed and born with

---

[3] On the dating of Filmer's works, see Johann P. Sommerville's introduction to Robert Filmer, *Patriarcha and other Political Writings*, ed. Johann P. Sommerville (Cambridge, 1991), pp. xxxii–xxxvii.

[4] Michel Foucault, *The Order of Things: an Archeology of the Human Sciences* (New York, 1971).

freedom from all subjection, and at liberty to choose what form of government it please'. This would mean, as Filmer saw it, that all existing governments had originally been established by consent, 'at the discretion of the multitude'.[5] To this, Filmer replied that no one had ever been born free. God had given to Adam, the first man, absolute and unconditional dominion over the world, over Eve, and over Eve's offspring. This absolute power had since been fragmented spatially (that is, the world was now broken up into several distinct governments) and had been transferred from one ruler to another in many different ways, but it remained the same kind of power. Therefore, no one had ever been born free from subjection to an absolute authority. Filmer referred to this divinely granted absolute power as 'the right of fatherhood', or 'fatherly right'.

Virtually all the lengthier theoretical works produced by Whig writers during the exclusion crisis were framed as responses to *Patriarcha*; the list includes not only John Locke's *First Treatise of Government* and Algernon Sidney's *Discourses Concerning Government* but also James Tyrrell's *Patriarcha non Monarcha* (1681) and Thomas Hunt's *Mr Hunt's Postscript for Rectifying some Mistakes in some of the Inferior Clergy* (1682).[6] A look at some Whig readings (or misreadings) of Filmer reveals important differences among Whigs, but also shows what united them.

Algernon Sidney's critique of Filmer centred on the problem of transferring authority over time. He presented Filmer (oddly, as we shall see), as an advocate of hereditary succession to the throne via primogeniture, which he regarded not only as a bad political system but also as a violation of the natural, patriarchal order. Sidney had no trouble accepting Filmer's scenario of original sovereign authority residing in Adam or Noah. He regarded paternal authority, both in the beginning of society and in real families, as legitimate and natural. He balked, however, at the notion that paternal authority could be inherited from a father by one of his sons. A brother cannot assume a position of authority over his own brethren, for 'no man can be my father but he that did beget me; and it is absurd to say that

---

[5] Filmer, *Patriarcha*, p. 2.

[6] Whether this was because *Patriarcha* accurately represented Charles II's strongly absolutist position, or because its extremism made it a convenient target, remains a matter of scholarly debate. For Filmer's place in the exclusion crisis, see Mark Goldie, 'John Locke and Anglican Royalism', *Political Studies* 31 (1983), 727–46; cf. James Daly, *Sir Robert Filmer and English Political Thought* (Toronto, 1979). See also Alan C. Houston, *Algernon Sidney and the Republican Heritage in England and America* (Princeton, 1991), ch. 2.

I owe that duty to one who is not my father, which I owe my father, as to say he did beget me, who did not beget me'.[7]

Having proved, that the right of fathers is from nature and incommunicable, it must follow, that every man doth perpetually owe all love, respect, service, and obedience, to him that did beget, nourish, and educate him, and to no other under that name. No man can therefore claim the right of father over any, except one that is so . . . the extent and perpetuity of the duty which every man owes to his father, renders it impossible for him to owe the same to any other . . . no man can owe to his brother that which he owed to his father, because he cannot receive that from him which he had from his father.[8]

In short, what is appropriate in the relationship between father and son is not appropriate in relations among brothers. Consequently, Sidney objected to primogeniture because, if fatherhood is incommunicable, then all sons must inherit equally. Moreover, Sidney lamented, in a system of hereditary succession, 'women and children are patriarchs; and the next in blood, without any regard to age, sex, or other qualities of mind or body, are fathers of as many nations as fall under their power'.[9] Filmer threatened real paternal authority, Sidney argued, by setting up 'chimerical fathers' (i.e. kings) to supplant natural ones.

Sidney thus portrayed himself as the defender of real patriarchal authority, while casting Filmer as a threat to it. He drove the point home by pushing Filmer's equation of kings and fathers to the point of perversity. For example, picking up on Filmer's acknowledgement that kingship by conquest is legitimate, Sidney suggests that this would, in Filmer's language, make the conqueror the 'son' of the ruler he conquered, and therefore a parricide: 'Filmer alone is subtle enough to discover that Jehu, by extinguishing the house of Ahab, drew an obligation of looking on him as his father.'[10] Sidney also lovingly elaborated the incestuous possibilities of patriarchalist language: 'If Claudius was the father of the Roman people, I suppose the chaste Messalina was the mother, and to be honored by virtue of the same commandment [i.e. "honor thy father and mother"]: But when [sic] I fear that such as met her in the most obscure places, were not only guilty of adultery, but of incest.'[11] Filmer was thus, for

---

[7] Algernon Sidney, *Discourses Concerning Government* [1698], 3 vols. (New York, 1805), I, 396 (1.16). Chapter and section numbers are given in parentheses.
[8] *Ibid.*, II, 395–6 (3.1).   [9] *Ibid.*, I, 311 (1.introduction).
[10] *Ibid.*, III, 80 (3.16).   [11] *Ibid.*, I, 425 (1.19).

Sidney, a violator rather than an upholder of the natural order; he 'delights in monsters'.[12]

Locke's 'Filmer' delighted in a different kind of monster: a tyrannical paternal authority which works to the destruction rather than benefit of the children, thereby perverting the fundamental intention of nature that mankind should increase and multiply. Pointedly, Locke tied political absolutism and ideological patriarchalism to population decline. In chapter 4 of the *First Treatise*, he posed the question of whether God after the Flood had made Noah sole lord and owner of the world (as Filmer would have it), or whether his blessing was intended for Noah and his sons in common (as John Selden had argued). Since the blessing contained the words 'be fruitful and multiply', and since Noah had no more children after the flood, Locke concluded that Selden was right; unless, Locke jocularly added, Filmer meant to say that the sons 'must ask leave of their father Noah to lie with their wives'. He then expanded the joke to suggest a relationship between absolutism and depopulation:

[Filmer] takes great care there should be monarchs in the world, but very little that there should be people; and indeed his way of government is not the way to people the world. For how much absolute monarchy helps to fulfill this great and primary blessing of God almighty, *be fruitful and multiply and replenish the earth* . . . may be seen in those large and rich countries, which are now happy under Turkish government, where are not now to be found 1/3, nay in many if not most parts 1/30, perhaps, I might say not 1/100 of the people, that were formerly.[13]

The same point was made more luridly later in the text, where Locke presented an account of Peru, drawn from the *Commentarios Reales* of Garcilaso de la Vega as the *reductio ad absurdam* of what he took to be Filmer's concept of 'paternal power'. In some provinces, Locke noted, they were 'so liquorish after man's flesh' that

they spared not their own children which they had begot on strangers taken in war; for they made their captives their mistresses and choicely nourished the children they had by them, till about thirteen years old they butchered and eat them, and they served their mothers after the same fashion, when they grew past childbearing, and ceased to bring them any more roasters.[14]

This wilful exaggeration of Filmer's position allowed Locke to cast

---

[12] *Ibid.*, I, 392 (1.15).
[13] John Locke, *Two Treatises of Government*, ed. Peter Last (Cambridge, 1991), 1.33. Citations given by treatise (I or II) and section numbers.
[14] *Ibid.*, 1.57.

himself as the defender of morality, specifically a morality associated with the 'intention of nature'.

Be it then, as Sir Robert says, that anciently, it was usual for men to sell and castrate their children . . . Let it be that they exposed them; add to it, if you please, for this is still greater power, that they begat them for their tables to fat and eat them: If this proves a right to do so, we may, by the same argument, justify adultery, incest, and sodomy, for there are examples of these, too, both ancient and modern; sins which, I suppose, have their principal aggravation from this, that they cross the main intention of nature, which willeth the increase of mankind, and the continuation of the species, in the highest perfection, and the distinction of families, with the security of the marriage bed, as necessary thereunto.[15]

A third version of 'Filmer' might best be called 'Carole Pateman's Filmer', because it figures prominently in Carole Pateman's exegesis of the gender politics of Filmerian patriarchalism. Pateman takes Filmer's statement that 'God at the creation gave the sovereignty to the man over the woman, as being the nobler and principal agent in generation' to mean that Filmer thinks that Adam has power over his children because he appears to generate them by himself. By imagining that men give birth autogenously, she argues, Filmer and the patriarchalists obscured the role of women in reproduction and hence hid the fact that men need to possess women through marriage in order to obtain power over their 'own' children.[16] Whig writers in the exclusion crisis similarly described their opponents as believing that men had power over their offspring because they beget them, although (significantly) they did not specifically name Filmer as the holder of that belief. Locke alluded to 'the argument, that I have heard others make use of, to prove that fathers by begetting them, come to have an absolute power over their children', which was 'that fathers have power over the lives of their children because they give them life and being'.[17] Tyrrell, similarly, noted 'some writers think they have done sufficiently when they tell us, that the father hath an absolute dominion over his child, because he got it'.[18] This version of 'Filmer' (or the generic patriarchalist) was especially convenient for Whigs because his arguments could be refuted simply by pointing out that children have biological mothers as well as fathers.

---

[15] *Ibid.*, 1.59.
[16] Pateman, *The Sexual Contract*, p. 87. The quotation is from Filmer's *Observations Concerning the Original of Government*, in Filmer, *Patriarcha*, p. 192.
[17] Locke, *Two Treatises*, 1.52.
[18] [James Tyrrell], *Patriarcha non Monarcha. The Patriarch Unmonarch'd* (1681), p. 14.

Each of these versions of Filmer – Sidney's, Locke's and Pateman's – relies to an extent on a misreading. Sidney's is most easily disposed of: although Sidney, who was himself writing at a time when hereditary succession to the throne was the central political issue, read Filmer as an advocate of primogeniture, Filmer himself never argued that kings had to succeed to the throne by primogeniture through the male line. Rather, he imagined that the crown could be transferred in many different ways: 'It skills not which way kings come by their power, whether by election, donation, succession or by any other means, for it is still the manner of government by supreme power that makes them properly kings, and not the means of obtaining their crowns.'[19]

Nor did Filmer claim that fathers had absolute power over their children because they literally begot them. Although Filmer did characterize men as the 'nobler agent in generation', he did not actually say in the passage that Pateman quotes that men have power over children because they beget them. There is no reason to suppose that he would have found such an argument polemically helpful. In fact, the question of whether a father is the biological parent of his child was of little concern to Filmer. Quite the contrary. In his *Observations concerning the Original of Government*, Filmer responds to Hobbes's comments on the uncertainty of paternal identity by saying that legal paternity is sufficient:

As to the objection [by Hobbes], that 'it is not known who is the father to the son but by the discovery of the mother', and that 'he is son to whom the mother will, and therefore he is the mother's', the answer is, that it is not at the will of the mother to make whom she please the father, for if the mother be not in possession of a husband, the child is not reckoned to have any father at all; but if she be in the possession of a man, the child notwithstanding whatsoever the woman discovereth to the contrary it is still reputed to be his in whose possession she is. No child naturally or infallibly knows who are its true parents, yet he must obey those that in common reputation are so, otherwise the commandment of 'honour thy father and thy mother' were in vain, and no child bound to the obedience of it.[20]

Finally, what of Locke's tyrannical, child-eating, population-shrivelling Filmerian patriarch? *Patriarcha* says virtually nothing about population and, unsurprisingly, does not endorse men's right

---

[19] *Patriarcha*, p. 44.
[20] *Ibid.*, p. 192. The argument to which Filmer responds is in Thomas Hobbes, *De Cive: the English Version*, ed. Howard Warrender (Oxford, 1983), p. 123 (ch. 9, section 3).

to eat or castrate their children. On close scrutiny, moreover, what *Patriarcha* actually has to say about relationships within families has been a matter of controversy amongst scholars. In the first serious treatment of the subject, Gordon Schochet has placed Filmer within a broad stream of 'patriarchalism', which he defines not as a single idea but as a cluster of analytically distinct but related notions: that hierarchies in nature, the state and the family are divinely ordained, that they are therefore in some sense analogous to one another, that they *depend* on one another, that obedience to kings can be justified in the same way as obedience to fathers (through the commandment 'honour thy father'), and that once upon a time fathers and kings were the same.[21] These notions, he argues, were widely shared by most seventeenth-century political thinkers, functioning often as unconscious habits of mind rather than fully defended theories. Their pervasiveness can be attributed to actual social experience. The seventeenth-century English family 'was indeed an authoritarian institution that was well-suited to be the basis of an absolutist political doctrine, and . . . for the vast majority of Englishmen in this period, the patriarchal justification of the duty to obey the state was an accurate translation of their regular experiences into political terms'.[22] Thus, Schochet describes Filmer as both a 'patriarchalist' political theorist and as a proponent of 'patriarchy' as a social institution.

Some historians, however, have questioned Schochet's account of how patriarchalist political theory was related to social practices and institutions. In *The Patriarch's Wife*, Margaret Ezell uses Filmer's unpublished manuscript, 'In Praise of the Virtuous Wife' to argue that when he turned his mind to domestic relationships as he himself experienced or hoped to experience them, Filmer accorded to women a great deal of autonomy and power within the household. His ideal woman was by no means an inferior, but a trusted second-in-command to her husband, credited with abilities and talents and expected to use them. It was precisely the fact that 'patriarchalism' was so flexible in practice, Ezell speculates, that made it acceptable in theory.[23]

---

[21] Gordon Schochet, *Patriarchalism in Political Thought: the Authoritarian Family and Political Speculation and Attitudes Especially in Seventeenth-Century England* (New York, 1975), ch. 1.

[22] *Ibid.*, p. 64.

[23] Margaret J. M. Ezell, *The Patriarch's Wife: Literary Evidence and the History of the Family* (Chapel Hill, 1987), chs. 5–6.

Ezell further suggests that women could be empowered by tensions within and elements of patriarchalist *theory*. The power of the patriarch in the patriarchalist ideal of the household comprised two elements: the power of a parent over his children and the power of a husband over his wife. Patriarchalist theorists did not usually bother to distinguish between the two, since both forms were in practice combined in the person of the male head of household. However, insofar as patriarchalism upheld *parental* authority, it could be marshalled as a justification of the power of women as mothers within the household.[24] Mary Beth Norton, in her study of colonial North America, has pushed this point even farther. The 'Filmerian world view', she notes, held all kinds of hierarchies, of status and age as well as gender, to be natural and God-given. This meant that women of high status, especially widows or 'fictive widows' who headed households, were held worthy of exercising political power.[25] Unlike Schochet, then, Ezell and Norton detect possibilities for the empowerment of *some* women within Filmerian political thought.

The reason that scholars can disagree about the gender politics of Filmerian patriarchalism is that Filmer's concept of 'fatherly right' was abstract and maddeningly elusive. It is by no means clear, for example, what it had to do with the power of fathers in actual families, or even with *Adam's* power as a father. At some points, Filmer equated rulership and actual fatherhood. He asserted that 'creation made man prince of his posterity', and drew on biblical history to demonstrate that the first kings were heads of families and 'eldest parents'.[26] He cited examples of the absolute power of fathers over their children in the ancient world: the Romans let fathers execute their children, Judah condemned his daughter-in-law Thamar to death.[27] Moreover, 'there is no nation that allows children any action or remedy for being unjustly governed [by their father]'.[28] On this basis, Filmer argued that the reason that humans are born in subjection is not merely because they are born subject to the holder of Adam's original power but because they are born subject to their own fathers. 'I see not then how the children of

---

[24] *Ibid.*, p. 139. See also Susan D. Amussen, *An Ordered Society: Gender and Class in Early Modern England* (Oxford, 1988), pp. 59–60.

[25] Mary Beth Norton, *Founding Mothers and Fathers: Gendered Power and the Forming of American Society* (New York, 1996), especially section III.

[26] *Patriarcha*, pp. 6, 7–11.

[27] *Ibid.*, pp. 18–19, 7.   [28] *Ibid.*, p. 35.

Adam, or of any man else, can be free from subjection to their parents. And this subjection of children is the only fountain of all regal authority, by the ordination of God himself.'[29]

Nonetheless, although Filmer associated 'fatherly right' with the original dominion of Adam over the earth and mankind, he cited at least two sources for Adam's authority that were not related to the power of fathers over children, but rather to the power of husbands over wives, or of humans over animals. The first was God's curse on Eve in Genesis 3:16 ('thy desire shall be to thy husband and he shall rule over thee') which Filmer took to be the origin of political power.[30] The second was God's blessing to man in Genesis 1:28, enjoining him to 'have dominion over the fish of the sea, and over the fowl of the air, and over every living thing that moveth upon the earth'.[31] Neither one of these passages says anything about paternal power *per se*. Moreover, kings were not really the fathers of their people, and Filmer knew it. He indicated, for example, that the power of magistrates superseded the power of fathers to put their children to death. It was important to him that 'the power of a father over his child gives place to and is subordinate to the power of the magistrate' because it proved that the power of magistrates was as natural as the power of fathers.[32]

In fact, it is (and was) possible to read Filmer as a subverter of the powers of actual fathers in favour of the powers of kings. As we saw, Sidney did so in his *Discourses Concerning Government*. A similar argument has been made more recently by R. W. K. Hinton. Hinton contrasts Filmer with a 'true patriarchalist' like Bodin: the latter, Hinton explains, was interested in enhancing the power of actual fathers alongside that of kings, because 'he saw himself as living in a society of infinite chaos where there was plenty of room for both kings and fathers to have more power at the same time'. The role of Bodin's 'patriarchal' king was therefore to defend the power of fathers over their families. Significantly, this meant that Bodin was able to *distinguish* kings from fathers, treating their respective powers as similar but not identical. Filmer, by contrast, went a step farther

---

[29] *Ibid.*, p. 7.
[30] *Ibid.*, pp. 138, 145 [from *The Anarchy of a Limited or Mixed Monarchy*].
[31] Filmer, *Patriarcha*, pp. 236, 217–18 [from *Observations on Aristotle's Politics* and *The Original of Government*].
[32] *Ibid.*, p. 12. Filmer assumes here that if the power of magistrates were only conventional it could never supersede what is 'natural'.

than Bodin by equating kings and fathers. He thus, Hinton argues, failed to sidestep the fundamental dilemma: 'if kings are fathers, fathers cannot be patriarchs . . . patriarchal kings and patriarchal fathers are a contradiction in terms'.[33] As a result, Filmer magnified the power of kings at the expense of fathers: 'Filmer's ultimate statement on fathers and rulers – though he did not make it – was that between them a great gulf was fixed. Rulers were sovereign, fathers nothing: rulers had all power, fathers had none.'[34]

Whether one agrees with Schochet, Ezell, Norton or Hinton, the important point is that Filmer's beliefs about actual relationships in real families can be interpreted in many different ways, precisely because he had so little to say on the subject. For Filmer, the family was a way to make a point about order: it is the site upon which he raised, and answered in the negative, the question of whether anyone can exist without being subject to a higher authority. Once the point was made, Filmer was uninterested in discussing actual relationships among members of actual families. This silence allowed Filmer's Whig critics to present his views on familial relations in whatever light they thought would make him look worst. Some, like Locke, cast Filmer as *too* patriarchal; others, like Sidney, as not patriarchal enough. In each case, Filmer was dragged onto the terrain of the family for the purpose of discrediting him.

Whig writers, by contrast, were refreshingly concrete on the subject of the family, and made a point of being so. They treated fatherhood (or parenthood) as a particular relationship that could not be abstracted or transferred. 'To expect relative duties without relation, is most unnatural', wrote the Whig Thomas Hunt: the duty of parents toward children was so personal 'that it cannot be transferred, or permitted absolutely to any other person by the parents; nor can any challenge a right, or discharge the father from it, or require the same affection, submission and reverence that is due from a child to his father'.[35] Similarly, James Tyrrell argued that parental power could not be transferred to kings, because even 'if parents are to be trusted with this absolute power over their children, because of the natural affection they are always supposed to bear them; then princes ought not to be trusted with it, since none but

---

[33] R. W. K. Hinton, 'Husbands, Fathers and Conquerors (part I)', *Political Studies* 15 (1967), 291–300, p. 294.

[34] *Ibid.*, pp. 299–300.

[35] *Mr Hunt's Postscript for Rectifying Some Mistakes in Some of the Inferior Clergy* (1682), p. 72.

parents themselves can have this natural affection towards their children'.[36] Sidney's outrage at Filmer's substitution of 'chimerical' for actual fathers reflected the same view that fatherhood is a concrete, particular relationship that cannot be transferred.

The gap between Filmer and the Whigs, then, was even wider than one would think from reading Whig caricatures of Filmer. The difference was not, however, that Filmer advocated patriarchal tyranny and the Whigs rejected it; rather, it was that Filmer was not writing about 'families' and Whigs were. For Filmer, the family was a metaphor; for Whigs in the exclusion crisis, the family was an institution in which children were produced and cared for, and (as a means to these, also as an end in itself) through which the transfer of property between generations was organized.

CHANGE OVER TIME

The Whig view of the family is best described as an approach and an orientation rather than an ideology. Along with many other people in the late seventeenth century, Whigs shared a cluster of concerns revolving around two problems: first, how to ensure an expanding and productive population, and second, how to organize the transfer of property in families over time. These were perceived to be connected to one another, and together they shaped thinking on a host of issues. Late-seventeenth-century writers were fascinated by the question of how systems for organizing sexuality, determining paternity, transferring estates and caring for children would affect morality and society. These concerns were not entirely new, although some aspects of what will be discussed below – the development of new conveyancing techniques, and the rise of a commercially oriented 'political arithmetic' that located the source of wealth in people rather than land – have been associated specifically with this period.[37] But significantly, these concerns were not present in

---

[36] Tyrrell, *Patriarcha non Monarcha*, p. 22.

[37] On conveyancing, see H. J. Habbakuk, 'Marriage Settlements in the Eighteenth Century', *Transactions of the Royal Historical Society*, fourth series, 32 (1950), and his 'The Rise and Fall of English Landed Families', *Transactions of the Royal Historical Society*, fifth series, 29 (1979). On commercially oriented conceptions of wealth, see the suggestive remarks by Steve Pincus, 'Neither Machiavellian Moment nor Possessive Individualism: Commercial Society and the Defenders of the English Commonwealth', *American Historical Review* 103:3 (1998), 705–36. See also Joyce Appleby, *Economic Thought and Ideology in Seventeenth-Century England* (Princeton, 1978).

Filmer's works, whereas they had a powerful impact on the *political* writings of the later-seventeenth century.

The need to increase the number of people preoccupied late-seventeenth-century social thinkers. The principle that more reproduction was better was endorsed on a multitude of grounds in the late-seventeenth century. The popular medical-marital handbook, *Aristotle's Masterpiece*, frankly taught that God endowed men and women with the capacity for sexual pleasure so that they would naturally fulfil the commandment to 'increase and multiply'. Procreation was further essential to health, as barrenness deprived a woman of 'that full perfection of health which fruitful women do enjoy because they are not rightly purged of the menstrual blood and superfluous seed, which two are the principle causes of most uterine diseases'. The book helpfully offered 'directions to both sexes for the performing of that act [intercourse] as may make it efficacious to the end for which nature designed it'; this included advice to the woman to avoid coughing and sneezing, which by 'its violent concussion of the body is a great enemy to conception', and to the man 'not to part too soon from the embraces of his wife, lest some interposing cold should strike into the womb and occasion a miscarriage, and thereby deprive them of the fruits of their labours'.[38]

Reproduction was also central to social thought. As Joyce Appleby has noted, 'the most significant change of opinion about the poor was the replacement of the concern about overpopulation at the beginning of the seventeenth century with fears about a possible loss of people at the end'. Economic thinkers believed that a larger population would lead to greater national wealth.[39] This assumption also lay behind William Petty and John Graunt's development of the science of 'political arithmetic', a method of analysing economic issues mathematically in terms of the relationship between land and population.[40] Petty's thesis, that 'labor is the father and active principle of wealth, as lands are the mother', was clearly echoed (even in its colourfully gendered language) in Locke's explanation of how private property comes into being. When a man gathers nuts from 'nature's common store', Locke tells us in the *Second Treatise*, it is

---

[38] *Aristotle's Masterpiece Compleated, in Two Parts: the First Containing the Secrets of Generation . . . the Second Part Being, a Private Looking-Glass for the Female Sex* (1698), pp. 61, 93–4. The first version of *Aristotle's Masterpiece* was published in 1684.

[39] Appleby, *Economic Thought*, pp. 135–7.

[40] See Webster, *Great Instauration*, especially ch. 5.

the act of gathering itself that makes them his: 'That labour put a distinction between them and common. That added something more to them than nature, the common mother of all, had done, and so they became his private right.'[41] Land that is left uncultivated, Locke asserts, is mere waste; therefore, 'numbers of men are to be preferred to largeness of dominions'.[42] Henry Neville's proto-Crusoesque novel, *The Isle of Pines* (1668), albeit with distopian intent, reflected the spirit of the times, chronicling the peopling of a desert island by a shipwrecked clerk and his four female companions with alarmingly industrial efficiency, so that the narrator can end his life proudly numbering his descendants at 1,789 and 'praying God to multiply them'.[43]

There was also an ethical or even religious dimension to the late-seventeenth-century concern with reproduction. It is telling that *Marriage Promoted*, although rehearsing every possible secular argument for the political, military and economic benefits of a larger population, began by quoting the biblical injunction to 'be fruitful, multiply, and replenish the earth'.[44] As Charles Webster has argued, the project of promoting the 'multiplication of mankind' developed during the interregnum under the impetus of a quasi-millenarian optimism that the earth could be turned into a flourishing garden and that man's duty was to care for and cultivate it.[45]

This meant, however, not merely that it was desirable to produce many children, but that it was necessary to produce healthy, flourishing and ultimately productive children as well. The obligation of parents to care for children was one aspect, but a particularly powerful one, of Locke's ethical system, which, as John Marshall has argued, emphasized the obligation of every human being to care for and preserve God's creation. This 'ethic of care' tied together Locke's interest in agricultural experiment, his gentlemanly sense of an obligation to charity and liberality, the centrality of the right to

---

[41] Locke, *Two Treatises*, ii.28.
[42] *Ibid.*, ii.42; see also ii.40–1, 1.33. For Locke's interest in political arithmetic, see Karen Iverson Vaughn, *John Locke, Economist and Social Scientist* (Chicago, 1980).
[43] [Henry Neville], *The Isle of Pines: or, a Late Discovery of a Fourth Island in Terra Australis Incognita* (1668). The distopian dimension is evident in the extension/sequel, *A New and Further Discovery of the Isle of Pines* (1668). The point about industrial efficiency is made in Michael McKeon, *The Origins of the English Novel, 1600–1740* (Baltimore, 1987).
[44] *Marriage Promoted* (1690), p. 1.
[45] Charles Webster, *The Great Instauration: Science, Medicine and Reform 1626–1660* (London, 1975), especially ch. 4.

self-preservation in his political theory and his interest in education.[46] Locke was not alone in this emphasis on care. Lawrence
Stone and J. H. Plumb have both noted the rise of negative attitudes
towards corporal punishment over the long eighteenth century, and
suggested that (in Plumb's words) the 'autocratic, indeed ferocious'
attitude of the seventeenth century was replaced by a gentler
approach to children.[47] It is hard to say how deeply the change in
attitude ran, or whether it was as dramatic a change as Stone and
Plumb make it out to be. The actual feelings of parents for their
children are notoriously hard to discover.[48] For our purposes,
however, the evidence of discursive shifts noted by Stone and Plumb
is sufficient. The idea that the family exists for the benefit of children
(rather than for the benefit of fathers, or the keeping of order)
became so deeply rooted in the writings of Whig thinkers that it was
assumed rather than defended.

The ethic of care led naturally to concerns about inheritance.
Giving property to one's children was a form of caring for them, and
was assumed to be a parental duty. But this statement hardly captures
the practical and symbolic weight carried by inheritance in the late
seventeenth century. Although the arrangements for the transfer of
property across generations made in wills and marriage settlements
were expressed in notoriously arcane jargon, both men and women
of the property-holding classes had a surprisingly strong grasp of the
relevant legal terminology. The author of a 1732 handbook on law
written specifically for a female audience expected his reader to
comprehend a sentence like: 'A man is seised of lands in fee, and hath
issue two daughters, and makes a gift in tail to one of them, and then
dies seised of the reversion in fee, which descends to both sisters, the
donee, or her issue, is impleaded, she shall not pray in aid of the
other co-parcener, either to recover *pro rata*, or to deraign the
warranty paramount.'[49]

It was around issues of property settlement that people in seventeenth-century England engaged with questions of love, obligation,
justice and power in the family. Family estates connected the fates of

---

[46] John Marshall, *John Locke: Resistance, Religion and Responsibility* (Cambridge, 1994), pp. 169,
177, 293, 297 and *passim*.

[47] J. H. Plumb, 'The New World of Children in Eighteenth-Century England', *Past and Present*
67 (1975), 64–95; Stone, *The Family, Sex and Marriage in England 1500–1800* (New York, 1977),
pp. 439–40.

[48] Linda Pollock, *Forgotten Children: Parent-Child Relations from 1500–1900* (Cambridge, 1983).

[49] *A Treatise of Feme Coverts: or, the Lady's Law* (1732), p. 20.

individuals together; one person's economic future hinged upon another's death, or luck at marriage or childbearing. Emotional bonds and predicaments were figured in terms of property and bequests. Joan Thirsk has noted that as the practice of primogeniture spread amongst the English gentry in the seventeenth century it was accompanied by an angry literature protesting the harsh treatment of the neglected younger sons.[50] John ap Robert's popular and much reprinted *The Younger Brother his Apologie* conveys the emotional intensity of such literature. The elder brother squandering the family estates that he undeservedly inherited is, says ap Robert, a 'civil monster' who 'consumes the womb of his family (viper-like) wherein he was born: and without all remembrance of his obligement to the dead (whom, as having his being from them, he ought to honour) or respect to the living (to whom he should be a comfort) devours in some sort, them of his own species, society and blood: all which, the cannibals do not.'[51]

Brotherhood was only one of the familial relationships rendered fraught and complicated by the evolving strategies of the propertied classes to insure the perpetuation of estates. Fatherhood was perhaps more profoundly affected. Sometimes, fathers were demonized in the contemporary literature on primogeniture. James Harrington, who likened the 'flinty custom' of primogeniture to the common treatment of newborn puppies ('take one, lay it in the lap, feed it with every good bit, and drown five!') blamed the practice on the 'cruel ambition' of the father, who foolishly sought immortality by raising 'a golden pillar for his monument, though he have children, his own reviving flesh'.[52] But, as the passage from John ap Robert quoted above suggests, fathers (and ancestors) could be seen as the *victims* of the custom. Paternal power was potentially diminished by the development of conveyancing techniques (strict settlement and entailment) which secured the integrity of a family estate by allowing the owner to determine how the estate was to be settled in future generations; a father would be unable to discipline his children by threatening disinheritance, since such an act was now out of his power.[53] Lacking leverage over his heirs and bound by the planning

---

[50] Joan Thirsk, 'Younger Sons in the Seventeenth Century', *History* 54 (1969), 358–77.

[51] [John ap Robert], *The Younger Brother his Apologie* (1671), pp. 35–6. According to Thirsk, 'Younger Sons', the first known edition is 1618; it was reprinted in 1624, 1634 and 1641.

[52] James Harrington, *The Commonwealth of Oceana* [1656], ed. J. G. A. Pocock (Cambridge, 1992), p. 109.

of a distant ancestor, the male head of household was further vulnerable to betrayal by his wife. The sad plight of men whose wives became pregnant whilst committing adultery was a prominent theme in the literature of the period: these husbands lost not only masculine authority (to be cuckolded was a sign that one could not control one's family) but also the right to pass their estate on to the children of their own loins. Thus, reformers who argued in favour of permitting divorce on grounds of adultery almost always pointed out that female adultery had especially serious ramifications because of its implications for the inheritance property, amounting essentially to a form of theft.[54]

The notion that passage of property through generations is a basic human activity is embedded in Whig writing, especially that of Locke. The instinct of parents to pass on property to children is mentioned in the same breath as their instinct to produce them. 'God planted in men a strong desire also of propagating their kind, and continuing themselves in their posterity, and this gives children a title, to share in the property of their parents, and a right to inherit their possessions.'[55]

Having established the fact that children have a natural right to inherit from their parents, Locke can then marshal it to defend other parts of his argument. The natural right to inherit is, for example, invoked in Locke's chapter on conquest. Here, Locke explains that conquest does not establish political right. Even in the case of conquest in a just war, the conqueror only acquires a dominion over the lives and property of the individuals who made war against him. He cannot, however, become a permanent ruler because this right does not extend to the lives and property of the innocent *children* of the guilty individuals, because the children have a natural right to inherit.[56]

Even more importantly, Locke uses the idea that children naturally have a right to inherit to distinguish between the inheritance of

---

[53] On these developments, see Habbakuk, 'Marriage Settlements' and his 'The Rise and Fall of English Landed Families'. For their effect on paternal power, see Ralph Houlbrooke, *The English Landed Family 1450–1700* (London, 1985), pp. 231–2.

[54] Such arguments are discussed at length in Rachel Weil, *Political Passions: Gender, the Family and Political Argument in England, 1680–1714* (Manchester, 1999), ch. 5, and in Lawrence Stone, *The Road to Divorce* (Oxford, 1990). Examples in William Lawrence, *Marriage by the Moral Law of God Vindicated* (1680); *Reasons for the earl of Macclesfield's Bill in Parliament* [1697]; *Conjugium languens: or, the natural, civil and religious mischiefs arising from conjugal infidelity and impunity* (1700).

[55] Locke, *Two Treatises*, I.88.

[56] *Ibid.*, II.182.

property on the one hand and the inheritance of dominion on the other.

> The right a son has to be maintained and provided with the necessaries and conveniences of life out of his father's stock, gives him a right to succeed to his father's property for his own good, but this can give him no right also to succeed to the rule, which his father had over other men. All that a child has a right to claim from his father is nourishment and education, and the things nature furnishes for the support of life: but he has no right to demand rule or dominion from him.[57]

In the context of the exclusion crisis, this distinction allowed Locke to question the inheritance of political power via primogeniture without undermining the inheritance of property.

The passage of property thus emerged in late-seventeenth-century Whig writing as the symbol of what families are for, the epitome of care and nurturance, the moral justification for the existence of the family. The image of a man passing on property to his children seems to stand for the bond between a parent and child in this period, in much the same way that the image of a mother nursing a child at the breast might do in another.

The twin preoccupations about population and inheritance did not produce a coherent dogma. As I have argued at length elsewhere, the Whig writers who responded to Filmer did not agree over how much power a father or husband should have, whether biological paternity was essential to fatherhood, whether property should descend via primogeniture, or whether polygamy was a good idea.[58] Indeed, it could be argued that some of the most commonplace and treasured ideas of Whig writers were incompatible with one another. The giving of property to children was, in somewhat contradictory fashion, described as a duty, an instinct and a right. Thinkers also swung between the endorsing conventional monogamy and speculating about the feasibility of alternative sexual arrangements. The notion that the increase of mankind is the ultimate good could lead thinkers to ask whether the existing organization of sexuality was the best way to achieve population growth. William Petty, in his unpublished papers on 'the multiplication of mankind', suggested that men and women might engage instead in 'short marriages', or 'covenants'. These were to be agreements concerning '1. the time of

---

[57] *Ibid.*, 1.93.
[58] Differences among Whig thinkers are discussed in Weil, *Political Passions*, ch. 2.

cohabitation 2. the allowance to the woman 3. the disposal of the children and the power of inheritance, portion, name etc'. They could be 'dissolved in six months, in case of no conception, to be proved by proper signs; otherwise to continue till the delivery of the woman'. Men and women 'may cohabit upon any covenant they please, which the magistrate shall see well performed'.[59] More spectacularly, he described with apparent approval in his un-published essay on 'Californian marriages' a complex system of polygamy and polyandry that he believed to be practised among the natives of the American northwest. In California, he tells us, one 'great man' (known as the 'hero', and 'excelling in strength, nimble-ness, beauty, wit, courage, and good senses') was given a sexual monopoly on four 'ingenious healthy women' while at the same time 'one great rich woman had five men at her command, and was absolute mistress of them all'. Lest the creative energies of the five men were underused, they were given in turn 'one woman in common to them all', although 'none of the said five men meddled with the common woman without leave of the mistress, and unless she had no need'. Amongst the advantages, 'the hero and the mistress have their full and choice of venery', 'the increase of children will be great and good', and 'no controversy about jointure, dower, main-tenance, portion etc'.[60]

John Locke, too, was led by his interest in the increase of mankind to question conventional notions of sexual morality. His diary contains several entries describing plans for an imaginary society, 'Atlantis'. In one, Locke proposes that 'he that is already married may marry another woman with his left hand . . . the ties, duration and conditions of the left hand marriage shall be no other than what is expressed in the contract of marriage between the parties'.[61] Writing in his commonplace book on the subject of 'vice and virtue', he questions the necessity of marriage in its existing form: 'Thus, for a man to cohabit and have children by one or more women, who are at their own disposal, and when they think fit to part again, I see not how it can be condemned as a vice, since nobody is harmed,

---

[59] *The Petty Papers: some Unpublished Writings of Sir William Petty from the Bowood Papers*, ed. Marquis of Lansdowne, 2 vols. (London, 1927), vol. II, ch. 13.
[60] *Ibid.*, vol. II, ch. 13.
[61] Printed in John Locke, *Political Essays*, ed. Mark Goldie (Cambridge, 1997), p. 256. The entry is dated 15 July 1678.

supposing it done amongst persons considered as separate from the rest of mankind.'[62]

There were limits, however, to how far, and how publicly, Locke was willing to speculate. The free sexual exchange that he imagined possible amongst 'persons considered as separate from the rest of mankind' was 'a vice of deep dye' in the context of most societies:

> For if a woman, by transgressing those bounds which the received opinion of her country or religion, and not nature or reason, have set to modesty, has drawn any blemish on her reputation, she may run the risk of being exposed to infamy and other mischiefs, among the least of which is not the danger of losing the comforts of a conjugal settlement, and therewith the chief end of her being, the propagation of mankind.[63]

Moreover, the notion that a man had a right to pass his property to the children of his own loins suggested that women should be strictly controlled to prevent their bastards from taking their husband's property. Locke's remarks on the 'security of the marriage bed' quoted above reflect this concern, as does much of the commentary on divorce throughout the period. The logic of political arithmetic, similarly, could be used to argue against polygamy as well as for it. The *Observations on the Bills of Mortality* (1676), variously attributed to William Petty, to John Graunt, or to some combination of the two, cited the fact that males outnumbered females in the city of London to show 'that the Christian religion, prohibiting polygamy, is more agreeable to the law of nature, that is, the law of God, than Mohametism, and others that allow it: for one man his having many women, or wives, by law, signifies nothing, unless there were many women to one man in nature also'. The medical commonplace that a woman copulating with more than one man will fail to conceive was invoked to explain 'why the law is, and ought to be so strict against fornications and adulteries: For, if there were universal liberty, the increase of mankind would be but like that of foxes [who copulate without restriction but produce few offspring] at best'. The author concludes that 'it is no wonder why states, by encouraging marriage and hindering licentiousness, advance their own interest as well as preserve the laws of God from contempt and violation'.[64] A belief

---

[62] *Political Writings of John Locke*, ed. David Wootton (New York, 1993), pp. 241–2. The entry is dated 1681 (hereafter, Locke, *Political Writings*).

[63] *Ibid.*, pp. 241–2.

[64] *The Economic Writings of Sir William Petty*, ed. Charles H. Hull, 2 vols. (Cambridge, 1899), II, 374–8. See also *Marriage Promoted*, pp. 16–18 for similar arguments.

that population growth is the intention of nature could thus be reconciled with conventional morality.

Insofar as late-seventeenth-century Whig writers shared an attitude toward women, marriage and the family, it was a common recognition that laws, practices and institutions varied among societies, that they might change over time, that different systems were appropriate to different situations. Neville's *Isle of Pines* implied that what was necessary and appropriate for one generation was not so for another: after peopling his island with polygamy and incest, George Pine enjoins modesty and monogamy upon his descendants.[65] Relativism was fed by travel literature, whereby English readers learned that, for example, amongst the natives of Virginia the kingdom descends 'not to [the king's] sons, but first to his brethren, and after their decease to his sisters, and to the heirs of his eldest sister';[66] that in China, 'the king hath one wife, but many Concubines, whose children inherit if the lawful wife be barren';[67] or that because in South Asian societies 'it was the custom that the *Bracman* had the first nights company with the bride, supposing the ground of better value by that holy seed', the king, 'to make sure work used to confer his command upon his sister's issue; assured it seems that she was of his blood and they of his [blood] by consequence'.[68] There were many different ways of attributing paternity, of apportioning responsibility for the care of children, and of deciding who the legitimate heir would be. In Malabar, some women 'have six or seven husbands, fathering their children on which of them she pleaseth best'.[69] In Benin, there was a class of widows, called '*regetairs* or nurses', belonging to the king, who 'considering they need not stand in fear of a husband, choose as many single men as they like, to whom they prostitute themselves at pleasure: and when any of them prove with child, and bear a son, they are free from paying of tribute; but if they have a girl, it becomes the king's due to dispose of'.[70]

---

[65] [Neville], *The Isle of Pines; A New and Further Discovery*. The latter in particular emphasizes the problem of change.

[66] Samuel Clarke, *A True and Faithful Account of the Four Chiefest Plantations of the English in America* (1670), p. 11. See Edward G. Cox, *A Reference Guide to the Literature of Travel: the New World* (Seattle, 1938) for a comprehensive bibliography.

[67] G. Meriton, *A Geographical Description of the World*, 3rd edn (1679), p. 213.

[68] [Thomas Herbert], *Some Years Travels into Diverse Parts of Africa and Asia the Great*, 4th edn (1677), p. 337.

[69] Meriton, *Geographical Description*, p. 201.

[70] John Ogilby, *Africa* (1670), p. 472.

Although the tone of these accounts ranged from the proto-ethnographic and sympathetic to the sensationalist and derogatory, they all endowed their readers with the empowering knowledge that inheritance practices, as well as marital arrangements, varied across cultures. Thus, when John Locke wanted to provide examples of beliefs and behaviours that would fall into the category of 'things indifferent' (that is, things about which God had given no positive command but which for the sake of social peace were subject to regulation by the magistrate) he hit upon the subjects that concern us in this chapter: 'I say all practical principles or opinions by which men think themselves obliged to regulate their actions with one another, as that men may breed their children, or dispose of their estates as they please, . . . that polygamy and divorce are lawful or unlawful: these opinions and the actions following from them [are] things indifferent'.[71]

While Locke accepted the need to make laws about such things, he did not see such laws as based on foundations firmer than those of 'convenience'. As this suggests, there was by no means absolute consensus as to what was right and wrong with respect to Locke's list of subjects.

The lack of consensus about particulars made the family more rather than less interesting to Whig thinkers of the late seventeenth century. And this is what made them different from Filmer. It was important to Whig theorists that when they wrote about the family they actually wrote about 'real' families and not about a metaphor for something else. This is not to say, of course, that the 'real' was really real, i.e. that Whigs were describing relationships in families as they actually existed. But Whigs talked about the family as if it was real families that they had in mind.

Some of the same could be said for Tories in the 1680s. Insofar as the preoccupations with population and inheritance described above were widespread in the late seventeenth century, they shaped Tory thought as well as Whig. Thus, for example, Tories invoked the inalienable right of heirs to inherit property to defend the duke of York's claims to the throne.[72] But in the context of the exclusion

---

[71] Locke, *Political Writings*, p. 191.

[72] *A Letter to a Friend Reflecting upon the Present Condition of this Nation* (1680), pp. 4–5. See also *An Answer to Pereat Papa* [1681], p. 2; *Great and Weighty Considerations* [1679], p. 7; [John Nalson], *The Character of a Rebellion, and what England May Expect from One* (1681), pp. 7–10; [John Nalson], *The Complaint of Liberty and Property* (1681).

crisis, Tories who talked about the family did so in terms of order rather than property and reproduction. In part this was because Filmer's presence inhibited the proliferation of alternatives; more fundamentally, it was because the fear of disorder, expressed through metaphors of familial chaos, was the Tories' strongest polemical card. It is a sign of Tory *confidence*, then, that Tories did not feel compelled to discuss the family with much rigour or detail. The author of *A Letter to a Friend Shewing from Scripture* apparently felt he had sufficiently addressed the nature of familial relationships with one flippant, dismissive passage: 'If all power be originally in the people, then it will by consequence follow, that the lawful authority of a father over his children, and a husband over his wife, are derived from the children and wife, and the children and wife in some cases may resume their power . . . and their native liberty: If our author will aver so, he is to be cudgelled, not to be answered.'[73] What else was there to say? Whig writers had to put much more intellectual energy into refuting this argument than the Tories did into making it.

The only Tory (that I have found) to embark upon systematic, extended discussions of the familial relationships in the 1680s was Edmund Bohun, who defended Filmer against polemical attacks by both Algernon Sidney and James Tyrrell. The pressure of responding to Whig critics forced Bohun to be far more explicit than Filmer had been about the precise nature of power within the family; in effect, he filled in the blanks left by Filmer's rather cursory treatment. Yet, Bohun is an exception that proves the rule. Like Filmer, Bohun treated paternity as an abstract concept, applicable in all relationships between superiors and subordinates. Tyrrell was wrong, he insisted, to deny that kings could feel for their people the same 'natural affection of a father' for his children, for God 'has in his hands the hearts of all princes, and endows them with such affections as he thinks fit, not only towards the people in general but towards each particular person'.[74] Paternity was so widely transferable, in fact, that Bohun used it (in a way that might have fascinated Freud) to describe all other relationships within the family. Accordingly, he dismissed the distinction, dear to the hearts of Whig theorists,

---

[73] *A Letter to a Friend Shewing from Scripture, Fathers and Reason, How False that State-Maxim is, Royal Authority is . . . in the People* (1679), p. 7. The Whig author attacked here is unidentified.

[74] Edmund Bohun, 'Preface,' in Robert Filmer, *Patriarcha: or, the Natural Power of Kings* (1685), 1.51. Hereafter, Bohun, *Preface to Patriarcha*. Citations are by part and section numbers.

between paternal and conjugal power.[75] 'Adam having no superior but God, Eve owed him a filial subjection as well as [the children].'[76] Because Eve was created out of Adam, 'Adam was a kind of father to his wife. That marital, as well as all other power, might be founded in paternal jurisdiction.'[77] But Bohun also admitted that his description of the relations of Adam, Eve and their children was irrelevant to the experience of people in the present, since the civil law restrained the power that fathers had claimed in their original, natural state.[78] Like Filmer, he appeared uninterested in the situation of actual, contemporary families.

There is some justification, then, in speaking of the tendency to talk about the family in terms of reproduction and property as distinctly 'Whig' as well as distinctly late seventeenth century – although, as I argue elsewhere, the lines between Whig and Tory modes of talking about the family become hazier after 1688.[79]

The preceding discussion should cause us to question the conventional wisdom that the Whigs removed the family from political thought by separating the family and the state. Certainly, the Whigs did not allow the family to stand as a metaphor for the state, or for all authority, as Filmer had. But rather than say they eliminated the family from political thought, it is more accurate to describe them as inserting the family into political thought in a different way. The applicability of this point to Locke and Sidney particularly merits discussion here, since they are, of all Whig thinkers, the ones most closely associated with the family–state distinction, and therefore are the toughest test cases.

Sidney on first glance separated the family and the state definitively. His desire to retain the 'real-life' patriarchal family undisturbed could only be reconciled with the metaphor of political society as a band of brothers because the two were, in Sidney's mind, completely cordoned off from one another: 'For the question is not concerning the power that every householder in London hath over his wife, children and servants; but whether they are all perpetually subject to one family; and I intend not to set up their wives, prentices and children against them.'[80]

---

[75] *Ibid., Preface to Patriarcha*, 1.27.   [76] *Ibid., Preface to Patriarcha*, 1.31.

[77] Edmund Bohun, *A Defence of Sir Robert Filmer against the Mistakes and Misrepresentations of Algernon Sidney* (1684), p. 13.

[78] Bohun, *Preface to Patriarcha*, 1.67.

[79] See Weil, *Political Passions*, especially part II.   [80] Sidney, *Discourses*, II, 74–5 (II.9).

And yet, it would be misleading to describe this as a 'separation' of the family and state, since the idealized vision of fraternal love and equality that informs Sidney's view of the state was a familial metaphor, based on and energized by ideas about the proper relationships in families, including the relationship of dominance of fathers to sons. Notions about the family were thus not purged from Sidney's political thinking, but deeply embedded in it.

The same can be said of Locke. His preoccupation with the production and care of children inserted the family into political argument in a new way. The imperative to reproduce and care for children became the standard by which the family was judged, and the fulfilment of the obligation was a clinching argument in a court of moral appeal. The gender politics of this could cut in more than one direction. Locke's notion that the primary purpose of the family is to produce and care for children led him to suggest that when this task is accomplished, the couple could consent to part.[81] As Mary Shanley has argued, there was a feminist dimension to this claim.[82] On the other hand, if one places the emphasis differently – the couple *cannot* part until the task is accomplished – the effect of Locke's pronouncement was to establish that women are carers and producers of children first, and individuals later.

We are now heading back in the direction of emphasizing the diversity amongst Whigs and the complexity of the gender politics in the writing of any one of them. It is worth making it clear again that the basic underlying assumptions of Whig thought in the exclusion crisis that I have been trying to tease out here did not guarantee any consensus. Within a shared sense of what the family is for, there was much about which people could disagree: *how* to increase population, what kind of system of inheritance is fair, or what makes a father a father. But that is another story. What I have tried to do here is to explain how these became issues about which people *bothered* to disagree. By uncovering the unity that lies beneath the diversity, we can begin to illuminate the specificity and perhaps novelty of the terms in which Restoration political discourse was conducted.[83]

---

[81] Locke, *Two Treatises*, II.81
[82] Shanley, 'Marriage Contract and Social Contract'.
[83] This essay uses material appearing in chs. 1, 2 and 5 of my *Political Passions: Gender, the Family and Political Argument in England 1680–1714* (Manchester, 1999), and appears with permission of the publisher.

CHAPTER 5

Understanding popular politics in Restoration Britain

Tim Harris

Long before it became trendy to talk about the emergence of the 'public sphere', Restoration historians had recognized the need to pay attention to the growing importance of popular political agitation and opinion 'out-of-doors' under the later Stuarts. The very fact that a new word, 'the mob', was coined during the 1680s to describe those who participated in political rallies and demonstrations is in itself a clear indication that something significant was going on.[1] Max Beloff gave us a valuable study of popular disturbances in the period 1660–1714 as far back as 1938, whilst the growing importance of opinion 'out-of-doors' was a major reason why J. R. Jones felt able to conclude in 1961 that the exclusion crisis saw the emergence, for the first time, of party politics in England.[2] In 1987 I offered my own investigation of the political culture of the London masses, suggesting new ways of approaching the study of crowd politics and showing why it is necessary to take those out-of-doors seriously.[3] With the great growth of interest in Restoration history in recent years has come a concomitant increase in attention to opinion out-of-doors; many historians charting political developments after 1660, it now seems, appreciate the need to extend their accounts beyond the elite, and to look at

---

[1] Roger North, *Examen; or, an Enquiry into the Credit and Veracity of a Pretended Complete History* (1740), p. 574. Earlier versions of this chapter were delivered as talks at the Huntington Library, the University of Warwick and the North East Conference on British Studies meeting at Dartmouth College. I would like to thank the various audiences at all three venues for their constructive comments and criticisms. The research and writing of this article was supported by a fellowship from the John Simon Guggenheim Memorial Foundation.

[2] Max Beloff, *Public Order and Popular Disturbances, 1660–1714* (London, 1938); J. R. Jones, *The First Whigs: the Politics of the Exclusion Crisis, 1678–83* (Oxford, 1961).

[3] Tim Harris, *London Crowds in the Reign of Charles II: Propaganda and Politics from the Restoration until the Exclusion Crisis* (Cambridge, 1987).

the concerns, attitudes, aspirations and activities of the middling sorts and lower orders.[4]

Given this growing interest in politics or opinion out-of-doors, it is perhaps time to sit back and reflect upon whether we are going about it in the right way. My own approach was to work from the bottom up. Thus *London Crowds* began with an attempt to reconstruct the political culture of the people, and only later turned to a considera- tion of how political propagandists sought to reshape and redefine people's political affiliations and identities. Others appear to take more of a top-down, centre-out approach, placing emphasis on the ways members of the elite reached out to the masses and sought to politicize them through their exploitation of the press. 'Divisions within the elite', John Miller has recently argued, 'led its members to seek support among their social inferiors', particularly during the exclusion crisis; 'both parties', he continues, 'used a variety of media – above all the press – to woo popular support'.[5] Mark Knights, in his sophisticated and detailed analysis of politics and opinion during the exclusion crisis, chose to start with high politics, at Westminster, before going on to look next at the press and then finally at expressions of public opinion. The organizational structure is re- vealing. For all the valuable light this book sheds on mass petitioning activity, in particular, it is essentially a study of how 'the crisis at the centre' affected 'London and the localities', of how people in 'the localities' were drawn 'into national politics', with the press being central to the process.[6] If we are interested in learning about how people in the localities got drawn into national politics, there seem to be compelling reasons for focusing on the press. There is a common- sense view, which derives from what is now somewhat dated socio- logical thinking, that the media 'are largely responsible for the

---

[4] For studies which take popular political aspirations or opinion out-of-doors seriously, see in particular Richard L. Greaves, *Deliver Us from Evil: the Radical Underground in Britain, 1660–1663* (Oxford, 1986), *Enemies under His Feet: Radicals and Nonconformists in Britain, 1664–1677* (Stanford, 1990) and *Secrets of the Kingdom: British Radicals from the Popish Plot to the Revolution of 1688–89* (Stanford, 1992); Gary De Krey, 'The London Whigs and the Exclusion Crisis Reconsidered', in Lee Beier, David Cannadine and James Rosenheim (eds.), *The First Modern Society: Essays in English History in Honour of Lawrence Stone* (Cambridge, 1989), pp. 457–82; Mark Knights, *Politics and Opinion in Crisis, 1678–81* (Cambridge, 1994); John Miller, 'Public Opinion in Charles II's England', *History* 80 (1995), 359–81; Steven Pincus, '"Coffee Politicians Does Create": Coffeehouses and Restoration Political Culture', *Journal of Modern History* 67 (1995), 807–34.

[5] Miller, 'Public Opinion', p. 375.

[6] Knights, *Politics and Opinion* (quotes on pp. 153, 356).

creation of public opinion',[7] and the most powerful mass medium in the early-modern period was surely print. Kathleen Wilson describes the press as 'that preeminent instrument of politicization in the eighteenth century'; its 'political impact', she asserts, 'lay in its ability to organize knowledge, shape expectations, mobilise identities and proffer ideals, perspectives and attitudes through which politics could be interpreted'.[8] It was during the seventeenth century that the political press first came into being; there was a huge outpouring of printed news and polemic in the 1640s, with the breakdown of censorship on the eve of the civil war, and although restrictions on the freedom of the press were restored in the 1650s and after the Restoration, they were never fully effective, and broke down again from 1679, with the temporary lapsing of the Licensing Act. During Charles II's reign, moreover, printed materials came to be disseminated more widely than they had ever been before, thanks in large part to the growing numbers of coffee houses that were springing up all over Britain, which served as meeting places where all classes of people could go to read, or have read to them, the latest political news.[9] C. John Sommerville has recently argued that the seventeenth-century news periodical 'created a new kind of society, the informed public . . . Editors provided the ingredients for the coffee house discussion which generated an authentic public opinion.' In his chapter on the exclusion crisis, Sommerville repeatedly refers to how the press (or the news periodical) created public opinion.[10] Following such logic, it has been suggested that we witness a new development in the later seventeenth century – one which had its roots in the 1640s, to be sure, but which came to fruition in the Restoration period – namely, the rise of public opinion, or even of the public sphere: political debate was carried out-of-doors by the press, into the coffee houses, thereby heightening the political consciousness of the populace, who became drawn more and more into the political struggles of the elite.[11]

[7] D. McQuail, *Towards a Sociology of Mass Communications* (London, 1969), quoted in Tom Burns, 'The Organization of Public Opinion', in his *Description, Explanation and Understanding: Selected Writing, 1944–1980* (Edinburgh, 1995), p. 259.

[8] Kathleen Wilson, *The Sense of the People: Politics, Culture and Imperialism in England, 1715–1785* (Cambridge, 1995), pp. 29, 53–4.

[9] Pincus, 'Coffeehouses and Restoration Political Culture'; Harold Love, *Scribal Publication in Seventeenth-Century England* (Oxford, 1993), pp. 12, 203–7.

[10] C. John Sommerville, *The News Revolution in England: Cultural Dynamics of Daily Information* (Oxford, 1996), pp. 15, 90, 94.

[11] Pincus, 'Coffeehouses and Restoration Political Culture'; Love, *Scribal Publication*, pp. 192–5;

The intention of this chapter is to invite a critical exploration of some of these assumptions. I do not wish to deny the importance of the press, nor the coffee houses, nor the fact that those out-of-doors came to be seen as an increasingly significant force in politics at this time. I do, however, want to warn against a top-down approach or attributing too much influence to the medium of print in shaping public opinion. In our approach to popular politics, we should focus less on the press and pay more attention to the social and cultural processes whereby the masses became politicized: these would include inherited political, cultural and religious traditions, as well as the impact of government at the grass-roots level. The media certainly played an important role in heightening political awareness. But in addition to print we need to recognize that more traditional media remained vitally important; sermons, oral communication, rumour, visual display, all need to be brought into the equation. With this change of emphasis, we begin to see more continuities: in fact, there seem to emerge quite a few similarities, so far as politics out-of-doors is concerned, between the Restoration period, and, say, the reign of Henry VIII. What, then, were the differences? Here we need to reflect on long-term structural changes, something which political historians are somewhat reluctant to do nowadays. Demographically, sociologically and culturally, England was a very different place by the 1670s and 80s from what it had been in the 1530s; population densities were different, as were class structures and literacy profiles. We must also recognize the impact of the English civil war. Public opinion became important in the Restoration because Charles II realized that he could not afford to ignore it, as his father had done to his cost. In order to appreciate what was new about the Restoration with regard to popular politics, we need to place emphasis on these lessons of experience set against longer-term structural changes which resulted in the masses being seen as a more threatening or less controllable force than they had once been.

Any attempt to understand popular politics in Restoration Britain must start with the people themselves, and how their own identities were formed. We are not dealing with a *tabula rasa*, obviously, but

Jürgen Habermas, *The Structural Transformation of the Public Sphere: an Enquiry into a Category of Bourgeois Society*, translated by Thomas Burger with the assistance of Frederick Lawrence (Cambridge, MA, 1989); Dagmar Freist, *Governed by Opinion: Politics, Religion and the Dynamics of Communication in Stuart London 1637–1645* (London, 1997).

with people brought up with certain ways of looking at the world. These would be in part a reflection of class background, religious upbringing, and cultural environment. Then we have the experiences of the 1640s and 1650s, which undoubtedly led to a more politically self-conscious population; in that sense the legacy of the civil war was to make Britain after 1660 significantly different from what it had been prior to 1640. One of the biggest legacies of the civil war and interregnum was a politically and religiously divided society. Although the restoration of monarchy was welcome to most people, there certainly were some who retained sympathies for a republic. The severest tensions, undoubtedly, existed on the religious front: between episcopalians, Presbyterians, independents, various separatist groups, and, of course, Roman Catholics.[12] Yet it was not simply that the civil war made political partisans out of people; we have to recognize other legacies that are sometimes more difficult for the historian to get a handle on. One, certainly, was a profound fear of the same thing happening again. This could at times lead to a desire to seek compromise, or to hold back from pushing one's agenda too far; hence perhaps why some moderates, who formerly had been sympathetic to exclusion, rallied to the crown after 1681.[13] More typically, however, it could lead to heightened anxieties, suspicions and paranoia – a fear that what one's neighbour was up to, or what the political elite were up to, might threaten civil peace. Instead of promoting greater harmony, in other words, this fear of going down the same path again could provoke instability. One might cite, as an example, the suspicions that many English people had of their Presbyterian neighbours, on the whole a rather peaceful group who believed in hierarchy in church and state, but who during the exclusion crisis came to be feared as radical political and religious subversives.[14] A more telling case in point is that of the Scottish Presbyterians; fear of what they might be up to in their conventicles led the episcopalian establishment to embark on a ruthless policy of persecution, particularly in the south-west of Scotland, with the

---

[12] Harris, *London Crowds*, ch. 3; Greaves, *Deliver Us from Evil*.

[13] Jonathan Scott, *Algernon Sidney and the Restoration Crisis, 1677–83* (Cambridge, 1991), esp. part 1. For a more balanced view, see Knights, *Politics and Opinion*; Tim Harris, *Politics under the Later Stuarts: Party Conflict in a Divided Society* (London, 1993), ch. 4; Tim Harris, 'The Parties and the People: the Press, the Crowd and Politics "Out-of-Doors" in Restoration England', in Lionel Glassey (ed.), *The Reigns of Charles II and James VII and II* (Basingstoke, 1997), pp. 125–51.

[14] Harris, *London Crowds*, chs. 6–7.

result that eventually the Presbyterians there did rise in revolt against the government (on two occasions, in 1666 and 1679), in protest against their oppressions. Significantly, those in the south-east of Scotland, who were left relatively unmolested by the authorities, remained peaceful during the reign of Charles II.[15]

Another legacy of the civil war experience was that it encouraged a more developed sense amongst people that they possessed certain rights – whether inalienable birthrights, inviolable rights at law, or even obligations owed to them by their social and political superiors.[16] The Restoration for many people, of all classes and political and religious outlooks (including the Anglican clergy and Cavalier gentry), meant a restoration of the rule of law and constitutional propriety.[17] For example, in their remonstrance of November 1659, which called for the restoration of the monarchy, the London apprentices said that they looked upon the laws as their 'Birth-right', and that they would assert with their 'Lives and Fortunes the Laws of this Land and the Liberty of the Subject'.[18] Similarly, the corporation of Dublin, which joined in the conspiracy to restore Charles II to his three kingdoms, declared in February 1660 that they regarded 'a full and free parliament in England' as the 'birthright of the people of England'.[19]

People's political identities, therefore, were shaped by inherited or culturally conditioned outlooks. These identities were further refined or reshaped by how they experienced the workings of government. Government policy had a direct impact on the lives of ordinary people; they did not need to read about what the government was up to in the press, because they actually felt it themselves. They felt it in their purse. 'The vulgar' were most likely to stir, contemporaries thought, when 'pricked by exactions of money'.[20] Grievances centring around the high level of taxation imposed by an unconstitutional regime in order to support a standing army lay behind much of the public agitation against the republic in the winter of 1659–60 and helps explain why so many people in England looked favourably

---

[15] I. B. Cowan, *The Scottish Covenanters, 1660–1688* (London, 1976).

[16] *An Express from the Knights and Gentlemen now engaged with Sir George Booth* (1659); *To the Right Honourable, the Lord Mayor . . . The Humble Petition of Divers Well-Affected Householders and Freemen* (1660); Harris, *London Crowds*, ch. 3; Paul Seaward, *The Cavalier Parliament and the Restoration of the Old Regime, 1661–1667* (Cambridge, 1989), pp. 45–6.

[17] Harris, *Politics under the Later Stuarts*, pp. 36–7.

[18] *The Remonstrance of the Apprentices in and about London* (1659).

[19] *Calendar of the Ancient Records of Dublin*, ed. John T. Gilbert, 16 vols. (Dublin, 1889, 1913), IV, 179.

[20] *Calendar of State Papers Domestic, 1661–2* (hereafter *CSPD*), p. 412.

towards the possibility of a restoration of monarchy.[21] Continuing high and regressive taxes after the Restoration, in the form of the excise and the hearth tax, on the other hand, was one reason for the rapid growth of disillusionment with the new regime.[22] Economic policy, more generally speaking, could create dissatisfaction with the government. In Ireland, commercial interests, both Protestant and Catholic, resented the restrictions imposed on the freedom of economic enterprise imposed by the mother country, through measures such as the Navigation Acts, the Cattle Act or the Wool Act. The confirmation of the Navigation Acts at the start of James II's reign left the merchants of Ireland 'much dejected', commented one Protestant correspondent.[23] In 1686, the Dublin clothiers begged the Lord Lieutenant of Ireland, the earl of Clarendon, to intercede with the king to suspend the act prohibiting the export of Irish manufactures to 'his Majesty's plantations', otherwise they would be ruined, their trade being 'at best . . . but small, seldome affording a competent Subsistance'.[24] It was the Catholic majority in Ireland who felt most aggrieved by the government-backed policy of economic discrimination. Lack of access to land, trading privileges and jobs does much to explain the hostility of Irish Catholics to English domination, even amongst working-class Gaels, who could not read the English newssheets in the Irish coffee houses even if they could afford the price of a cup of coffee.[25] Although the economic pinch of government was undoubtedly important, it was perhaps the religious codes of the Restoration monarchy that most noticeably impacted on the lives of ordinary people. In England dissenters, from a wide variety of social backgrounds, lost their 'lives, liberties and estates' as a result of religious persecution.[26] The penal laws were most brutal in Scotland. Here, Presbyterian nonconformists might suffer not just fines and imprisonment, but be subject to punitive

---

[21] Harris, *London Crowds*, ch. 3; Harris, *Politics under the Later Stuarts*, pp. 29–30.
[22] Algernon Sidney, *Court Maxims*, ed. Hans W. Blom, Eco Haitsma Mulier and Ronald Janse (Cambridge, 1996), pp. 5, 75, 167; Corporation of London Record Office, Sessions File, July 1663, ind. of Samuel Lewys; David Underdown, A *Freeborn People: Politics and the Nation in Seventeenth-Century England* (Oxford, 1996), p. 123.
[23] *HMC, Egmont*, ii, 157.
[24] Bodleian Library, MS Clarendon 88, fol. 290; *Calendar of Clarendon State Papers Preserved in the Bodleian Library*, ed. F. J. Routledge, 5 vols. (Oxford, 1872–1932), v, 670.
[25] Tim Harris, *British Revolutions* (Harmondsworth, forthcoming).
[26] Tim Harris, '"Lives, Liberties and Estates": Rhetorics of Liberty in the Reign of Charles II', in Tim Harris, Paul Seaward and Mark Goldie (eds.), *The Politics of Religion in Restoration England* (Oxford, 1990), pp. 217–41.

taxation, the dragooning of troops, judicial torture, and even – in the 1680s – summary execution.[27] Nor was it just the victims of the law who experienced government policy in this way. In recent years we have come to appreciate the widespread popular participation in the machinery of government at the local level, particularly in the area of law enforcement – through participation on juries, service as constables, beadles, nightwatchmen, in the militia, or even just appearing as a witness or informer. In an era when people could be fined for their refusal to help bring nonconformists to justice, or financially rewarded when they did, many who were not dissenters had to decide where they stood with regard to the government's policy towards dissent. For some, it was the tough choice of whether to abandon one's neighbours and friends in time of need or stand by them and risk the consequences.[28]

The way governments policed their subject peoples was a further factor that shaped people's political outlook. Hostility towards the army's role provoked disturbances in London in the autumn and winter of 1659; the army was hated in part because its financing required the imposition of heavy taxes, which the soldiers themselves were responsible for collecting, but also because of the ruthless way it dealt with popular disorder. Colonel Hewson's decision to order his troops to fire on a crowd of somewhat unruly petitioners on 5 December, killing half a dozen youths, provoked a storm of reaction, with threats from the inhabitants of London that they would oppose violence with violence if the soldiers were not removed from the city.[29] Troops billeted in the Scottish south-west in the later 1670s not only consumed all their landlords' food and robbed them of money, but 'behaved themselves in so beastial a manner, that no Marriageable-Woman could with safety stay at home'.[30] There was much resentment in England against James II's build-up of his standing army in the aftermath of the Monmouth rebellion – not just because of the presence of Catholic officers, but because of the way the

---

[27] Cowan, *Scottish Covenanters.*

[28] J. A. Sharpe, 'The People and the Law', in Barry Reay (ed.), *Popular Culture in Seventeenth-Century England* (London, 1985), pp. 244–70; Harris, *London Crowds,* pp. 18–22, 72–3; Harris, *Politics under the Later Stuarts,* pp. 16–17; Mark Goldie, 'The Hilton Gang: Terrorising Dissent in 1680s London', *History Today* 47 (October 1997), 26–32; Paul Griffiths, Steve Hindle and Adam Fox (eds.), *The Experience of Authority in Early Modern England* (Basingstoke, 1996), introduction.

[29] Harris, *London Crowds,* pp. 43–4.

[30] *A Brief and True Account of the Sufferings of the Church of Scotland* (1690), pp. 3–4.

soldiers behaved when stationed in various parts of the country. When the duke of Norfolk's regiment was billeted in the east end of London in mid August 1685 there were reports not only that they 'stoll all that ever they could lay theire hands on' but also that they were 'very abussiffe' to the local householders and threatened to rape their wives.[31] Mistreatment at the hands of Catholic soldiers in Ireland, intruded into the army by the earl of Tyrconnell, did much to alienate Protestants in Ireland from James II's regime. One Protestant clergyman later complained how the Catholic troops 'ruined all the Protestant Inns of Ireland, partly by oppressing them with Quarters, partly by paying nothing for what they had in their Quarters, and partly by driving away other Guests by their rudeness'.[32] In April 1687, when a disgruntled innkeeper confronted some soldiers about the money they owed him, they 'tossed him in a blankett' so severely that he died the next day.[33]

My remarks have been necessarily brief. The examples could be extended almost indefinitely, however, to show the variety of ways in which government intruded into the lives of ordinary people and therefore helped to shape their attitudes towards those who were ruling them. One might even argue that 'the preeminent instrument of politicization' in Restoration Britain was the government – and what it was doing to people – not the press. Amongst the most politically troublesome group in Restoration Scotland were the wild hill men, as contemporaries called them, of the Presbyterian southwest. These were not well-educated people; many were indeed illiterate.[34] They lived in a remote area, where communications were poor, and where printed materials coming from the presses in London or Edinburgh did not easily penetrate. Their politicization was the result of inherited traditions, upbringing in the Presbyterian faith, and reaction to government policies such as religious persecution, dragooning and punitive taxation.[35] This is an extreme example; there were not many places in England that were quite as

---

[31] BL, Add. MSS 41,804, fol. 48.
[32] [William King], *The State of the Protestants of Ireland under the Late King James's Government* (1691), p. 55. Cf. p. 121.
[33] Dr. Williams's Library, Roger Morrice, Ent'ring Book, Q, p. 129; BL, Add. MSS 41,804, fol. 279; *HMC, Ormonde*, NS VIII, 350. For the army under James II, and conflicts with the civilian population more generally, see John Childs, *The Army, James II, and the Glorious Revolution* (London, 1980).
[34] [James Stirling], *Naphtali; or, the Printed Wrestlings of the Church of Scotland* (1680), p. 220.
[35] *A Declaration of the Rebels Now in Arms in the West of Scotland* [1679], p. 2.

wild and remote. Yet it is revealing because it enables us to isolate the variables. Even in areas that were not well integrated into the national communications network or the burgeoning consumer print culture, we still find a politicized and politically self-assertive population, capable of co-ordinating political activity themselves and even posing a considerable amount of trouble for the government of the day (through the rebellions of 1666 and 1679).

Let us now turn to a consideration of the media. The press undoubtedly was very important, as was the fact that printed materials were made widely available to those who could not afford to buy them through places like the coffee houses. The government certainly recognized the power of the press, hence why it sought to control it through measures such as the Licensing Act of 1662 and the enforcement of the law of seditious libel, and hence why it tried to control the coffee houses and stop them from carrying scandalous papers, books and libels (as it did in the winter of 1675–6).[36] When controls over the press broke down during the exclusion crisis, the government sought to beat the opposition at its own game. As the licenser of the press, Roger L'Estrange, put it when he launched his periodical the *Observator* in April 1681: the press had 'made 'um [the people] Mad' and 'the Press must set 'um Right again'.[37] One of the most effective pieces of printed propaganda at this time, as the work of Knights has shown, was Charles II's *Declaration To All His Loving Subjects, Touching the Causes and Reasons that Moved Him to Dissolve the Two Last Parliaments* of April 1681, which helped generate a significant loyalist reaction in the aftermath of the exclusion crisis.[38]

Yet we should be cautious of placing too much emphasis on the impact of print culture, especially once we move away from the more literate urban cultures. In a society where the majority of people remained illiterate – and where many people who had basic literacy skills would have had difficulty reading Charles II's relatively short *Declaration* of April 1681, let alone the much lengthier reply to it by Algernon Sidney[39] – traditional forms of oral communication

---

[36] Corporation of London Record Office, Journal 48, fols. 189–91; Harris, *London Crowds*, pp. 28–9, 92; Love, *Scribal Publication*, pp. 240–2.

[37] Roger L'Estrange, *Observator*, no. 1, 13 Apr. 1681.

[38] Knights, *Politics and Opinion*, ch. 10. In *London Crowds* I placed great emphasis on the part played by popular propaganda in helping define the political outlooks of the London masses: Harris, *London Crowds*, chs. 5, 6.

[39] [Algernon Sidney and William Jones], A *Just and Modest Vindication of the Proceedings of the Two Last Parliaments* (1681); Scott, *Sidney and the Restoration Crisis*, pp. 184–97.

remained vitally important. One of the most powerful tools for the dissemination of political information and ideas was the sermon. Again, this was something Restoration governments recognized – hence the decision to crack down on nonconformist conventicles. The motivation was not religious – the government persistently denied allegations that it was engaged in persecuting people for their religious beliefs; rather, conventicles were feared as nests of sedition. It is hard to find out much about what was taught at conventicles, since the sermons were not printed; we do know that the government was convinced that nonconformist ministers were teaching doctrines of resistance.[40] By contrast, Anglican sermonizing played a crucial role in building up loyalty to Charles II's government during the years of the Tory reaction, in turning people against their non-conformist neighbours and persuading them to denounce dissenters before the law courts, and in cementing a commitment to the hereditary principle and the accession of James II in 1685.[41] James II himself recognized the power of the pulpit, especially when the Anglican clergy started turning against him, and he tried to prevent the clergy of the established church, in all three of his kingdoms, from broaching controversial subjects. In England in the early months of 1686, as is well known, he took initiatives to stop anti-Catholic sermonizing, which brought him into conflict not just with the rector of St Giles in the Fields, but also with Bishop Compton of London, and resulted in the setting up of the Ecclesiastical Commission to discipline recalcitrant clergymen.[42] Similar measures were taken in Ireland at the same time, where the earl of Clarendon, as viceroy, was ordered to reprimand those clergy who were stirring up the people against popery. James was prompted to action by a report that the bishop of Meath, in a sermon preached before Clarendon himself, had taken 'a greater liberty' on the subject of popery 'than became him', although the overworked lord lieutenant may well have slept through it, since he reported back to James II that the bishop was 'a very dull preacher', and that was why he, 'as well as others . . . minded him [not] so much' as they ought to have done.[43]

---

[40] Samuel Parker, *History of His Own Time*, trans. Thomas Newlin (1727), pp. 366–7.
[41] Harris, *Politics under the Later Stuarts*, pp. 121–3. This is a line of argument I develop more fully in my forthcoming *British Revolutions*.
[42] John Miller, *James II: a Study in Kingship* (London, 1989 edn), pp. 154–5.
[43] *The Correspondence of Henry Hyde, Earl of Clarendon and of His Brother Laurence Hyde, Earl of Rochester; With the Diary of Lord Clarendon from 1687 to 1690*, ed. Samuel Weller Singer, 2 vols. (1828), I, 258, 282.

In October 1685 the Scottish secretary of state in London ordered
the bishop of Edinburgh to put a stop to 'seditious speeches . . . in
the Pulpits' which were stirring people up against the king and 'the
Popish religion'. Despite the bishop's attempts to enforce the direc-
tive, he found it difficult to keep his clergy in line. One minister who
continued to poke fun at the Catholic religion from the pulpit
defended his action by saying that he thought 'a ridiculous religion
might be treated in ridicule'.[44] Indeed, anti-Catholic sermonizing
appears to have been responsible for prompting the widespread anti-
Catholic rioting in Edinburgh on 31 January and 1 February 1686.[45]

Even when we are dealing with written materials, we have to
recognize that often they came to be transmitted orally. Charles II's
Declaration of Reasons of April 1681 was so effective as propaganda
because the king instructed the archbishops of Canterbury and of
York to see to it that their clergy read it aloud to their congregations
in all churches and chapels throughout the land.[46] News that broke
from the London presses and found its way, through the medium of
print, to provincial centres, nevertheless often ended up being
circulated through the surrounding countryside by word-of-mouth.
In December 1678, shortly after the Privy Council's search of the
papers of Edward Coleman, the duke of York's former secretary, had
uncovered incriminating papers seemingly pointing to the reality of
a popish plot, a man from Paisley, in Renfrewshire, recorded how
someone had recently ridden 'throw the place declaring that there
are two Letters of Colemans found', and explaining that he had seen
a copy of the first at Edinburgh.[47] During the time of the exclusion
crisis, we can find examples of Whig agents in the provinces reading
pamphlets aloud in the streets for the edification of passers-by.[48]
Steven Pincus's work on Restoration coffee houses shows that these
were places where people went to hear gossip as much as read

---

[44] Sir John Lauder of Fountainhall, *The Decisions of the Lords of the Council and Session from June 6th,
    1678, to July 30th, 1713*, 2 vols. (Edinburgh, 1759–61), I, 371, 412.
[45] A *Complete Collection of State Trials*, ed. T. B. Howell, 33 vols. (1809–26), XI, cols. 1003–1024;
    The Register of the Privy Council of Scotland, 1685–6 (hereafter *RPCS*), pp. 544–5; *RPCS, 1686*,
    pp. 7–16; Fountainhall, *Decisions*, I, 399–407; *Historical Selections from the Manuscripts of Sir John
    Lauder of Fountainhall. Volume First, Historical Observations, 1680–1686* (Edinburgh, 1837), p. 243.
    The rioting may well have been triggered, in part, by James Canaries's assault on Chancellor
    Perth and other Catholic converts from the pulpit of the East Church of St Giles on the
    preceding 14 February: James Canaries, *Romes Additions to Christianity* (1686).
[46] All Souls Library, Oxford, MS 257, no. 96.
[47] National Library of Scotland, Wod. MSS Qu. xxx, fol. 59.
[48] *CSPD, 1682*, pp. 303, 456.

pamphlets; printed materials were there for anyone who had the leisure or ability to read them, but many spent their time talking about politics, and others just popped in to obtain a quick verbal report of what the latest news held.[49] Thomas Coningsby, MP for Leominster in the second Exclusion Parliament, sent detailed written reports about transactions at Westminster back home to a local agent, who in turn took care 'to distribute all the news . . . about the corporation . . . advising the mobeley every post of that corporation of all the proceedings in Parliament'. The choice of the word advise, together with a statement in the same report that after the Parliament was dissolved 'all the *discourse* [my emphasis] was of the unjust, unlawful and unwarrantable proceedings in so frequently dissolving Parliaments', suggests this news was disseminated orally.[50] It may be that some of the cases we can uncover from the legal records of prosecutions for seditious words in reality reflect the process whereby educated members of the elite conveyed their book (or pamphlet) learning to a wider audience through oral communication. In January 1684 the Surrey Grand Jury drew up a presentment against Richard Onslow, MP for Guildford, in the three Exclusion Parliaments, charging that during the height of the exclusion crisis he 'did openly take upon him to prove and maintain this . . . seditious position, That all power was originally in the people and the king had noe power but what he Received from them'. Onslow allegedly spoke these and similar words 'in several Companyes', one being at the Red Lyon pub.[51] From Bath at the end of 1682 we have a report of a local lawyer 'holding forth to a parcel of apron men in a public house', arguing that it was not 'fit the prerogative and so great power should be in the Crown', and that 'the Late House of Commons did very well in denying to give the king any money'.[52] In Dublin in James II's reign newsletters from unofficial sources in England found their way into the coffee houses, where they would then be discussed and reviewed and the news they contained subsequently spread by word-of-mouth. Indeed, we have the ironic situation of the head of the government

---

[49] Pincus, 'Coffeehouses and Restoration Political Culture'. Cf. Steven C. A. Pincus, *Protestantism and Patriotism: Ideologies and the Making of English Foreign Policy, 1650–1668* (Cambridge, 1996), pp. 276–80, where the emphasis is placed first on gossip, discourse and the hearing of news.

[50] *CSPD, 1682*, pp. 506–7.

[51] Guildford Muniment Room, 111/10/14/1–14.

[52] *CSPD, 1682*, p. 587.

in Ireland during 1686, the earl of Clarendon, learning more about the royal agenda for Ireland from stories he heard on the streets than from what he was told in writing by the king, or his prime minister, the earl of Sunderland.[53] It was a situation that provided a fertile ground for the spreading of rumours.

This leads to a further consideration, namely the importance of rumour as a medium of political communication. Rumour may be described as improvised news.[54] It should not be seen as 'false news' in contradistinction to the 'true news' one could read in the press. Rumours could at times prove true; often they did not, but then again many of the reports carried in the news periodicals of the exclusion crisis were distortions of reality, or based on no more than hearsay, or even complete fabrications, invented for polemical effect or to boost sales.[55] The unstable situation that existed in Restoration Ireland, and the sharp tensions between Catholics and Protestants that became particularly manifest during the reign of James II, resulted as much as anything else from the prevalence of rumour and speculation. For example, there appears to have been little, if any, genuine Monmouthite conspiracy in Ireland at the time of the rebellion of 1685. The Irish, however, who had seen much of their land taken away by Cromwellian settlers, were convinced that the English in Ireland were all at heart republicans and 'devoted to Monmouth', which led in turn to 'hot discourses . . . about the country', and fears that the English were waiting their opportunity to rise and 'cut their throats'.[56] Similarly, there were rumours in several parts of the country in the autumn of 1686 of 'great meetings in the night of armed men', both 'Scotch and English', who were 'coming to destroy the Irish'. Troops were dispatched to patrol the areas where these reports were coming from, but such action merely confirmed the suspicions of the local residents. At Mullingar in County Westmeath, for example, witnesses saw 100 horsemen march in rank and file through the town and concluded that they must be 'Presbyterians, for honest men did not use to meet and march by

---

[53] *Clarendon Correspondence*, I, 189, 270, 297, 305, 308–9; *HMC, Ormonde*, NS VII, 415.

[54] Tamotsu Shibutani, *Improvised News: a Sociological Study of Rumor* (Indianapolis, 1966); Freist, *Governed by Opinion*, ch. 5.

[55] Remarks found in contemporary correspondence that such a report was 'no more than a Rumour, and a false one too' or that 'rumors . . . nowadayes . . . are so comonly false' imply that contemporaries recognized that rumours could be true. See: BL, Sloane MS 1008, fol. 252; BL, Add. MSS 28,876, fol. 5.

[56] *HMC, Egmont*, II, 158.

night', or that they were 'Whigs, because . . . in Monmouth's time they did use to meet and march at night'. At nearby Athlone, the townsfolk were awoken from their sleep on the night of 10 November by a report that 'they were all undone' because a body of 100 horse and 300 men had been seen entering the town. Clarendon's enquiries revealed that the armed men who had been seen were none other than the troops that had been dispatched to deal with the rumoured threat of an uprising.[57] It was not just the Irish who harboured such fears. The English were similarly convinced that the Irish were plotting against them, and that there was going to be a massacre of Protestants. On 21 June 1685, for example, the town of Borrisokane in County Tipperary was alarmed by a rumour that there was to be 'a rising . . . of the Irish' and that all the Protestants 'should have their throats cut by them'. To defend themselves the Protestant inhabitants decided to keep watch that night, parading the streets armed with swords, staves, or guns. Such action, of course, merely served to convince Catholics that the Protestants were out to get them.[58]

Ireland may have been particularly sensitive to the spread of rumour; of the three kingdoms that comprised the Britannic archipelago, its culture was probably the most oral, and printed media played a less significant role in the distribution of news there than on the island of Britain itself. Yet even in England and Scotland, rumour was important. During the 1670s and 1680s fears of the French threat or of the crown's absolutist ambitions were fuelled by gossip and the spreading of stories by word of mouth. In December 1679 Francis Tranchard of Badgworth in Somerset returned from a trip to London with reports that 'there was a Peace concluded betweene our King and the French . . . and that the Parliament shall not sit these five yeares and the French King will give our King two hundred thousand pounds to keepe the Parliament from sitting'.[59] When one James Ledger, returning home from the capital to Charing in Kent shortly after the accession of James II, was asked 'what news from London', he replied: 'it was Reported the king would govern by a Standing Army'. Such remarks were treated as seriously as if one had authored or published seditious literature: the Kentish quarter sessions sentenced Ledger to be fined, pilloried and

[57] *Clarendon Correspondence*, II, 73−9, 81−3, 105−6, 145.
[58] *HMC, Ormonde*, NS VII, 365−7, 371, 373−4, 378, 380−1, 387, 394, 399.
[59] Somerset Record Office, Q/SR/142/1.

whipped.[60] The politically savvy at times sought to manipulate the medium of rumour by deliberately planting false reports; the Irish scare of December 1688, which provoked anti-Catholic rioting in both England and Scotland, is a powerful case in point.[61] Yet the Irish scare took hold because people had already been led to expect that the Irish were once more planning to rise and massacre Protestants, and again the medium for the transmission of such fears was oral, notably the word-of-mouth reports spread by those Protestants fleeing Ireland. Thus at the beginning of Lent 1688, Joseph Sagget, a man who had left Ireland 'for fear of a massacre', said in a house in Wiveliscombe in the heart of rural Somerset, 'that they were afraid to Lye in their beds in Ireland for fear they should have their Throats cut'.[62] Rumours that spread through Edinburgh on Sunday 9 December 1688 that 'a great number of Papists had got in the Town and designed to burn it that Night' prompted two days of violent anti-Catholic rioting: crowds chanting 'No Pope, No Papist, No Popish Chancellor, No Melfort, No Father Petres' besieged the Catholic chapel at Holyrood House, ransacked Chancellor Perth's lodgings, and also attacked the residences of other leading Catholics. The fact that on the night of the 9th the apprentices and students proclaimed at the town cross the offer 'of Four Hundred Pounds sterling to any who should bring Perth . . . dead or alive' was the main reason why the Catholic chancellor decided to resign his position and flee the capital.[63] (For those interested in the history of cross-dressing, Perth was eventually found

---

[60] Centre for Kentish Studies, Q/SB/17/1.

[61] Edmund Bohun, *The History of the Desertion* (1689), p. 88; *Five Letters from a Gentleman in Scotland to His Friend in London* (1689), p. 4; G. H. Jones, 'The Irish Fright of 1688', *Bulletin of the Institute of Historical Research* 55 (1982), 148–57; J. G. Simms, *Jacobite Ireland 1685–91* (1969), pp. 47–8.

[62] Somerset Record Office, Q/SR/174/17.

[63] National Library of Scotland, MS 7026, fols. 81–2, 87; Colin Lindsay, 3rd earl of Balcarres, *An Account of the Affairs of Scotland, relating to the Revolution of 1688* (1714), pp. 34–5, 38, 39–42; Narcissus Luttrell, *A Brief Historical Relation of the State of Affairs from September, 1678, to April, 1714*, 6 vols. (Oxford, 1857), I, 39; BL, Add. MSS 28,850, fol. 93; Robert Chambers, *Domestic Annals of Scotland. Volume III: From the Revolution to the Rebellion of 1745* (Edinburgh, 1861), p. 12; *Scotland Against Popery* (1689); *Five Letters*, pp. 1–4; [Thomas Morer], *An Account of the Present Persecution of the Church in Scotland, in Several Letters* (1690), p. 15; [Charles Leslie], *An Answer to a Book, Intituled, The State of the Protestants in Ireland Under the Late King James's Government* (1692), sig. b2v; [Alexander Monro], *An Apology for the Clergy of Scotland* (London, 1693), p. 8; *RPCS, 1686–9*, p. lv; Robert Wodrow, *History of the Sufferings of the Church of Scotland, From the Restoration to the Revolution*, 2 vols. (Edinburgh, 1721–2), II, 650–2; J. S. Clarke (ed.), *The Life of James II*, 2 vols. (London, 1816), II, 338; Gilbert Burnet, *History of His Own Time* (London, 1850), p. 510; R. A. Houston, *Social Change in the Age of Enlightenment: Edinburgh, 1660–1760* (Oxford, 1994), pp. 306–8.

on board a sea vessel in the Forth disguised in women's clothing on 20 December, trying to make his escape to the continent, and he was hastily dispatched to Stirling Castle.) In short, rumour played a vitally important part in bringing down James's regime in both England and Scotland, and also in helping to create a revolutionary climate in Ireland.

If we turn to the question of where people met to talk about politics and exchange information and ideas, we should not over-estimate the importance of the coffee house. Although contemporary critics might have liked to convey the impression that coffee houses swarmed with multitudes of people from all social classes, we may wonder whether they were really home from home for many of the labouring poor from town and countryside. My own examination into the evidence of seditious words, crowd unrest, popular conspiracy, petitioning activity and organized demonstrations suggests that, next to the streets, the single most important locale where people engaged in political discussion was the alehouse – as indeed it had been for a long time.[64]

The above remarks invite a more general reflection on what might be termed 'alternative media' – alternative, that is, to the traditional organs we identify with early-modern society, namely the pulpit and the press. Rumour would qualify as one example. Public demonstrations would be another. For example, one could 'read' the elaborate London pope-burning processions of the exclusion crisis rather like one could read a Whig anti-Catholic broadside. Governments had long appreciated the value of organized display to get a particular political message across, and it was a medium that disaffected members of the political elite frequently exploited. But it was a medium which the masses themselves could also exploit. People could create news by staging a news-worthy event. And if processions could be read like pamphlets, people could in a sense write their own pamphlets by staging a dramatic ritual, which observers could witness, and which the writers of news or political commentary could then carry accounts of in their manuscript newsletters or printed broadsides. One of the earliest pope-burnings of the exclusion crisis was a ritual staged at Lewes on 5 November 1679, which was quickly

---

[64] Peter Clark, *The English Alehouse: a Social History 1200–1830* (London, 1983); T. J. G. Harris, 'The Politics of the London Crowd in the Reign of Charles II', Cambridge University PhD thesis (1985), p. 299; Miller, 'Public Opinion'; Greaves, *Deliver Us from Evil, Enemies Under His Feet* and *Secrets of the Kingdom*.

picked up on by the Whig press, who held it up as an example for Londoners to follow.[65] In early December 1688 the students of Edinburgh University held a mock trial of the pope to protest against the policies of James VII and Chancellor Perth. They marched through the town, chanting 'No Pope, No Papist' before descending on the Parliament House, where they forced their way in, and 'having got upon the Bench, they arraigned his Holiness before his Judges, and gave the Jury their Commission, who brought him in Guilty; whereupon they sentenced him to be burnt publickly at the Cross' on Christmas Day.[66] (We have a published account of this demonstration, but it came out several weeks after the event, and it was not produced by the students.) An even more elaborate display was put on by the students of St Andrews in early January 1689: after a long procession of Catholic clergy through the town centre, and a short play depicting the downfall of the 'Scarlet Whore' and the kingdom of Babylon, they proceeded to hold a mock trial of the pope for his 'High Treason against . . . God', and for being 'an enemy to Religion, Monarchy and Government, and an open and avowed Murderer of Mankind', before sentencing him to be burned to ashes at the market cross.[67]

Let us summarize. Although the press was important in Restoration Britain, we should be careful not to exaggerate its role in the formation of public opinion. Indeed, we might go further and suggest that if we are interested in unravelling popular political consciousness, the press is not the appropriate place to start. People's political outlooks were shaped by their personal backgrounds and by their individual experiences of government; these were in turn refined and altered as a result of what people were told by preachers, or heard about through rumour, personal communication and discussions they had with acquaintances in the streets or the ale-house, or saw in visual spectacles and public demonstrations. Those who could read could also have access to printed materials, and some illiterates certainly had written materials read to them, but people could equally well be politicized if they were cut off from access to printed media. When we start looking at the problem like this, and place greater emphasis on experience, on the pulpit, on rumour and the alehouse, we may wonder how different things were in the 1680s

---

[65] *Domestick Intelligence*, no. 39, 18 Nov. 1679.
[66] *Five Letters*, p. 1.
[67] [Robert Reid], *The Account of the Popes Procession at Aberdeene, the 11th of January, 1689* (1689).

compared to, say, the 1530s.[68] Do we have an emerging public sphere
in the England of the Henrician Reformation? Opinion out-of-doors
certainly mattered, and the Pilgrimage of Grace arguably had an
important impact on government religious policy, prompting
perhaps the conservative reaction that began to set in from 1537.
What then, if anything, had changed by the reigns of Charles II and
James II?

One difference, of course, was the rise of print culture. The output
of the press was much greater under Charles II than it had been in
Tudor times, and more people could have access to printed materials,
both because literacy rates were much higher by the 1680s than they
had been in the 1530s, and because printed material was being more
widely disseminated through places such as the coffee houses. Even if
rumour remained important in the 1680s, rumour was nevertheless
informed by print culture in a way that it had not been in the past.
These are clearly very important developments. Yet we need to think
carefully about their significance. Did the rise of printed media have
a transformative effect? Did the dissemination of printed materials,
in other words, fundamentally alter the ways in which people could
have access to news and political information, thereby effecting a
profound transformation of people's political understanding? Or
should we see printed propaganda as an additional, enriching factor,
providing just one more way in which people could have their views
on politics shaped and influenced? If the former, then the crucial
transformation surely occurred with the great flourishing of the press
on the eve of the civil war, which still leaves us wondering what, if
anything, was new in the Restoration. I would suggest, however, that
whereas printed materials undoubtedly did play an important role in
shaping the political opinions of those out-of-doors, the existence of
an articulate and sophisticated popular political consciousness was
not necessarily dependent upon the dissemination of news through
print. We should, in other words, resist the assumption that the mass
of the population could only become politicized through the press, or
the view that, by the time of Charles II's reign, it was invariably
through access to printed materials that people were able to achieve
a political education.

In considering why politics out-of-doors was different by the

---

[68] Geoffrey Elton, *Policy and Police: the Enforcement of the Reformation in the Age of Thomas Cromwell*
(Cambridge, 1972). See also Roger B. Manning, 'Violence and Social Conflict In Mid-Tudor
Rebellions', *Journal of British Studies* 16 (1977), 18–40.

1680s compared to what it had been in the 1530s, we need to reflect
on long-term, structural changes. The population of England and
Wales approximately doubled between the 1530s and the 1650s.
With this demographic growth came significant shifts in population
concentrations; whilst some areas saw virtually no increase, others
witnessed huge expansion, as hordes of people migrated looking for
employment opportunities. Many ended op in the towns. London's
population, which stood at about 200,000 in 1600, had reached
nearly half a million by the end of the seventeenth century, a
staggeringly large number of people crammed into a small urban
environment with narrow streets.[69] London had always been notoriously difficult to police; rapid population growth made it more so.
Provincial towns came nowhere near London in terms of size, but
they too could have sizeable and growing populations, whilst many
parts of the countryside – notoriously the forest and sheep-pasture
areas – were swarming with people, many of whom had moved
from arable areas where the excess population could not be easily
absorbed.[70] Inevitably the class structure of England began to
change: we see the rise of 'masterless men', as Christopher Hill
termed them.[71] The vertical ties that had once held lord and
servant together were beginning to fracture, and the system of
clientage and dependency that had provided one type of social
cohesion in late-medieval England was breaking down. The implications for our understanding of popular politics become apparent
if we compare the Pilgrimage of Grace of 1536 with the Monmouth
rebellion of 1685. In the former, the power of vertical allegiances
and clientage ties are still readily apparent.[72] Not so in the latter;
Monmouth drew his recruits from the ideologically committed and
the under- and unemployed workers of the more densely settled
parts of the west country.[73] The loosening of traditional vertical ties
by the seventeenth century meant that there was a potential for

[69] Roger Finlay and Beatrice Shearer, 'Population Growth and Suburban Expansion', in A. L.
      Beier and Roger Finlay (eds.), *The Making of the Metropolis: London, 1500–1700* (London, 1986),
      pp. 38–9, 48–9.
[70] Keith Wrightson, *English Society 1580–1680* (London, 1982); David Underdown, *Revel, Riot
      and Rebellion: Popular Politics and Culture in England 1603–1660* (Oxford, 1985).
[71] Christopher Hill, *The World Turned Upside Down: Radical Ideas During the English Revolution*
      (Harmondsworth, 1975), ch. 3.
[72] M. L. Bush, *The Pilgrimage of Grace: a Study of the Rebel Armies of October 1536* (Manchester, 1996);
      Geoffrey Elton, 'Politics and the Pilgrimage of Grace', in his *Studies in Tudor and Stuart
      Government and Politics*, 3 vols. (Cambridge, 1974–83), III, 183–215.
[73] Underdown, *Freeborn People*, pp. 125–8; Robin Clifton, *The Last Popular Rebellion: the Western*

people to pursue their own political agendas, freer from the influence of the traditional elite than had hitherto been conceivable. In areas of large population concentrations, if such people did get restless, there could be serious problems, especially given the fact that there was no professional police force.

One might object that there is no chronological fit here: the changes that have been outlined apply to the sixteenth and early seventeenth centuries, not the later Stuart period; indeed, in the century after 1660 the population of England and Wales as a whole (despite a continuing increase in London) stabilized, and may even have declined. This is where we need to bring in the experiences of the struggles of the first half of the Stuart century. Both James I and Charles I had sought to keep their distance from the people. This was partly an ideological position, based on a belief that kings, as God's lieutenants on earth, should be able to expect the loyalty of their subjects, and that it would be demeaning to their royal majesty to court the opinion of the masses. It was also a reflection of their personalities; both James and Charles were clearly nervous about appearing in front of huge crowds.[74] It would be wrong to suggest that the early Stuarts were totally insensitive to the need to cultivate the support of their subjects; during the 1620s, in particular, we see some attempt to appeal to opinion out-of-doors through the media of the press, pulpit, and manuscript letters and poems, and to justify and defend royal policies in the face of increasing public criticism of the crown's foreign policy. But the efforts were of limited scope and effect, whilst during the 1630s the government's preferred strategy appears to have been to shut down public debate rather than engage with it.[75] Such an approach proved fatal to Charles I; he lost the hearts and minds of many of his English subjects before the civil war

---

Rising of 1685 (London, 1984), ch. 9; Peter Earle, *Monmouth's Rebels: the Road to Sedgemoor* (London, 1977), appendix.

[74] R. Malcolm Smuts, 'Public Ceremony and Royal Charisma: the English Royal Entry in London, 1485–1642', in Lee Beier, David Cannadine and James Rosenheim (eds.), *The First Modern Society: Essays in English History in Honour of Lawrence Stone* (Cambridge, 1989), pp. 65–93; Judith Richards, '"His Nowe Majestie" and the English Monarchy: the Kingship of Charles I before 1640', *Past and Present* 113 (1986), 70–96.

[75] Thomas Cogswell, 'Underground Verse and the Transformation of Early Stuart Political Culture', in Susan Amussen and Mark Kishlansky (eds.), *Political Culture and Cultural Politics in Early Modern England* (Manchester, 1995), pp. 277–300; Thomas Cogswell, 'The Politics of Propaganda: Charles I and the People in the 1620s', *Journal of British Studies* 29 (1990), 187–215; Joad Raymond, *The Invention of the Newspaper: English Newsbooks 1641–1649* (Oxford, 1996), pp. 87–100.

started, and most frightening of all, he lost control of the city of
London, which saw mass demonstrations, at times of quite a violent
nature, in 1640–2.[76] It was not until the eleventh hour, on the eve of
civil war, that royalists began to engage in a serious way in the battle
for public opinion, by which time it was already too late.[77]

The later Stuarts were determined not to make the same mistakes.
Opinion out-of-doors could not be ignored – less so after 1660 than
before 1640 because of the process of politicization that had resulted
from the experiences of the 1640s and 1650s. But traditional forms of
control that had been available to late-medieval and Tudor monarchs, by tapping into the vertical links that tied this society together
through a court-based system of co-option, clientage and dependency, could no longer work.[78] The Restoration regime felt desper-
ately insecure, and the sorts of groups it feared is revealing, and lends
confirmation to the analysis offered here. There was considerable
concern about the traditions of political and religious radicalism
bequeathed by the civil war; hence successive administrations
remained particularly attentive to the alleged subversive activities of
ex-Cromwellian soldiers, erstwhile Levellers or their relatives, and
religious nonconformists, those who had refused to accept the
reestablishment of the old order in the church.[79] Restoration authorities were also nervous about the possibility of unrest in major urban
centres, particularly in London. Many of those who were to take to
the streets in protest during the reigns of Charles II and James II
were the traditional trouble-makers in the towns, namely apprentices
and students, so we might not think there was anything new here.
The reason for the heightened sensitivity of Restoration governments
was partly because of the troubles that had been caused by urban –
and particularly London – crowds on the eve of the civil war, partly
because London was now so much bigger and getting bigger every

---

[76] Brian Manning, *The English People and the English Revolution* (Harmondsworth, 1978; 2nd edn,
1991); Keith Lindley, *Popular Politics and Religion in Civil War London* (Aldershot, 1997).

[77] We still await a full-scale, scholarly analysis of royalist propaganda during the first civil war.
Useful insights can be gleaned from Joyce Malcolm, *Caesar's Due: Loyalty and King Charles
1642–6* (London, 1983); Anthony Fletcher, *The Outbreak of the English Civil War* (London,
1981); Freist, *Governed by Opinion;* Ethan Howard Shagan, 'Constructing Discord: Ideology,
Propaganda, and English Responses to the Irish Rebellion of 1641', *Journal of British Studies*
36 (1997), 1–34; Ethan Howard Shagan, '"Remonstrating Downwards": Media and
Propaganda in the Outbreak of the English Civil War', Brown University Honors Thesis
(1994).

[78] Cf. Tony Claydon, *William III and the Godly Revolution* (Cambridge, 1996), ch. 2.

[79] Alan Marshall, *Intelligence and Espionage in the Reign of Charles II, 1660–1685* (Cambridge, 1994).

day, but also because of fears of what might happen if the youths were joined by the heirs of the civil war radicals and the hordes of depressed, semiskilled and under-employed workers from the urban slums. When news of the alleged Rye House plot broke in the summer of 1683, the duke of Ormonde learned that 'Most, if not all, the meaner sort that were in the conspiracy' were 'Anabaptists or Independents, and many of them broken or indigent tradesmen'.[80] So concerned was the government about the possibility of an explosive situation developing in the east end of London, that it poured poor relief into the area, in an attempt to prevent a feared uprising of some 5,000 weavers.[81] Whether the weavers would ever have risen is perhaps not the point; what is important is the government perception of where the problem lay. Sensitivities about possible disaffection amongst the depressed cloth-workers of the west country are well brought out by a loyal address from the Company of Clothiers in the City of Worcester at the accession of James II, which was featured prominently in the *London Gazette*. The master, wardens and assistants of the company saw it necessary to beg James to pardon his 'misguided Subjects', claiming that their eyes were 'at last Universally open'd', though they admitted at the same time that 'some of us were too fond of a bold and daring Man that fled in the Face of his Majesty', namely the duke of Monmouth.[82]

For Restoration governments, then, there appeared to be new social forces that posed a formidable threat to their security. Given that it proved difficult for the restored monarchy to reimpose effective controls over the media, it eventually became apparent to those who held the reins of power that they would have to engage, in a serious way, in the battle for public opinion: even to the point of courting the crowd, encouraging demonstrations, mass petitions and collective manifestations of support. Contemporaries were sometimes amazed by what they saw going on. The Scottish lawyer, Sir John Lauder of Fountainhall, for example, was stunned by Charles II's *Declaration* of April 1681 explaining why he had dissolved the last two Parliaments: 'some think a prince at a losse', he wrote, 'when he is put to give ane accompt of his actions, or to apologize to his subjects'.[83] Most modern historians recognize it as brilliant propa-

[80] *HMC, Ormonde*, NS vii, 64.
[81] *CSPD, 1683–4*, p. 269; Harris, *London Crowds*, pp. 209–10.
[82] *London Gazette*, no. 2027, 20–23 Apr. 1685.
[83] Fountainhall, *Historical Observations*, p. 34.

ganda coup. Whereas for a long time Charles had proved hostile to
mass petitioning, by 1681 he was actively encouraging the presentation of loyal addresses – even from groups such as apprentices,
cooks, or Cornish tinners – all of which were reported in the *London
Gazette*, so that the reading public would be aware that this was what
the government expected.[84] Referring to the loyal addresses that
were being drawn up in 'all Counties and towns', one correspondent
wrote in June 1681 that 'the affaires now transacting . . . do staggar
very many', whilst the political diarist, Narcissus Luttrell, admitted
he found the loyal addresses 'a mystery'. The royal court, however,
received them with 'great commendations', praising 'the seasonable-
ness of them and loyalty of the persons' who subscribed, and went so
far as to reward some of those who presented such addresses with
lavish feasts.[85] The crown even encouraged loyalist demonstrations
in the streets. For example, when the Scottish Privy Council received
a letter from Charles towards the end of October 1680 informing
them that the duke of York was shortly to arrive in Edinburgh to
head up the government in Scotland, Lord Chancellor Rothes
responded (whether on his own initiative or at the king's is unclear)
by instructing the councillors that there should be 'publick Demonstrations of Joy' as soon as the duke landed.[86] Similarly, when
Charles decided to bring his brother back to London in the spring of
1682, he wrote to the lord mayor in advance instructing him to give
the duke 'such receptione as became him'; although the lord mayor
was to 'keep the peopell from tumulting, and order the trained Bands
to be in armes', the king added that he 'doubted not but his loyall
apprentices in London would make a body for his Receptione'.
Charles, in short, was asking the lord mayor to ensure that a loyalist
crowd would be out in force, even though he was well aware of the
potential risks involved and the possibility of provoking disorder;
indeed, Charles said in his letter that he realised a Whig crowd
would assemble – 'the silly Rabble that last presented the Addresse',
as he called them – but he thought they would be 'Inconsiderable'.
There was indeed trouble in London on the day of York's return, as
Whig crowds armed with long canes paraded through the streets

[84] Knights, *Politics and Opinion*, pp. 329–45.
[85] BL, Sloane MS 1008, fol. 309; Luttrell, *Brief Historical Relation*, I, 85, 87; *Loyal Protestant Intelligence*, no. 43, 2 Aug. 1681; Library of Congress, MS 18,124, VIII, fol. 220, 10 Aug. 1682.
[86] *RPCS, 1678–80*, pp. 565–6; Wodrow, *History of Sufferings*, II, 153; *A True Narrative of the Reception of their Royal Highnesses at their Arrival in Scotland* [1680]; *London Gazette*, no. 1561, 1–4 Nov. 1680.

shouting 'a Monmouth, a Monmouth, no York, no York' and tried to extinguish all the bonfires lit in honour of the duke, and violent clashes erupted between Whig and Tory groups at a number of places.[87] Nevertheless, efforts continued to be made to drum up public demonstrations of support for the duke in the English capital. When York attended the Artillery Company's feast on 20 April 1682 crowds were out in force to cheer him as he made his way to Merchant Tailors' Hall, though the royal guards who lined the route had been primed 'to put the Boys and Mobile in mind of their Duty, to shout and Hallow'.[88] Another reception was laid on for York at Whitehall on 27 May, after a brief return trip to Scotland, with this time an order being issued in advance by the lord mayor and court of aldermen 'that every Landlord as a signe of their Loyalty to his Majesty and respect to the Branches of the Royall family, should have . . . their Bonfires ready' by eight o'clock at night, under pain of 'a great penalty'.[89] The novelty of these developments is revealed by Fountainhall's expression of surprise that a reigning monarch would even think it appropriate just to permit such demonstrations on behalf of his successor during his own lifetime.[90]

Not that all this loyalist activity out-of-doors was sponsored by the crown, by any means; much of it was spontaneous, or encouraged by loyalist activists in the localities. Nevertheless, it is apparent that it was welcome to the crown.[91] James II was prepared to play the same game, and tried to encourage loyalist demonstrations and addresses in all his three kingdoms at various times during his reign – for his accession, his birthday, the defeat of the Monmouth and Argyll rebellions, the declarations of indulgence, the birth of the Prince of Wales. Again, such loyalist activity was reported in the *London Gazette*, in an attempt to show that public opinion was on the king's side. The flipside of this strategy was the attempted suppression of any opinions hostile to the government; hence both Charles II and James II sought to clamp down on the opposition media, whether by that we mean the press, the pulpit, demonstrations, or the spreading of rumour or

---

[87] Library of Congress, MS 18,124, VIII, fols. 27, 40; *Impartial Protestant Mercury*, no. 101, 7–11 Apr. 1682; *Loyal Protestant Intelligence*, no. 140, 11 Apr. 1682; L'Estrange, *Observator*, no. 122, 12 Apr. 1682; Harris, *London Crowds*, p. 179.

[88] *Impartial Protestant Mercury*, no. 104, 18–21 Apr. 1682, and no. 105, 21–25 Apr. 1682; *True Protestant Mercury*, no. 135, 19–22 Apr. 1682; Library of Congress, MS 18,124, VIII, fol. 45.

[89] Library of Congress, MS 18,124, VIII, fol. 63.

[90] Fountainhall, *Historical Observations*, I, 49–50.

[91] Knights, *Politics and Opinion*, pp. 329–45; Harris, 'The Parties and the People'.

seditious gossip. In short, the struggle in the 1680s was over who could lay claim to have public opinion on their side. It was a battle from which Charles II emerged triumphant; it was one which James II lost, with disastrous consequences.[92]

Let me offer some brief remarks by way of conclusion. This essay is reacting against a top-down, centre-out approach to popular politics, where politics is seen as essentially happening 'up there', in parliament or at the court, with information about what was going on filtering out to the masses in a trickle-down way. It is also reacting against what, for want of a better term, might be styled the intellectual approach to popular politics – that the people were politicized as a result of their exposure to political ideas and news as conveyed through the medium of print. Both approaches encourage the view that the further one was away from where things were *really* happening – whether socially (further down the social hierarchy), geographically (out in remote rural parts), or culturally (further down the literacy hierarchy) the less politicized one was likely to be. Such a conclusion is not sustainable, as the remarks about what was going on in the remoter parts of Scotland and Ireland have shown. Instead, this essay is arguing for what might be termed a social history approach, one that places emphasis on the social processes at work that helped create and shape political awareness amongst the masses and also provided the context for how members of the elite responded to a politically conscious populace. In short, any attempt to understand popular politics must start at the grassroots level, and work upwards. We must look at the experiences of the people (which would include, of course, their experience of print); we need a materialist approach (in the broadest sense), rather than an ideational one. The argument developed here has implications not just for the study of popular politics but for politics more generally speaking. If we look at the issues that Restoration politicians had to deal with, they were issues that permeated their society; it was not just that the masses were responding to what was coming from above, but the elites were also responding to what was coming from below. If we look at the major sources of domestic political tension in Restoration England – the threat of political insurrection at home, the tensions over religious

---

[92] This case will be argued at length in my forthcoming *British Revolutions*.

dissent, concerns about the abuse of the law, fears about the standing army, concerns about the regulation of the economy – it was not that the elites put these issues on the agenda and tried to convince the masses that they should be concerned about these sorts of things; they were on the agenda because they were issues of real concern in Restoration society.

If we want to appreciate what was new, or different, about popular politics in Restoration Britain, the answer perhaps is to be sought less in changes in the means whereby the people achieved a political education, but rather in the extent to which those who held the reins of power, including even the reigning monarchs themselves, showed themselves ready (even believed it essential) to appeal to those out-of-doors, cultivate public opinion and encourage mass demonstrations of support. The reasons why the crown felt compelled to do this again need to be sought in a contextualized social history – those 'from above' were responding to pressures and circumstances that were not of their creation and which were to a large extent beyond their control. They found, as a result, that they needed to develop new and more refined methods of political management, especially with regard to the control or manipulation of opinion out-of-doors.

One final issue remains to be addressed, which concerns just how distinctive the Restoration period was. Given the current state of my research and on-going thinking about how the Restoration period fits into the longer historical perspective, my remarks here are necessarily speculative, intended simply to pose questions for future historical enquiry, rather than offer firm conclusions. I have suggested that the way the restored monarchs responded to opinion out-of-doors was different when our point of comparison is with the early Stuarts. Some might object that the real turning point comes in the 1640s, which is when we first see a serious attempt by royalist propagandists to develop strategies for appealing to and cultivating the opinions of the lower orders. More work is needed comparing the propaganda campaigns of the exclusion crisis to those of the first civil war before we can resolve this issue; the similarities and contrasts would surely be highly illuminating.[93] What one can say with confidence is that there was an awareness, amongst supporters of the

---

[93] For a beginning, see Tim Harris, 'Propaganda and Public Opinion in Seventeenth Century England', in Jeremy Popkin (ed.), *Media and Revolution: Comparative Perspectives* (Lexington, KY, 1995), pp. 48–73. See now also David Zaret, *Origins of Democratic Culture: Printing Petitions and*

crown during the exclusion crisis, that what had been done by
royalists on the eve of the civil war was too little too late, and that it
was imperative not to allow the situation to become as critical for the
crown again as it had in 1641. As a result (it might be suggested), Tory
efforts to woo public opinion in the early 1680s were more committed, extensive and deliberate – and, because of the experience
one had to build upon and the developments in the various news
media over the past forty years, also more sophisticated – than the
efforts of royalists some forty years earlier (although this is a hypothesis that needs to be tested by further research).

On the other hand, accepting my position on the early Stuarts, it
could be maintained that it was James I and Charles I who were the
odd ones out, and that Charles II was simply showing the same
sensitivities and political sagacity in recognizing the need to appeal
to and manage public opinion as did Queen Elizabeth;[94] the sociopolitical (and religious) context was different in the late 1670s and
early 1680s from what it had been a century earlier, but a recognition
by the crown that it had to play to the public sphere was nothing
new. There is something to this argument. Nevertheless, I would
suggest that the context was so different that what we see happening
in the final years of Charles II's reign was in essence a very different
phenomenon from what happened under the virgin queen. Queen
Elizabeth projected an image of majesty and splendour to her
subjects in an attempt to impress and awe; her people were invited to
celebrate and rejoice in the glory of the crown and what the
Protestant monarchy stood for. It could never be that straightforward
for Charles II. The troubles of the seventeenth century had led to a
demystification of majesty, and to the rise of a more articulate and
assertive popular political culture which had proven that it could be
a seriously destabilizing force for the crown. Charles II therefore had
to negotiate with his subjects, appeal to their sensibilities, convince
and persuade – in short, he had to solicit their support by showing
that his policies were designed to protect their interests and welfare,
and in the process he ended up making certain promises to his
subjects to rule in a particular way. When James II failed to rule in

the *Public Sphere in Early-Modern England* (Princeton, 2000), which appeared after this chapter
was submitted for publication.
[94] Roy Strong, *The Cult of Elizabeth: Elizabethan Portraiture and Pageantry* (London, 1977); Roy
Strong, *The Tudor and Stuart Monarchy: Pageantry, Painting, Iconography. II: Elizabethan* (Woodbridge, 1995).

that way, all his attempts to exploit Elizabethan-type techniques for the manipulation of public opinion – royal progresses, the celebration of royal birthdays and so forth – were to no effect.[95] The world had become a very different place.

[95] This argument will be developed in full in my forthcoming *British Revolutions*.

CHAPTER 6

The War in Heaven and the Miltonic sublime[1]

Nicholas von Maltzahn

Late in *Paradise Lost*, when Michael tells Adam the story of the future, Milton famously has the archangel denounce the corruption of the later Christian ministry, which 'Spiritual laws by carnal power shall force / On every conscience.' 'What will they then,' he questions, 'But force the spirit of grace it self, and bind / His consort liberty?'[2] This is at the beginning of the *saeculum*, that 'interval between fall and *eschaton* where coercive justice, private property and impaired natural reason must make shift to cope with the unredeemed effects of sinful humanity'.[3] But Michael's narration comes late in a long epic. Much of Milton's poem has been given instead to imagining the work of love in creation, the cosmic governance of divine reason before and beyond the 'original violence' that John Milbank has described as a 'thread of continuity between antique reason and modern, secular reason'.[4] To this end Milton had strained his powers in *Paradise Lost* in achieving an extraordinary expansion of mid-seventeenth-century poetics. Central to his project was the revision of the epic mode to produce a profound critique of such 'original violence' and its consequences – what Milton calls 'outward' or 'worldly' or 'fleshlie

[1] I am especially grateful for my discussions of secularization with Phillip Donnelly, whose research on mid-seventeenth-century rationalism, and Milton's especially, has much stimulated the revision of this chapter, first delivered as a paper at the 1997 Seventeenth Century Conference at the University of Durham. Our work has been supported by the Social Sciences and Humanities Research Council of Canada.
[2] *Paradise Lost*, 12: 508, 521–2, 524–6.
[3] John Milbank, *Theology and Social Theory: Beyond Secular Reason* (Oxford, 1990), p. 9.
[4] 'Antique thought and politics assumes some naturally given element of chaotic conflict which must be tamed by the stability and self-identity of reason. Modern thought and politics (most clearly articulated by Nietzsche) assumes that there is only this chaos, which cannot be tamed by an opposing transcendent principle, but can be immanently controlled by subjecting it to rules and giving irresistible power to those rules in the forms of market economies and sovereign politics.' *Ibid.*, p. 5.

force'.[5] Central to this critique and to his epic was his description of the War in Heaven.

In the late seventeenth and early eighteenth centuries, the War in Heaven was much commended by early readers of *Paradise Lost*. The sublimity of Milton's treatment found special recognition. Later poets eagerly adapted it for their own needs.[6] But Milton's distinctive poetics, which had in Book 6 found memorable expression, did not much govern the responses to this part of his epic. Between the mid and the late seventeenth century, something had profoundly changed in English literary culture, in a way that found further expression in Milton's most influential promoters in the early eighteenth century. Such was the transformation that even Milton's later 'friends' and admirers responded to *Paradise Lost* in ways deeply inconsistent with its critique of 'fleshlie force'.

The Platonism and apocalypticism that had so animated Milton's godly poetics were increasingly overlooked in favour of more mimetic and secular readings of the heroic. This is evident especially in the influence of *Paradise Lost* on English poetry, which grew most markedly after the Glorious Revolution. That was a literary as well as a political watershed, as appears in occasional poetry from the 1690s and early 1700s. In heroic poetry honouring William III, the idiom of Milton's War in Heaven played an increasing part, and the more so in later poetry celebrating episodes in the War of the Spanish Succession, especially Marlborough's triumphs in the continental campaigns of 1704 and 1706. Poets saw in Miltonic verse a method for vivid narrative description, not least for narratives of artillery

---

[5] *Complete Prose Works of John Milton* (hereafter *CPW*), gen. ed. Don M. Wolfe, 8 vols. (New Haven, 1953–82), VI, 797–9; VII, 256–7 and passim.

[6] Only later would critical misgivings regarding Book 6 lead to modern doubts about its value, making it perhaps the least cherished part of Milton's epic, at least until some recent studies again revived its interest. See especially Stella Revard, *The War in Heaven*, which revisits the literary and theological context in which it was written; for the comic dimension, Arnold Stein, *Answerable Style* (Minneapolis, 1953), pp. 17–37; for the allegorical and Christological dimensions, W. G. Madsen, *From Shadowy Types to Truth* (New Haven, 1968), pp. 87–8, 110–13, J. H. Adamson, 'The War in Heaven: the *Merkabah*', in J. H. Adamson, W. B. Hunter, and C. A. Patrides, *Bright Essence* (Salt Lake City, 1971), pp. 103–13, and W. B. Hunter, 'The War in Heaven: the Exaltation of the Son', *Bright Essence*, pp. 115–30; for the biblical dimension, Michael Lieb, *Poetics of the Holy* (Chapel Hill, 1981), esp. pp. 282–301; for the ethical, James Freeman, *Milton and the Martial Muse* (Princeton, 1980), pp. 151–6, 172–3; and for the philosophical, especially Stephen M. Fallon, *Milton among the Philosophers* (Ithaca, NY, 1991), pp. 223–42. Nearest to the present account is the suggestive description of Dennis and Addison on the War in Heaven in Leslie Moore, *Beautiful Sublime* (Stanford, 1990), pp. 108–33. William Kolbrener's *Milton's Warring Angels* (Cambridge, 1997) is concerned with broader figurations, only incidentally touching on Book 6 (pp. 147–54).

combat.[7] This sublime aspect of Book 6 seemed a step beyond the classical originals. It answered some questions about what heroic poetry might achieve faced with the changing methods and scale of modern warfare.[8] At first the poetic resources of Miltonic poetry were exploited chiefly by Whig writers such as John Dennis and Richard Blackmore. With the further impetus of Oxford men of letters like Joseph Addison and John Philips, imitations of Milton became a staple in later war poetry from many hands. But Milton's questioning of military heroism in Book 6 of *Paradise Lost* was strangely neglected in the heroic poetry that drew on his example. His ambivalence about militarism had led him much to inflect the martial conventions of the epic. It was to be in his idiom, however, that the description of new techniques of war, of which he had been so critical, became a central feature of a triumphally nationalist poetry.

I

In *Paradise Lost*, the angelic rebellion and War in Heaven dramatize how charity is lost in 'original violence' as well as in later 'outward force', both of which cloud sense and dull judgement, as spiritual transgression leads to tyrannic militarism. The terms of Milton's critique of 'outward' or 'fleshlie force' colour his contemporary prose works. In the chronology of his writings, the last books of *Paradise Lost* fall significantly between his tracts on the eve of the Restoration and *Of True Religion* (London, 1673).[9] In his *Treatise of Civil Power in Ecclesiastical Causes* (London, 1659), he attacked the Erastian emphases of the Westminster Confession and the Savoy Declaration of 1658, further baleful consequences of the Assembly of Divines that he had excoriated long before. Earlier he had lamented their lack of faith in the 'spiritual power of thir ministrie' and 'evangellic perswasion', and denounced their aim 'to have set up a spirtual tyrannie by

---

[7] That this might even be held against Milton appears from Samuel Morland, *The Urim of Conscience* (London, 1695), p. 14, who disparages Book 6 citing the use of 'Powder, Bullets and great Guns (it is pity that Bombs were not in use when he wrote that treatise).'

[8] Michael Murrin, *History and Warfare in Renaissance Epic* (Chicago, 1994), esp. pp. 123–36, 141, 241, although this diminishes the point of Milton's description of the second day of the War in Heaven; cf. Robert Fallon, 'Michael Murrin's Milton and the "Epic without War": a Review Essay', *Milton Quarterly* 31 (1997), 119–23.

[9] N. von Maltzahn, 'The First Reception of *Paradise Lost* (1667)', *Review of English Studies* n.s. 47 (1996), p. 479.

a secular power'.[10] Now he again opposed the 'state-tyranie over the church'. He wished to prove 'That it is not lawfull for any power on earth to compell in matters of Religion', although history had long shown 'force on the one side restraining, and hire on the other side corrupting the teachers' of the church. Moreover, his *Treatise* against 'force . . . restraining' was one of two companion tracts, the other published some months later as *Considerations Touching the Likeliest Means to Remove Hirelings out of the Church* (London, 1659). There Milton explained more fully the need to extricate Christians as well as nations from involvement in a national church. He now rousingly recalled the example of the Council of State under the Commonwealth, and especially its virtue in 'so well joining religion with civil prudence, and yet so well distinguishing the different power of either'. The distinction was an essential one. In emphasizing it Milton claimed to be motivated by 'an inward perswasion' of his Christian duty.[11] In particular, he is concerned to express the growth of experience as we move from the law to the gospel. The latter is 'our new covnant, upon the heart of every beleever, to be interpreted only by the sense of charitie and inward perswasion'.[12]

Thus Milton proposes a communicative rationality of a profoundly Christian kind. Its failure he dramatizes in the War in Heaven. Vital to such communal reasoning is the double aspect of 'the sense' of charity, as felt as well as known. In *Of True Religion* he returned to the subject. Crucial was the experience of our 'own diligent study' and 'constant reading of Scripture', which rescues us from the desperation of 'implicit faith, ever learning and never taught', and helps us 'to mutual forbearance and charity towards the other, though dissenting in some opinions'. This follows from scriptural exhortation, and is confirmed by the experiential benefit of having 'Senses awakt, . . . Judgement sharpn'd' because 'we not only tolerate . . . but patiently hear . . . and seriously read'.[13] Such activity was what 'popery' threatened.

Against claims like Milton's, however, the English national church in the Restoration was neither inactive nor silent. The political and ecclesiological arguments for religious intolerance were supported by more fully theorized claims especially 'in the heyday of Charles II's

---

[10] *CPW,* v, 447.
[11] *CPW,* vii, 231, 239–41, 252, 274–5, 277.
[12] *CPW,* vii, 259–60. See his *De doctrina,* esp. *CPW,* vi, 118–24.
[13] *CPW,* viii, 434–7.

Anglican polity, between 1675 and 1685', when Catholic arguments about the relation of coercion to conscience superseded even Erastian ones.[14] The belief 'that coercion is a justifiable and effective instrument of education and persuasion' again found Augustinian sanction. Latter-day Donatists might be supposed to require the marriage of 'force . . . with edification' to bring them into the national church.[15] Augustine has been defended on the basis that it was the church not the state that did the coercing, and that 'his hold upon the concept of "the state" was not firm enough to force him to question whether its absorption by the "Church" in the exercises of religious coercion was consistent with his theology of society'.[16] Milton had less difficulty in making the distinction and in insisting on the injurious consequences of collapsing or ignoring it.

The opposed claims about conscience were not soon reconciled. The tension between them found some resolution, however, in a literary realm increasingly constituted as such. This aestheticization often appears in the later secularization of mid-century poetics. Here the promotion of the sublime might include the revival of *furor poeticus* as a praiseworthy poetic 'enthusiasm'. Such enthusiasm could then be combined with another component of the mid-century republican inheritance: civil religion. This was dear to many of Milton's most ardent admirers, although not to Milton himself. Contesting Milton's plea for the separation of church and state, the republican James Harrington had insisted on the need for a national church founded like the commonwealth on natural principles.[17] Such innovative claims for civil religion were to complicate Milton's legacy in the 1690s, as they influenced some notable Miltonists – John Dennis, John Toland, Sir Richard Blackmore, Charles Gildon – whose interest in the sublime was strengthened by Whig hopes of the cohesion that might be wrought through a broader politics of self-transcendence and 'elevation of soul'. In their hands, the celebration of power in a Miltonic idiom found various expression, but most

---

[14] Mark Goldie, 'The Theory of Religious Intolerance in Restoration England', in Ole Grell, Jonathan Israel and Nicholas Tyacke (eds.), *From Persecution to Toleration* (Oxford, 1991), pp. 331–68, p. 368.

[15] Goldie, 'Theory of Religious Intolerance', pp. 334, 333–45, 350–3.

[16] Robert Markus, *Saeculum: History and Society in the Theology of St Augustine* (Cambridge, 1970), pp. 148–53.

[17] *CPW*, VII, 84, 518–21; *The Political Works of James Harrington*, ed. J. G. A. Pocock (Cambridge, 1977), pp. 111–13, 765–7.

influentially, it proved, in occasional poetry celebrating national triumphs.

The impulse to aestheticize and secularize Miltonic poetry also followed from the interests of more truly liberal Whigs. Closer to Milton on the separation of church and state was the toleration being mooted in the 1690s, especially by John Locke, who, despite having at the Restoration sought to legitimate 'the ruler's imposition of forms of religious worship', later turned to the position for which he is famous, in which 'the ecclesiastical sphere and "civil concernments", are more firmly separated.[18] Here was a deeper suspicion of enthusiasm; but here also was a firmer sense of how private interest might contribute to the requirements of public good. The tension between the two found some resolution in a more autonomously constituted aesthetics. Like Locke and like Locke's student the third earl of Shaftesbury, the hugely influential Joseph Addison was suspicious of enthusiasm. At the same time he deeply admired *Paradise Lost*, as had Dennis, Toland and Gildon before him. He therefore diminished the claims of revelation in his reading of Milton's epic.[19] With reference to Milton's growing reputation, it has been proposed by Steven Knapp that the growth of toleration fostered this aestheticization of his work, especially owing to Addison's polite resolution of competing demands, namely 'a desire to possess the power of alien or archaic belief while at the same time avoiding its absurd or violent consequences'.[20] In the same vein, Victoria Kahn further emphasizes the seventeenth-century debate over *adiaphora*, or 'things indifferent', and tries to maintain that 'theological and rhetorical indifference' is central to Milton's works.[21] But what Knapp has claimed of Milton's reception in the late seventeenth and early eighteenth centuries should not be too much read back into his mid-seventeenth-century poetics, to which the later aestheticization is in part a reaction. There had indeed been a transformation, by the proponents of civil religion as well as by politer Whigs, in which stylistic preoccupations displaced the profound submission to the authority of the Bible in *Paradise Lost*. The

---

[18] John Locke, *Political Essays*, ed. Mark Goldie (Cambridge, 1997), pp. xvii–xviii.
[19] N. von Maltzahn, 'The Whig Milton: 1667–1700', in D. Armitage, A. Himy and Q. Skinner (eds.), *Milton and Republicanism* (Cambridge, 1996), pp. 252–3.
[20] Steven Knapp, *Personification and the Sublime: Milton to Coleridge* (Cambridge, MA, 1985), pp. 130–41, esp. 140–1.
[21] Victoria Kahn, 'Allegory, the Sublime, and the Rhetoric of Things Indifferent in *Paradise Lost*', in David Quint et al. (eds.), *Creative Imitation* (Binghamton, NY, 1992), pp. 127–52, 131.

epic asks searching questions of our 'own diligent study' and 'constant reading of Scripture', of our patience and seriousness in hearing and reading. These are at a remove from the quieter enjoyments of the Milton essays in Addison's *Spectator*, which so profoundly reflected and then also influenced contemporary responses to Milton and *Paradise Lost*.

The persuasion of *Paradise Lost* lay in its massive renarration of tradition, which was 'only to be recovered by an argumentative retelling of that narrative . . . in conflict with other argumentative retellings'.[22] Milton had too much invested in 'Christian libertie' to allow its decline into civil religion, or any specifically national church in which the scope for such persuasions was reduced. International Protestantism was to supersede competing national or imperial pretensions and their Erastian concomitants, and the peace of believers to offer a reformed version of the *pax ecclesiae*. The stronger the nations, the stronger the conflict between nations: Milton does not quite write *contra gentiles*, but he proclaims fraternity in his contributions to a Christian universalism, as when he wishes to share his *De doctrina christiana* with 'men of every land and, particularly, all Christian men', and 'with as many people as possible'.[23] Other narrower rivalries were to be sunk in the integrative toleration demanded by the common cause.

In Book 6 of *Paradise Lost*, moreover, the argumentative retelling of the much-told story of the War in Heaven was at the same time a critical renarration of other stories celebrating military virtue. Milton's critique of the heroic sets his work at odds with other contemporary explorations of heroic in relation to social virtue, especially in the drama. At issue were contending versions of the sublime, which can be styled the rational and the pathetic. For Milton, famously, 'reason is but choosing', with the actions of choice defining the will. The dynamism of this rationalism shows increasingly in Milton's later works, as he attempts to resolve competing claims, on one hand for right reason, in terms analogous to those of other mid-century English Platonists, and on the other a more

---

[22] The formulation is borrowed from Alasdair MacIntyre, 'Epistemological Crises, Dramatic Narrative, and the Philosophy of Science', in Stanley Hauerwas and L. Gregory Jones (eds.), *Why Narrative? Readings in Narrative Theology* (Grand Rapids, MI, 1989), p. 146 (repr. from *Monist* 60 (1977), 453–72).

[23] *CPW*, IV, 537; VI, 121, 124. Whether or not the *De doctrina* is Milton's, and the preface in particular, this sentiment is consistent with his objective in *Paradise Lost* to 'justify the ways of God to men'.

reductive instrumental rationalism, which he followed while he also adapted Ramist claims. We may recall Stanley Hauerwas's concern that the rationalizing and universalizing impulse in 'liberal' theology can restrict the very imagination 'that makes it possible to avoid resorting to coercive violence'.[24] Milton possessed the rationalizing and universalizing impulse to an unusual degree. But the 'reason' in question was not the instrumental, depersonalizing style of knowledge that Walter Ong has taught us to suspect; nor does Milton thus treat literally or objectify terms of cognition whose metaphoric origin has been ignored.[25] 'To orators and poets should be left their own account of method', concludes Milton's *Artis logicae*, emphatically restricting the totalizing tendency of Ramist thinking.[26] In the work of orator and poet 'some homogeneous axioms will be suppressed', Ramus had observed, 'and certain heterogeneous ones will be appropriated, such as digressions from the point and dwelling on a point. And especially will the order of things be inverted.' Just so, Milton must have thought, and it was the dramatization of choice that was to govern his own inversion of 'the order of things', setting his richer conception of reason at the heart of heroism.

The War in Heaven ends with Christ's triumph. This is central to Milton's epic and to his evocation of the rational sublime. By contrast, the more affective thrust of the pathetic sublime we may associate especially with the heroic drama of the Restoration,[27] and its increasingly nationalist aesthetics, and secondarily with Dryden's influence on the aesthetics of Dennis, Gildon, Blackmore and others in the 1690s. For Dryden's Whig acolytes after the Revolution, the sublime seemed especially useful as a means of gaining consensus in national issues, a coercion without coercion, which we might style

---

[24] This is linked to his concern that the identity of nations is much sustained by wars between nations, also since war 'is an institution which arises among peoples who can claim sufficient commonalty to transform violence into power'. Stanley Hauerwas, *Against the Nations* (Minneapolis, 1985), pp. 12, 61–65, 176–82; and see also the lively restatement of Hauerwas's position in John Milbank, *The Word Made Strange* (Oxford, 1997), p. 30.

[25] Walter Ong, *Ramus, Method and the Decay of Dialogue* (Cambridge, MA, 1958, 2nd edn 1983), esp. pp. 107–16, 288–92. On this point I am indebted to the research assistance of Phillip Donnelly; in work not yet published, Donnelly further explains how Milton uses 'Ramist principle to maintain the independence of his epic poetry from the methodizing of Ramist logic'.

[26] *CPW,* VIII, p. 395.

[27] Milton's anxieties about this new development have been explored by Steven Zwicker, 'Milton, Dryden, and literary controversy', in Gerald MacLean (ed.), *Culture and Society in the Stuart Restoration* (Cambridge, 1995), pp. 137–58.

propaganda or more broadly ideology. Their embrace of power politics was complete. It seemed to them that contending passions might best be harmonized when the arts contributed more directly to national occasions, thus helping to foster civil religion.[28] And the achievement of Milton in epic fired them with the possibilities of a nation transformed, in a fantasy of social and political cohesion powerfully underwritten by literature. Whatever the outcome of this fantasy, for present purposes it should instead be emphasized how far the terms in which it was proposed already represent a significant transformation of mid-century poetics, and of Milton's in particular. Passions were to be harnessed to the work of reason, but this was reason of a thinner, more instrumental kind than he had conceived, with a more secular bent than the Christian temper commended in *Of Civil Power.*

The godliness of the 'godly revolution' of 1688/89 was of a different spirit than that of the interregnum. It is a mistake to underestimate the alterations of 'theological language' between the mid seventeenth century and the 1690s.[29] This appears in the transformation in aesthetics that contributed to the accelerating success of *Paradise Lost* in the 1690s and after, and the growing admiration for its style at the expense of its content. The technology of knowing was now directed toward the mastery of an objectified world, even in the political sphere, at a remove from the dialectical desire of the created for the creator that Milton had sought to describe. In this climate, Milton's 'friends' could therefore be as dangerous to him in their embrace of his style as his enemies were in other respects.

In the Whig heroic poetry of the 1690s and early 1700s we can trace the growing vogue for a Miltonic style much indebted to his epic, an influence that came to displace the pindarics of an earlier generation. This became especially the case with the War in Heaven, as imitators adapted it to narrower ends, in particular the demands of occasional poetry celebrating national triumphs. It was bold of occasional poets to use the War in Heaven to glorify international warfare, reading Milton back into his Homeric sources and the

---

[28] Justin Champion, *The Pillars of Priestcraft Shaken* (Cambridge, 1992), esp. pp. 170–96; Mark Goldie, 'The Civil Religion of James Harrington', in Anthony Pagden (ed.), *The Languages of Political Theory in Early Modern Europe* (Cambridge, 1987), pp. 197–222.

[29] Cf. Tony Claydon, *William III and the Godly Revolution* (Cambridge, 1996), pp. 4–5, and passim.

titanic struggles of the theogonies.[30] But the indifference on the part of later rationalists to the implications of Book 6 may seem equally at odds with Milton's purpose. Here still other 'friends' of Milton might also mislead. Deists did not harken to the epic's comparison of false, solipsistic reasoning with the fuller working of *ratio* as *logos* (the etymology of 'logic' on which Milton insists from the beginning of his *Artis logicae*).[31] Voltaire, for example, who could admire Milton, found the War in Heaven suspicious because it seemed a carry-over from the deception of priestcraft, and more conducive to *l'infâme* than to the growth of civil power. The Italian Patriot Paolo Rolli could a few years later observe Voltaire's rejection of 'certain qualities of fantasy' as proceeding from his 'sternly rationalistic' emphasis.[32] But reason of what kind? In Milton's most notable departure from traditional sources, reason or *ratio*, the content of difference, becomes central to his renarration of this common story, especially its conclusion, as he unusually describes the victory as that of the Son of God rather than of Michael.[33] Scholarship has much cited the subordinationism of Milton's Christology. He much compensates for this heterodoxy, however, by enlarging his description of the role of the Son, notably in His triumphal glory in Book 6, and then in Creation in Book 7. This means of glorifying the Son, or reason over rebellion, was not much acknowledged in the subsequent aestheticization of literature away from Milton's prophetic aims. But from the standpoint of Milton's poetics, any narrower rationalism seems more akin to the solipsism in which the War in Heaven begins. There Satan sought to deny truer *ratio*, in a wilful imposition of himself on infinitude, in order to escape his unease about the 'new' creature who is not the same as himself.

When, in a fuller critique of the War in Heaven, Daniel Defoe claims that Milton made of the Son 'a meer *je ne scay Quoi*', it was not just the novelist's realist expectations of epic that had diminished the

---

[30] Again Dryden had led the way, using Milton to translate Ovid's description of the Giant's War, qv. John R. Mason, 'To Milton through Dryden and Pope', University of Cambridge PhD (1987), pp. 286–94; for the early perception of Milton's debt to the Orphic hymns, see Patrick Hume, *Annotations on Milton's Paradise Lost* (London, 1695), *passim*; and to Hesiod's *Theogony*, especially William Broome, *Poems on Several Occasions* (London, 1727), p. 220.

[31] *CPW*, VIII, p. 217.

[32] Voltaire, *An Essay upon the Civil Wars of France* (London, 1727), pp. 117–20; George Dorris, *Paolo Rolli and the Italian Circle in London, 1715–1744* (The Hague, 1967), p. 200.

[33] Stella Revard, *The War in Heaven: 'Paradise Lost' and the Tradition of Satan's Rebellion* (Ithaca, NY, 1980), pp. 235–63.

complexity and the coherence of Book 6.[34] Revealingly, Defoe uses
the French neoclassical term *je ne sais quoi* to negative effect. The term
itself had been born of a suspicion of transportedness, and in the
seventeenth century the Platonist potential for enthusiasm had
instead come in neoclassical criticism to be expressed by the discourse of the sublime. For this Defoe, who may stand as an
embodiment of revolution principles, had little sympathy. The cavils
about the War in Heaven in his *Political History of the Devil* reveal a loss
in the potential meanings of reason, an incapacity to sustain the
'effortless Baroque integration of the "modern" discovery of human
making into a traditional Platonic, participatory framework'.[35]

II

The cultural transformation in which this 'Baroque integration' was
lost can be traced in the transition from the poetics governing the
composition of *Paradise Lost* to the aesthetics governing its reception
and growing fame. Longinus may be thought the key figure in this
change. His treatise on the sublime appeared in an influential
translation by Boileau in 1674, the same year as the repackaging of
Paradise Lost in a second edition. There is evidence that Milton's first
readers were quick to value his emulation of and rivalry with classical
poetry, and classical epic in particular. The benefits of such influence
they appreciated in terms that often disclose a Longinian frame of
reference.[36] Such Longinian appreciations much define the excellence of Milton's epic in the years to come, but the uses of Longinus
were themselves in flux. When Milton's nephew Edward Phillips, for
example, claims that a learned readership immediately valued the

---

[34] Daniel Defoe, *The Political History of the Devil* (London, 1726), p. 69. Defoe seems to have
drawn on Charles Leslie, *The History of Sin and Heresie Attempted, from the First War that they
Rais'd in Heaven* . . . (London, 1698), A2r–A3v, etc.

[35] Milbank, *Theology and Social Order*, p. 12.

[36] Longinus had been available for some time, and is now thought to have influenced
republican poetics already in the 1650s: Annabel Patterson, *Reading between the Lines* (London,
1993), pp. 258–70; Nigel Smith, *Literature and Revolution in England 1640–60* (New Haven,
1994), pp. 189, 215; David Norbrook, *Writing the English Republic* (Cambridge, 1999). Longinus
had been published in continental editions since the mid sixteenth century, and was also
available in English translation since the 1650s, not least among Milton's acquaintance to
whom the translator, John Hall of Durham, belonged. Cf. Samuel Holt Monk, *The Sublime*
(New York, 1935), pp. 18–28; Bernard Weinberg, 'Translations and Commentaries of
Longinus, *On the Sublime*, to 1600: a Bibliography', *Modern Philology* 47 (1949–50), 145–51;
Jules Brody, *Boileau and Longinus* (Geneva, 1958), pp. 9–23.

sublimity of Milton's argument and invention, it bears emphasis that it was as a rhetorical category that Phillips used the adjective *sublimitas* in summarizing early responses to the poem.[37] Such rhetorical evaluations as those of Phillips, however, were before long replaced in criticism of the epic by a Longinian aesthetics that was much less categorical. Under Boileau's influence, rhetorical classifications of the sublime style began to yield to more direct testimonies to the sublime itself, if not yet quite in a Kantian sense.

The cultural transformation in which the sublime evolved led readers and writers away from the critique of tyrannic militarism in Book 6 of *Paradise Lost*. Longinian criticism tended to divorce Milton's poetic technique from his theological or moral teaching, with admiration for the *techne* of style coming to displace the *agape* of content. Thus the technique might the more readily lend itself to national and partisan claims to political and martial virtue. Whig heroic poetry secularized Christian epic by rewriting Milton's archetypal war into present military occasions. There is a more than incidental connection between the fascinations in reproducing what may be termed the technology of Milton's verse and in celebrating the technology of war. Moreover, in response to the moral allegory of the War in Heaven, the tradition at first favoured the insistent externalization of inner argument into outward spectacle, the displacement of tensions within into violences without.

The challenge confronting Milton's readers in the late seventeenth and early eighteenth century, especially those more versed in neoclassical and Restoration aesthetics, should not be underestimated. The commonplace that his political writings needed separating from his poetry has obscured the degree to which his baroque poetics, especially in *Paradise Lost*, demanded an acceptance of its synthetic claims, whether at the level of phrase or of episode, and this in subordination to the biblical pretexts to which Milton had been so extraordinarily attuned. One of the answers to the challenge lay in the limiting approach to Platonist thought available in Longinian discourse. This invited the more affective and enthusiastic response to Milton's sublimity that becomes increasingly common from the

---

[37] Edward Phillips, *Tractatulus de carmine dramatico poetarum*, in Johann Buchler, *Sacrarum profanarumque* . . . (London, 1669), p. 399; William Godwin, *Lives of Edward and John Phillips* (London, 1815), p. 145; Edward Phillips, *Theatrum poetarum* (London, 1675), 'The Modern Poets', pp. 113–14. Phillips was most likely trained in Longinian analysis by Milton himself, whose educational programme had included study of *On the Sublime*: *CPW*, II, 402–3.

1670s to the early 1700s. Phillips's claims notwithstanding, we have it from Dryden that *Paradise Lost* had early been threatened by neoclassical reactions faulting the extravagance of 'this or that expression' in the epic, and 'tax[ing] Milton, as our false Critiques have presum'd to do, for his choice of a supernatural argument'.[38] The danger was averted when the mimetic emphasis of neoclassical theory was relaxed in order to accommodate the experience of the sublime (rather than through allegory). A broader appeal to experience could thus collapse 'Universal Tradition' into 'right Reason'. This more empirical criticism increasingly came to value transcendence by referring to its effects on the reader.

There was a breakthrough, then, in which Milton's 'supernatural argument' was naturalized. This emerges in some key responses to *Paradise Lost* in the 1670s – those of Samuel Barrow, Andrew Marvell and John Dryden – which helped present the epic to its widening audience. Early readers of the poem were encouraged to a Longinian reading in part by the time of publication of the new epic, which coincided with the reemergence of Longinian discourse as the new criticism of the 1670s and after. For readers of *Paradise Lost* in the second and third editions (1674, 1678), the introductory poems by Barrow and Marvell further invited such an approach. Barrow and Marvell cite the sublimity of Milton's achievement, with Marvell specifically using the term. Moreover, especially Barrow's elegiac distichs '*In paradisum amissam summi poetae Johannis Miltoni*' make the War in Heaven the central feature of Milton's epic. For Barrow, a former army doctor, and would-be historian of the civil wars, *Paradise Lost* seems to have been more about the fall of angels than the fall of man. Unlike Marvell, the impeccably royalist Barrow did not need to be circumspect in his applause of Milton: in 1674, not many could thus write in celebration of '*magni ... Miltoni*'![39] Barrow speaks of *Paradise Lost* as a '*grandia . . . carmina*' in which we read about all things, their *primordia, fata* and *fines*.[40] His praise centres in Milton's

---

[38] *The Works of John Dryden*, ed. Vinton Dearing et al., 20 vols. (Los Angeles, 1956–), XII, 90, 97, 352.

[39] Barrow had attended General Monck and his army in the north in the 1650s, and his services and good counsel at the Restoration positioned him to become a royal doctor in the 1660s and 1670s. N. von Maltzahn, ' "I admird Thee": Samuel Barrow, Doctor and Poet', *Milton Quarterly* 29 (1995), 25–8; also Michael Lieb, 'S.B.'s *In paradisum amissam*: Sublime Commentary', *Milton Quarterly* 19 (1985), 71–8.

[40] '[Robortello], Gabriel de Petra, and Gerard Langbaine also give "grandis" as an alternative' for *sublimis*. A. F. B. Clark, *Boileau and the French Classical Critics in England (1660–1830)* (Paris, 1925), p. 371.

Homeric achievement, recalling the opening to the twentieth Iliad, and perhaps the famous chapter in which Longinus's valuation of that Battle of the Gods led to his commendation of the passage from Genesis where God bids 'Let there be light.'[41] Barrow nowhere refers to Longinus, but his style of commendatory appreciation is in a notably Longinian vein, with the characteristically demonstrative approach especially apparent in the exclamatory style of the middle lines of Barrow's poem (six exclamation marks in eight lines). And with the growth of Longinian criticism, Barrow's praises of the War in Heaven might still more easily become critical commonplaces, contributing to a Longinian reading of *Paradise Lost*.

Barrow's note of wonder is complemented by the insistent ironies of Marvell's 'On Mr Milton's Paradise Lost'.[42] This poem foregrounds the 'sublime' as most nearly resolving the uncertainties explored in this tribute. The strain to which Marvell was subjected by Milton's poetics appears in his elaboration of these ironies, sophisticated even by Marvell's standards, as he addresses Milton and a Restoration audience alike. His larger strategy is to intimate Milton's evocations of transcendence to a sceptical audience, while reserving his own judgement and proclaiming instead the success of Milton's sublime style. Marvell acknowledges, for example, that Milton 'above humane flight [does] soar aloft', but his own claim to be 'transported' is in the same breath limited to transport only 'by the Mode [for rhyme]'.[43] Even so, when Marvell's narrator proceeds to model the transition toward a more transformative reading of *Paradise Lost*, his account of Milton as epic poet manages to herald some experience of the sublime, in which the poet's boldness becomes a virtue. Again, in keeping with Milton's early reputation, the compliment responds first of all to his humanist technical achievement; here Marvell is only commending what even Milton's

---

[41] 'Longinus', *On Sublimity*, trans. D. A. Russell (Oxford, 1965), 9.6, 9.9 (pp. 10–12).

[42] *The Poems and Letters of Andrew Marvell*, ed. H. M Margoliouth and P. Legouis, 2 vols. (Oxford, 1971), I, 137–9, 335–8. Especially the ironies at Dryden's expense have often been noted but not fully explained. For example. while touching on the difficulty of of Milton's situation in the Restoration Marvell also mocks Dryden's services in the Protectorate, when the latter writer, Marvell and Milton had worked as 'Secretarys of the French and Latin Toungs': hence the knowing comment now to Milton that 'none will dare / Within thy Labours to pretend a Share' (lines 25–6), which sharpens the humour at the expense of Dryden's 'less skilful hand . . . tag[ging]' *Paradise Lost* 'With tinkling Rhime' (lines 18, 45–50).

[43] On the selection of appropriate materials – 'Thou has not miss'd one thought that could be fit, / And all that was improper dost omit' (lines 27–8) – Marvell also echoes Longinus, *On Sublimity*, x.7 (p.16).

enemies would concede, his humanist gifts. But he does then invite some further celebration of that which Milton's technique exalts, or his *agape*.

That Marvell acknowledges Milton's wondering love of God appears from the two defining subtexts of 'On Mr Milton's Paradise Lost', one from Lucretius and the other from the Book of Wisdom. Their provenance and partial concealment may be thought to signal his diffidence about the Miltonic sublime. But the subtexts mark the stages of the poem as it models for readers a changing response to Milton and his teaching: from suspicion to emotion, and from emotion to conviction. The suspicion is presupposed: it follows, of course, from Milton's notoriety as an anti-monarchical writer. The emotion Marvell is concerned to portray more fully: it lies in the 'delight and horrour' he professes in response to Milton's singing with 'so much gravity and ease'. This recalls a passage from Lucretius – '*divina voluptas / percipit atque horror*' – where that author had praised Epicurus, and the testimonial is the more striking if returned to its original context, where Lucretius had celebrated Epicurus as a writer who brings light out of darkness.[44] When Marvell responds readily to the 'gravity and ease' of Milton's song it is not therefore as technique alone but as a way of evoking 'delight and horrour' as a means to an end, the sublime of the epic's revelation. The conviction Marvell presents more cautiously still. But his fascination with the Miltonic sublime appears more plainly in his final commendation of 'Thy verse created like thy Theme sublime'. This still seems caught in rhetorical categories, on one hand the formalist issue of Milton's choice of blank verse, on the other the 'theme' as a propositional object of thought, in which the Sublime *per se* has not yet fully emerged. As Marvell justifies the ways of Milton to men, he stands poised between his admiration for Milton's technique and the great urgency in the content of the epic. The sublime is here connected with Marvell's concluding praise for Milton's 'Number, Weight and Measure', in verse and in theme. This witty tribute has deeper implications owing to its recollection of a commonplace from Wisdom, 11:20, in which the praises of divine wisdom working through history include some meditation on God's capacity for even greater punishments of the fallen. Marvell thus emphasizes the

---

[44] Lucretius, *De rerum naturae*, trans. W. H. D. Rouse, 2nd edn (Cambridge, MA), 1975 III, 9–18 (p. 189).

restraint of Milton's power, of his measure or *ratio* in judging the fallen, even as he again speaks to questions of technique and of blank verse in particular.

The sublimity of Milton's poetry was to find much more comment than the *ratio* or 'measure' of his judgement, and the sublimity came to seem more and more available for imitation and commodification. Famously Marvell's dedicatory verse to the second edition of *Paradise Lost* already attacks Dryden's present attempt 'the whole Creations day / To change in Scenes, and show it in a Play', the play or opera being *The State of Innocence*. In Marvell's view, of course, Milton's work is unreproducible in any such fashion. It is noteworthy, therefore, then that Dryden's preface to *The State of Innocence*, written a few years later, should prove his most Longinian work, as he defends Milton's boldness and his own boldness in emulating Milton's 'Original', which he here claims to be 'undoubtedly, one of the greatest, most noble, and most sublime Poems, which either this Age or Nation has produc'd'.[45] In the next twenty years *The State of Innocence* outsold *Paradise Lost*, and Dryden's perspective here and elsewhere in his criticism helped define how Milton's epic should be read.

Dryden's Longinian impulse goes beyond his commendation of 'the boldest strokes of Poetry, . . . manag'd Artfully'.[46] At the heart of the matter is what Dryden calls 'imaging' and the emphasis on description in this aesthetics.[47] Already in its extravagantly courtly dedication to Mary of Modena, for example, *The State of Innocence* emphasizes the relation between 'Admiration' and 'extasie', with a not unplatonist reference also to 'that Love which is more properly a Zeal than Passion'.[48] Citing Longinus, Dryden describes imaging as 'the very heighth and life of Poetry': 'a Discourse, which, by a kind of Enthusiasm, or extraordinary emotion of the Soul, makes it seem to us, that we behold those things which the Poet paints, so as to be pleas'd with them, and to admire them'. This unusually positive application of 'enthusiasm' to the self-transcendence available in poetry reveals the new possibilities in the discourse of the sublime.

---

[45] Dryden, *Works*, xii, 86. This testimony John Dennis later thought among the first recognitions of Milton's achievement, *Critical Works of John Dennis*, ed. E. N. Hooker, 2 vols. (Baltimore, 1939–43), ii, 169.

[46] Dryden, *Works*, xii, 90, also 91–4.

[47] I argue the case more fully in 'Dryden's Milton and the Theatre of Imagination', in Paul Hammond and David Hopkins (eds.), *John Dryden, Tercentenary Essays* (Oxford, 2000), pp. 32–56.

[48] Dryden, *Works*, xii, 83.

When Dryden defends Milton against the presumption of 'our false Critiques', who have blamed that poet 'for his choice of a supernatural Argument', he notes scriptural descriptions even of 'Immaterial Substances', where 'the Text accommodates it self to vulgar apprehension, in giving Angels' a human likeness. The justification was, in Dryden's view, that 'sublime Subjects ought to be adorn'd with the sublimest, and (consequently often) with the most figurative expressions'.[49] Where Marvell ironized in his discussion of Milton's epic and emphasized style, Dryden, by shifting from style to its effects, assisted the impulse in reading Milton less to participate in the rational sublime than to respond to the pathetic sublime.

Fuller arguments about the sublime were to be forthcoming only in later idealist philosophy, relating mimesis to self-transcendence. But issues of elevation, transport and passion were joined in Dryden's emphasis on 'imaging'. This helped shape the work of Whig theorists of the 1690s and after, who much extended the discussion of sublimity. Moreover in poetic description it was to be 'Sense', in the phrase of Dryden's friend, the poet Nathaniel Lee, that 'clear'd' what he termed Milton's 'mystic reason'.[50] The context of Lee's remark further narrows his meaning. The sublime was to be presented in terms of physical experience, in which metaphysical issues were joined chiefly for metaphorical purposes (and often only in the hyperbole of occasional verse). A sensational rather than mystical sublime had been proposed, one more pathetic than rational, in which Milton before long became increasingly implicated. We catch the drift in John Aubrey's comment about Milton's sonnets for Cromwell and Fairfax, 'two admirable Panegyricks (as to sublimitie of Witt)': 'Were they made in the commendacion of the Devill, 'twere all one to me. 'tis the *upsos* that I looke after.'[51]

III

From Barrow and Marvell's commendations especially, as well as others' similar praises, early readers of *Paradise Lost* knew to expect a sublime poem on the 'Warring Angels'. The evidence is that this is what they then found.[52] Even Milton's critics might admire the way

---

[49] *Ibid.*, XII, 94–5, 97.
[50] John Dryden, *The State of Innocence* (London, 1677), sig. A4v.
[51] John Aubrey to Anthony Wood (postmark 24 May 1684), Bodleian MS Wood F. 39, f. 372r.
[52] *The Poems of John Oldham*, ed. Harold Brooks and Raman Selden (Oxford, 1987), pp. 131–2

his 'rapt Muse did tell / How in th'Aetherial War th'Apostate Angels fell'.[53] Moreover, as well as sensation Longinian aesthetics stressed emulation. This the writers of the next generation were eager to practice, whether in their Longinian wonder at Milton's achievement, or in the related impulse to reproduce his successes themselves, especially that of the War in Heaven. The visual emphasis of Longinian aesthetics helped shape the emerging poetic strategies for imitating Milton, especially for passages of description, where the Miltonic sublime was to have its widest impact in the decades following. The change can be traced in the outpourings of occasional verse in the 1690s and the first decades of the 1700s, especially in 1694/5 (the death of Queen Mary), in 1702 (death of William, accession of Anne), in 1704 (Marlborough's great victories, at Blenheim especially), and again in 1706 (Marlborough victorious at Ramillies), at the Union (1707), and even in the poetry celebrating the Peace of Utrecht, which belatedly describes the preceding wars in terms borrowed from Milton. There was an excitement to these laureate occasions. As poets became alert to the possibilities of Miltonic description, and began to revel in the sublime, they showed a Longinian enthusiasm about their modern subject, as well as a delight at these opportunities for sales and patronage, especially with Marlborough's successes on the continent. To modern judgements schooled in Kantian claims about the disinterestedness of the sublime, the occasional poems of the 1690s and early 1700s seem anything but sublime in their palpable designs on their readership, whether patron or wider populace. The poets' conception of the public good as the object of self-transcendence, however, is consistent with the version of the sublime promoted by a theorist like Dennis. In describing the Christian marvellous, he proclaimed that passions, 'the chief thing in Poetry', should run to enthusiasm, in which the cause of the passions 'is not clearly comprehended by him who feels them'.[54] Civil religion should draw on the exaltation of heroism and restraint, for example in the person of Marlborough. In this pre-

('Bion'); Nahum Tate, *A Poem, Occasioned by his Majesty's Voyage to Holland* (London, 1691), p. 5; *The Athenian Mercury* 8:6 (17 Sept. 1692); Cobb, *Poetae Britannici* (London, 1700), sig. B2r; see also the second edition of the earl of Roscommon's *Essay on Translated Verse* (London, 1685), which now includes 'An Essay on Blanc Verse out of the 6th Book of Paradise Lost'.

[53] *Poems to the Memory of that Incomparable Poet Edmond Waller* (London, 1688), p. 22.

[54] Dennis, *Critical Works*, I, 216; Douglas Lane Patey, *Probability and Literary Form* (Cambridge, 1984), pp. 274–80.

Kantian sublime, a poetry of admiration was to rouse patriotic passion in a wider readership.

Longinian criticism was now in full flow. Early in the 1690s, for example, a young Joseph Addison could already admire how 'bold, and sublime' Milton's poetry was, 'above the criticks nicer Laws'; he would later admire as 'Milton's chief Talent, and indeed his distinguishing Excellence . . . the Sublimity of his Thoughts'. That his was a Longinian valuation appears also from his formulaic reference to the 'terror and delight' experienced by the reader of *Paradise Lost*, most of all 'When angel with arch-angel copes in fight! / When great Messiah's out-spread banner shines . . .'[55] For Addison, Milton's 'imaging' deserves special praise. Milton's theology, which we may think of as central to his sublimity, never much engages the later critic, and we are closer to Addison's preoccupations where he advises us to read Longinus on Homer in order to find glories that are paralleled in *Paradise Lost*. This Longinian emphasis also governs Addison's hugely influential *Spectator* essays on *Paradise Lost* (1712), especially his fervent admiration of 'the Battel of the Angels', the height of Milton's achievement. Here he could propose that 'The Author's Imagination was so inflamed with this great Scene of Action, that where-ever he speaks of it, he rises, if possible, above himself . . . [and that] the Poet never mentions any thing of this Battel but in such Images of Greatness and Terrour, as are suitable to the Subject.'[56] Praising these 'utmost Flights of Human Imagination', Addison admires 'the Master-Stroaks' that abound in Book 6, for which he also cites Roscommon's authority, and he decides on the propriety even of the second day's engagement – that is the Satanic artillery and the angelic counterattack with mountains. Well might the later elegist for Addison, his biographer and editor Thomas Tickell, suppose that the great man, now in heaven, would particularly 'delight [now] to hear bold Seraphs tell / How Michael battel'd, and the Dragon fell'.[57]

The transformation from Milton's poetics to Addison's aesthetics is marked by the shift from a universal to a national emphasis. The public spirit Addison wished to foster originated in a more private orientation, in which a narrower conception of interest could still

---

[55] Joseph Addison, *Miscellaneous Works*, ed. A. C. Guthkelch, 2 vols. (London, 1914), I, 33; *The Spectator*, ed. Donald Bond, 5 vols. (Oxford, 1965), II, 587 (no. 279).

[56] *Spectator*, III, 227–8 (no. 333).

[57] Addison, *Miscellaneous Works*, I, xxiv.

lead to public good. His patriotism did not require the prescriptions imagined by a Dennis, Gildon, or Toland, but his more conventional Anglicanism might like their civil religion begin to seem 'autonomous, cut loose from its evangelical authority'.[58] His manipulations were less direct than those attempted by the more radical Whigs, but his writings may be thought the more political for being so polite, modelling a sociable rationality. Thus Addison eases and aestheticizes the radical Whigs' subordination of private to public interest. His indulgence of private interest, however, still includes some invitation to self-transcendence, in part owing to his related invitation that the individual invest in the public good of Credit. In the literary realm, the author as well as the reader might be encouraged to engage in such self-transcendence, which became increasingly central in theories of the sublime.

Addison, before his later fame, exemplifies the vogue for Milton's poetry in the Oxford of the 1690s and after, which would so favour his reception in the early eighteenth century. *Paradise Lost* was much promoted by members of the University, and of Christ Church in particular, who did much to shape Milton's reputation. There was a difficulty, for Milton's was a double legacy: his bad reputation as a republican controversialist vying with his increasing fame as a great poet, whose English Protestant epic even Tories could wish to celebrate. The Tory consensus had deplored Milton as 'the great Anti-monarchist';[59] the enduring scandal of his political writings was recalled in the much publicized Oxford Decree and book-burning of 1683, and in many a polemical tract linking Milton's with Whig seditions. On the other hand, the Oxford contribution to Tonson's illustrated folio *Paradise Lost* (1688) helped transform the reputation of the epic. The assistance came from that Tory bastion, the Christ Church of Henry Aldrich and a young Francis Atterbury, where *Paradise Lost* further gained a following owing to the extraordinary challenge to Tory allegiances presented by the reign of James II. That king's promotion of Roman Catholicism, especially in Oxford itself, prompted in Aldrich and Atterbury a fierce defence of the

---

[58] For the critical definition of civil religion, see Oliver O'Donovan, *The Desire of the Nations: Rediscovering the Roots of Political Theology* (Cambridge, 1996), pp. 224–6; for changing constructions of virtue in the reformation of manners, Shelly Burtt, *Virtue Transformed* (Cambridge, 1992), esp. pp. 13, 15–63; for a broader description of the 'sublime Milton' in the early eighteenth century, Moore, *Beautiful Sublime*, pp. 1–55.

[59] Anthony Wood's note in Bodleian, Wood 363, flyleaf 1^v. The next sentences are based on my 'Wood, Allam, and the Oxford Milton', *Milton Studies* 31 (1995), 155–77.

church of England. Now even Tories might fear the growth of popery and arbitrary government, as Whigs had done for a decade and more. Thus they might the sooner join with Whigs in supporting and subscribing to the sumptuous folio of *Paradise Lost*, in which Milton's English Protestant epic emerged as the great national poem, in that extraordinary year 1688.

Of the Christ Church group, especially the young John Philips helped assure the place of Miltonic imitation in early-eighteenth-century poetry, and with it the Miltonic sublime. We should recall that before 1700 the number of poems visibly influenced by Milton's example is surprisingly small. After 1700 this soon changes, to the point that Milton's wide influence can become difficult to define, so mediated does it become by intervening examples of poetry in various versions of his style. In the occasions for poetry in 1694/5 and 1702, the deaths of Mary and then William, there are some Miltonic moments, from poets we know of from other evidence as dedicated Miltonists.[60] But except for John Dennis, they reveal no obvious sense of how Milton might serve present occasions, and even Dennis was at first loath to leave the Pindarics so typical of occasional poetry of the day.[61] In the 1690s, he was already theorizing the sublime in strongly political terms, as a cultural crucible in which national passions might be heated and the dross of faction purged; in Dennis's Whig politics, a Miltonic poetics was therefore designed to foster the public spirit, in a surprisingly secular national religion. But Dennis was an exception and not yet that influential. As late as William's death in 1702, Milton's influence does not often colour occasional poetry.[62]

---

[60] von Maltzahn, 'The Whig Milton', pp. 243–5; Patrick Hume, *Poem Dedicated to the Immortal Memory of . . . Q. Mary* (London, 1695); Samuel Wesley, *Elegies on the Queen and Archbishop* (London, 1695).

[61] John Dennis, *The Court of Death* (London, 1695), sig. a2ʳ, pp. 4–5. The exceptions prove the rule: Henry Denne, *A Poem on the Taking of Namur* (London, 1695), pp. 3–4; *A Poem Occasion'd by the Happy Discovery of the Horrid and Barbarous Conspiracy to Assassinate his Most Sacred Majesty* (London, 1696), pp. 1–2.

[62] Dennis's *The Monument* (London, 1702) is the great exception, where he boldly ventures a Miltonic blank verse, which he is glad to justify with reference to that poet's example. When he denounces the French, for example, he describes their tyranny in terms borrowed from Milton's description of Satan, in a way that would soon become a commonplace: such tyrants are 'Too faithful Copies of their proud Original, / The great Destroyer, and the Foe of men, / The first and grand Artificer of Fraud; / The pow'rful Prince of all th'infernal Pow'rs; / Mighty to act, sagacious to contrive, / Who with capacious comprehensive thought / Sits brooding o'er his dark and damn'd Design / Of captivating all the Race of Men, / And fixing Universal Monarchy . . .' (p. 7). See also Francis Manning, *The Shrine* (London, 1702), pp. 10–11, which is only perhaps Miltonic; Marshall Smith, *A Pindarique*

The real breakthrough in Miltonic imitation came a few years later, in 1704, with Marlborough's continental triumphs, especially at Bleinheim. The renewed need for heroic poetry now seemed to invite the wider use of Milton in order to narrate the admirable events of that year's campaigns. Again Dennis was to the fore. His *Britannia triumphans* shows at length the new freedom in narrative poetry available through Miltonic imitation, and in elaborately defending blank verse, Dennis cites 'the spreading Fame of Milton' as warrant for his own practice.[63] In the poem itself the Miltonic influence is much more visible than in Dennis's earlier efforts: it appears in the invocation, in subsequent characterizations of the French tyrant, in the glorification of Marlborough, whether as a rational Adam or, when he turns the battle, like a Miltonic version of 'Homer's Jove'. Dear to Dennis and his contemporaries were the poetic opportunities in the mass drowning of the routed French in the swollen Danube, a welcome opportunity to describe a Homeric river of blood. Indeed, for Dennis the gory flood so cries out for Miltonic treatment that he just invokes that poet:

> Here Heavenly Goddess couldst thou but impart
> To my weak Mind the Force, th'immortal Force,
> To paint with lively Strokes the dismal Scene . . .
> Not Milton's wond'rous Piece should mine transcend
> In which Messiah with his Thunders arm'd
> Drove down th'infernal Tyrants warring Host
> With Terrors and with Furies thro' th'Abyss . . .[64]

Others too, especially Samuel Wesley again, drew on Milton more incidentally.[65]

But it was now John Philips who really made his mark, and in doing so demonstrated the value and ease of Miltonic description. Might the success of Addison's poem *The Campaign*, a Whig celebration of

Poem Sacred to the Glorious Memory of King William III (London, 1702), where the influence is again questionable, although Smith draws much on Milton elsewhere; *The Mournful Congress* (London, 1702), pp. 9–10, 12; Richard Daniel, *The Dream: a Poem Occasion'd by the Death of his Late Majesty, William III* (London, 1702), pp. 19–20, 76–8, which more plainly draws on Milton's example as Homeric gods are given Miltonic description and then voice.

[63] John Dennis, *Britannia triumphans* (London, 1704), sig. a4r. Now he too can at last comfortably derogate Dryden's *State of Innocence*.

[64] Dennis, *Britannia triumphans*, 67.

[65] Samuel Wesley, *Marlborough; or, the Fate of Europe* (London, 1705), pp. 3–7, esp. 7; John Geree, *A Poem to his Grace the Duke of Marlborough* (London, 1705), pp. 4–8; Nahum Tate, *The Triumph, or Warriors Welcome* (London, 1705), pp. 1, 4.

Marlborough's triumph, be answered by some answering Country production? Philips was commissioned to write one by Robert Harley.[66] Philips, famous for his indolence, eventually hit upon the answer in his *Blenheim* (London, 1704). As a Christ Church wit in the 1690s he had delighted in parodying Milton in *The Splendid Shilling*, which Addison would kindly style 'the finest burlesque poem in the British language'.[67] Having begun his poetic career by imitating Milton in jest, he was now ready to do so in earnest. Milton's legacy was a double one. *Paradise Lost* afforded Philips models for topographical and personal description; its elaborate similes also offered a means of attempting the sublime. The descriptive impulse in Philips's earlier burlesque could be directed toward more sober ends, in the heroic style of the panegyric, or in what might be styled the celebratory georgic, at once Virgilian and encomiastic (*Cyder*, 1708). Philips's answer in *Blenheim* was closely to rewrite Addison into Miltonian verse, in a process we can trace from section to section of the poem, and often from line to line. In sum, Philips translated Addison's work into a more descriptive blank verse that in its self-consciously Miltonic passages evoking scene and image moved away from the hortatory mode of celebration that Addison had perfected.[68] Philips's poem is therefore doubly derivative: he uses Addison's *Campaign* as his template, and *Paradise Lost* as a means of escaping Addison. His later shame over the work, perhaps not only owing to its praises of Marlborough, emerges in a story told by Harley himself: Philips 'was with some of his old acquaintance who fell foul upon him for his Blenheim: after they had teezed him awhile, says Jack, I could not help it, Mr Secretary Harley made me write it – but God forgive him; then, after some pause – & God forgive me

---

[66] I am grateful to John Baird for alerting me to his 'Whig and Tory Panegyrics: Addison's *The Campaign* and Philips's *Blenheim* Reconsidered', *Lumen* 16 (1997), 163–77, in which he argues the case for Philips's commission having preceded Addison's success. Even so, the evident debt of Philips to Addison shows that Philips needed that example finally to perform his obligation.

[67] *The Tatler*, ed. Donald Bond, 3 vols. (Oxford, 1987), III, 272–3 (no. 249).

[68] Even Philips's departures reflect his source: thus where Addison charts the progress of 'Our god-like leader' against continental tyranny, and the governing trope is his movement across the map, eastward 'to[ward] the rising Sun' (lines 47–85), Philips, in describing the relief Churchill's approach offers from such tyranny, produces an elaborate Miltonic simile about the delight of those in the extreme north at the sun's return (lines 55–81). Where Philips appears to depart still more widely from the *Campaign* – especially where he uses Milton's Battle in Heaven as the model for the spurning boasts of the French at the Britons' advance (*Blenheim*, lines 82–120) – it still proves that these despicable Frenchmen are jeering at a heroic tableau straight out of Addison's poem.

also'.[69] The speed at which Philips worked bears noting, however, and seems to have been noted by his fellows. Addison's *Campaign* appeared in mid-December 1704; the wholly derivative *Blenheim* was in print two and a half weeks later. Its success was second only to that of Addison's work, finding republication also with government support in London, Edinburgh and Dublin, and prompting the swift pirating of Philips's *Splendid Shilling*, even before it could be brought out again by Philips's own bookseller.[70]

Philips had shown how readily the Miltonic sublime might be used to transpose work in another key. The example was not lost on his contemporaries, who marvelled how 'Sublime Philips with Majestick Style' could write 'With such heroick Ardour'.[71] *Blenheim* showed how a Miltonic descriptive style could advance beyond the more hortatory or expostulatory poetics common in occasional verse of the time. In 1706, with Marlborough's great success at Ramillies, poet after poet joined in the chorus singing his praises, and the proportion suddenly rises of those using conspicuously Miltonic techniques – and notably blank verse – to sensationalize war.[72] Dennis contributed once more, now in the 132 octavo pages of his *The Battle of Ramillia ... A Poem. In Five Books*, verse shot through with Miltonic elements and allusion. There were other ambitious efforts, among which the anonymous *Joshua* stands out in devoting many folio pages to a Miltonic blank verse celebration of Marlborough in terms of the Old Testament hero. John Philips was not roused again, but another John Phillips may for the purposes of conclusion take his place.

This John Phillips was Milton's nephew, now at the very end of his life. In earlier years he had quite disowned his notorious uncle, whom he may have once satirized as 'blind Milton'. Now, however, as early as the title-page of his *Vision of Mons. Chamillard concerning the Battle of Ramilies* (London, 1706) he advertises himself as 'a Nephew of the late Mr John Milton', and the poem is dedicated to the Lord Chancellor Somers, a significant promoter of *Paradise Lost* in Tonson's

[69] Bodleian, MS Rawl. letters 30–31, f. 290: William Brome – Richard Rawlinson (26 Feb. 1730/31).

[70] D. F. Foxon, *English Verse: 1701–1750*, 2 vols. (Cambridge, 1975), I, 226–33, 246–7; II, 68–9.

[71] Huntington Library, MS EL 8796: Sarah Fyge Egerton, 'The Essay / Address'd to the Illustrious Prince and Duke of Marlbrow / after the long Campaigne 1708', f. 3.

[72] E.g. *A Letter to Mr Prior* (London, 1706); *Joshua: a Poem in Imitation of Milton* (London, 1706); Charles Johnson, *Ramelies. A Poem* (London 1706); John Paris, *Ramillies. A Poem* (London, 1706); Nicholas Rowe, *A Poem upon the Late Glorious Successes* (London, 1707); Bolton, *Prince Eugene* (London, 1707); Thomas D'Urfey, *The Trophies* (London, 1707), esp. pp. 14–15.

illustrated folio subscription edition of 1688. Of Chamillard, Louis XIV's secretary of war, here satirically linked to Madame Maintenon, Phillips makes a Satanic figure in keeping with the common practice of thus portraying the French. The French troops are 'Like Locusts form'd into a pitchy Cloud / Warping on th'Eastern Wind', and, recalling the War in Heaven, this 'Martial Host / Waving their bristly Spears look'd stern, anon / Clash'd on their sounding Arms the Din of War, / Hurling defiance tow'rds the Vault of Heav'n . . . ' Elsewhere Phillips improbably describes them as rolling 'their baleful Eyes, / That witness'd fierce Revenge, and high Disdain / Mix'd with obdurate Pride, and Stedfast Hate'; their artillery Phillips also heralds in visibly Miltonic terms: 'the Brazen Tubes of Death they brought, / Which speak the last, and fix'd Resolves of Kings / In flaming Language, and with Accent dire, / Exhaling Anger with sulphureous Breath!' It is the War in Heaven that is again being echoed when the English artillery responds with its own barrage: 'the Deep-throated Cannons 'gan to roar, / And with an hideous Orifice gaping wide, / Thick Vollies of Missive ruin discharg'd'.[73] The chief difficulty is that this pastiche of Miltonic poetry, thick with quotations and half-quotations from *Paradise Lost*, also uses such references uncritically in developing Marlborough as the hero of the piece. Phillips draws variously on Milton's descriptions of Satan, Death and Beelzebub to convey Marlborough's greatness. But Phillips' interest lay especially in evoking the new realities of continental warfare, to which he frequently applies his Miltonic techniques.[74] Moreover, the confusions as soon as Phillips much departs from his pastiche point up the value of his Miltonic technique, which provides a descriptive method and narrative impulse plainly not otherwise natural to this poet. By the time of Ramillies, after the example of the Blenheim poetry of a few years before, it was possible to be a very bad poet and by writing in a Miltonic style to achieve some minimally acceptable form of occasional poetry.

A Miltonic sublime drawn especially from the War in Heaven had by 1706 become a reproducible poetic mode, one capable of much imitation and adaptation in the decades to come – a vital part of eighteenth-century verse, as it would prove. The poets' excitement about this new resource is writ large in these folios of panegyric. And

---

[73] John Phillips, *Vision*, pp. 1, 3, 4, 6, 7.
[74] *Ibid.*, pp. 4, 7–8.

so marked was the rush to Miltonize that it drew comment about the methods that, in a contemporary's words, 'our lesser Poets use, / To force a Genius, and provoke a Muse'.[75] It is perhaps easy in reading these poets to forget the fuller inflections of Milton's original, especially the 'mystic reason' that informs the central episode of *Paradise Lost*. Whether the analysis of alienation, pride and envy, that informs Raphael's narrative, or the levels of analogy through which the War in Heaven proposes Milton's theodicy, by the time Milton's nephew John Phillips publishes *The Vision of Mons. Chamillard* these seem a distant memory. It may be claimed that allowance needs to be made for generic considerations. But how much? Longinian criticism in this period invited the sensationalizing of the sublime, and higher valuation of narrative technique than theological vision, of representation rather than reality, or, in biblical terms, of chaff rather than wheat. 'Th'Aetherial War' is indeed sublime, but its sublimity asked questions of that category that the Miltonic mode in the eighteenth century did not soon answer.

---

[75] Richard Daniel, *The British Warriour* (London, 1706), p. 4. See also Cambridge University Library, MS Add. 42, f. 17: 'Why not some Heroe deck'd with Borrow'd Praise. / Give him the lawrell & my self the bays: / From Dryden[,] Milton take some mighty line / Tune it to Malboroughs [sic] Praise & make it mine'; Richard Blackmore, *Advice to the Poets* (London, 1706), p. 10; *The Taylor Turn'd Poet. An Inscription Sacred to the Memory of the Author of Late Poem (Intitl'd Rammillies.) Written in Imitation of Milton* (London, 1706); Nicholas Amhurst, *The British General; a Poem, Sacred to the Memory of his Grace John, Duke of Marlborough* (London, 1722), p. 3.

CHAPTER 7

The Cowleyan Pindaric ode and sublime diversions[1]

Joshua Scodel

Generally considered the summit of lyric poetry during the Restoration, the Pindaric ode spoke forcefully to the times by displaying an intense concern with diverting disruptive passions from destructive to constructive ends. Late-seventeenth-century Englishmen continued to celebrate military heroism as the manly virtue that sustained English might abroad. Yet in response to successive political conflicts and crises and the ever-present fear of renewed civil war, military heroism was increasingly contested as an ideal.[2] Pindaric odes by such poets as Abraham Cowley, John Dryden and Aphra Behn celebrated figures whose sublime heroism or bold anti-heroism resided in their channelling of potentially bellicose or unruly impulses into nonviolent poetic, intellectual and personal realms that posed no threat to political order. Such odes simultaneously praised an ethics and enacted a poetics of 'diversion'. Pindaric and mock-Pindaric odes of the period by John Oldham and (a disillusioned) Dryden also questioned the efficacy of such 'diversion' and thereby helped to bring the genre into disrepute. Nevertheless, the late-seventeenth-century vogue for Pindaric odes forcefully contributed to the intellectual tendencies that fuelled eighteenth-century aesthetics, which posited against the disorderly political domain an alternative realm of artistic excellence.[3]

---

[1] For comments on drafts of this essay I thank Richard Kroll, Glenn Most, Janel Mueller, Steve Pincus, Richard Strier, Alok Yadav and Steven Zwicker. See also my 'Lyric Forms, 1650–1740', in Steven P. Zwicker (ed.), *The Cambridge Companion to English Literature, 1650–1740* (Cambridge, 1998), pp. 122–5.

[2] On suspicion of the military hero in the late seventeenth century, see the essays by James William Johnson, W. B. Carnochan and Peter Hughes in Robert Folkenflik (ed.), *The English Hero, 1660–1800* (Newark, DE, 1982); Derek Hughes, 'Dryden's *Don Sebastian* and the Literature of Heroism', *The Yearbook of English Studies* 12 (1982), 72–90; and Michael West's 'Dryden and the Disintegration of Renaissance Heroic Ideals', *Costerus* 7 (1973), 193–222; and 'Shifting Concepts of Heroism in Dryden's Panegyrics', *Papers in Language and Literature* 10 (1974), 378–93.

[3] On the rise of the aesthetic as a refuge from the political, see Elizabeth A. Bohls,

The widespread notion that unruly passions should be diverted because they could not be suppressed was a distinctive early-modern intellectual phenomenon, a new third way between the long-standing alternatives for handling the passions, which were traditionally thought to be conquerable by either reason or force. Aristotle argued that the virtuous few obey reason and therefore respond to those who 'exhort [them] . . . to virtue on moral grounds', while the vicious majority resists reason and must therefore be controlled by the 'pain' of punishment (*Nicomachean Ethics* 10.9.10).[4] Echoing Aristotle, Gilbert Sheldon, the hard-line bishop of London and later archbishop of Canterbury, insisted in 1662 on harsh measures against nonconformists on the grounds that those 'who will not be governed as men by reason and persuasions should be governed as beasts by power and force'. Yet for Sheldon as for many early-modern Englishmen, the binary opposition between the persuasion suitable for the rational few and the force needed to subdue the beast-like many was not exhaustive. Writing upon the death of Jeremy Taylor in 1667, Sheldon noted that the well-respected but intermittently heterodox divine, whom he considered 'of a dangerous temper apt to break out into extravagancies', was prevented from causing too much 'trouble' by Sheldon's ability 'to find diversions for him'.[5]

Asserting the populace's need for harmless recreations to prevent discontent and lawlessness, James I and his son Charles I had controversially authorized traditional country festivals and pastimes.[6] Responding first to the prolonged national crisis of the civil war and interregnum and then to the intense politicization of Restoration life, members of the sociopolitical elite during the mid and late seventeenth century increasingly suggested that all social ranks, including the highest, needed a variety of appropriate pleasures to divert violent or disruptive impulses. Linguistic usage registers the elite's growing recognition of various pleasures' sociopolitical usefulness *as*

'Disinterestedness and Denial of the Particular: Locke, Adam Smith, and the Subject of Aesthetics', in Paul Mattick, Jr (ed.), *Eighteenth-Century Aesthetics and the Reconstruction of Art* (Cambridge, 1993), pp. 16–51.

[4] All citations and translations from classical texts are taken from the Loeb Classical Library editions.

[5] John Spurr quotes Sheldon in *The Restoration Church of England, 1646–1689* (New Haven and London, 1991), pp. 47, 397.

[6] See Leah Marcus, *The Politics of Mirth: Jonson, Herrick, Milton, Marvell, and the Defense of Old Holiday Pastimes* (Chicago, 1986); and Peter Stallybrass, '"Wee feaste in our Defense": Patrician Carnival in Early Modern England and Robert Herrick's "Hesperides"', *English Literary Renaissance* 16 (1986), 234–52.

'diversions'. From the 1640s onwards, the verbs 'to divert' and 'to divertise' are increasingly deployed in the newly fashionable sense of 'to entertain' while still suggesting the older meaning of 'to cause (the mind, attention, etc.) to turn *from* one channel *to* another' (*OED*, s.v. 'divert', 5, 6), and the nouns 'diversion' and 'divertisement' are increasingly used in the newer sense of 'entertainment' while retaining the older sense of 'distraction' from something else (*OED*, s.v., 'diversion', 4, 4b).[7]

The championing of diversionary pleasures of various sorts was encouraged by the Neoepicurean currents within late-seventeenth-century English culture.[8] While ancient Epicureans recommended achieving tranquil pleasure by rationally moderating one's desires, English Neoepicureans followed Michel de Montaigne and his French heirs in their scepticism regarding reason's ability to moderate the passions. The seventeenth-century English vocabulary of diversion derives directly and indirectly from France, the home of so many Royalist exiles during the mid seventeenth century, where 'diversion', 'divertissement', and 'divertir' were deployed from the late sixteenth century onwards in senses that prefigure common seventeenth-century English usage. Montaigne is a major source for the theory of diversion.[9] His essay 'Of Diversion' ('De la diversion') claims that human beings will generally not submit to reason and therefore require diversions. 'Of Diversion' promotes their use in both the personal and political realms: Montaigne recalls that sexual liaisons provided him with 'vehemente diversion' or 'Powerful Diver-

---

[7] The *OED*'s first instance of 'divert' and the now obsolete 'divertise' in the sense of 'entertain' date from 1660 and 1651 respectively, while its first citations of 'diversion' and 'divertisement' in the sense of 'entertainment' date from 1648 and 1642. Despite earlier examples (see note 10 below), the dictionary accurately registers the surge in popularity of these terms in the mid seventeenth century.

[8] On late-seventeenth-century English Epicureanism, see Howard Jones, *The Epicurean Tradition* (London and New York, 1989), ch. 8; Richard Kroll, *The Material Word: Literate Culture in the Restoration and Early Eighteenth Century* (Baltimore, 1991); Thomas Franklin Mayo, *Epicurus in England (1650–1725)* (College Station, TX, 1934); and Maren-Sofie Røstvig, *The Happy Man: Studies in the Metamorphoses of a Classical Ideal, 1600–1700*, 2 vols. (Oslo and Oxford, 1954), 1, 311–434. None of these works notes the deviation from ancient Epicureanism charted in this chapter. I owe a general debt to Albert O. Hirschman's influential discussion of early-modern thinkers' loss of confidence in the power of reason and their consequent search for ways of transforming rather than repressing the passions in *The Passions and the Interests: Political Arguments for Capitalism before its Triumph* (Princeton, 1977), pp. 7–66. Hirschman, however, treats neither the Neoepicurean celebration of 'diversion' nor its literary ramifications, which are my major focus.

[9] Leo Lowenthal briefly analyses Montaigne as a theorist of 'diversion' in *Literature, Popular Culture, and Society* (Englewood Cliffs, NJ, 1961), pp. 15–16.

sion' (to cite Charles Cotton's felicitous Restoration translation) from displeasure and that he diverted a prince from cruelty by tempting his ambition with the glory of clemency. In contiguous essays Montaigne also emphasizes the diversionary powers of literature and imagination, noting that he reads enjoyable books and cultivates 'young and Foolish Thoughts' in order to divert his mind from the depression of old age.[10] Often recalling Montaigne favourably or unfavourably, debate about 'divertissements' raged among seventeenth-century French thinkers between Neoepicureans who regarded them as essential for the management of the passions and religious moralists who deemed them sinful distractions.[11]

The Pindaric ode, as influentially fashioned by Cowley in his *Pindarique Odes* of 1656, was the major later-seventeenth-century innovation in English lyric poetry. Cowley, who had returned to England in 1654 from exile at Henrietta Maria's court in France, published the poems while under arrest as a Royalist spy. Transforming a classical genre by applying a Neoepicurean notion of diversion, Cowley created a poetic vehicle for diverting his countrymen from rebellious, disruptive ambitions by celebrating daring in nonpolitical spheres. Critics have normally treated Cowley's interregnum and Restoration odes separately, arguing or implying that they were radically different in purpose and form because of the differing political and intellectual climates in which they were written.[12] I will

---

[10] Michel de Montaigne, *Les Essais* (ed.) Pierre Villey, rev. V. L. Saulnier, 2 vols. (Paris, 1965), II, 835, 829, 841; Michel de Montaigne, *Essays in Three Books*, trans. Charles Cotton (1685–6; rpt. London, 1738), III, 56–7, 49, 63. John Florio's 1603 translation of Montaigne provides an early instance, unnoted in the *OED*, of the English domestication of French 'diversion'; see 'Of Diverting and Diversions' in Michel de Montaigne, *Essayes* (1603), trans. John Florio, 3 vols. (London, Toronto and New York, 1910), III, 51–62. Robert Burton in 1621 provides another important early-seventeenth-century English example of Montaigne's influence when arguing that if 'wee cannot moderate our passions . . . we must divert them' (*The Anatomy of Melancholy*, ed. Nicolas K. Kiessling, Thomas C. Faulkner and Rhonda L. Blair, vol. II (Oxford, 1990), p. 186 (Part 2, section 3)).

[11] The Neopicurean *libertin* Charles Saint-Evremond, for example, who from 1661 onwards dwelt in English courtly circles, followed Montaigne in arguing that life was bearable only if 'divertissemens' provided 'diversion' from melancholy (*Œuvres en Prose*, vol. IV, ed. René Ternois (Paris, 1969), pp. 12–13). Montaigne's Jansenist antagonist Blaise Pascal, by contrast, condemned 'diversions'; see Lowenthal, *Literature, Popular Culture, and Society*, pp. 16–18; and Nannerl O. Keohane, *Philosophy and the State in France: the Renaissance to the Enlightenment* (Princeton, 1980), pp. 274–9.

[12] On Cowley's interregnum Pindaric odes, see Annabel M. Patterson, *Censorship and Interpretation* (Madison, 1984), 152–66; Stella P. Revard, 'Cowley's *Pindarique Odes* and the Politics of the Interregnum', *Criticism* 35 (1993), 391–418; and David Trotter, *The Poetry of Abraham Cowley* (London, 1979), pp. 109–42. Patterson claims that the Restoration odes 'have none of the characteristics and make none of the claims of the interregnum pindarics'

argue, by contrast, that both the continuities within Cowley's own
Pindaric practice and the great popularity of the Cowleyan Pindaric
form throughout the late seventeenth century indicate how much
Restoration literary culture was haunted by the political and aesthetic issue of 'diversion' that was first urgently raised for Englishmen by
the civil war and interregnum.

I. PINDARIC ODES AND CULTURAL DIVERSIONS

Annabel Patterson has shown how Cowley designed his interregnum
Pindaric poems not to be 'precisely understood' so that they could
simultaneously encode both acquiescence to and criticism of the
Protectorate.[13] In her reading, the major feature of Pindar's odes
adopted by Cowley is their grandiloquent obscurity, which makes
interpretation difficult and licenses ambiguity. Yet Pindar's subject
matter also provided a positive vision upon which Cowley could
build. Pindar's odes celebrate the athletic victories of a ruler or
aristocrat as heroic achievements, equal to military victory, that
glorify an entire community. In the preface to his 1656 volume,
Cowley advances several contradictory views of poetry's mission and
his own writings, but one formulation helps explain his particular
attraction to Pindar's odes. Calling poetry an 'exercise, or rather
divertisement', he argues that a 'warlike . . . age is . . . worst to *write
in*' because the poet must be 'in good humor' in order to 'communi-
cate delight to others; which is the main end of *Poesie*'.[14] Cowley's
Pindaric odes are, among other things, an attempt to 'divert' himself
and his audience by representing peaceful achievements that are –
unlike the civil war and Parliamentary victory – unambiguous causes
for celebration.

Cowley's Montaignesque identification of poetry with 'divertisement' may be found among other defeated Royalists who during the
interregnum promoted (however disingenuously or provisionally) the
production and/or consumption of literary 'diversions' as an alternative to continued strife. In 1653, Margaret Cavendish, the wife of

---

(p. 165); Trotter invokes a 'different intellectual milieu' (p. 140) to explain what he sees as
major differences between the interregnum and Restoration ode. Nicholas José stresses
continuities in Cowley's poetry but only briefly discusses the Pindaric odes in *Ideas of the
Restoration in English Literature, 1660–1671* (Cambridge, MA, 1984), pp. 67–96.

13 Patterson, *Censorship and Interpretation*, 165.
14 Abraham Cowley, *Poems*, ed. A. R. Waller (Cambridge, 1905), p. 7.

the exiled Royalist general William Cavendish, the duke of New-castle, published her *Poems and Fancies* with a preface that disclaimed any subversive intent against the interregnum government by pre-senting her poetry as an innocent diversion. Declaring her 'Ambi-tions' for fame 'great' but her 'designes . . . harmlesse', Cavendish claimed she wrote poetry, an innocent 'Pasttime' more suitable for a woman than 'Politicks', to 'divert' her 'discontented Thoughts' concerning her husband's and her own unhappy plights. In his playful 1654 commentary on *Don Quixote*, Edmund Gayton, who had been ejected from his Oxford beadleship by the Puritans, defended plays, romances and other 'recreations' (including, implicitly, his own text) as a means of 'divert[ing]' people lest they 'become troublesome Judges of the State and Church'. Gayton thus simultaneously expressed his distaste for the Puritan revolution, which had brought down the established 'Church and State' and closed the theatres, and advised the new regime to avoid further disorder by tolerating 'diversions'. In 1655 Gayton had the chance to implement the policy he had advised when he composed the text for the first interregnum Lord Mayor's Day pageant, which he published as an example of the 'innocent and delightful diversions' promoted by all prudent govern-ments.[15]

During his exile in France, Cowley associated with William Davenant, who in 1650 published a preface to his epic *Gondibert* that acknowledged Cowley's supportive criticism. Arguing like Gayton that wise statesmen provided public 'diversions' to keep the 'People' in 'obedience', Davenant's preface noted that the ancient Athenians used entertainments to 'divert' criticism of the government.[16] Dave-nant was probably indebted to contemporaneous French debates concerning the utility of theatre as 'divertissement'.[17] He addressed, however, a politically divided English audience. While his concern with preventing popular rebellion had a Royalist cast, he also appealed to the victorious Parliamentary elite with his Athenian example, which underscored that popular governments as well as

---

[15] Margaret Cavendish, duchess of Newcastle, *Poems and Fancies* (1653), sig. A4v–A5r, A7r–v; Edmund Gayton, *Pleasant Notes on Don Quixot* (1654), pp. 270, 273; *Charity Triumphant . . . exhibited on . . . the Lord Mayor Day* (1655), p. 4.

[16] See William Davenant, *Gondibert*, ed. David F. Gladish (Oxford, 1971), pp. 270–1, 24, 40.

[17] On French debates regarding dramatic 'divertissement', see Henry Phillips, *The Theatre and its Critics in Seventeenth-Century France* (Oxford, 1980), pp. 151–73; on Davenant's general debt to French dramatic theory, see Susan Wiseman, *Drama and Politics in the English Civil War* (Cambridge, 1998), p. 144.

monarchies needed 'diversions' to avoid subversion. In 1653 Davenant published an anonymous tract urging the interregnum government to allow theatrical entertainments that would 'divert the people from disorder'; in a 1656 letter to the Protectorate's secretary of state William Thurloe, he argued that the London theatres should be reopened because the English 'People', being 'inclin'd to that melancholy that breeds sedition', need 'divertisements'.[18] Conceding the Royalists' defeat, Davenant offered 'divertisements' – and his artistic services – in place of continued dissension.

While his friend Davenant wished to 'divert' the common 'people', Cowley's learned Pindaric odes seek to 'divert' the educated – and divided – social elite. Cowley begins his interregnum collection with two loose translations of Pindar that suggest his commitment to a poetic 'divertisement' that would accommodate the new regime. In his preface, Cowley had claimed that now that the civil war was over, Englishmen should practice an '*Art* of *Oblivion*' concerning recent divisions. Such an '*Art*', Cowley implies, would extend far beyond the 1652 Parliamentary 'Act of Oblivion', which had done little to alleviate Royalist sufferings or to heal divisions.[19] In his opening translation of *Olympian* 2, Cowley freely renders a Pindaric passage treating Theron of Acragas's chariot victory as a recompense for the violent sufferings of his mythical ancestry in order to suggest the need for Englishmen to forget the recent past: 'For the past sufferings of this noble Race / . . . / Let *present joys* fill up their place, / And with *Oblivions silent stroke* deface / Of foregone Ills the very *trace*.'[20] This passage could be read as Cowley's call for Englishmen to accept the Protectorate as the happy end of civil war; but it could also be read as Cowley's exhortation to his countrymen to divert their attention from political and military strife to the '*present joys*' conjured by Cowley's own Pindaric '*Art* of *Oblivion*'.

Cowley's Pindaric celebrations of ancient Greek games has pointed topical significance. As the Greek orators Lysias (*Olympic Oration* 1–3) and Isocrates (*Panegyricus* 43) emphasized, the Panhellenic athletic competitions, which were accompanied by a general truce

---

[18] James R. Jacob and Timothy Raylor reprint and discuss Davenant's tract in 'Opera and Obedience: Thomas Hobbes and *A Proposition for Advancement of Moralitie* by Sir William Davenant', *The Seventeenth Century* 6 (1991), 205–50. I cite p. 245. C. H. Firth reprints the letter in 'Sir William Davenant and the Revival of the Drama during the Protectorate', *English Historical Review* 17 (1903), 319–21.

[19] Cowley, *Poems*, p. 455.

[20] Cowley, 'Second Olympique Ode', stanza 3, in *Poems*, p. 158.

between the often warring Greek city-states, gathered Hellenes together for friendly competition rather than violence. In his two Pindaric translations and the glosses he provides, Cowley elaborates upon Pindaric glorifications of athletic competition in order to evoke a peaceful but heroic alternative to civil war. Cowley's notes to *Olympian* 2 describe the Greek games as 'a *Sacred bloodless War*'. Referring to Pindar's praise of an ancestor of Theron for victory in 'contests' (*aethlois*) (line 43), which Cowley translates as 'warlike sports', he points out in his notes that the '*publique Games* . . . were in that age, no less honourable than *Victories* in *War*'.[21] Cowley's head-note to *Nemean* 1 similarly accentuates the 'incredible honor' accruing to 'Conquerors' in the Greek games. In his preface Cowley calls for '*Amity*' between '*Conquered*' Royalists and the Parliamentary '*Conqueror*'; his application of the military term 'Conquerors' to athletic victors – which the *OED* cites as its first instance of 'conqueror' in the pacific sense of 'victor in a contest of skill or strength, in a game' (s.v., 'conqueror', 1d) – underscores that 'warlike sports' channel the bellicose impulses all too evident in recent years into peaceful competition.[22]

In several passages Cowley diverges from Pindar to make the odes more pacific. Pindar's *Olympian* 2 praises Theron and his brother's double athletic victories as a release from the 'anxieties' (line 52) of competition; Cowley describes their victories as 'kind pious glories' that 'deface / The old *Fraternal* quarrel' of their ancestors. 'Kind . . . glories' encapsulates the irenic heroism with which Cowley counters civil war. Pindar claims Theron will posthumously dwell in the Island of the Blest with heroes like Achilles; suppressing Pindar's list of belligerent Achilles's victims (lines 80–3), Cowley instead claims that 'great *Achilles*' is 'wrathful . . . no more' in the 'peaceful' Island. By purging 'great' Achilles of the violent anger that caused bitter discord among the Greeks, as readers would remember from Homer and Horace (*Epistle* 1.2.14), Cowley reimagines him as an example of peaceful greatness, like an athlete.[23] Pindar claims in *Nemean* 1 that the Syracusans, whose tyrant's brother-in-law Chromius won the chariot race, were 'enamored of bronze-armored war' and 'often . . . crowned / with golden olive leaves / from Olympic festivals' (lines

---

[21] Cowley, 'Second Olympique Ode', stanza 5, and notes 1, 5 in *Poems*, pp. 159, 163, 166.

[22] Cowley, *Poems*, pp. 170, 455. For other Cowleyan references to athletic 'Conquerors', see Cowley, 'The Praise of Pindar', stanza 3 and note 3 in *Poems*, pp. 179, 181.

[23] Cowley, 'Second Olympique Ode', stanzas 7–8 and note 8 in *Poems*, pp. 160–1, 167.

16–18). After praising like Pindar the Sicilians as both 'Wise in *Peace*, and Bold in *Wars*', Cowley's translation concludes a stanza by adding a triplet with a final seven-foot line which grandly stresses that peaceful athletic conflict provides no less honour than war: 'Nor let their *warlike Lawrel scorn*, / With the Olympique *Olive* to be worn, / Whose gentler *Honors* do so well the *Brows* of *Peace* adorn.'[24]

Cowley terms ancient athletic competitions 'exercises' as well as 'sports'.[25] They resemble poetry itself, described in Cowley's preface as an 'exercise' or 'divertisement'. Pindar's athletic games could only be an inspiring metaphor for the kinds of 'heroic' diversionary activities in which Cowley and his contemporaries might themselves indulge in place of war. Cowley treats his own poetic emulation of Pindar, however, as a glorious alternative to violence akin to the ancient athletic contests. The Greek poet himself often analogizes his rivalry with other poets to the athlete's competition. Drawing attention to Pindar's *agon* with other poets, Cowley's notes to *Olympian* 2 claim that Pindar boasts of his poetic talent 'in derogation of' his 'adversary' Bacchilides. Yet while Pindar's odes are full of self-praise, his primary panegyric subject is always the athletic victors. By contrast, Cowley's third ode, an imitation of Horace's *Ode* 4.2 in praise of Pindar's 'impetuous' poetic power as exemplified by his (supposed) prosodic freedom, takes as its theme the poet as hero. A Cowleyan addition to his Horatian model underscores that Pindar's poetic virtues are the same as those of the peaceful athletic 'Conquerors' he praises: Cowley claims with strict parallelism that 'the *Swift*, the *Skilful*, or the *Strong*' athletes are 'crowned' in Pindar's '*Nimble, Artful, Vigorous* Song'.[26]

In his preface to the odes, Cowley presents his own engagement in such glorious poetic competition. He justifies his loose translation of Pindar on the grounds that to copy Pindar exactly would lead to aesthetic failure because 'men resolving in no case to shoot *beyond* the *Mark*, it is a thousand to one if they shoot not *short* of it'.[27] Cowley uses Pindar's own archery image to proclaim his ambition to outdo the Greek poet. In *Olympian* 2, Pindar describes himself (in

---

[24] Cowley, 'Second Olympique Ode', stanza 5; and 'First Nemean Ode', stanza 3 in *Poems*, pp. 159, 171–2.
[25] Cowley, *Poems*, p. 163.
[26] Cowley, 'Second Olympique Ode', notes 1 and 9; and 'The Praise of Pindar', stanza 3 and note in *Poems*, pp. 157, 168, 179, 181.
[27] Cowley, *Poems*, p. 156.

Cowley's rendition) as a 'noble *Archer*', and Cowley's note compares Pindar's claim in *Olympian* 13 that he must not shoot 'beyond the mark' ('para skopon').[28] Cowley's prefatory defence of 'shoot[ing] *beyond* the *Mark*' thus implies that by going beyond the Greek poet's own self-imposed limits, Cowley seeks to rival Pindar in glorious but peaceful emulation.

Cowley also praises contemporaries as intellectual, pacific 'Conquerors'. His ode on the doctor Charles Scarburgh begins by praising Scarburgh's medical skill as a powerful antidote to murderous 'Civil Wars'; the poem concludes by declaring that Scarburgh has won a '*Crown*' (like Pindar's athletic victors) for his peaceful 'Conquests' of nature. Cowley's ode on Thomas Hobbes compares the philosopher's reason to Aeneas's impregnable magic shield; but whereas (as Cowley's note points out) Aeneas's military weapon 'frightened' all observers, Hobbes's reason supposedly manages to 'delight' even 'the enemies' forced to acknowledge defeat in intellectual '*Combat*'.[29]

Cowley associates Pindaric verse, his own emulation of the Greek poet and such intellectual heroes as Hobbes with a sublime but peaceful 'boldness'. Cowley's preface to his poems notes that Pindar's figuration is '*bold, even to* *Temeritie*'.[30] Cowley's ode 'The Muse' celebrates his own 'bold' Muse freely ranging across time and space. The subsequent ode on Hobbes, in which Cowley 'dare[s] boldly' declare his support for his controversial contemporary, recalls 'The Muse' in order to suggest a parallel between Cowley's boldness as a Pindaric poet and Hobbes's daring as a philosopher: just as Cowley's 'bold' Pindaric Muse discovers a '*New world*' of imagination, so Hobbes is the daring 'Great *Columbus*' of '*new Philosophies*'. Cowley suggests that he and Hobbes are similarly audacious in their contestation of ancient restraints. Lauding Hobbes's challenge to Aristotelianism, Cowley praises Hobbes's sailing beyond the 'slender-limb'd Mediterranean' of classical thought.[31] Here Cowley himself challenges Pindar's ancient timidity: Pindar often warns against hubris by claiming that no mortal should dare sail beyond the Mediterranean's bounds, the 'pillars of Hercules' (*Olympian* 3.43–5,

---

[28] Cowley, 'Second Olympique Ode', stanza 9 and note 9 in *Poems*, pp. 161, 168.
[29] Cowley, 'To Dr Scarborough', stanzas 1 and 5; and 'To Mr Hobs', stanza 5 and note 5 in *Poems*, pp. 197, 200, 190–1.
[30] Cowley, *Poems*, p. 11.
[31] Cowley, 'The Muse', stanza 2; and 'To Mr Hobs', stanzas 1 and 4 in *Poems*, pp. 185, 188–9.

Nemean 3.19–23, *Isthmian* 4.11–13). Cowley thus anoints himself the bard and Hobbes the philosopher of modern boldness.

The boldness that Cowley honours in Pindar, in his own Pindaric poetry and in contemporary intellectuals displaces the traditional ideal of military boldness, exemplified by the Sicilians of *Nemean* 1 whom Cowley, following Pindar, praises as 'Bold in *Wars*'. More specifically and topically, poetic or intellectual daring figure as alternatives to the violent boldness of rebellion, which Cowley treats with fascinated ambivalence. Cowley's 'Brutus', the poem that most directly treats contemporary events, both praises and rejects such violence. The poem first defends Brutus's killing of Julius Caesar as one of 'Th'*Heroick Exaltations* of *Good*' that are misunderstood as '*Vice*'. In the final stanza, however, Cowley commands Brutus to 'restrain' his 'bold' '*Disdain*' and represents Christ's passion as super-seding Brutus's tyrannicide, now associated with mortal 'pride'.[32] The topical application is notoriously – and prudentially – ambigu-ous. If Caesar is read as Charles I and Brutus as Cromwell, Cowley initially praises Cromwell's heroic virtue but then implies that the Puritan revolution was too proud for Christians, who should pas-sively suffer like Christ. If Caesar is read as Cromwell (excoriated by Royalists as a tyrant), then Brutus becomes a figure for Royalists who heroically but vainly wished to continue battling the interregnum regime instead of humbly accepting Providence.[33] In either case, however, Cowley expresses both admiration and fear of such bold-ness and seeks an alternative in Christian passivity.

Cowley's about-face concerning Brutus's ethical status re-enacts a long-standing debate concerning heroism. Brutus's '*Heroick Exalta-tions*' of virtue that are mistaken for 'Vice' recall Aristotle's claim in his *Nicomachean Ethics* that 'heroic' (*hêroikê[n]*) virtue is an 'excess' (*huperbolê[n]*) of virtue (7.1.1–2, translation mine). Such heroic 'excess' could well seem like vice because it is an awkward and under-developed exception to Aristotle's conception of ethical virtue as a mean between the vicious extremes of 'excess' (*huperbolê*) and defi-ciency. Early-modern writers, however, seized upon Aristotle's brief discussion of 'heroic virtue' in order to glorify leaders who exceeded ordinary ethical standards. Baldesar Castiglione, for example, praises the prince whose 'heroicall' virtue (in Thomas Hoby's Elizabethan

---

[32] Cowley, 'Brutus', stanzas 2 and 5 in *Poems*, pp. 195, 197.
[33] See Patterson, *Censorship and Interpretation*, pp. 160–2.

translation) 'passe[s] the boundes' of human nature. Implying its disruptive potential as an ideal in strife-torn England, Cowley pays tribute to but then fearfully rejects such heroism. He turns to the alternative association of 'heroic virtue' with Christ and Christian martyrdom propounded in the Scholastic and Neoscholastic commentaries on Aristotle often used at Cambridge, Cowley's alma mater.[34] Christlike submission to Providence emerges as the highest political conduct. Yet Cowley's celebration in the *Pindarique Odes* of 'boldness' in athletic, poetic and intellectual spheres reveals his strong sense that however laudatory Christian passivity might be, men must still find active outlets for their 'heroic' ambitions to exceed and excel.

Cowley's commendation of passivity in the political sphere continues in the Restoration: his 'Ode. Upon his Majesties Restoration and Return' (1660) praises Charles I the martyr and hails Charles II as the *'unarmed King'* whose imitation of Christ's *'suffering Humanity'* made possible his political triumph.[35] Cowley's 'A Discourse by way of Vision, Concerning the Government of Oliver Cromwell' (1661) provides a palinode for the ambiguities of the 'Brutus' ode with an unambiguous attack upon Cromwell's political daring. While the interregnum Cowley praised Pindar's 'Bold' figures and 'vast' verse,[36] the Restoration Cowley condemns Cromwell's 'bold, and vast' political designs as 'Brutish' (with a pun on 'Brutus'?) 'Madness'.[37] As the two extremes beyond ordinary virtue and vice,

---

[34] On Renaissance notions of 'heroic virtue', see Merritt W. Hughes, 'The Christ of *Paradise Regained* and the Renaissance Heroic Tradition', *Studies in Philology* 35 (1938), 254–77, which cites Castiglione (p. 263); and John M. Steadman, 'Heroic Virtue and the Divine Image in *Paradise Lost*', *Journal of the Warburg and Courtauld Institute* 22 (1959), 88–105; on Scholastic notions, see Rudolf Hofmann, *Die Heroische Tugend: Geschichte und Inhalt eines theologischen Begriffes* (1933; repr. Hildesheim, 1976). On Cambridge instruction in ethics, see Harris Francis Fletcher, *The Intellectual Development of John Milton*, 2 vols. (Urbana, 1961), I, 157–65. In an unpublished work of 1645–7, Cowley's contemporary Robert Boyle mingles Scholastic and Renaissance formulations with examples of both active and passive 'heroic virtue': he argues (presumably with reference to Cromwell) that God 'to worke . . . som . . . notable change in Kingdoms or Commonwelths . . . excite[s] Heroick Spirits'; he also, however, celebrates Joseph, who chose 'Misery with Chastity' and a 'Dungeon rather [than] Mistres', and argues that Christ had 'all Vertues in a heroicall Degree' (*The Early Essays and Ethics of Robert Boyle*, ed. John T. Harwood (Carbondale, IL, 1991), pp. 130–2). In the 1680s Boyle identifies 'heroic virtue' with Christian martyrdom (*The Works of . . . Robert Boyle*, ed. Thomas Birch, 6 vols. (London, 1772), v, 260).

[35] Cowley, 'Ode. Upon his Majesties Restoration . . .', stanzas 9 and 12 in *Poems*, pp. 425–6, 428. Cf. Cowley's Restoration ode, 'Christs Passion' (pp. 402–4).

[36] Cowley, 'The Praise of Pindar', stanza 1 in *Poems*, p. 178.

[37] Cowley, *Essays, Plays, and Sundry Verses*, ed. A. R. Waller (Cambridge, 1906), p. 365.

Aristotle had paired heroic virtue with bestiality (*Nicomachean Ethics* 7.1.1–3); Cowley dismisses the view that Cromwell's political boldness exemplified the former by identifying it with the latter.

Yet in Restoration odes on cultural heroes and heroines, Cowley continues to celebrate diversionary outlets for heroic ambitions by praising extreme 'boldness' that is confined to nonpolitical domains. His ode on the Royal Society, which prefaces *The History of the Royal-Society* (1667) by his friend Thomas Sprat, praises the 'bold work' of the Royal Society scientists, who are described as 'great Champions' in the 'glorious' – but peaceful – 'Fight' against nature.[38] Cowley's ode thus supports Sprat's own promotion of scientific activity as a diversion of energies from civil strife to peaceful activities. Sprat's text describes the proto-Royal Society's meetings during the civil war period in terms of the participants' desire, amidst national 'distresses', for 'private diversion' rather than religious and political controversy. Arguing like Montaigne that diversion is more able than reason to quell disorderly passions, Sprat generalizes that scientific activity provides 'innocent' and '*diverting Delights*', calms '*ambitious disquiets*' with the 'glory' of discovery, and 'sweeten[s]' the 'peevishness' that leads men to 'Rebellion'.[39]

In his two Restoration odes on Katherine Philips, Cowley represents a woman's poetic accomplishments as yet another mode of irenic heroism. Treating Philips as the embodiment of modern English literary achievement, Cowley influentially extends the praise of bloodless but glorious struggles to a woman's successful rivalry with male tradition. In a 1663 Pindaric on Philips's death, Cowley declares that Philips outdid men in both 'Wit' and 'Virtue'; she was a pacific conqueror whose 'tender Goodness' rendered 'powerless' the 'furious Bullets' of 'violent Passion'. In 'On *Orinda*'s Poems. Ode' (1664), Cowley celebrates her 'bold' but peaceful 'sally' against male dominance in 'Wit' that ends in her victory because of her poetic androgyny – she is 'than Man more strong, and more than Woman sweet'.[40]

---

[38] Cowley, 'To the Royal Society', stanzas 6–7, 9 in *Poems*, pp. 451–52.

[39] Thomas Sprat, *The History of the Royal-Society of London* (1667), ed. Jackson I. Cope and Harold Whitmore Jones (St Louis, MO, 1958), pp. 55–6, 343, 345, 428.

[40] Cowley, 'On the death of Mrs Katherine Philips', stanza 4; and 'On *Orinda*'s Poems. Ode', stanzas 1 and 3 in *Poems*, pp. 443, 404–5. On Cowley's trope of androgyny, see also Joanna Lipking, 'Fair Original: Women Poets in Male Commendatory Poems', *Eighteenth-Century Life* 12 (1988), 60–2. Carol Barash's dark reading of Cowley as 'punish[ing] the poetically fecund and aggressive Philips' is vitiated by misinterpretation; see *English Women's Poetry, 1649–1714:*

Cowley rewrites traditional images of the *virago* to emphasize the unthreatening peacefulness of Philips's poetic ambitions:

> The warlike *Amazonian* train,
> Who in *Elysium* now do peaceful reign,
> And wits milde Empire before Arms prefer,
> Hope 'twill be setled in their sex by her.
> . . . .
> Ev'n *Boadicia*'s angry Ghost
> Forgets her own misfortune, and disgrace,
> And to her injur'd Daughters now does boast,
> That *Rome*'s o'ercome at last, by a woman of her Race.[41]

Recalling his transformation of Achilles into a posthumously peaceful hero, Cowley transforms violent women – the Amazons and the Amazon-like Boadicea, who with 'barbarian cruelty' (Tacitus, *Agricola* 16) rebelled against Britain's Roman conquerors – into posthumous supporters of Philips's irenic heroism. The ode's contrast between 'Wits milde Empire' and 'Arms' recalls an interregnum ode in which Cowley lauded the 'mild' battle of the sexes as the happy alternative to civil war: in his Pindaric epithalamion upon the 1657 marriage of Maria Fairfax, the daughter of the former Parliamentary general, and George Villiers, the duke of Buckingham, an erstwhile Royalist who made peace with the interregnum regime, Cowley contrasts the bride's 'Triumphs' in the 'milder War' of love with her military family's 'rougher Victorie[s]'.[42] The Philips odes similarly encode Cowley's hope that peaceful battles can replace civil war.

Pindaric odes after Cowley continue to depict women's rivalry with men as a peaceful cultural battle. In the light of the fractiousness of Restoration politics, the fear of renewed civil war, and the intense constitutional and religious conflicts surrounding the exclusion crisis of 1678–81, the battlecry of the slim, anonymous volume *The Triumphs of Female Wit* (1683) seems deliberately diversionary. The preface to this work declares women's 'diverting Wit' as well as 'Wisdom' equal to men's and introduces 'The Emulation, A Pindaric Ode' by declaring that women will 'bold[ly]' let their 'Wit sally out upon' male

---

Politics, Community, and Linguistic Authority (Oxford, 1996), pp. 84–6 (quotation on p. 85). Cowley compares Philips the mother of 'immortal' poetic 'Progenie' to the 'great Mother' goddess '*Cybele*' (Cowley, 'On Orinda's Poems. Ode', stanza 2 in *Poems*, p. 405). Confusing Cowley's powerfully fecund '*Cybele*' with the tragically overreaching Semele, Barash argues that Cowley's comparison conveys 'Philips's sexual and poetic hubris' (p. 85).

[41] Cowley, 'On Orinda's Poems. Ode', stanza 5 in *Poems*, p. 406.
[42] Cowley, 'To the duke of Buckingham . . .', stanza 4 in *Essays*, p. 464.

'Enemies'.[43] The ode itself, which simultaneously exemplifies and defends women's 'diverting Wit' as well as their 'Wisdom', protests that men have deprived women's 'unbounded Mind' of the learning with which they could challenge male 'Empire' (lines 16, 37). The poem glorifies female emulation of male achievement by associating it with the Pindaric ode's praise of athletic and poetic competition and decorously deploys the metrical liberty with which Cowley associated the form to espouse female freedom from tyrannical male constraints. Yet the poem not only explicitly circumscribes the female challenge to the cultural realms of 'Learning', Wit' and 'Poetry' (lines 61, 87) but also somewhat contradictorily declares that 'peaceful' women 'desire to reign' only over their own passions and seek no 'braver' 'Conquest' (lines 55–6).[44] Thus the poem defuses the threat of a violent challenge to male dominance and patriarchal order.

John Dryden recognized the diversionary functions of both literary production and consumption. In 1664 he commended the heroic dramas of Roger Boyle, the earl of Orrery, written during the author's attacks of gout, as 'Diversion[s]' of the author's 'Pain' that also 'divert others'.[45] In *An Essay of Dramatick Poesie* (1668), Dryden argued that his 'sullen' countrymen were 'diverted' by comedies. Like his friend and sometime collaborator Davenant's claim that diversions were necessary for Englishmen lest their 'melancholy' breed 'sedition', Dryden's characterization of his countrymen as 'sullen' hints at the rebelliousness 'diverted' by plays.[46] In his 1685

[43] *The Triumphs of Female Wit* (1683), sig. B1r–v.

[44] I cite 'The Emulation' from Germaine Greer et al. (eds.), *Kissing the Rod: an Anthology of 17th Century Women's Verse* (London, 1988), pp. 309–14 (quotations on pp. 310–12).

[45] *The Works of John Dryden*, ed. Edward Niles Hooker, H. T. Swedenberg, Jr, et al., 20 vols. (Berkeley, 1956–), VIII, 96. All citations of Dryden's prose are from the California Dryden, hereafter cited as *Works*.

[46] Dryden, *Works*, XVII, 48. Cf. the 'Moody, Murmuring' (line 45) Jews/English in *Absalom and Achitophel* (1681) and the 'sullen' (line 284) religious dissenters in *The Medal* (1682); see *The Poems of John Dryden*, ed. James Kinsley, 4 vols. (Oxford, 1958), I, 218, I, 260. (All citations of Dryden's verse are from this edition, hereafter cited as *Poems*.) The significance of Dryden's claim that English comedy 'divert[s]' his 'sullen' countrymen is underscored by his debt to the 1664–5 debate concerning English temperament and drama between Samuel Sorbière and Thomas Sprat. With implicit reference to the civil war period, the Frenchman accused the English of a 'Haughty' 'Rudeness' threatening to monarchy and dismissed their drama as 'Diverting' trivia. Conceding that the English might 'incline' to 'Disobedience' in a 'discontented Age' though not in a 'secure Time' like the 'present', Sprat denied the English were 'Sullen' and defended English drama's 'diverting' gaiety as proof ([Samuel] Sorbière, *A Voyage to England, Containing many Things relating to the State of Learning . . . with Thomas Sprat, Observations on the Same Voyage* (1709), pp. 54–5, 59, 69–71, 123, 168–9, 178). George Williamson noted Dryden's debt in his *Essay* to Sprat's defence of English drama ('The Occasion of *An Essay of Dramatic Poetry*', *Seventeenth Century Contexts*, rev. edn (Chicago, 1969),

Pindaric ode 'To the Pious Memory of . . . Anne Killigrew', prefaced to Killigrew's posthumous book of poetry, Dryden followed Cowley in celebrating a woman's artistic accomplishments as a glorious diversion of potentially dangerous ambitions.[47]

Dryden explicitly associates the deceased with Philips, closely echoes at various points Cowley's two Pindaric odes on Philips and represents Killigrew as a similarly androgynous figure.[48] Dryden praises Killigrew's sole reliance as a poet on her natural 'Vigour' – a quality traditionally ascribed to males – rather than upon 'Art' or poetic craft: 'Art she had none, yet wanted none; / For Nature did that Want supply / So rich in Treasures of her Own, / She might our boasted Stores defy: / Such Noble Vigour did her Verse adorn' (lines 71–5).[49] Dryden underscores Killigrew's masculinist poetic strength by echoing Pindar's own proud boasts of 'natural' excellence as translated by Cowley: whereas other poets' '*Art*' is 'weak and poor', Pindar lays claim to the 'unexhausted store' of '*Nature*'; 'My *Muse*', he declares, writes 'by *Nature*'.[50] Dryden's echoes decorously acknowledge the Pindaric power that Killigrew claimed for herself in her ode 'The Discontent' when she bid her Muse no 'Art or Labour use'.[51] Figuring Killigrew's untutored 'nature' as Pindaric power, Dryden follows Killigrew herself in turning female cultural disadvantage – Killigrew's lack of the classical education deemed necessary for access to 'art' – into a sign of 'masculine' strength.[52]

In his depiction of such 'masculine' force, Dryden treats the

---

pp. 272–88; see Dryden, *Works*, XVII, 343–6, 374), but Dryden combines Sprat's positive assessment of English drama with Sorbière's negative characterization of English temperament, thereby implying the political function of English drama's 'diverting' power.

[47] Dryden, *Poems*, I, 459–65.

[48] On the Killigrew ode's relation to Cowley's Philips poems, see Lipking, 'Fair Original', pp. 62–4; on the ode's androgynous representation, see James Anderson Winn, '*When Beauty Fires the Blood': Love and the Arts in the Age of Dryden* (Ann Arbor, MI, 1992), pp. 91–108.

[49] On 'Vigor', see Winn, *When Beauty*, pp. 91–2.

[50] Cowley, 'Second Olympique Ode', stanza 9 and 'First Nemean Ode', stanza 4 in *Poems*, pp. 161, 172. Cowley notes that Pindar 'frequently' prefers nature to art (*Poems*, p. 168). Killigrew's 'Vigour' is equally Pindaric: Dryden's *Preface to the Sylvae* (1685) declares 'Vigor of Fancy' the Pindaric ode's 'Soul' (Dryden, *Works*, III, 17).

[51] Anne Killigrew, 'The Discontent', lines 1–2 in *Poems* (1685), intro. Richard Morton (Gainesville, FL, 1967), p. 51.

[52] Ignoring Killigrew's poetic 'Vigour' and identifying her 'Nature' without 'Art' with a feminine ethical 'artlessness', Laura L. Runge argues that Dryden celebrates Killigrew's blameless feminine character instead of praising her literary achievement; see *Gender and Language in British Literary Criticism, 1660–1790* (Cambridge, 1997), pp. 76–7. Yet in her own excellent discussion of Dryden's gendering of literary qualities, she notes that Dryden associates imaginative vigour with masculinity, formal 'regularity' and 'perfection' (i.e. the 'Art' that Killigrew lacks) with femininity (pp. 40–61).

problem of violent energies and their diversion to peaceful spheres in a fashion similar to, though more tonally complex than, Cowley. Dryden emphasizes Killigrew's Pindaric boldness when characterizing her decision to paint as well as write verse: 'But what can young ambitious Souls confine?' (line 91). Yet his description of Killigrew's 'masculine' ambition is laden with apparent criticism. The details in Dryden's analogizing of Killigrew to a conquering monarch who could not be 'content' with a 'Spacious Empire' and therefore took over a 'Province' with a '*Chamber of Dependencies*' (lines 88–98) glance satirically, as numerous critics have noted, at Louis XIV's foreign conquests. Dryden seems explicitly to treat Killigrew's ambition, like Louis's, as overweening when he suggests that her ambition caused her death: 'To such Immod'rate growth her Conquest rose, / That Fate alone its Progress could oppose' (lines 147–8). Dryden's military analogy works on two levels. On the one hand, the analogy censures the ambitions of violent monarchs, and Dryden may be using Killigrew's death, as John M. Wallace suggested, to obliquely warn his own 'warlike' king, James II, against a belligerent policy like the French king's.[53] Yet the analogy cannot be meant seriously as a judgement upon Killigrew, whose combination of poetry and painting was hardly destructive. Dryden's playful, hyperbolic analogy rather recalls Cowley's simultaneous praise of intellectual achievements in martial terms and condemnation of actual war, and his question – 'But what can young ambitious Souls confine?' – serves to remind readers that Killigrew's ambitious mind *was* in fact confined – to artistic realms. Dryden often praised purely artistic ambition: in 1670 he claimed that poets should be 'bold and dare' even unto 'rashness'; in 1677, he averred that 'Ambition is so far from being a Vice in Poets, that it is almost impossible for them to succeed without it.'[54] Unlike Louis XIV's, Killigrew's ambition harmed nobody, and Dryden implicitly asks readers to weigh Killigrew's artistic successes *against* male violence.

Dryden once more relies upon values Killigrew herself professed. Killigrew herself had contrasted masculine violence with female accomplishments: her volume opens with a fragmentary 'Alexendreis' celebrating Alexander the Great's discontent after conquering the 'spacious World' (line 3), followed by the palinode 'To the Queen',

---

[53] John M. Wallace, 'Dryden and History: a Problem in Allegorical Reading', *English Literary History* 36 (1969), 275–9.

[54] 'Prologue to *Tyrannic Love*', lines 12, 21 in Dryden, *Poems*, I, 118; Dryden, *Works*, 12:81.

which rejects such 'Frantick Might' as far 'inferiour' to Mary of Modena's 'sublime' virtue (lines 3, 17, 22, 33).[55] Dryden's military analogy implies that Killigrew, the innocent but forceful Pindaric androgyne, did not simply reject masculinist ambitions. Instead she diverted such ambitions to the literary domain – and thereby morally transmuted them.

Dryden certainly worried that the same unruly energies that the Pindaric ode celebrated could have harmful consequences when *not* confined to the artistic realm. Two years before the Killigrew ode, Dryden associated the Pindaric ode with the unruly crowd's lust for power in *The Medal* (1682); addressing the mob, he claims, in an extra-metrical line that mimics the Cowleyan Pindaric's prosodic freedom, 'Thou leap'st o'er all eternal truths, in thy *Pindarique* way' (line 94).[56] The mob embraces outsized Pindaric ambition and liberty in politics; the Killigrew ode, by contrast, celebrates the diverting of unconfined ambitions to an aesthetic realm.

Thomas Heyrick's elephantine Pindaric ode of 1691, a 67-page underwater tour of the world's oceans entitled *The Submarine Voyage*, provides a late instance of the Pindaric treatment of poetic ambition as heroic diversion. Responding to the factional party strife of late-seventeenth-century English life, Heyrick announces in his preface that he writes on 'Subjects of Indifferency' that will not disturb 'Quiet and Peace'. He proposes thereby 'to draw Men's Minds, that are Idle, from . . . Dangerous . . . Speculations' and 'Evil-Maxims against Church and State'.[57] His Pindaric tour of the oceans attacks the 'unruly Appetite' of the 'Ambitious', whom 'never Bounds or Limits could contain', for leading to 'Anarchie'. Heyrick tries to divert his countrymen from dangerous thoughts and unruly ambitions by trumpeting poetry's own innocent ambitions. His Pindaric ode proclaims its author's 'boundless Mind', 'bold Ambition', 'bold course'.[58] The collection's prefatory puffs by Heyrick's university cronies, several of which are Pindaric odes, similarly laud Heyrick's sublime ambitions: Heyrick's 'boundless . . . Mind' encompasses the 'Vast abyss'; he has set upon a 'more adventurous Course' than

---

[55] Killigrew, *Poems*, pp. 1, 6–7.
[56] Dryden, *Poems*, 1, 256.
[57] Thomas Heyrick, *The Submarine Voyage* (1691), pp. iv–vi.
[58] Heyrick, 'The Submarine Voyage' (Pindaric ode), stanzas X, VII, IX, XVI, XXIIII, pp. 7, 5–6, 46 (separately paginated). Heyrick also recalls Cowley's trope for modern intellectual and poetic boldness by travelling the 'boundless Ocean' beyond 'Hercules Pillars' (stanza XXVI, p. 66).

Cowley; his 'tow'ring Mind / To . . . low Station could not be confin'd'; he outdoes Alexander the Great in scorning 'Bounds'.[59] Such ludicrous hyperboles reveal an intense desire to aggrandize poetic diversion and thus render poetry a suitably heroic substitute for disruptive aspirations in the public sphere.

Heyrick's attempt at poetic diversion may be glossed by William Temple's discussion of poetic diversion in an essay published the year before. Temple's *Of Poetry* (1690) treats literary diversions in a Neoepicurean manner that recalls Montaigne. Temple praises poetry for providing 'innocent amusements' that 'divert the violent passions and perturbations of the greatest and the busiest men'. Temple goes on to praise those who 'content themselves' with such diversions rather than 'trouble the world'. *Of Poetry* initially associates literary diversion with the servile French: Temple claims that Richelieu set up the French Academy to 'divert' 'wits' 'from raking into his politics'. Yet Temple's view that England's laudable liberty of opinion and religion has produced subjects who 'will not be constrained' and has 'raised' factions suggests why poetry is necessary to divert Englishmen from mischief. By coupling Temple's paean to poetic diversion with his earlier remark that 'the genius of poetry' is 'too libertine to be confined' to 'constraints', one may derive the cultural 'logic' of so many odes, in which unconstrained liberty remains safely in a realm of poetic, Pindaric imagination.[60]

II PINDARIC ODES AND GLORIOUS RETIREMENT

Late-seventeenth-century authors also invoked diversion to glorify country retirement. In a work published anonymously in 1659, the Neoepicurean John Evelyn attacked interregnum England for lacking 'innocent. . . diversion'. During the Restoration, as part of his agenda for revitalizing England, Evelyn produced his oft-reprinted *Kalendarium Hortense, or The Gard'ner's Almanac* (1664), which promoted gardening among the upper classes as the most 'innocent and laudable . . . Diversion'. Evelyn dedicated his second edition to Cowley, whom he noted found 'easy . . . Diversions' in retirement.[61]

---

[59] *Ibid.*, pp. viii, x, xiv, xviii.

[60] William Temple, *Five Miscellaneous Essays*, ed. Samuel Holt Monk (Ann Arbor, MI, 1963), pp. 197–200, 202–3.

[61] *The Writings of John Evelyn*, ed. Guy de la Bédoyère (Woodbridge, UK, 1995), pp. 87, 351, 353, 355.

In his own posthumously published Neoepicurean celebration of retirement, *Essays, in Verse and Prose* (1668), Cowley similarly praises the diverse innocent 'divertisements' that rural life grants the cultured individual.[62]

Cowley insists that retired diversions represent a glorious alternative to military heroism. While echoing the classical retirement poetry of Horace and Virgil, throughout his *Essays* Cowley emphasizes his sense of the grandeur of retirement by contrasting it with the Augustan poet's humble subservience to their bloody patron Augustus. Attacking Augustus's supposed 'greatness' as based upon 'Falshood' (*sic*) and 'guilt' and rejecting Virgil's denigration of the retired life as 'ignoble ease' ('ignobilis oti', *Georgics* 4.564) in comparison to Augustus's military accomplishments, Cowley proudly celebrates his own 'no unactive Ease, and no unglorious Poverty'.[63]

Cowley's use of the Pindaric ode in his *Essays* underscores his association of retirement with a sublime form of heroism. While the opening stanza of the ode 'Upon Liberty' celebrates retired Epicurean contentment with the 'Golden Mean' between 'Poor' and 'Great', in an expansive countermovement the third stanza compares the poet's retired freedom to do as he pleases to the 'soaring boldly' of 'Heroic' birds who are not 'so mean' as to give up their 'Native Liberty'.[64] Cowley's move from a positive to a negative sense of 'mean' underscores his ascent from contented moderation to a sublime register. Though the opening of the final stanza contrasts Cowley's retirement 'Pindarique way . . . / . . . loose and free' with a 'more Heroique strain', Cowley concludes by adapting Pindar's sublime self-representation as eagle (*Olympian* 2.86–8, *Nemean* 3.80–2, 5.20–1), which Cowley praised in the notes to his interregnum Pindarics as '*nobly extravagant*'.[65] Cowley compares the retired man's roving spirit to the 'Imperial Eagle' who scorns 'meaner Birds'.[66] The retired figure's eagle-like nature transfigures the highflying ambitions, condemned elsewhere in the *Essays*, of those who have or seek worldly power, those whose possession of or desire for 'Imperial Grandeur' leads them to prey upon others and

[62] Cowley, *Essays*, p. 394.
[63] *Ibid.*, pp. 420–1, 431. I discuss Cowley's self-portrait as a hero of retirement in relation to the Augustan poets in *The English Poetic Epitaph: Commemoration and Conflict from Jonson to Wordsworth* (Ithaca, NY, 1991), pp. 217–19.
[64] Cowley, 'Ode. Upon Liberty', stanzas 1 and 3 in *Essays*, pp. 388–90.
[65] Cowley, 'Second Olympique Ode', note 9 in *Poems*, p. 168.
[66] Cowley, 'Ode. Upon Liberty', stanza 6 in *Essays*, p. 391.

whose 'Heroical' but rebellious 'attempt[s]' at 'scaling Heaven' can never lead to 'Tranquility'.[67]

Other poets of the 1670s and 1680s use the Pindaric ode to aggrandize the retired life but in so doing undermine Cowley's moral distinction between retirement and disruptive worldly passions. Consider how, for example, Montaigne's translator Cotton evokes country life in his Pindaric 'The Retirement' (1676):

> Oh my beloved rocks! that rise
> To awe the earth, and brave the skies,
> From some aspiring mountain's crown
> How dearly do I love,
> Giddy with pleasure, to look down.[68]

Cotton recalls Lucretius's celebration of retired Epicurean wisdom, which allows one to 'look down' (*despicere*) with pleasure upon others' anxious toil to reach the 'pinnacle' (*summas*) of worldly triumph (*De rerum natura* 2.9–13). Lucretius boldly adapts the worldly image of 'making it to the top' in order to claim that the retired philosopher, rather than the ambitious man, reaches the acme of true success. Yet the odd tone of Cotton's stanza undermines Lucretius's contrast. 'Giddy with pleasure' as he stands upon the 'aspiring mountain's crown', Cotton sounds less like an Epicurean, tranquil in his rejection of worldly desires, than like the ambitious men scorned in Cowley's retirement verse, who 'Upon the slippery tops of humane State, / . . . proudly stand' and 'The giddy danger . . . beguile, / With Joy, and with disdain look down on all, / Till . . . down they fall.'[69] Cotton's blunting of the distinction between retirement and its exciting but dangerous worldly opposite betrays that he has not sought an alternative to worldly glory but tried to recover it within his retirement landscape.

Aphra Behn's Pindaric ode 'A Farewel to Celladon, On his Going into Ireland', published in 1684 and written sometime in the late 1670s or early 1680s, depicts a retirement figure as glorious in such a way as to blur the difference between retired diversions and a specifically courtly form of worldliness.[70] She celebrates the unidentified Celladon, a man of 'lavish Fortune' (line 52) whom Charles II has appointed to public office in Ireland, as a 'nobler Soul' made 'For

[67] Cowley, *Essays*, p. 433.
[68] *Poems of Charles Cotton, 1630–1687*, ed. John Beresford (London, 1923), p. 47.
[69] Cowley, *Essays*, pp. 399–400.
[70] *The Works of Aphra Behn*, ed. Janet Todd, 7 vols. (Columbus, OH, 1992–1996), I, 35–9.

Glorious and Luxurious Ease' (lines 46–7). 'Glorious . . . Ease' recalls – and intensifies – Cowley's claims to 'Ease, and no unglorious Poverty'. Cowley's *Essays* used the term 'luxury' antithetically both to attack courts' 'guilty and expenseful Luxury' and to glorify the paradoxical 'cheap and virtuous Luxurie' of Epicurean retirement.[71] Behn, by contrast, collapses these two opposite senses in praise of wealthy, courtly Celladon's retired 'Ease'.

Behn's 'Luxurious' also has a specifically erotic resonance, suggesting a 'lascivious' and 'voluptuous' (*OED*, s.v. 'luxurious', 1, 3) courtly lifestyle that Behn declares nobler than anti-court prudes can imagine.[72] With his 'Luxurious Ease', Celladon sounds like an avid imitator of his royal master Charles II, who notoriously cared for little except (to quote Samuel Pepys) his 'lusts and ease'.[73] Behn wishes that Celladon may find opportunities for specifically erotic diversion in retirement:

> Divert him all ye pretty Solitudes,
> And give his life some softning Interludes:
> That when his weari'd mind would be,
> From Noise and Rigid Bus'ness free;
> He may upon your Mossey Beds lye down,
> . . . .
> With some dear Shee . . .
> . . . .
> [whose] soft tale of Love . . .
> Is Musick far more ravishing and sweet,
> Then all the Artful Sounds that please the noisey Great.

(lines 83–96)

In the stanza celebrating Celladon's 'Luxurious Ease', Behn also declares his 'Loyalty' during the exclusion crisis, when 'unmov'd he stood' while others perpetrated 'Rebel *Crimes*' (lines 58, 60, 66–7). A hedonistic appetite for luxury and diversion, Behn suggests, keeps noble natures from busy, sordid rebellion.[74]

---

[71] Cowley, *Essays*, pp. 403, 424 ('The Garden', stanza 6); cf. Cowley's praise of 'the Wholesome Luxurie' of 'Roots and Herbs' (*Essays*, p. 406).

[72] Cf. the 'Luxuriant' sexual 'Raptures' in Behn's 'On a Juniper-Tree, cut down to make Busks' (lines 57–8) (Behn, *Works*, I, 40).

[73] On the politics of Charles II's sexuality, see Harold Weber, *Paper Bullets: Print and Kingship under Charles II* (Lexington, KY, 1996), pp. 97–9 (Weber quotes Pepys on p. 98); Rachel Weil, 'Sometimes a Scepter is Only a Scepter: Pornography and Politics in Restoration England', in Lynn Hunt (ed.), *The Invention of Pornography: Obscenity and the Origins of Modernity, 1500–1800* (New York, 1993), pp. 125–53; and Steven N. Zwicker, *Lines of Authority: Politics and English Literary Culture, 1649–1689* (Ithaca, NY, 1993), pp. 90–129.

[74] Behn elsewhere underscores the political function of 'diversions'. In her dedication to *The*

Half-heartedly celebrating Celladon's service to his monarch in public office, Behn briefly justifies retired diversion as a way of preserving the health of one who labours for the public good: 'Mix thus your Toiles of Life with Joyes, / And for the publick good, prolong your days' (lines 97–8). Yet for Behn, Celladon's erotic proclivities are not truly subordinate to public office, for his pursuit of erotic diversion most clearly establishes his credentials as a Carolean courtier. Behn elsewhere represents rural erotic 'diversion' as a court prerogative: her 'Epilogue' to *The Young King* (1686) notes that 'Courts do oft divert in Cottages, / And prize the Joys with some young Rural Maid, / On Beds of Grass, beneath a lovely Shade' (lines 5–7). Such philandering befits courtiers because it is, by Behn's libertine accounting, the 'noblest' activity: in the dedication to the first part of *Love-Letters between a Noble-man and his Sister* (1684), Behn bids her gentle addressee 'divert the toils of life' with 'noble' love, which provides all life's 'charms'.[75] Behn's Pindaric ode transforms Cowleyan attacks on worldly greatness and ambition to eulogize a court and its courtiers whose erotic diversions reveal the nobility that justifies their negligent rule.

III OLDHAM, DRYDEN, AND THE UNDERMINING OF HEROIC DIVERSIONS

The blurring of the distinction between retirement diversions and worldly passions found in late-seventeenth-century Pindaric poetry reveals the instability and vulnerability of Cowley's Neoepicurean 'project' of diversion. It is not surprising that some seventeenth-century English divines, like contemporaneous French moralists, denied its efficacy: the Cambridge Platonist Benjamin Whichcote, for example, claimed that religion, not all-too worldly 'Diversion',

---

Luckey Chance (1687), Behn cites the recently translated treatise on theatre by the French critic François Hédelin, Abbé d'Aubignac, to argue that 'Plays and publick Diversions' are 'essential' to 'Good Government' (VII, 213). Like Davenant, d'Aubignac contends that theatrical 'Diversions' prevent 'idle People' from 'doing ill' see François Hédelin, Abbé d'Aubignac, *The Whole Art of the Stage* (1684), p. 6–7; for the French, see *La pratique du théâtre* (1657), ed. Pierre Martino (Algeria, 1927), pp. 10–11. In the light of Monmouth's rebellion and growing Protestant opposition to James II, Behn invokes d'Aubignac to present 'public Diversions' as a way of deflecting the idle from political mischief. Celladon's erotic escapades are a courtly analogue to the 'public Diversions' that keep men from disruptive impulses.

[75] Behn, *Works*, VII, 150; II, 7. Cf. the declaration in *Lycidus* (1688), Behn's translation of a French work, that erotic 'diversion' is the 'great end of Man' (IV, 397).

could alone deliver men from corrupting passions.[76] Similarly, some late-seventeenth-century Pindaric poets themselves self-consciously explode, even as they exploit, the poetics of diversion.

In his Pindarics of the 1670s, for example, John Oldham both praises and problematizes alternatives to heroic violence. In several odes Oldham glorifies alternatives to the ultimate violent ambition, the desire for universal conquest that Restoration Englishmen so often perceived and condemned in their foreign enemies.[77] Circa 1675 Oldham eulogizes his deceased friend Charles Morwent for a 'Soul . . . big enough' to 'pity Kings' and to regard 'Empires as poor humble things'; in despising political power, he was as 'Great' as Alexander with his 'boundless mind'. An epithalamion of 1677 recommends that William of Orange, in contrast to his Alexander-like enemy Louis XIV, find in conjugal bliss the true universal monarchy: 'Think You in her far greater Conquests gain, / Then all the Pow'rs of France have from your Country ta'ne, / In her soft Arms let Your Ambition bounded ly, / And fancy there an Universal Monarchy.' A panegyric of 1678 proclaims Ben Jonson the 'Founder' of poetry's 'new Universal Monarchy'.[78] Heroic ambition in each case is fulfilled (or fulfillable) in a peaceful realm, whether personal, conjugal, or literary.

Adopting the Aristotelian identification of heroic virtue as an 'excess' or '*huperbolē*' of virtue while rejecting Aristotle's general identification of ethical virtue with the eschewal of extremes, Oldham praises his peaceful heroes for excess. He declares Morwent a '*Hyperbole*' in whom 'Extreams were joyn'd' and more virtuous than Aristotle's 'scant *Ethics*' could conceive.[79] Scorning the Aristotelian distinction between liberality as a virtuous mean and prodigality as a vicious excess (*Nicomachean Ethics* 4.1), Oldham's

---

[76] See the posthumously published sermon reprinted in *The Cambridge Platonists*, ed. C. A. Patrides (London, 1969), p. 74; cf. Henry More's 1660 declaration that 'diversions' are inadequate against 'passion' in *The Conway Letters: the Correspondence of Anne, Viscountess Conway, Henry More, and their Friends, 1642–1684*, ed. Marjorie Hope Nicolson, rev. Sarah Hutton (Oxford, 1992), p. 165.

[77] On the English fear of continental monarchs' desire for universal monarchy, see Steven Pincus, 'The English Debate over Universal Monarchy', in John Robertson (ed.), *A Union for Empire: Political Thought and the British Union of 1707* (Cambridge, 1995), pp. 37–62.

[78] John Oldham, 'To the Memory of Mr Charles Morwent', lines 387, 389; 'Upon the Marriage of the Prince of Orange with the Lady Mary', lines 64–7; 'Upon the Works of Ben Jonson', line 182 in *The Poems of John Oldham*, ed. Harold F. Brooks and Raman Selden (Oxford, 1987), pp. 302, 280, 199.

[79] 'To . . . Morwent', lines 403–4, 551, in Oldham, *Poems*, pp. 302, 307.

Pindaric elegy on Harman Atwood, composed circa 1677, lauds Atwood's 'holy Prodigality'.[80]

Oldham's cult of excess helps explain his fascination with military conquerors, whose greatness he assumes even when he praises virtuous alternatives: he declares Morwent to be as great, but not greater, than Alexander and he bids William of Orange 'fancy' his spouse the 'Universal Empire' that William (alas!) does not have. Oldham's ode on Homer, presumably also from the mid 1670s, praises 'mighty' Homer not only for his 'bold' and 'boundless' poetic 'Discoveries' (thus echoing Cowley) but also for inspiring Alexander's 'boundless Conquests'.[81] While at odds with the pacific values Oldham espouses elsewhere, this celebration of world conquest expresses Oldham's overall contempt for limits. It also reveals his sense that greatness and violence are more closely linked than Cowley's 'bold' aesthetics of diversion dared fully acknowledge.

Both Oldham's fascination with heroic violence and his sense that 'diversions' are implicated in that violence are most evident in his mock-Pindarics of the late 1670s. An ambivalent member of John Wilmot, earl of Rochester's circle, he composed odes whose libertine speakers laud transgression. While Oldham's Pindaric panegyrics trouble the Cowleyan distinction between peaceful and violent heroism, his greatest mock-Pindaric ode, 'Sardanapalus', not only lampoons but also aggrandizes hedonistic diversion and military heroism as analogous modes of excess.[82] The poem purports to praise an infamously debauched ancient monarch who resembles Charles II and his libertine courtiers.[83] Like retired Cowley, Sardanapalus finds grandeur in scorning heroic ambitions: the 'Great Prince' is content with a 'blest Retreat, / Free from the Trouble, and Impertinence of State' (lines 71–2). Unlike Cowley, however, Sardanapalus undermines the moral distinction between retirement and violent ambition. Rejecting conquerors' 'Restless Ambition' to 'disturb Mankind' in favour of a 'vast Dominion' of mistresses,

---

[80] 'To the Memory of . . . Mr Harman Atwood', line 88, in Oldham, *Poems*, p. 316.

[81] Oldham, 'The Praise of Homer,' lines 13, 38–39, 89 in Oldham, *Poems*, pp. 122–4.

[82] Raman Selden discusses Oldham's poetic response to Rochester's circle as an 'unstable, polysemic . . . discourse which slides between the ironic . . . and the heroic' and as a 'discourse of excess' with 'its own momentum'; see 'Rochester and Oldham: "High Rants in Profaness"', *The Seventeenth Century* 6 (1991), 89–103 (quotations on pp. 91, 93). Selden does not link this unstable 'discourse of excess', as I do, with Oldham's cult of virtuous excess in his Pindaric panegyrics.

[83] Oldham, 'Sardanapalus. Ode', in *Poems*, pp. 344–51.

Sardanapalus made 'C-t the only Field' in which to be 'Great', on the grounds there was no crucial difference between having 'Fought, or F-k'd for Universal Monarchy' (lines 5, 14, 35, 54). The ode thus depicts as equally insatiable libertines like Charles II and imperialists like Louis XIV. By describing how Sardanapalus tries to preserve his 'Sovereign Pr-k's Prerogative' by immolating himself along with a 'mighty Hecatomb' of virgins whom he rapes (lines 93, 169), Oldham invokes the widespread association of Charles's libertinism with violent tyrannical tendencies. He thus depicts the 'luxurious Ease' and courtly 'diversions' celebrated by Behn as tainted with violence.

Yet as Rachel Weil notes, Oldham's poem also grants its male readers, who can identify with Sardanapalus's priapism, pornographic titillation. Oldham's hyperbolic grandiloquence indeed magnifies as well as diminishes his subject by imagining excesses of vast Pindaric disproportions. Weil argues that pornographic indulgence allows Oldham to voice opposition to the court without appearing a Puritanical killjoy.[84] In the light of Oldham's other Pindaric odes, one can add, more generally, that Oldham is able to satirize courtly diversions while fully indulging his own delight in excess.

Like Oldham's mock Pindarics, Dryden's 'Alexander's Feast, or the Power of Music' (1698), the last and perhaps the greatest of Dryden's Pindaric odes, both celebrates grand diversion and questions its viability as an alternative to violence. In his mocking, Oldham-like portrait of Alexander the Great at his revels as drunken, vain, lecherous and violent, Dryden, a Jacobite loyal to the deposed James II, satirizes the new king William III, who was praised as another Alexander by Dryden's poetic contemporaries.[85] Dryden's evocation of one of Alexander's drinking parties focuses on the connection between the military leader's diversions and his destructive belligerence.

The poem demonstrates poetry's power by depicting how the shifting melodies of the bard Timotheus, a 'Mighty Master' (line 93), aroused a gamut of passions in the helpless, carousing Alexander.[86] The ode partially encodes Dryden's fantasy of conquering with

---

[84] See Weil, 'Sometimes a Scepter', pp. 128–36.
[85] On Alexander as William III, see Earl Miner (ed.), *Poems on the Reign of William III*, Augustan Reprint Society no. 166 (Los Angeles, 1974), pp. v–vii. On the ode's Jacobitism, see James Winn, *John Dryden and his World* (New Haven, 1987), pp. 495–6; and Howard Erskine-Hill, *Poetry of Opposition and Revolution: Dryden to Wordsworth* (Oxford, 1996), pp. 40–5.
[86] Dryden, *Poems*, III, 1428–33.

poetry England's despised conqueror. Yet Dryden also mocks and distances himself from Timotheus, and in so doing denigrates the Cowleyan Pindaric project of diversion that Dryden had himself practised in the Killigrew ode. Timotheus begins by flattering Alexander into believing himself a god and ends by inciting him to a shameful rampage in which Alexander torches the Persian capital (lines 25–41, 123–50). Dryden pointedly modifies Plutarch's account of how Alexander slipped from drunken diversion to irrational destruction. As rendered by Evelyn in the 1680s translation of Plutarch for which Dryden provided a dedication and life of the author, Plutarch describes how Alexander 'diverted himself' along with his officers and their mistresses at a drinking party in the Persian capital. According to Plutarch, Alexander's wily mistress, the Athenian courtesan Thais, charmed the drunken Alexander into burning down Persepolis 'in sport'.[87] Dryden, by contrast, has the bard recklessly incite the inebriated conqueror from drunken diversion to destructive frenzy.

Timotheus rouses Alexander and his men by conjuring with his song a vision of Greek Furies demanding revenge upon their Persian enemies:

> Revenge, revenge! *Timotheus* cries,
>   See the Furies arise!
>   See the Snakes that they rear,
>   How they hiss in their Hair,
>   And the Sparkles that flash from their Eyes!
>   Behold a ghastly Band,
>   Each a Torch in his Hand!
> . . . .
> The Princes applaud, with a furious Joy,
> And the king seyz'd a Flambeau, with Zeal to destroy;
>   *Thais* led the Way,
>   To light him to his Prey,
>   And, like another *Hellen*, fir'd another *Troy*.   (lines 131–50)

An allusion to Virgil's *Aeneid*, which Dryden completed translating the year he wrote 'Alexander's Feast', underscores the madness of the scene. Timotheus's evocation of 'Furies' with firebrands, which he uses to instigate 'furious' (mad, raging, excessive) 'Joy' and senseless,

[87] *Plutarch's Lives*, trans. by 'several hands', 5 vols. (1683–6; rpt. London, 1711), IV, 287. For a different account of Dryden's use of Plutarch, see Ruth Smith, 'The Argument and Contexts of Dryden's *Alexander's Feast*', *Studies in English Literature* 18 (1978), 476–7.

fiery destruction, recalls Virgil's description in the *Aeneid* of how the brand-throwing Fury Allecto brought on unnecessary war by inflaming Latins and Trojans alike with furor, a mad passion imaged as fire (*Aeneid* 7.341–482). Yet there is a crucial difference. Virgil treats the war between Romans and Latins as a replay of the tragic Trojan war that nevertheless has a happy ending: the founding of Rome.[88] Dryden treats Alexander's burning of the Persian capital as a bathetic, gratuitous replay of the Trojan war that leads to nothing except, if one remembers Plutarch, regret.

Timotheus plays Allecto the Fury, but for all his horrifying power he only arouses passions in Alexander and his drunken companions to which they are already inclined. The progress of 'Alexander's Feast' from drunken revelry to mindless violence reveals the bitter truth that the theory and aesthetics of diversion since Montaigne had repressed. Timotheus triumphantly concludes by inciting the revellers to 'furious Joy' because he recognizes that for Alexander and his irascible soldiers, violence is the highest, most intense pleasure. Sixteenth-century political theorists like Jean Bodin and Giovanni Botero advised rulers to wage wars to occupy their irascible subjects, who would otherwise disrupt the state. Botero described such wars as a 'diversion' ('diversione') for 'peccant humors' ('humori peccanti').[89] Intent on promoting peaceful diversions, Montaigne denounced those like Botero who recommended diverting 'peccant Humours' ('humeurs peccantes') with wars.[90] While early in the Restoration Dryden himself had hailed the end of internecine strife as a glorious opportunity to turn on 'forraign Foes' (*Astraea Redux*, line 118, *Poems*, I, 19), other Restoration authors committed to peaceful diversions followed Montaigne in denouncing violent ones, which they conveniently associated with foreign imperial powers. In the second part of *The Siege of Rhodes* (1663), for example, Davenant had his Turkish sultan Soleyman lament his need for 'new Towns to Sack, new Foes to Kill' as the 'accurs'd diversion' of his belligerent people who would, if not so engaged, destroy 'peace / . . . at home'. In an essay published in 1680, Temple, a major proponent of peaceful diversions, sardonically noted that Louis XIV's France continually sought 'some

---

[88] See David Quint, *Epic and Empire: Politics and Generic from Virgil to Milton* (Princeton, 1993), pp. 50–96.

[89] Jean Bodin, *Les six livres de la république*, 6 vols. (1576; rpt. of 1596 edition, Paris, 1986), V, 137–42; Giovanni Botero, *Ragione di stato* (Venice, 1589), p. 232.

[90] Montaigne, *Essays*, trans. Cotton, II, 409; III, 51; *Les Essais*, I, 683; II, 831.

war or other' to 'amuse' its people, who might otherwise resent 'their condition at home'.[91] Dryden's Jacobite poem implies that the English and their imperial monarch are now as much attracted to violent forms of diversion as the most belligerent empires in history.

In provoking his audience to the violence to which they are prone, Timotheus plays not only Allecto the Fury but also the daring Pindaric poet. In 1677 Dryden defended the 'boldness' of images in Cowley's Pindaric odes in terms of Longinus's celebration of *phantasia* (*On the Sublime*, 15) or (in Dryden's rendering) 'Imaging', the sublime method by which a poet or orator vividly sees, and makes his audience see, what he describes.[92] 'Alexander's Feast' dramatizes the dark side of such sublime Pindaric power. Timotheus's vision of slain Greeks as 'Furies' crying out for revenge upon the Persians recalls not only Virgil but also Longinus's first example of sublime *phantasia*, the Aeschylean Orestes's mad vision of his dead mother and the Furies, with their horrible snakes and bloodshot eyes, demanding vengeance (*On the Sublime*, 15.1). Longinus notes how such visualization, combined with a call to action, can enslave an audience (*On the Sublime*, 15.9), and Timotheus's visualization of 'Furies', combined with his cry for revenge, contagiously enslaves his audience with 'furious' passion. While Dryden's Killigrew ode had optimistically posited bold poetic diversion as an alternative to the violence of the great, his Alexander ode breaks down the distinction between the poet's sublime diversion and brutal violence. Thus Dryden bids farewell to the Cowleyan project of setting Pindaric diversions *against* the violence of the times.[93]

After Dryden it is perhaps not surprising that Cowley's Pindaric project of celebrating heroic or grandly anti-heroic diversion increasingly came to seem hollow and was gradually abandoned. Edward Young's preface to 'Imperium Pelagi' (1729), his lengthy series of Pindaric celebrations of British commercial empire, recalls Cowley

---

[91] William Davenant, *The Siege of Rhodes: a Critical Edition*, ed. Ann-Mari Hedbäck (Stockholm, 1973), p. 66 (Part 2, II.ii.53–64); Temple, 'A Survey of . . . Constitutions and Interests . . . in the Year 1671' (1680) in *Works*, II, 225.

[92] Dryden, *Works*, XII, 93–4.

[93] In 1696 Dryden dismissively compared farces to grotesque paintings that 'divert' the 'vulgar'. While alluding to Davenant's *Gondibert* preface on the political usefulness of theatrical diversions, Dryden distinguished such diversions from the 'just Images of Nature' that provided the true 'pleasures of the Mind' (Dryden, *Works*, XX, 56). Alexander/William III and the 'vulgar' complicit in his reign are the high and low audiences that the post-Glorious Revolution Dryden has given up trying to 'divert'.

by declaring the would-be modern Pindaric poet's necessary independence from his Greek model. Within the poetic series itself,
Young contrasts his heroic, patriotic theme with the 'diversion light
and glory vain' of Pindar's athletes. Instead of 'diversion light',
Young's Pindaric project could be uncharitably dubbed 'diversion
ponderous'. Young exalts merchants 'o'er proudest heroes' for
providing material 'blessings' rather than wars' 'pain'. Despite
Oldham and Dryden's debunking of the project of heroic diversion,
Young's celebration of merchants as new forms of peaceful heroes
envisages the Pindaric ode in Cowleyan fashion as diverting ambitious energies from passionate bellicosity into sublime beneficence.
Yet Young's attempt to rescue trade from 'the shore of Prose' fails to
reach sublime crests.[94]

Early-eighteenth-century aesthetics continues the project of diversion in a more urbane, 'polite', less grandiose fashion. With allusions
to the civil war of the previous century, in the early 1710s Joseph
Addison presents his *Spectator* papers as 'draw[ing] Men's Minds off
from the Bitterness of Party, and furnish[ing] them with Subjects of
Discourse that may be treated without Warmth or Passion'; perusing
Addison's essays, the reader 'diverts himself with . . . innocent
Amusements'. Addison's 'Pleasures of the Imagination', his major
contribution to eighteenth-century aesthetic theory, are designed to
make 'the Sphere' of 'innocent Pleasures as wide as possible' so that
Addison's cultured reader can distinguish himself or herself from the
mob whose 'every Diversion . . . is at the Expence of . . . Virtue'.
Contemplating the sublime 'greatness' both of nature and 'vast'
artistic imaginations provides one such innocent diversion. Addison
regards the sublime, however, as something his contemporaries
should admire but not attempt. He praises Pindar's 'vast Conceptions' and 'noble Sallies of Imagination' but condemns his modern
imitators as 'Men of a sober and moderate Fancy' who misunder-
stand their talents and their age.[95] According to the cultural arbiter

---

[94] *The Poetical Works of Edward Young*, ed. John Mitford, 2 vols. (London, 1896), ɪɪ, 335–93
(citations from ɪɪ, 336, 357, 372).

[95] *The Spectator*, ed. Donald F. Bond, 5 vols. (Oxford, 1965), ɪɪ, 128, 519, ɪɪɪ, 536, 538–40, 564–7.
Robert Phiddian argues that Addison's concern with diversion exemplifies his culture's
'central anxiety' concerning the 'chaos of the previous century' in *Swift's Parody* (Cambridge,
1995), pp. 24–30. Addison's praise of innocent diversions is part of the *Spectator* 's general
programme for the polite refinement of otherwise dangerous passions discussed in John
Brewer, *The Pleasures of the Imagination: English Culture in the Eighteenth Century* (New York, 1997),
pp. 104–6.

Addison, he and his readers live in a modest age of criticism and must find exciting diversion through contact with an Other (nature, the ancients) rather than in themselves. The age of sublime heroes, even the pacific heroes celebrated by Pindaric poets like Cowley and his followers, is over.

CHAPTER 8

Plays as property, 1660–1710[1]

Paulina Kewes

In pious times, ere Authors did begin, before to plagiarise was made a sin . . .[2]

Christopher Ricks, 'Plagiarism'

Was there really a time when there were no authors and when plagiarism was not judged an offence? In one sense, as Christopher Ricks has recently reminded us, ever since classical antiquity authors have asserted the right to their compositions, protesting vociferously against plagiarism as did, in the first century AD, the Roman poet Martial.[3] 'Thus may we perceive', wrote Sir Thomas Browne in the middle of the seventeenth century, 'that the Ancients were but men, even like our selves. The practice of transcription in our daies was no monster in theirs: Plagiarie had not its nativitie with printing; but began in times when thefts were difficult, and the paucity of books scarce wanted that invention.'[4] Yet the apparent similarity between the past and the present can be deceptive. For even if the notion of plagiarism as the wrongful appropriation of another writer's work has

---

[1] I am grateful to Rob Hume and Blair Worden for comments, advice and criticism; and to Oxford University Press for permission to reproduce, in an altered form, some material from my *Authorship and Appropriation*.

[2] 1998 British Academy Lecture, in *Proceedings of the British Academy*, 97 (Oxford, 1998), pp. 149–68, at p. 156.

[3] 'Plagiarism', pp. 155–6. Ricks quotes William Cartwright's translation of Martial's Epigrams i.67 which begins: 'Th'art out, vile Plagiary . . .'. See Cartwright's *Comedies, Tragi-Comedies, With other Poems* (London, 1651), p. 253. That volume contains commendatory poems 'To Mr *Thomas Killigrew* on his two Playes, the Prisoners, and *Claracilla*' and 'To the Memory of *Ben Johnson*. Laureat', which engage with the issue of authorial self-sufficiency. The former praises Killigrew's plays for 'here no small stoln Parcels slyly lurk / Nor are your Tablets such *Mosaique* Work, / The Web, and Woof, are both your own' (p. 259); the latter uneasily excuses Jonson's borrowings from the classics: 'What though thy culling Muse did rob the store / Of Greek and Latine Gardens, to bring o'r / Plants to thy Native Soyl? their Vertues were / Improv'd far more, by being planted here . . . . / Thefts thus become Just works . . .' (p. 315).

[4] *Pseudodoxia Epidemica: or, Enquiries into Very many Received Tenets, And commonly Presumed Truths*, 2nd edn (London, 1650), p. 16. See also the marginal note to this passage: 'The Antiquity, and some notable instances of Plagianisme, that is, of transcribing or filching Authours' (p. 16).

been with us at least since Martial's time, conceptions of authorship and attitudes toward appropriation have changed significantly over the last two millennia, the advent of copyright law in the eighteenth century being but one manifestation of the change. However 'regressive' this state of affairs may appear to champions of the author's moral rights such as Ricks, the condition of authorship in Shakespeare's time – when practices of appropriation and collaboration were widespread and generally unremarked – was such as to offer little, if any, recognition of the individual dramatist's right in his work. So when and how did authors gain the moral claim to what they wrote? When and how did imaginative works come to be regarded as the intellectual property of their authors? The transformation from Renaissance conceptions of authorship toward modern ones, I shall argue, was the product of the half century after the Stuart Restoration in 1660. In that transformation, the rising commercial and cultural stature of the dramatic profession was the driving force.

I

In the modern world, both the right to perform a play and the right to publish it belong to the dramatist. For example, the copyright notice prefaced to the London edition of Arthur Miller's latest full-length play, *Broken Glass*, stipulates that 'The author has asserted his moral rights.' It is accompanied by an additional note of 'caution':

Professionals and amateurs are hereby warned that this play is subject to a royalty. It is protected under the copyright laws of the United States of America, and of all countries covered by the International Copyright Union . . . and of all countries covered by the Pan-American Copyright Convention and the Universal Copyright Convention, and of all countries with which the United States has reciprocal copyright relations. All rights, including professional, amateur, motion picture, recitation, lecturing, public reading, radio broadcasting, television, and the rights of translation into foreign languages, are strictly reserved. Particular emphasis is laid upon the question of readings, permission for which must be secured from the author's agent in writing.[5]

The modern author's right of ownership in a play extends beyond the legally sanctioned control of its reproduction: he or she enjoys moral authority over and property in the dramatic work which neither performance nor publication can alienate.

[5] (London, 1994, repr. 1995).

The contrast with Shakespeare's day is striking. The practices of the early-modern theatrical marketplace denied the dramatist any enduring association with, let alone enduring reward from, a play. The provider of a script ceded all further rights in it upon the receipt of a fee from a theatrical company which thereafter owned it. Acting companies tended to withhold their scripts from the press.[6] To this end they inserted prohibitive clauses into their contracts with the writers attached to them and frequently appealed to the Lord Chamberlain for protection of their property in the scripts they put on. Despite these safeguards many plays found their way into print. Irrespective of how the publisher obtained a copy (whether from a mercenary actor, from an unscrupulous playwright, or from a company who judged the piece no longer worthy of being protected), the right to publish it remained his once he had entered the title on the books of the Stationers' Company. So acting companies and publishers, not playwrights, were the 'owners' of plays, and lasting beneficiaries of performance and print publication, respectively. The playwright had virtually no control over the dissemination of his work on the stage or in print. His identity usually remained unknown to the audience and, if the play was published, his name was frequently omitted from the title-page.[7]

After the Restoration, the division of property rights in plays changed radically. That change was a direct consequence of the institution of a theatrical duopoly by the king in 1660, when two patent companies, the King's and the Duke's, were established. Each

---

[6] On the restrictions upon publication before 1642 see G. E. Bentley, *The Profession of Dramatist in Shakespeare's Time, 1590–1642* (Princeton, 1971), pp. 264–92; Stephen Orgel, 'What is a Text?', *Research Opportunities in Renaissance Drama* 24 (1981), 3–6; Joseph Loewenstein, 'The Script in the Marketplace', *Representations* 12 (1985), 101–14; Timothy Murray, 'From Foul Sheets to Legitimate Model: Antitheatre, Text, Ben Jonson', *New Literary History* 14 (1983), 641–64. For a hypothesis that Shakespeare refrained from publishing his plays because as house playwright, sharer and actor with the King's Men, he subscribed to the company ethos in terms of which his scripts were company property see Richard Dutton, *Licensing, Censorship and Authorship in Early Modern England* (Basingstoke, 2000). I am grateful to Professor Dutton for sending me a typescript of his book in advance of publication.

[7] See Bentley, *Profession of Dramatist*; Orgel, 'What is a Text?'; Peter Stallybrass, 'Shakespeare, the Individual, and the Text', in Lawrence Grossberg, Cary Nelson and Paula Treichler (eds.), *Cultural Studies* (New York, 1992), pp. 593–610. The near-anonymity of professional playwrights was to a large extent a function of the collaborative nature of contemporary playwriting. See Jeffrey Masten, *Textual Intercourse: Collaboration, Authorship, and Sexualities in Renaissance Drama* (Cambridge, 1997); Kewes, *Authorship and Appropriation: Writing for the Stage in England, 1660–1710* (Oxford, 1998), pp. 130ff. and Appendix A.

company had exclusive rights to its own repertory.[8] The property rights in old drama were confirmed in successive royal grants which discouraged the piracy of plays assigned to the competition. The King's Company under Thomas Killigrew secured rights to virtually all worthwhile Elizabethan, Jacobean and Caroline scripts by sustaining their claim to the old King's Men's plays.[9] The Duke's Company led by Sir William Davenant had no repertory to fall back on. He was constrained to petition for rights to perform at least some pre-Commonwealth scripts, including his own early plays, in order to keep his theatre open. So unequal a division of older drama between the two patent companies stimulated the production of new plays in the 1660s. The emergent pattern of competition boosted the demand for fresh scripts and furnished a favourable environment for the re-emergence of professional writing for the stage after an eighteen-year hiatus.

So far as we know, no official document regulated the rights to new plays. Yet the universal understanding seems to have been that a script became the property of the company that first mounted it. Its provider, whether a professional attached to a company or a free-lance writer, was regularly awarded the net profits of the third night. Unlike early-seventeenth-century professionals,[10] Restoration play-wrights were not entitled to a fee for a script prior to performance. Under this system of remuneration, the author's financial reward was directly dependent upon the reception of the play by the audience.

---

[8] For discussions of the repertory of early Restoration acting companies see Gunnar Sorelius, 'The Rights of the Restoration Theatre Companies in the Older Drama', *Studia Neophilologica* 37 (1965), 174–89, and 'The Early History of the Restoration Theatre: Some Problems Reconsidered', *Theatre Notebook* 33 (1979), 52–61; John Freehafer, 'The Formation of the London Patent Companies in 1660', *Theatre Notebook* 20 (1965), 6–30; Leslie Hotson, *The Commonwealth and Restoration Stage* (Cambridge, MA, 1928), pp. 197–280; Robert D. Hume, 'Securing a Repertory: Plays on the London Stage 1660–5', in Antony Coleman and Antony Hammond (eds.), *Poetry and Drama, 1570–1700: Essays in Honour of Harold F. Brooks* (London, 1981), pp. 156–72.

[9] In January 1669, the King's Company received a grant affirming their property in 108 of these old plays. The titles in question were listed in 'A Catalogue of part of his Ma^tes Servants Playes as they were formerly acted at the Blackfryers & now allowed of to his Ma^tes Servants at ye New Theatre' (LC 5/12, pp. 212–13).

[10] In Shakespeare's time, professional playwrights attached to an acting company received a salary and a benefit which comprised the net proceeds from one day in the play's initial run, usually the second or third. Professional playwrights who had no fixed attachment to a company were granted a fee upon delivery of the script, though cash advances were common. By the early seventeenth century, they too had been granted a benefit. For an account of pre-Restoration playwrights' earnings and contractual obligations see Bentley, *Profession of Dramatist*, pp. 88–144.

That writer stood to earn most whose work they enjoyed most and were readiest to pay to see.

Dramatists had a pecuniary interest in filling the theatres, especially on their benefit night. Great bills advertised premières and benefit performances, but neither the bills nor, so far as we know, the spoken announcement of the next day's offering given out in the theatre mentioned the name of the author. (The unprecedented publicity accompanying the revival of Congreve's *The Double-Dealer* in March 1699 drew from Dryden the tart comment: 'the printing an Authours name, in a Play bill, is a new manner of proceeding, at least in England'.)[11] So playwrights alerted friends and acquaintances to the première and the date of the benefit performance. They also sold tickets, sometimes at higher than standard prices. The author acted as script-writer, director and marketing agent. His or her personal stake in the success of the show was boosted in the 1690s with the introduction of a second benefit, on the sixth night of the opening run. After 1700 dramatists normally received the proceeds from every third performance throughout at least the first nine nights if the play lived that long.

The later-seventeenth-century playwright was no longer an employee of the company, as most of the pre-Commonwealth playwrights had been, but an entrepreneur and an investor of sorts. Although his or her long-term income from the theatre may not have been as stable over the years as that of early-seventeenth-century professionals, the author's potential profit from any one play could well have exceeded theirs, not least because the practice of collaborative playwriting which entailed the division of profit among the contributors was now virtually defunct. The loss of what we would today call greater job-security was compensated for by an unprecedented opportunity for a speculative investment of one's talent, time, and skill in the hope of earning an equally unprecedented financial return.

The growing social and economic visibility of professional playwrights was cause and consequence of the evolution of benefit arrangements. The rise in the cultural status of dramatic authorship, too, was stimulated by the reconstitution of the theatrical marketplace after the Restoration. A development of crucial importance was the acquisition by playwrights of the unrestricted right to publish

---

[11] *The Letters of John Dryden With Letters Addressed to Him*, ed. Charles E. Ward (Durham, NC, 1942), p. 113.

their scripts. In the context of the post-1660 theatrical duopoly, publication in no way endangered a company's performance rights. When printed, a play did not fall into the public domain, for a rival company was barred from mounting it. We may suppose that the management felt no urge to retain control over the reproduction of the manuscript, for even attached professionals such as John Dryden and Thomas Shadwell seem to have been free to have their plays printed. Their contracts presumably contained no provisos comparable to the one to which Richard Brome had been obliged to subscribe earlier in the century in his contract with Salisbury Court in August of 1638, which explicitly denied him the right to sell his play-scripts to a bookseller.[12]

After the Restoration, playwrights were at liberty to sell their copies to publishers. In the absence of statutory authorial copyright, the transaction of sale confirmed the playwright as owner, that is, as the party *de facto* entitled to dispose of the copy. The author's property in the manuscript also emerged as distinct from the rights to performance vested in a theatrical company. Although the sums of money involved were apparently too insignificant for the actors to mind, the payment from the bookseller did provide the author with a supplement to the uncertain theatrical benefit.[13] Moreover, the printed play enabled the playwright to insert a dedicatory address to a wealthy and generous patron, or one with the power to be of assistance in other ways. The public nature of the commendation accompanying the gift and imprinted in each copy of the playbook endowed it with permanence and prestige.[14] In the earlier part of the

---

[12] The articles of the contract survive in a suit brought against Brome by his employers. See Ann Haaker, 'The Plague, the Theater, and the Poet', *Renaissance Drama*, n.s. 1 (1968), 283–306. G. E. Bentley has conjectured that such contracts probably bound earlier attached professionals (*Profession of Dramatist*, pp. 112ff).

[13] For sample payments see Shirley Strum Kenny, 'The Publication of Plays', in Robert D. Hume (ed.), *The London Theatre World, 1660–1800* (Carbondale, 1980), pp. 309–36, at pp. 310–11. For a more detailed documentation of dramatists' earnings see Judith Milhous and Robert D. Hume, 'Playwrights' Remuneration in Eighteenth-Century London', *Harvard Library Bulletin*, n.s.10 (1999), 3–91. I am grateful to the authors for sending me their draft in advance of publication.

[14] For essays on late-seventeenth-century patronage of the drama see Deborah C. Payne, 'Patronage and the Dramatic Marketplace under Charles I and II', *Yearbook of English Studies* 21 (1991), 137–52; 'The Restoration Dramatic Dedication as Symbolic Capital', *Studies in Eighteenth-Century Culture* 20 (1990), 27–42; ' "And Poets Shall by Patron-Princes Live": Aphra Behn and Patronage', in Mary Anne Schofield and Cecilia Macheski (eds.), *Curtain Calls: British and American Women and the Theater, 1660–1820* (Athens, OH, 1991), pp. 105–19. On women as patrons see David Roberts, *The Ladies: Female Patronage of Restoration Drama, 1660–1700* (Oxford, 1989).

century, John Fletcher had enjoyed the munificence of the Hunting-dons without ever having dedicated a published play to his patrons.[15] For the late-seventeenth-century playwright, by contrast, the relationship between patronage and print was one of absolute interdependence: the favour of the great had to be solicited and its receipt celebrated through the public medium of the printed epistle. About half of the plays published in the period were in fact prefaced with elaborate panegyrics designed to elicit a financial bonus, however modest.[16]

Late-seventeenth-century dramatists – no longer semi-anonymous script-writers or mere suppliers of live entertainment, as their predecessors in the earlier period had been – were increasingly thought of as individuals who carried their own identity and authority, and from whom the printed artifact originated. The author's stake in his or her script was implicit, as we have seen, both in the benefit arrangement with the theatrical company and in the bargain with the bookseller. Yet this ownership was not officially recognized by law or demonstrable upon display of a deed of entitlement. Once the benefit day was past and the play entered in the Stationers' Register, the performance rights belonged to the company and the right in copy to the publisher. The playwright had no further claim to either. The company might consult an experienced writer such as Dryden about some details of production or casting when a piece of his was to be revived; and the publisher, swayed by the commercial appeal of novelty, might countenance authorial revisions and alterations prior to bringing out a new edition. But the dramatist had no control over the future fortunes of a play on the stage or in print.

Notwithstanding the lack of further rewards following performance and publication, by the end of the seventeenth century playwrights had come to enjoy substantially improved circumstances. The patent duopoly and the enforcement of exclusive performance rights by the Lord Chamberlain had created conditions in which theatrical companies permitted writers to sell scripts to publishers for their own profit. Regular publication had in the course of a

---

[15] G. E. Bentley has delineated the pattern of publication of Fletcher's plays in his *Profession of Dramatist*, pp. 275–9. For an account of Fletcher's relations with his benefactors see Gordon McMullan, *The Politics of Unease in the Plays of John Fletcher* (Amherst, 1994), pp. 11–36.

[16] Stanley L. Archer, 'The Epistle Dedicatory in Restoration Drama', *Restoration and Eighteenth-Century Theatre Research* 10 (1971), 8–13, at p. 8.

generation helped to give plays the status of literature. Playwriting could now be taken seriously by writers with literary pretensions. Of the other genres open to them, the novel was far from respectable, while poetry, though respectable, was not a paying proposition. 'All other Poetry (Dramatick only excepted,) turns to so little Account', observed George Powell, actor-*cum*-playwright, 'that the Toyl's as hopeless as labouring for the Philosopher's Stone; the Undertaker is certain to gain nothing by it'.[17]

Not until 1710 were authors formally recognized as legitimate copyright holders by Queen Anne's Act for the Encouragement of Learning. Not until 1774 were the provisions of the Act clarified in courts, and the claims of publishers to perpetual copyright demolished. Yet between 1660 and 1710 a quiet revolution had occurred. Plays had become valuable commodities. A single benefit in the small playhouses of the 1660s is unlikely to have yielded more than £50. Two or even three benefits in the larger theatres of the years around 1700 could amount to as much as £150 or even £200. A fee from a publisher added anything from £10 to £50 or more.

Thus rising profits and the growing prestige of dramatic poetry combined to elevate the status of playwriting at the century's end. That development, we shall now see, took place against a background of mounting public discussion of the status and methods of playwriting.[18]

II

The emergent notion of the author as owner of his or her work was more conspicuous in respect of drama than it was in poetry and prose fiction. One reason why late-seventeenth-century debates over literary property focused on plays rather than on poems or novellas was the greater economic viability of playwriting. The potential earning power of theatrical scripts, whether 'original', 'adapted', or 'stolen', meant that the question of the propriety of reaping profits from someone else's labour was particularly pressing with regard to writing for the stage. But there was another, perhaps more important

---

[17] Dedication to *The Treacherous Brothers* (1690), sig. A2ᵛ.

[18] For an account of the status of playwriting and attitudes toward literary borrowing in the eighteenth century see my '"A Play, which I presume to call *original*": Appropriation, Creative Genius and Eighteenth-Century Playwriting', *Studies in the Literary Imagination* 34 (2001), 17–47.

reason. It was in relation to drama that the processes of appropriation, adaptation and plagiarism were most apparent and easiest to demonstrate. With vast numbers of old and new plays available in printed form, the reliance of a recent play on a source or sources could be ascertained by those keen to do so, though, of course, the very urge to perform such a comparative analysis was a novel one. What, then, were the areas in which the incipient concern about the propriety of appropriation manifested itself? And what were the implications of that concern for the conception of dramatic authorship in the period?

In the Renaissance, the practice of appropriation had gone generally unremarked. By contrast, the later seventeenth century witnessed an unprecedented surge of interest in matters of authorship and attribution of plays, and a concomitant preoccupation with the legitimacy of literary borrowing. When, in 1582, Stephen Gosson published his blast against the theatre, *Playes Confuted in five Actions*, he treated the use of various kinds of sources by playwrights as a matter of course: 'the *Palace of pleasure*, the *Golden Asse*, the *Aethiopan historie*, *Amadis of Fraunce*, the *Rounde table*, *baudie Comedies in Latine, French, Italian*, and *Spanish*, have beene throughly ransackt, to furnish the Playe houses in London'.[19] What he objected to was not plagiarism but the fact that the borrowed materials made the resulting plays irreverent, dissolute and obscene, and thus the more likely to corrupt the morals of those who saw them. When John Cotgrave, in the preface to his *The English Treasury of Wit and Language* (1655), looked back on pre-Civil War drama from the perspective of the Cromwellian Commonwealth, he too referred to the multiplicity of sources, notably foreign ones, which had gone into the making of past dramatic scripts. Bent on combating the anti-theatrical prejudice typified by such as Gosson, William Prynne and the Puritan authorities of his day, Cotgrave drew attention to the appropriative character of Renaissance plays so as to buttress the erudition, learning and refinement of those who produced them:

And indeed the Drammatick Poem seemes to me (and many of my friends, better able to judge then I) to have beene lately too much slighted, not onely by such, whose Talent falls short in understanding, but by many that have had a tolerable portion of Wit, who through a stiffe and obstinate prejudice, have (in neglecting things of this nature) lost the benefit of many rich and

---

[19] (London, 1582), sig. D5^{v}.

usefull Observations, not duly considering, or believing, that the Framers of
them, were the most fluent and redundant Wits that this age (or I think any
other) ever knew, and many of them so able Schollers, and Linguists, as they
have culled the choicest Flowers out of the greater number of Greeke,
Latin, Italian, Spanish, and French Authors (Poets especially) to embellish
and enrich the English Scene withall, besides, almost a prodigious
accrewment of their own luxuriant fancies.[20]

Far from compromising their creative faculties, he suggests, the
reliance of pre-civil war dramatists on materials drawn from classical
antiquity and from continental literature enhances the quality of
their plays. Yet Cotgrave stops short of specifying the sources
Shakespeare and his contemporaries had used. He neither attributes
the dramatic extracts which he prints in his anthology to their
authors, nor provides the titles of the plays from which they derive.

By the time of the Restoration, the climate had changed sufficiently for anthologists, publishers and writers to become more
circumspect and fastidious in matters of attribution and acknowledgement of sources. When, in 1662 and 1673 respectively, Henry
Marsh and Francis Kirkman published their collections of drolls
(short pieces which had been performed in taverns and at fairs in the
years when legitimate theatres had been suppressed) called *The Wits,
or Sport upon Sport*, Parts I and II, they inserted catalogues listing the
source-plays of the drolls (though, for the most part, they omitted the
names of their authors).[21] In the following decades acknowledge-
ments of sources and extended justifications of appropriation by
playwrights become increasingly common. By the late 1680s and
early 1690s, we encounter substantial literary-critical projects such as
Gerard Langbaine's *Momus Triumphans: or The Plagiaries of the English
Stage* (1688) and *An Account of the English Dramatick Poets* (1691), which
set out to list and attribute all plays ever written in English, and to

---

[20] See his *The English Treasury of Wit and Language, Collected Out of the most, and best of our English
Drammatick Poems; Methodically Digested into Commonplaces For Generall Use* (London, 1655), sig.
A3[r].
[21] Marsh's *The Wits, or Sport upon Sport. In Select Pieces of Drollery, Digested into Scenes by way of
Dialogue . . . Part I* (London, 1662) includes '*A Catalogue of the severall Droll-Humours, from what
Plays collected, and in what page to be found in this Book*', sig. A4[v]; Kirkman's *The Wits, or, Sport upon
Sport. Being a Curious Collection of several Drols and Farces* (London, 1673) uses the catalogue of
sources as an advertising ploy: 'If you please to Turn over the Leaf, you may find from what
Plays these several Droll Humours are Collected: and if you please to come to my Shop
being the Next Door to the Sign of the Princes Arms, in Saint Pauls Church-Yard, you may
be Furnished; not only with all those Plays themselves, but also with all the English Stage
Playes that were ever yet Plaid.'

detail the materials on which they were based.[22] More than that, Langbaine's aim was to discuss and circumscribe the proprieties of dramatic appropriation, and to stigmatize as plagiarists those who, in his view, have transgressed against them.

Langbaine's campaign against literary thieves, especially John Dryden, has been seen as obsessive, and as uncharacteristic of the period as a whole. However, the concerns which Langbaine's work exemplifies had grown steadily since the Stuart Restoration in 1660, and are apparent in several distinct kinds of textual records, both manuscript and printed ones, which predate his compilations. Those include: statements by playwrights prefaced to editions of their plays and included in prologues, epilogues and personal correspondence; critical projects such as Dryden's *Essay of Dramatick Poesie*; literary journals; dramatic burlesques and satirical vignettes of playwrights in comic drama; and a succession of poems and prose pieces written in the tradition of the so-called 'Sessions of the Poets'.

Dryden's pronouncements on literary borrowing are well-known and have been the subject of intense scholarly scrutiny.[23] I have elsewhere analysed the numerous prefatory defences against charges of plagiarism which from the 1660s onward were mounted not only by Dryden but by Shadwell, Settle, Behn, Otway, Crowne, Cibber, Tate and other playwrights.[24] In this chapter I shall focus on those kinds of evidence that have so far received little critical attention, notably the figurations of plagiarism in plays and in verse and prose satire.

Those figurations are present from early in the Restoration. The first new burlesque, Sir William Davenant's *The Play-house to be Let* (1663), evinces an almost obsessive preoccupation with novelty. As its title suggests, the piece humorously depicts repertory decisions that have to be taken by actors intent on making money by renting out their theatre in the Long Vacation. The focal question is: What is

---

[22] For a detailed discussion of Langbaine's catalogues of plays and his conception of plagiarism and appropriation, see my *Authorship and Appropriation*, ch. 3: 'Plagiarism and Property', pp. 96–129.

[23] See for example Robert D. Hume, *Dryden's Criticism* (Ithaca, NY, 1970); David Bruce Kramer, *The Imperial Dryden: The Poetics of Appropriation in Seventeenth-Century England* (Athens, GA, 1994); Jennifer Brady, 'Dryden and Negotiations of Literary Succession and Precession', in Earl Miner and Jennifer Brady (eds.), *Literary Transmission and Authority: Dryden and Other Writers* (Cambridge, 1993), pp. 27–54; Michael Werth Gelber, *The Just and the Lively: the Literary Criticism of John Dryden* (Manchester, 1999).

[24] *Authorship and Appropriation*, ch. 2: 'The Proprieties of Appropriation', pp. 32–95. See also Laura J. Rosenthal, *Playwrights and Plagiarists in Early Modern England: Gender, Authorship, Literary Property* (Ithaca, NY, 1996); Brean S. Hammond, *Professional Imaginative Writing in England, 1670–1740: 'Hackney for Bread'* (Oxford, 1997).

most likely to appeal to audiences? The answer that Davenant's skit gives is that the most promising course is to present something novel, surprising, and full of variety. However, as the allusions to early Restoration translations from the French and Spanish indicate, such novelties may well include redactions of foreign plays or travesties of previously produced scripts.[25] *The Play-house to be Let* was itself an instance of such a potpourri, recycling as it did Davenant's own earlier operatic shows, *The History of Sir Francis Drake* and *The Cruelty of the Spaniards in Peru*, as well as Molière's *Sganarelle, ou le Cocu Imaginaire* and the story of Antony and Cleopatra.

Even though *The Play-house to be Let* was no more than a makeshift concoction, Sir William is almost certain to have claimed the author's benefit for it. That surmise is confirmed by the play's portrayal of a Poet who advises the players to put on his rendition of heroic tragedy in 'Verse Burlesque' or, as he also calls it, 'the Travesti' and 'the Mock-heroique'. The Poet's suggestion is accepted, and in return for putting the show on, he is promised the profit of 'the second day' (Act I, pp. 75, 76). Albeit in a comic vein, Davenant's play raises the issue of remuneration for a script which has little claim to originality.

By the time the most renowned dramatic burlesque of the Restoration, the duke of Buckingham's *The Rehearsal*, was produced in December 1671, the plagiaristic playwright who preys on the intellectual productions of others had become a stock figure. Buckingham's portrait of Bayes–Dryden – a hack who 'transverses' and 'transproses' sundry texts, who eavesdrops on gentlemenly conversations so as to seize *bon mots* that he might recycle in comic repartee, and who plunders a 'book of *Drama Common places*' to make up for his creative aridity[26] – proved so memorable and influential as to spawn a number of dramatic and nondramatic imitations. One of the earliest theatrical offshoots of *The Rehearsal* was W. M.'s *The Female Wits: or, The Triumvirate of Poets At Rehearsal*, staged by the Patent Company in 1696. Its subtitle a deliberate allusion to the venerable triumvirate of Shakespeare, Jonson and Fletcher, *The Female Wits* sets out to debunk the literary pretensions of three women playwrights,

---

25 *The Play-house to be Let*, in *The Works of Sr William Davenant* (London, 1673), Act I, pp. 75–7. See also the Prologue: 'Since you affect things new, what I'm to say, / Shall be as great a Novel as our Play, / Custom would have me speak a Prologue now, / But that we may intire adherence show / To Novelty (which in the Mode of Plays / Like soveraign Nature over Custom sways) . . .' (p. 67, second pagination).

26 George Villiers, second duke of Buckingham, *The Rehearsal*, ed. D. E. L. Crane (Durham, 1976), esp. 1.i.84–138.

Delarivière Manley (Marsilia), Mary Pix (Mrs Wellfed) and Catherine Trotter (Calista), whose plays enjoyed substantial success in the preceding theatrical season. As was the case with Bayes, the abiding impression is that despite their repeated professions of self-sufficiency and creative independence, these women are unable to produce a script without filching ideas and lines from earlier drama. 'Mr *Praiseall*, is not that Simile well carried on?', asks Marsilia, eagerly fishing for a compliment from her admirer. 'To an Extreamity of Thought, Madam', replies he, only to whisper to the audience: 'But I think 'tis stole.'[27] Marsilia is further mocked for her plan to revise Jonson's *Catiline*, which argues her both artistically sterile and ridiculously vain.[28]

The Rehearsal became a long-term favourite, being not only frequently revived but also giving rise to a line of 'rehearsal' plays, many of them taking up its critique of derivative play-making.[29] Yet the appearance of another plagiary in a closet play by a clergyman and amateur writer Robert Wild corroborates the pervasiveness of anxieties about appropriative playwriting. Though it found its way into print after Wild's death, *The Benefice* probably dates from *c.* 1641. In it Pedanto, A School-Master, is 'making a *Play*'. Too dull to invent the plot for, and to write up the dialogue of, this piece himself, Pedanto 'hath all the Play Books in the Country to help him. Like the Cuckooe, he sucks other's Eggs: Here he steals a Word, and there he filches a Line'.[30] As Wild's play shows, not only professional dramatists but also amateurs could be satirized for their lack of invention and a propensity to pilfer.

In common with those of Bayes–Dryden and Marsilia–Manley, many other satirical portrayals of playwrights as thieves in Restoration and eighteenth-century plays caricature living individuals. The victims include Sir Robert Howard in Thomas Shadwell's *The Sullen Lovers* (1668); Dryden in Shadwell's *The Humorists* (1670) and Joseph Arrowsmith's *The Reformation* (*c.* 1672–3); Elkanah Settle in Shadwell's

---

[27] *The Female Wits: or, The Triumvirate of Poets At Rehearsal* (1704), The Augustan Reprint Society, no. 124 (Los Angeles, 1967), Act II, p. 30.

[28] 'I have laid a Design to alter *Cateline's Conspiracy*', she says, 'Nay, I intend to make use only of the first Speech' (Act I, pp. 9–10). See also Act II, pp. 23, 39; Act III, pp. 60, 65.

[29] For an account of burlesque plays in the Restoration and the eighteenth century see Dane Farnsworth Smith, *Plays about the Theatre in England from The Rehearsal in 1671 to the Licensing Act in 1737 or, The Self-Conscious Stage and its Burlesque and Satirical Reflections in the Age of Criticism* (New York, 1936); and Dane Farnsworth Smith and M. L. Lawhon, *Plays about the Theatre in England, 1737–1800 or, The Self-conscious Stage from Foote to Sheridan* (Lewisburg, 1979).

[30] (London, 1689), Act I, pp. 7–8.

and the duke of Newcastle's *The Triumphant Widow, or The Medley of Humours* (1674); Susannah Centlivre in the Pope–Gay–Arbuthnot *Three Hours After Marriage* (1717); and Colley Cibber in Henry Fielding's *The Historical Register for the Year 1736* (1737). They culminate with an inspired spoof of Richard Cumberland as Sir Fretful Plagiary in Richard Brinsley Sheridan's *The Critic* (1779).

As I have argued in the opening section of this chapter, the literary standing of plays rose in the late seventeenth century owing, in large measure, to the extensive availability of both old and new drama in printed form. Yet the confident assertions, made by Dryden and others, of the superiority of modern plays to those by Shakespeare, Fletcher, Jonson and other pre-civil war playwrights coexisted uneasily with a perception that the methods by which new plays are composed are not worthy of an artistic form with claims to cultural respectability. That perception is apparent in self-conscious discussions of current stage offerings to be found in several contemporary plays. Again, the claim that modern playwrights are outright appropriators with no shred of imagination and invention is a common one. For instance, *Sir Hercules Buffoon* by the actor John Lacy likens the business of writing plays to such common trades as cobbling and tinkering. Sir Hercules, 'a Lover of Wit and Learning', wishes to bind his son, the Squire, apprentice to a poet. The Squire himself wants to become apprentice to a comic poet. In the course of the play father and son issue a damning assessment of modern dramatists:

HER. . . . some of 'em will filch and steal out o'th' old Plays, and cry down the Authors when they've done.
SQ. They have no more invention than there is in the head of a souc'd Makeril: now they're turned Coblers, they vamp and mend old Plays.
HER. Or rather turned Tinkers, who stop one hole and make ten; so they mend one fault, and make twenty.[31]

Sir Hercules and the Squire may be the comic butts of the play (the former has himself written a play which has been rejected by the actors), yet their view of authors in general and of the dramatic profession in particular is one that prevailed in much comic and satiric writing of the period. For instance, *Poor Robin's Intelligence* for

---

[31] *Sir Hercules Buffoon: or The Poetical Squire* (London, 1684), II.iv., p. 16. The date of the first performance is uncertain; the *terminus ad quem* is 1681, the year of Lacy's death. Cf. also Thomas Wright's *The Female Vertuoso's* (London, 1693), in which one of the characters, Lovewitt, claims to 'have made an exact Collection of all the Plays that ever came out, which I design to put into my Limbeck; and then extract all the Quintessence of Wit that is in them, to sell it by drops to the Poets of this Age' (Act III, p. 23).

23–30 May 1676 contains a series of mock-advertisements, appropriately styled 'Divertisements', of 'Books printed for Poor Robin'. Among them we find the following item: '*Plagiarism improved*, shewing how any body that can but Translate or Transcribe, may in short time become a very considerable Author. To be lent to read.' Clearly, by the late seventeenth century the understanding that texts are made out of other texts was not only becoming widespread, but its implications for the status of authorship, dramatic or otherwise, were judged to be intensely negative.

The development of that judgement is vividly illustrated in a series of satirical texts which purport to stage imaginary 'Sessions of the Poets'. The basic structure is simple: scores of aspiring poets arrive at the court of Apollo, who then wittily (and often searingly) appraises the credentials of the various claimants to the bays. The genre was inaugurated by the poem of Sir John Suckling which was prompted by Ben Jonson's death in 1637. 'Sessions of the Poets' proliferated after the Restoration, with new generations of poetasters being held up to ridicule. Two features of the genre are pertinent here. First, in contrast to Suckling's original skit which promiscuously mixed poets, playwrights, historians and other learned writers such as Waller, Carew, Jonson, Davenant, Selden, Sandys and Falkland, post-Restoration 'Sessions' invariably focus on playwrights. Second, the resolution of the contest for the bays which these poems represent is predicated, with increasing frequency, upon the exposure of the literary thefts perpetrated by the pretenders to the laurel.

The first example of the genre in the Restoration, *The Session of the Poets* (published in 1668 but apparently written in 1664), centres on those who have supplied (or have striven to supply) recent theatrical offerings: Davenant; Buckingham; Thomas Killigrew (who is admonished by Apollo for printing his plays); Sir Robert Howard (who is said to have been rifled of a play by Dryden); Edward Howard; Sir Samuel Tuke; Robert Stapylton; William Cavendish, the duke of Newcastle (who arrives with his own plays and those of his wife); Sir William Killigrew; the aristocratic translators of Corneille's *La Mort de Pompée*; Thomas Porter; and Samuel Butler (who is rebuked for attempting to write a play); John Wilson; Sir Thomas Clarges; Richard Rhodes; Thomas Shadwell; and Sir George Etherege.[32] It is

---

[32] *The Session of the Poets* (1668), Bod. MS Don b. 8, printed in *Poems on Affairs of State; Augustan Satirical Verse, 1660–1714* (hereafter *POAS*), 7 vols. (New Haven, 1963–75), 1: *1660–1678*, ed. George deF. Lord, pp. 327–37.

telling that a literary satire composed at so early a date should pay so much attention to Dryden's robbing 'the sad Knight' (Sir Robert Howard) 'of his muse', and to his illicit appropriation of an old play in *The Wild Gallant*:

> Each man in the court was pleas'd with the theft,
> Which made the whole family swear and rant,
> Desiring, their Robin in'th' lurch being left,
> The thief might be fin'd for his *Wild Gallant*.   (lines 63–8)

In conclusion, Apollo judges the standard of modern stage-fare wanting, and bestows the laurel upon two actors, John Lacy and Henry Harris, 'Because they alone made the plays go off' (line 172).

In *A Session of the Poets* of 1676, the contenders for the bays are again predominantly playwrights (Dryden, Etherege, Wycherley, Shadwell, Lee, Settle, Otway, Crowne, Behn, D'Urfey, Rawlins), and, as in its predecessor, the laurel is conferred upon a player, Thomas Betterton, who:

> had made plays as well as the best,
> And was the great'st wonder the age ever bore,
> For of all the play scribblers that e'er writ before
> His wit had most worth and most modesty in't,
> For he had writ plays, yet ne'er came in print.[33]

Another 'Session' which concentrates on dramatists is Daniel Kenrick's *A New Session of the Poets, Occasion'd by the Death of Mr Dryden* (1700). Here we encounter not only playwrights such as D'Urfey, Farquhar, Crowne, Congreve, Southerne and Tate, but also miscellaneous writers and critics such as Rymer, Blackmore and Tom Brown. No contestant is deemed worthy to inherit the laurel from Dryden and it remains his. By the time of *The Tryal of Skill: or, A New Session of the Poets* (1704), playwrights begin to lose out to poets. Many writers of plays are mentioned: Peter Motteux, Abel Boyer, Thomas D'Urfey, Thomas Baker, Richard Wilkinson, Francis Manning, George Farquhar, Richard Steele, Nahum Tate, Charles Gildon, John Oldmixon, John Dennis, William Burnaby, John Vanbrugh, William Congreve, Thomas Southerne and Nicholas Rowe. But it is a poet, Dr Garth, who is accorded the greatest accolade.[34]

Though their aim was to castigate the triviality and worthlessness of modern plays, the concentration of successive late-seventeenth-

---

[33] *A Session of the Poets* (1676), in *POAS*, i, lines 97–101.
[34] *POAS*, vi, 681–711.

century 'Sessions' poems on the drama to the virtual exclusion of poetry and prose attests to its cultural centrality in the period. The same is true of an anonymous prose 'Session', a cultural document which is a particularly rich source of information about attitudes toward the dramatic profession and the practice of appropriation, and one which has not hitherto received the scholarly attention it deserves. Written some time in 1688 (the year of the publication of Langbaine's *Momus Triumphans* with which it shares a strong affinity), *A Journal from Parnassus* had remained in manuscript until early this century. The *Journal* follows, but also ingeniously modifies, the formula of the 'Sessions' poems. First, the medium of prose offered the author of the *Journal* greater scope to engage with a variety of issues relating to imaginative writing (above all playwriting with which it is for the most part concerned). Second, though its satire is as sharp as, if not sharper than, that of versified 'Sessions', the *Journal* is more obviously rooted in the political and commercial realities of its time. That rootedness is apparent in its representation of Parnassus as less an absolute kingdom than a parliamentary monarchy, with the 'Election (like that of other Parliaments,) being manag'd, for the most part, by Popular Votes'.[35] With old members being keen to retain their seats, and with new arrivals vying for membership of that august assembly, charges of plagiarism are characteristically invoked to discredit the self-advertising manifestoes of would-be sons of Apollo. Among them are: Bayes (Dryden) who is told by Flecknoe (Shadwell) that a simile of his 'was stolln from Virgil' (p. 11); Tate whose 'Plea', says Apollo, 'was very weak, for his own Plays had been damn'd, Shakespear's wrong'd, and his Siphylis excell'd by every Mounte-bank's Bill' (p. 16); and Crowne who is 'desir'd' by Apollo 'to circumcise your Jewish Play, & to restore some Scenes of it to a noble Peer: to Mr Wicherly your Surly or his Plain Dealer, & to a certain old exploded Author your Character & Story of the Callicoe-Merchant . . . This Charge of Plagiary hit the poor Culprit so home, that he sneak'd as abruptly from the Barr as his Sr Courtly did from the Stage, and with as great a Disappointment' (p. 18).

Yet, like Langbaine's *Momus Triumphans*, the *Journal from Parnassus* goes beyond *ad hominem* attacks on literary thieves. It considers the problem of appropriative composition and adaptation of old and

---

[35] *A Journal from Parnassus Now Printed from a Manuscript circa 1688*, ed. Hugh Macdonald (London, 1937), p. 5.

foreign drama in general terms, locating it firmly in the context of London's literary marketplace. That contextual grounding is introduced through a clever mimicry of parliamentary procedures established in England such as the hearing of petitions submitted by various interest groups and the relegation of contentious matters to committees. Thus petitions are presented to the House by 1. 'the Company of Booksellers & Printers' (pp. 35–7), 2. 'that part of the Nobility & Gentry commonly call'd Patrons' (pp. 40–2), 3. 'another sort of Sufferers call'd Readers' (pp. 44–6), and 4. 'his Maties. poor Subjects the Company of Players' (pp. 53–5). Those fictitious petitions provide a wealth of information about the interaction between the suppliers and the consumers of imaginative literature in the Restoration. In particular they demonstrate the urgency with which the issue of intellectual property was viewed in the period.

The *Journal* perceptively explores the artistic, moral and economic implications of the production and dissemination, whether in print or performance, of literary works that are adaptations or appropriations of earlier texts. Like Langbaine in the preface to *Momus Triumphans*, the author of the *Journal* stresses that the marketing of appropriated works is an imposition upon the reading and theatre-going public who, having paid for them, discover that what they have purchased is stale, second-hand matter. The formulation of that point in the Readers' Petition is worth quoting at length:

The extraordinary pleasures & satisfaction we have receiv'd in our frequent Conversation with your learned & elegant Works has of late been mightily disturb'd by the many avocations we have mett with from a Company of fullsome impudent Plagiaries that without fear or witt daily endeavour to impose upon us their sophisticated ware under the deceitfull title of a new Poem, which generally has nothing new but it's Name: & then to bespeak, or rather tire our Patience we are saluted in the Beginning with the complemental titles of Courteous, Gentle, Learned, Candid, & (as one terms us) Sugar-candid[36] Reader: yet all this does but serve to increase the wretched fatigue we endure in tiring our Eyes with reading, & our hands with turning till we come to their happy Finis. But our greatest greivance is that after all this toil & trouble, we find our time & our labour lost, & the Author's mighty Promise dwindled into a stale repetition or corruption of other men's Works. To that pass is the Poetry of this Age come, that our Writers are not contented to quote a Line or two of an Author in their Title-

---

[36] This is a reference to Aphra Behn's epistle to *The Dutch Lover* (London, 1673) which is addressed to 'Good, Sweet, Honey, Sugar-candied READER' (sig. A2^r). Again, we are reminded that the author of the *Journal* is primarily concerned with plays.

Page, but they must steal two or three hundred in their Book, & them so miserably cloath'd, so poorly disguis'd that the meanest capacity may see through the thin Cheat, & perceive that in all their Writings there is nothing their own but what they have made so by corrupt translation. In short, what part of their Book is free from Deceit? (pp. 44–5)[37]

In their plea for redress, the Readers are careful to emphasize that they and the Poets should make common cause, for the Poets ought to be 'equally concern'd to revenge their Thefts from You & their Injuries to us' (p. 46). Edmund Waller, a universally respected member of the House, admits that the Readers have a point:

And now, Gentlemen, we ought to hold our selves so far at least interess'd in this Affair, that if the Complaints of our Addressers move us not, our own Sufferings may: the Wrong is ours, the Theft from us, & the Injury to us; & which is worse, these Wrongs, Thefts, & Injuries are committed by those who pretend to be of us. (pp. 50–1)

To recognize a problem is one thing, to solve it is quite another. For though everyone would agree that to steal from the work of others is wrong, the consensus as to what constitutes literary theft is difficult, if not impossible, to reach. Waller's exhortation to his peers to punish plagiarists is followed by a protracted, animated and ultimately inconclusive debate. The first to speak are Ben Jonson and Dryden, '(both of whom thought themselves reflected upon for the freedome of the one with the Roman & of the Other with the French Authors)'. They maintain that 'some distinction ought to be made between those modest Writers who by an ingenuous Imitation & a happy Allusion to antient Authors did as it were naturalize forreign Witt & make it deservedly their own, & those lawless unmercifull Pirates that live upon the Spoil, & count all they meet with lawfull Prize'. The gist of their argument is that there is a difference between legitimate appropriation and plagiarism, and that the former 'Liberty as an antient Priviledge of the House' ought 'not to be parted with upon so slight an Accusation' (p. 51). With the House being equally divided between the proponents and opponents of instituting formal measures to discipline literary thieves, the casting vote is Apollo's. He rules that some such action should be taken. Accordingly, it is

---

[37] Cf. also the portrait of a plagiaristic hack later in the *Journal*: 'methoughts I saw a hungry Author in his Study sometimes pumping for Rhyme, sometimes for Sense, &, when Invention fails, turning his Drama-Common-places, or poaching for Conceits among the Latine, French, or Italian Authors; sifting & shifting & shuffling words & syllables to bring them into Metre, & patching together variety of Styles to dress up the same Matter' (p. 49).

resolved that all new works of literature are to be subjected to a quasi-chemical test that will distinguish what is 'spurious & unlawfull' from what is 'genuine & legitimate' (p. 52). However useful this test might prove in unmasking *covert appropriations*, it would do nothing to resolve another contentious issue, that of *acknowledged adaptation* of old drama. It is to this issue, which features prominently in the petition filed by the players, that I now turn.

The players are compelled to appeal to the literary parliament because of the deplorable condition of London's one surviving theatre, the United Company. (The King's Company and the Duke's Company had merged, or, rather, the former had been taken over by the latter, in 1682.) In the years following the merger, the United Company largely refrained from staging new plays, relying on revivals instead:

> no stale Nursery-Play has scap'd our Acting: we have rak'd up the Ashes of Antiquity, & have spar'd neither Cost nor Pains to furbish up, & put off whatever was vendible. We have exhausted Shakespear, Fletcher, & Johnson, are now plundering Terence, & must shortly go higher & borrow Plots from Plautus & Aristophanes. (p. 54)

Finding themselves in dire need of updating their repertory, the actors are now confronted by a dearth of fresh scripts, for the playwrights who used to supply them (and who found their offerings consistently rejected when competition disappeared), have since turned to the more dependable business of translation. (As Bayes puts it, 'we find Translation an easyer & a more thriving Trade', p. 56.)

In response to the Players' Petition, and with a view to improving the quality of 'Stage-Poetry' and to safeguarding both the moral rights and the financial security of dramatists, the House resolves upon a number of regulations. Those regulations are: a ban on farces and operas; an implementation of strict supervision of the practice of adaptation; and an institution of an additional authorial benefit. It is the last two measures that are noteworthy for what they tell us about the notion of dramatic authorship promoted by *A Journal from Parnassus*. Clearly, there is no blanket condemnation of adaptation here; however, injudicious rewritings of pre-Restoration plays are seen as detrimental to the reputations of their authors:

> Shakespear in the behalf of himself and his Friends the Ancient Play-wrights rose up & moved that some cognizance might be taken of the gross Abuses that had been put upon themselves & the Town in the dull Revival

of those Plays of theirs which some ignorant Admirers under the pretence of
liking them best, had render'd worse, & debas'd them from the general
Applause of Readers to the just Censure of Auditors: but withal so
lamentably patch'd so miserably disfigur'd, that the original Authors either
cou'd not, or wou'd not know them for their own; this they imputed . . . to
the dull diligence of those profess'd Plagiaries, by whom their Works might
more justly be said to be mortify'd than reviv'd. (pp. 57–8)

In order to protect the moral rights of the original authors, it is
decided 'that no Play should be so reviv'd as to receive any diminu-
tion or addition but what was first of all brought by the Revivers to
this House, & freely allow'd by the Author's consent' (pp. 58–9). But
the interests of adapters, too, have to be taken into consideration.
Once their revisions have been approved, they will be entitled to the
standard reward for a new play. And since the uncertainty of income
intrinsic in the system of third-night benefit is unfair to the playwright, who may find himself or herself deprived of any remuneration for a play s/he has expended a substantial amount of labour in
writing, the Poets and the Players agree that a second benefit, on the
sixth night, should be put in place:

Whereas the usual custome had been to allow the Poet the uncertain reward
of a Third Day, which, if the Play miss'd an Audience at that time (either
through the ignorance or malice of the Town) was a very mean encouragement to the Author, & if it found one no longer, was a great Damage to the
Actors; it was ordain'd & enacted by the Authority aforesaid that the time of
Approbation shou'd be doubled, & that if the Play lasted the sixth Day, the
Poets share shou'd be a sixth part to that of the Players; so that by those
means there might be neither want on the one side, nor loss on the other
. . . (p. 59)

As a matter of fact, the move from one to two benefits did occur
around that time, though the first allusion to the practice dates from
1691.[38] Hence it is revealing that a measure advocated in a satirical
piece of *c.* 1688 should have become a commercial reality so soon. It
is revealing, too, that *A Journal from Parnassus* should have provided so
comprehensive and astute an inquiry into the competing interests of
publishers, acting companies, patrons and, above all, authors. What
underlies this inquiry is the assumption – which it shares with

---

[38] In the dedication of his *Sir Anthony Love: or, The Rambling Lady* (London, 1691) to Thomas
Skipwith, Thomas Southerne boasts of 'the Favours from the Fair Sex . . . in so visibly
promoting my Interest, on those days chiefly (the Third, and the Sixth) when I had the
tenderest relation to the welfare of my Play' (sig. A2ᵛ). However, it is by no means clear that
Southerne was the first playwright to be granted a second benefit.

Langbaine's almost exactly contemporaneous *Momus Triumphans* – that literary texts in general, and plays in particular, are the rightful property of their authors.

III

Late-seventeenth-century law offered some protection to publishers from piracy but none to authors whose work had been plagiarised. *A Journal from Parnassus* equates plagiarism with the crime of illicit minting, and proposes that it too should incur lawfully ordained punishment:

> [the Poet] makes all he meets with not the subjects of his Imitation but the objects of his Theft, & like your thorough-pac'd Malefactor, is not contented to steal the Ore unless he adulterates it with his own base Alloy, marks it with his own counterfeit Stamp, & passes it upon the World for currant Coin. And truly it were to be wish'd that as our Laws take hold of that sort of Offenders, so there might be some very severe animadversion upon these Clippers & Coiners of Poetry, that are guilty not only of Sacriledge & Robbery from their Predecessors, but of a gross & apparent Cheat upon their Contemporaries. (pp. 49–50)

Those who are guilty of illicit appropriation, this passage suggests, transgress against both the moral rights of the original authors from whom they steal and the financial interests of their audiences and readers whom they force to pay a second time for what they have purchased before.

A Journal from Parnassus is a brief satirical skit which remained unpublished for two and a half centuries. Yet it was only one of a number of documents which illustrate the view that plagiarism constitutes a serious violation of what was coming to be recognized as intellectual property. Other writers, too, resorted to the language of law and called for some form of legal redress against literary theft. One of them was Langbaine:

> The last sort of Remarks, relate to Thefts: for having read most of our English Plays, as well ancient as those of latter date, I found that our modern Writers had made Incursions into the deceas'd Authors Labours, and robb'd them of their Fame . . . I know that I cannot do a better service to their memory, than by taking notice of the Plagiaries, who have been so free to borrow, and to endeavour to vindicate the Fame of these ancient Authors from whom they took their Spoiles. For this reason I have observ'd what Thefts I have met with throughout the Catalogue, and have endeavour'd a restitution to their right Owners, and a prevention of the

Readers being impos'd on by the Plagiary, as the Patrons of several of our Plays have been by our Modern Poets.[39]

John Dennis was more explicit than Langbaine. A year after the Copyright Statute of 1710 – a piece of legislation which for the first time officially recognized authors as 'Proprietors' – had come into effect, Dennis wrote: 'As Laws are made for the Security of Property, what pity 'tis that there are not some enacted for the Security of a Man's Thoughts and Inventions, which alone are properly his?'[40] Dennis was not concerned with the commercial ramifications of print publication which the Copyright Statute had been designed to regulate; rather, he was lobbying for a new act, one that would protect a literary work from plagiarism, not from piracy.

Most late-seventeeenth- and early-eighteenth-century debates about the legitimacy (or otherwise) of dramatic appropriation focused on the following topics: imitation of the classics, translation of foreign drama and adaptation of pre-civil war scripts by Shakespeare, Fletcher and others. Those debates thus predominantly centred on works by dead authors, foreign authors, or both. But in practice theft was also rife among living writers. I conclude this chapter with an account of a *fracas* over a stolen plot which occurred in 1697 and which involved two very minor (but very much alive) writers, George Powell and Mary Pix.

Powell (1668?-1714) was an actor and playwright who did not belong in the first ranks of either profession, though he seems to have had the talent, if not the self-discipline, to become a distinguished player.[41] In his playwriting he was an unscrupulous and opportunistic appropriator, gleaning materials from a variety of sources. The plot of his first tragedy, *The Treacherous Brothers* (1690), derives from a tedious prose romance *Herba Parietis: or, The Wall-Flower* (1650) by

---

[39] *Momus Triumphans*, sigs. A4ᵛ–a1ʳ.

[40] 'To the Spectator' (1711), in *The Critical Works of John Dennis*, ed. Edward Niles Hooker, 2 vols. (Baltimore, 1939–43), II, 27.

[41] For contemporary views of Powell see *The Spectator*, ed. Donald F. Bond, 5 vols. (Oxford, 1965), I, 172–3; *An Apology for the Life of Colley Cibber*, ed. B. R. S. Fone (Ann Arbor, 1968), p. 134; *A Comparison Between the Two Stages* (London, 1702), p. 199; a manuscript newsletter addressed to Madam Pole, Radbourne, Derbyshire, attached to the issue of *The Post-Man*, no. 1598 (9–11 April 1706), in the William Andrews Clark Library, Los Angeles, quoted in J. D. Alsop, 'The Quarrel Between Sir John Vanbrugh and George Powell', *Restoration and Eighteenth-Century Theatre Research*, Second Series, 5 (1990), 28; *The Female Wits*; Daniel Defoe, *More Reformation. A Satyr upon Himself* (London, 1703), p. 45. See also Philip H. Highfill, Jr, Kalman A. Burnim and Edward A. Langhans, *A Biographical Dictionary of Actors, Actresses, Musicians, Dancers, Managers and Other Stage Personnel in London, 1660–1800*, 16 vols. (Carbondale, IL, 1973–93), XII, 107–12.

Thomas Bayly. In tailoring the romance to the stage, Powell replaced
Bayly's villain with his titular treacherous brothers, condensed the
action by eliminating a number of subsidiary intrigues and love
affairs, and heightened the tension and suspense, in the process
enlivening the musty language of the original. The outcome was a
powerful tale of love, lust, ambition and betrayal, and a considerable
theatrical success; the play was reprinted twice in the next few years,
in 1696 and 1699, which may indicate revivals.[42] In his second play,
Alphonso, King of Naples, Powell borrowed the place of action, some
character names, and the broad outlines of the plot from James
Shirley's tragicomedy *The Young Admirall* (1637),[43] but discarded the
low comic scenes, thus turning his play into a straight affective
tragedy. The first two acts were practically transcribed verbatim.
From the third act onwards, the reviser developed a new story line,
more sensational and more tragic, which included an attempted
rape, a gory duel, suicide and a victorious rebellion resulting in the
deposition of the tyrant.[44] He amplified the focus on passion and love
by reducing the original cast of Shirley's four lovers (which allowed
for a happy ending), and instead placing one female, desired by two
men, centre-stage. Powell's third piece, *A Very Good Wife* (1693), set
something of a record, for it was a farrago of no fewer than four
early-seventeenth-century comedies: Thomas Middleton's *No Wit, No
Help Like a Woman's*, Richard Brome's *The City Wit* and *The Court
Begger* and James Shirley's *Hyde Park*.[45]

However heavily he drew upon pre-Restoration plays and romances, Powell felt no urge to document his sources in the prefatory
materials to the editions of his plays, emphasizing, instead, the *ad hoc*

[42] *The London Stage, 1660–1800. Part I: 1660–1700*, ed. William Van Lennep, Emmett L. Avery
and Arthur H. Scouten (Carbondale, IL, 1965), pp. 451, 504.

[43] John Genest, *Some Account of the English Stage, From the Restoration in 1660 to 1830*, 10 vols. (Bath,
1832), I, 11. Shirley's play was based on Lope de Vega's *Don Lope de Cardona*. See John Loftis,
The Spanish Plays of Neoclassical England (New Haven and London, 1973), p. 66.

[44] Written in the wake of the Glorious Revolution and clearly taking its cue from it, Powell's
play explicitly condones the rising of subjects against a despotic king: in the closing speech
the tyrant recognizes his own unworthiness and resolves to step down to make room for a
better ruler. See *Alphonso King of Naples* (London, 1691), v.iii, p. 47.

[45] Whether Powell relied on the original play by Middleton, or on its early Restoration
adaptation, *The Counterfeit Bridegroom* (1677), has been disputed. See Genest, *Some Account*, II,
50; M. S. Balch, *Thomas Middleton's 'No Wit, No Help like a Woman's' and 'The Counterfeit
Bridegroom' (1677) and Further Adaptations* (Salzburg, 1980), pp. 59–73. See also Paulina Kewes,
'The Politics of the Stage and the Page: Source Plays for George Powell's *A Very Good Wife*
(1693) in their Production and Publication Contexts', *Zagadnienia Rodzajów Literackich* 37
(1994), 41–52.

nature of his playwriting. By adopting this pose of self-denigration, he confines himself to the ghetto of actor-playwrights, a move which identifies him as a social and aesthetic inferior, but also ensures that his play will not be considered alongside those written by *bona fide* poets. To appreciate the pertinence of Powell's self-definition in the context of the prevalent attitudes, which were largely negative and condescending, toward players aspiring to the bays, one need only recall the discussion of actor-playwrights in *A Comparison Between the Two Stages*: 'The Players have all got the itching Leprosie of Scribling as *Ben. Johnson* calls it; 'twill in time descend to the Scene keepers and Candle-Snuffers' (p. 25). The prejudice against players was further exacerbated by the mounting fierceness of theatrical competition and the concomitant decline in the fortunes of the London theatres after the split in 1695.[46] With the companies vying to outdo one another, the number of premières soared, yet most of them met with disastrous reception. The last decade of the century witnessed a rapid shrinking of audiences. '[N]ow Two [companies] can hardly Subsist', complained James Wright in 1699.[47] Under such circumstances the plays of Powell, Mountfort, Underhill, Doggett and other actors were a formidable threat to professional playwrights whose living depended on the regular acceptance of their wares by the playhouses.

In addition to supplying the stage with makeshift scripts which he put together himself, Powell was also a sponsor of others' plays. He was thus one of those who, says Tom Brown, 'serve the Town in the double Capacity, of Poets and Players; and what by reviving, altering, and travesting old Plays; fathering other Peoples Productions, and filching Plots from some Authors, who trust their writings to their perusal, make a shift to get more Money than the true Poets'.[48] An author, either of an original piece or of an adaptation, might resolve to preserve anonymity by engaging somebody else to see his script to the stage. What this involved was not the transference of credit for composing the piece, but the ceding of potential benefits, the proceeds from the third night and the sale of copy to a bookseller. The sponsors (and beneficiaries) were usually players, an arrangement which, as Robert D. Hume has shown, in time gave rise to the

[46] See Shirley Strum Kenny, 'Theatrical Warfare, 1695–1710', *Theatre Notebook* 27 (1973), 130–45.
[47] *Historia Histrionica: an Historical Account of the English Stage . . . In a Dialogue, of Plays and Players* (London, 1699), p. 5.
[48] *Letters of Wit, Politics and Morality* (London, 1701), pp. 221–2.

formal actor benefit in London theatres.[49] After the split of the
United Company in 1695, Powell secured a senior position in
Christopher Rich's troupe performing at Drury Lane and Dorset
Garden. This explains why he was sometimes able to claim the
author's benefit for plays mounted under his aegis. Those were: *The
Cornish Comedy* (1696), *Bonduca: or The British Heroine* (1696), *A New
Opera; Called, Brutus of Alba* (which Powell brought to the stage with a
fellow actor, John Verbruggen, in 1697), and *The Fatal Discovery; or,
Love in Ruines* (1698).

Powell's habit of appropriation initially escaped critical assault,
perhaps because of the light-hearted self-disparagement of his prologues and prefaces. The case was altered, however, by the production in September or early October 1697 of *The Imposture Defeated:
or, A Trick to Cheat the Devil*, part of which he had stolen from the
manuscript of Mary Pix's *The Deceiver Deceived*. Pix's mildly smutty
and moderately witty farce revolves around the motif of pretended
blindness, which constitutes an old miser's ploy to evade the assumption of a costly public office. Powell appropriated the blindness trick,
added the devil to the cast, and turned the original play into a much
more smutty if less witty comic extravaganza, inclusive of special
effects, spectacular discovery scenes and songs.[50]

The force of the ensuing scandal compelled Powell to defend
himself in the preface to the printed version of his play:

I stand impeacht (at least the Publick Cry is loud upon that Subject) that I
have stolen a Character from a Comedy of Mrs. P___t's [sic], being the
Humour of *Bondi* the pretended blind Man. ___ I would not willingly be
thought so poor a Plagiary, and am far from being guilty of this accusation.
For, in the first place, I had that hint from a Novel, and that Play of her's
that has such a Character I declare I never Read. 'Tis true, such a one she
brought into the House, and made me a Solicitor to the Company to get it
Acted, which when I had obtain'd, she very mannerly carry'd the Play to

---

[49] 'The Origins of the Actor Benefit in London', *Theatre Research International* 9 (1984), 99–111.
[50] See the self-advertising prologue written and spoken by Powell:

> To this poor Treat, these Honour'd Guests t'invite,
> I come my own Embassador to Night,
> ....
> But though this Play in Wit be not so strong,
> 'T has that will do as well, it trouls along,
> With a whole train of Fiddles, Dance and Song.
> And tho to other heights, my Pen can't rise,
> What the Dish wants, the Garnature [sic] supplies.

(*The Imposture Defeated: or, A Trick to Cheat the Devil* (London, 1698), sig. A2ᵛ).

the other House; and had I really taken the Character from her, I had done her no more than a piece of Justice. (sig. A2^r)

As Powell himself admits, he did have the opportunity to read Pix's comedy in manuscript. His denial that he had done so sounds dubious at best and makes him seem highly irresponsible in having solicited performance of a script he says he had not read. Even more incriminating is his failure to produce the title of the novel from which he allegedly derived the disputed character. The only un-doubted piece of truth in Powell's account is that Mary Pix did not tolerate the theft. She publicized his dishonesty and had the original play staged by the rival company at Lincoln's Inn Fields, who were naturally elated to strike at the competition. Thomas Betterton, Elizabeth Barry and Ann Bracegirdle starred in the production of Pix's play in November 1697.[51]

The barbed prologue to the play denounces Drury Lane and its leading actor and would-be playwright, Powell:

> 'Tis t'other House best shows the slight of hand:
> Hey Jingo, Sirs, what's this! their Comedy?
> *Presto* be gone, 'tis now our Farce you see.
> By neat conveyance you have seen and know it
> They can transform an Actor to a Poet.[52]

The legal terms interspersed throughout ('Case', 'Fee', 'Councel', 'restitution', 'indite', 'prosecution') simulate a hearing in a court of law:

> Our Case is thus:
> Our Authoress, like true Women, shew'd her Play
> To some, who, like true Wits, stole't half away.
> We've Fee'd no Councel yet, tho some advise us
> T' indite the Plagiaries at *Apollo*'s Sizes?
> . . . .
> Besides, shou'd they be cast by prosecution,
> 'Tis now too late to think of restitution;
> . . . .
> Therefore to you kind Sirs, as to the Laws
> Of Justice she submits her self and Cause . . .

---

[51] The play was published shortly after the première. After having been advertised in the *Post-Boy* for 18–21 December 1697, *The Deceiver Deceived* was printed with the date 1698 on the title-page. In 1699 the unsold stock of the play was put back on sale with a new title-page and prologue, and some of the initial leaves cancelled, as *The French Beau, A Comedy*. See G. Thorn-Drury, 'An Unrecorded Play-Title', *The Review of English Studies* 6 (1930), 316–18.

[52] *The Deceiver Deceived* (London, 1698), sig. A3^r. See also the epilogue: 'Part of this Play though stoln was lately shown' (p. 47).

Even as it raises the issue of the protection of the author's property, the prologue foregrounds Pix's sex. For the first time in the history of English theatre a female writer arraigns a man for plagiarism. The audience is made equivalent to a jury, and its applause and support tantamount to a favourable verdict. What she seeks to accomplish in this provisional playhouse tribunal is a full vindication of her right in the play. She does this by having Powell metaphorically convicted of theft. Pix's use of the trope of the audience as judges deciding a case between her and Powell implicitly confers the status of property on her dramatic creation.

The complaint voiced by the prologue transcends the case in hand. In the final lines the perspective shifts from the particular to the general, and the closing couplet bluntly points to a significant gap in the law which fails to protect the author's right to his (or her) own creation: 'For to whom else shou'd a wrong'd Poet sue, / There's no appeal to any Court but you' (sig. A3ʳ). In the late seventeenth century, we must remember, nothing like the author's copyright existed. The Licensing Act which had lapsed a few years earlier, in 1695, would have been of no avail anyway, since it had protected the rights in copies held by publishers and not the manuscripts of authors.[53] Nor did common law recognize literary productions as property, although in the years to come increasing numbers of lawyers would argue retrospectively that it had.[54]

Perhaps the most startling aspects of the Pix–Powell squabble are the relative obscurity of the two parties and the third-rate status of their respective comedies, with the copy ironically enjoying greater popularity than the original.[55] None the less the furore aroused by the quarrel underscores the difference between the appropriation of

[53] On the emergence of the term 'copyright' see Donald W. Nichol, 'On the Use of "Copy" and "Copyright": a Scriblerian Coinage?', *The Library*, sixth series, 12 (1990), 110–11. On stationers' copyright see Lyman Ray Patterson, *Copyright in Historical Perspective* (Nashville, 1968), pp. 3–150; Ian Parsons, 'Copyright and Society', in Asa Briggs (ed.), *Essays in the History of Publishing* (London, 1974), 31–60; David Saunders, *Authorship and Copyright* (London, 1992), pp. 35–74.

[54] Mark Rose, 'The Author as Proprietor: *Donaldson v. Becket* and the Genealogy of Modern Authorship', *Representations* 23 (1988), 51–85, and *Authors and Owners: the Invention of Copyright* (Cambridge, MA, 1993); Trevor Ross, 'Copyright and the Invention of Tradition', *Eighteenth-Century Studies* 26 (1992), 1–27, at pp. 5–7; Margreta de Grazia, *Shakespeare Verbatim: the Reproduction of Authenticity and the 1790 Apparatus* (Oxford, 1991), pp. 181–4.

[55] Charles Gildon thought that 'the Scene where the Blind Man's Wife make's [sic] Love before his Face, is better manag'd in Mr *Powel*'s Play, than here [that is, in *The Deceiver Deceiv'd*], tho' in general, this is the better Play' (*The Lives and Characters of the English Dramatick Poets* (London, [1699]), Appendix, p. 178).

materials from a published text whose author was usually dead and plagiarism from an unpublished manuscript of a living author. Imitation and borrowing had been usually discussed in aesthetic and/or moral terms, but Pix's retaliation against Powell's theft from her manuscript was couched in a language not only of art and ethics but also of law. Like the author of *A Journal from Parnassus*, like Langbaine, like Dennis, Pix invokes a vocabulary closer to Arthur Miller's world than Shakespeare's.

The emergence of that vocabulary was predicated, as we have seen, on two parallel processes: the growth of financial rewards for playwriting and the rise in the literary status of plays after the Restoration. The incipient economic and cultural centrality of drama ensured that it was in relation to plays rather than poetry or prose fiction that the problem of appropriation became the most pressing and the language of law and property was first applied. As the profusion of satiric figurations of plagiaristic playwrights in contemporary comedies, burlesques and verse and prose 'Sessions of the Poets' attests, plagiarism was loudly and universally condemned as an injury to both the original author and the reading and theatre-going public. The belief that to unmask a literary thief was not a sufficient punishment steadily gained ground, and calls for legal retribution became widespread. By the end of the seventeenth century, then, the conceptual framework which treats literary compositions as the intellectual property of their authors was already in place.

Writing in the early 1950s, Alexander Lindey observed that 'The era [of plagiarism litigation] began around 1915, gained momentum in the roaring 20s, spurted through the troubled 30s, and bowled along merrily in the 40s'.[56] Since then there has been a veritable explosion of copyright infringement cases tried in courts and of accusations of plagiarism which have been extensively publicized in the media. Artists, critics and lawyers continue to debate the moral, aesthetic, legal and commercial ramifications of plagiarism and of copyright violation. In many ways the treatment of appropriation is far more stringent today than it was three centuries ago: practices which were normal at the time would now land the perpetrator in court, liable to heavy damages. Paradoxically, however, in other respects we have become far more indulgent toward appropriators.

---

[56] *Plagiarism and Originality* (New York, 1952), p. 134.

In the Restoration many commentators viewed not only furtive appropriations but even acknowledged adaptations of older plays and translations of foreign drama as thefts and a sign of artistic barrenness. By contrast, the postmodern consensus posits intertextuality as the pervasive and inevitable condition of all writing, thereby eschewing moral judgements of appropriation and questioning legal ones. This stance would have exasperated those such as Langbaine, the author of *A Journal from Parnassus*, and many others who, in the late seventeenth century, urged legal protection of the author's rights and for whom 'to plagiarize' was very much 'a sin'.

CHAPTER 9

Republicanism, the politics of necessity, and the rule of law[1]

Alan Houston

> public reason just,
> Honor and Empire with revenge enlarg'd,
> By conquering this new World, compels me now
> To do what else though damn'd I should abhor.
> So spake the Fiend, and with necessity,
> The Tyrant's plea, excus'd his devilish deeds.
>
> John Milton, *Paradise Lost*[2]

> Civil War in *Macchiavels* account is a Disease, but tyranny is the death of a State.
>
> Algernon Sidney, *Discourses Concerning Government*[3]

> A man will trust the law for a thousand pounds . . . but he will not trust a man for a hundred pounds; or if he do, he may repent it.
>
> James Harrington, *A Discourse*[4]

THE REPUBLICAN PARADOX

'Reason of State is the knowledge of the means by which . . . dominion may be founded, preserved and extended.'[5] Concerned

---

[1] Previous versions of this chapter were presented at conferences in Cambridge ('The Politics of Necessity and the Language of Reason of State') and Naples ('Prudenza civile, bene comune, guerra giusta: Percosi della ragion di Stato tra Seicento e Settecento') and at Princeton's seminar on 'Politics, Ethics and Public Affairs'. I would like to thank Istvan Hont, Gianfranco Borelli, Alan Ryan and the participants in these gatherings for their comments and suggestions.

[2] John Milton, *Paradise Lost*, book 4, lines 389–94.

[3] Algernon Sidney, *Discourses Concerning Government* (1698), III:40, p. 434.

[4] James Harrington, 'A Discourse upon this saying: the Spirit of the Nation is not yet to be trusted with Liberty' (1659), in *The Political Works of James Harrington*, ed. J. G. A. Pocock (Cambridge, 1977), p. 744.

[5] Giovanni Botero, *The Reason of State* (1589), trans. P. J. and D. P. Waley (London, 1956), p. 3. '*Raison d'état* is the fundamental principle of national conduct, the State's first Law of Motion. It tells the statesman what he must do to preserve the health and strength of the State' (Friedrich Meinecke, *Machiavellism: the Doctrine of Raison d'Etat and its Place in Modern History* (1925), trans. Douglass Scott (New Haven, 1957), p. 1).

241

with the art and science of political survival, it is frequently conceived in terms of a brute contrast between politics and morality, might and right, what is and what ought to be. As Machiavelli famously argued, 'there is such a difference between how men live and how they ought to live that he who abandons what is done for what ought to be done learns his destruction rather than his preservation'.[6] For states to endure, statesmen must be prudent; they must carefully weigh means and ends, giving greater attention to conflicts of power than to claims of justice. In times of crisis personal ideals must give way to public responsibilities. Necessity speaks in imperatives; reason of state is the voice of political realism.

The apparently amoral character of reason of state obscures the fact that it is itself a term of valuation, intended to justify specific actions. The term *ragion di stato* was coined during the sixteenth century to provide a rationale for the fiercely competitive struggles of the Italian peninsula. Diplomacy was its *métier*, secrecy and craft its principal arts. The wars of religion expanded its range of meanings, and by the early seventeenth century *ragion di stato* and its cognates – *ratio status*, *raison d'état*, *Staatsräson* and reason of state – were employed throughout Europe to describe and justify actions that were politically advantageous but contrary to accepted moral, political and religious norms. Reason of state was a form of prudence or practical wisdom.[7] Its touchstone was necessity, the claim that under certain circumstances the pursuit of the public good created an unavoidable obligation to act in politically ambiguous and morally suspect ways. As one Englishman put it in defence of Pride's Purge in 1648, 'Yea many of the Laws of God themselves, think it no disparagement unto them, to give place to their elder sister, the law of necessity.'[8]

Necessity takes many forms. Crises may be domestic or international, moral or material, regular or irregular, anticipated or unforeseen, transitory or enduring. They range from wars, revolutions and earthquakes to competition for scarce resources and unbounded sectarian strife. But regardless of the challenge, a stable and successful political order requires that some public agency be empowered to address it. Who, in the last instance, decides when a crisis has arisen? Using what criteria? What options do they have

[6] Niccolò Machiavelli, *The Prince*, in *Machiavelli: the Chief Works and Others*, trans. Alan Gilbert (Durham, 1989), I, 57–8.
[7] John Dunn, *Interpreting Political Responsibility* (Cambridge, 1990), pp. 39–40.
[8] John Goodwin, *Might and Right Well Met* (1648), p. 15.

available to them? How should they assess the costs and benefits associated with each? Answers to these questions were implicit in a variety of idioms deployed in early-modern Europe;[9] the language of reason of state brought them to the fore. In its most basic form, it constituted a meditation on the nature and purpose of discretionary political power.[10]

One of the most revealing discussions of the politics of necessity occurred in seventeenth-century England. By right English monarchs possessed broad discretionary powers. These royal prerogatives affected everything from the declaration of war to the determination of guilt. During the course of the seventeenth century a complex array of social, political and intellectual changes conspired with massive displays of royal ineptitude to call the prerogative into question. Woe, not weal, seemed the consequence of permitting kings too much latitude. Could the prerogative be restricted? If so, how? If not, what alternatives existed? By focusing attention on these questions, the language of reason of state served as a litmus test of English political sensibilities.

Nowhere was the case against the royal prerogative pressed with greater vigour than in the writings of republicans. 'Public reason' was hierarchical, mysterious and secretive. It lurked in dark corners where it could not be observed or controlled. In John Milton's famous words, it spoke of 'necessity' and in so doing 'excus'd' the tyrant's 'devilish deeds'. According to Algernon Sidney, it was 'reason of state' that led to 'the tragedy of St Bartholomew's Eve', just as it was the practice of 'Arcana Imperii' that sustained the tyranny of Oliver Cromwell.[11]

In the light of these claims it would be tempting to view

---

[9] Modern natural jurisprudence took as its starting point the right of self-preservation; theories of sovereignty focused attention on the juridical preconditions to public order; the concept of interest provided new tools for thinking about the relationship between public and private well-being. The relationship between these idioms and the language of reason of state will be explored below.

[10] My formulation is indebted to John Dunn's extremely lucid discussions of reason of state and the politics of trust in John Locke: *The Political Thought of John Locke* (Cambridge, 1969), pp. 148–64; 'The Concept of "Trust" in the Politics of John Locke', in Richard Rorty, J. B. Schneewind and Quentin Skinner (eds.), *Philosophy in History* (Cambridge, 1984), pp. 279–302; *Interpreting Political Responsibility*, pp. 26–44. I have also learned a great deal from Victoria Kahn, 'Political Theology and Reason of State in *Samson Agonistes*', *South Atlantic Quarterly* 95 (Fall 1996), 1065–98.

[11] Algernon Sidney, *Court Maxims, discussed & refelled* (Warwickshire Record Office, CR 1886), fol. 70.

republicanism as an alternative to, and a repudiation of, the language of reason of state. There would seem to be little room for the maxim *necessitas non habet legem* (necessity has no law) in a theory predicated on 'the empire of laws and not of men'.[12] But republicans were no less attentive to the politics of necessity than were their opponents. Tyranny was 'the death of the state'; it destroyed individual liberty, subjected the nation to the unfettered passions of a single man and undermined international strength and independence. To many, republicanism was the sole – hence necessary – alternative to it. More subtly, republican conceptions of law and politics did not eliminate political prudence; they adapted and transformed it to meet England's changing domestic and international needs. The key question was not *whether* there should be discretionary powers, but *how* they could be rendered trustworthy.[13] For law to rule, laws must be declared, interpreted and applied. Each facet of this process – from electing legislators to rendering verdicts in grand juries – was subject to searching scrutiny.[14]

In this chapter I explore a set of arguments mobilized by republicans against key aspects of the royal prerogative. My aims are historical, historiographical and conceptual. First, I seek to shed new light on an important chapter in the history of political thought. The writings of seventeenth-century English republicans were singularly influential in the development of modern political thought, particularly in the United States.[15] Despite extensive scholarly attention to the role of Machiavelli – or, perhaps, precisely because of the way

---

[12] Harrington, 'Oceana', in *Works*, p. 161. In an absolute monarchy everything depends 'on the person of a man and must therefore necessarily be perpetually wavering and uncertain according to the life of him that gives the Impulse to them. But in Common-wealths its not men but laws, Maxims, interests, and Constitutions that govern' (Sidney, *Maxims*, fol. 23).

[13] Contrast Quentin Skinner, who has argued that for English republicans 'if you wish to maintain your liberty, you must ensure that you live under a political system in which there is no element of discretionary power' (*Liberty Before Liberalism* (Cambridge, 1998), p. 74). Skinner skilfully draws attention to republican anxieties about personal dependence, but mistakenly treats these as equivalent to reflections on discretionary political power. As Philip Pettit has acknowledged, 'no matter how constrained a constitutionalist system is, there is always discretion in government' (*Republicanism: a Theory of Freedom and Government* (Oxford, 1997), p. 277).

[14] On the political character of the rule of law, see Judith N. Shklar, *Legalism* (Cambridge, MA, 1964), esp. pp. 1–28, 111–221.

[15] The literature on republicanism is enormous. For a partial (and now slightly dated) discussion, see Alan Houston, *Algernon Sidney and the Republican Heritage in England and America* (Princeton, 1991). Contrast Skinner's emphasis on the discontinuity of English republicanism with modern political thought in *Liberty Before Liberalism*.

the 'machiavellian moment' has been formulated – key aspects of republican thought have been overlooked. If we are to fully understand modern republicanism, then we must attend to its relationship to the politics of necessity. Second, I want to indicate, through this narrative, one of the limitations of recent historiography concerning the Restoration. Revisionist scholars have argued for the 'basic continuity of seventeenth-century English politics'.[16] This claim can be sustained only by deflecting attention from important political and intellectual changes in mid-Stuart England. Third, I hope to articulate a new perspective on several key concepts in modern politics. Popular sovereignty is often thought of as a moral ideal, a claim of right by the many against the government of the few. That is surely correct. But it is also a theory of political prudence, a complex set of claims concerning the social distribution of discretionary political power. A sovereign people does not literally rule itself; representation is the *sine qua non* of modern politics.[17] To be legitimate, in turn, representative government must be capable of ensuring the welfare and survival of the people. The republican 'empire of laws' was continuous with, and not distinct from, the politics of necessity.

Adversity is perennial; it is not possible to imagine a plausible theory of politics that does not take into account hardship and misfortune.[18] The social context of adversity, however, is essential to its identity. The politics of necessity must be explored comparatively and contextually. Changed distributions of power and authority, novel forms of political and economic organization, new moral and psychological ideals: each of these may compel us to rethink basic categories of analysis. Seventeenth-century English republicanism was predicated on the eclipse of feudalism; changes in the social context of political power made the royal prerogative uniquely dangerous. At the conclusion of this chapter I note the challenges to republicanism posed by the emergence of international commerce.

[16] John Morrill, *The Nature of the English Revolution* (London, 1993), p. 392.
[17] John Dunn, *Western Political Theory in the Face of the Future*, 2nd edn (Cambridge, 1993), pp. 1–28.
[18] Hence I am unable to accept Maurizio Viroli's categorical distinction between a morally praiseworthy language of 'politics' and an ignoble language of 'reason of state' ('The Revolution in the Concept of Politics', *Political Theory* 20 (August 1992), 473–95; *From Politics to Reason of State* (Cambridge, 1993), *passim*).

SALUS POPULI

In the politics of necessity, the pursuit of the public good rests on the existence of a power capable of acting in the absence of, and sometimes even contrary to, the law. In late-Elizabethan and early-Stuart England, this power was identified with the crown. As Chief Justice Fleming argued in Bate's Case (1606),

> The king's power is double, ordinary and absolute . . . That of the ordinary is for the profit of particular subjects, for the execution of civil justice, the determining of *meum*; and this is exercised by equity and justice in ordinary Courts, and . . . cannot be changed without Parliament . . . The absolute power of the king is . . . that which is applied to the general benefit of the people and is *salus populi* . . . and this power . . . is most properly named policy and government.

The king's 'absolute power' – his prerogative – included the right to tax, to create new courts and supervise the personnel of the old, to pardon criminals, to veto legislation, to suspend or dispense with specific laws, to summon and dismiss Parliament, and to declare war and peace. Fleming acknowledged the hazards of 'absolute power'. But 'the wisdom and providence of the king is not to be disputed by the subject . . . To argue *a posse ad actum* [from ability to action] to restrain the king and his power . . . is no argument for a subject.'[19]

The plea of necessity was frequently invoked by the crown to justify extra-parliamentary taxation. In 1585 Thomas Bilson asserted that monarchs 'may justly command the goods and bodies of all their subjects in time both of war and peace, for any public necessity or utility'. Dudley Carleton concurred; in 1610 he defended the king's power to impose taxes with the claim that 'reason of state is not . . . a monster . . . Reason of state is [the] preservation of the state and not the ruin of the state'.[20]

According to Richard Tuck, the 'background' to this plea was 'familiar from the history of other European states of middling size and power at this time: the impossibility of maintaining an effective military force within the old legal framework'. Custom and statute law derived 'from an earlier period laid down quite precise rules for

---

[19] 'Judgments in Bate's Case, 1606', in J. R. Tanner (ed.), *Constitutional Documents of the Reign of James I* (Cambridge, 1930), pp. 337–45.

[20] Johann Sommerville, 'Ideology, Property, and the Constitution', in Ann Cust and Richard Hughes (eds.), *Conflict in Early Stuart England* (London, 1989), p. 50; George L. Mosse, *The Holy Pretence: a Study in Christianity and Reason of State* (New York, 1957), p. 13.

the levy and training of soldiers', and Parliament was 'unwilling to provide new legal guidelines' adequate to the tasks of Stuart foreign policy. To advance his aims the king 'had to plead *necessity*, and to claim that the extra-legal use of his prerogative was justified by virtue of his general duty to protect the realm'.[21] Thus it was that in 1626 Charles I, faced with a recalcitrant Parliament and an ill-fated and under-funded war with Spain, sought to justify a forced loan in terms of 'reason of state': 'otherwise our common enemy will in an instant become master of all Germany and consequently of all the ports and parts where the mass and bulk of our cloth is vented'. The loans were a matter of 'unavoidable necessity': 'the safety and very substance of ourself and our people, the true religion of God . . . are in apparent danger of suffering inseparably'.[22]

The king's monopoly of discretionary powers was typically defended in terms of the moral and technical requirements of statecraft. In 1621 James I explained that foreign affairs were 'unfit Things to be handled in Parliament, except your King should require it of you: for who can have Wisdom to judge of Things of that Nature, but such as are daily acquainted with the Knowledge of Secret Ways, Ends, and Intentions of Princes, in their several Negotiations'. Since 'reasons of state and policie' sometimes necessitated secrecy, claimed John Everard, 'it doth not belong . . . to every private man, to make too curious a disquisition into the causes and occasions of his Soveraignes command'. 'My lord', argued attorney-general Heath in the critical Five Knights' Case of 1627, 'there be *arcana Dei, et arcana imperii*'. Mere mortals were not to question the decisions of the king.[23]

Not all Englishmen embraced the language of reason of state, of course, and many complained of the unusually large amplitude of power it seemed to grant the king. More than any other concept in the English political lexicon, it threatened to efface the distinction between Britain's constitutional government and the baroque monarchies of the continent. In 1610 Sir John Strangeways told the House that 'if the king be judge of the necessity, we have nothing and are

---

[21] Richard Tuck, *Philosophy and Government 1572–1651* (Cambridge, 1993), p. 224.

[22] David S. Berkowitz, 'Reason of State in England and the Petition of Right, 1603–1629', in Roman Schnur (ed.), *Staatsräson. Studien zur Geschichte eines politischen Begriffs* (Berlin, 1975), p. 181.

[23] Francis D. Wormuth, *The Royal Prerogative 1603–1649* (Ithaca, NY, 1939), p. 75; Johann Sommerville, *Politics and Ideology in England 1603–1640* (London, 1986), p. 35; 'The Case of the Five Knights', 1627, in S. R. Gardiner (ed.), *The Constitutional Documents of the Puritan Revolution 1625–1660*, 3rd edn (Oxford, 1906), p. 63.

but tenants at will'. William Hakewill concurred: if the king were permitted to determine what constituted an emergency, then 'will it not follow that the king may levy a tax at his own pleasure, seeing his pleasure cannot be bounded by law?'[24]

The king's plea of necessity rested on the plausibility of the claim that he represented the public interest, and that *salus populi* was identical to *salus regis*. With increasing frequency the ancient maxim *salus populi suprema lex* (the good of the people is the highest law) was used to drive a wedge between the king and the nation. As Johann Sommerville has noted, opponents of crown policy discovered that 'reason of state could be employed against as well as for the king'.[25]

This claim was formalized by the great parliamentary theorist Henry Parker. In *The Case of Shipmoney* (1640), Parker argued that 'the supreame of all humane lawes is *salus populi* . . . rather than a Nation shall perish, anything shall be held necessary, and legal by necessity'.[26] Parker gave this argument a radical twist by inserting it into a natural law account of the contractual origins of government. 'Power is originally inherent in the people . . . At the founding of societies, when the consent of societies convayes rule into such and such hands, it may ordaine what conditions, and prefix what bounds it pleases.' Political power was a 'trust' granted by the people to its government. It was 'conditionate and fiduciary', subordinate to 'the transcendent $\alpha\chi\mu\eta$ of all Politiques . . . Salus Populi'. In a crucial proviso, Parker argued that a nation could not consent to its own destruction.[27] This enabled him to invoke the community's right of self-preservation against the prerogative powers of the crown. 'We cannot imagine in the fury of warre (when lawes have the least vigour) that any *General-*

---

24 Sommerville, 'Ideology, Property and the Constitution', pp. 57–8. These fears seemed born out by a remark of the earl of Strafford was alleged to have made to the Privy Council in 1639: 'Your Majesty having tryed all ways, and [being] refused; in this Case of extream Necessity, and for the Safety of Your Kingdom and People, You are loose and absolved from all Rules of Government; You are acquited before God and Man; You have an Army in *Ireland*; You may imploy it to reduce this Kingdom' (quoted in Tuck, *Philosophy and Government*, p. 223).

25 Sommerville, *Politics and Ideology*, p. 74.

26 [Henry Parker], *The Case of Shipmony briefly discoursed* (1640), p. 7. Cf. [Henry Parker], *The Contra-Replicant, his Complaint to his Maiestie* (1643), pp. 18–19.

27 [Henry Parker], *Observations upon some of his Majesties late Answers and Expresses* (1642), pp. 1–2. 'It is not just nor possible for any nation so to enslave itself, and to resigne its own interest to the will of one Lord, as that that Lord may destroy it without injury, and yet to have no right to preserve it selfe: For since all naturall power is in those which obay, they which contract to obay to their owne ruine, or having so contracted, they which esteeme such a contract before their owne preservation are fellonious to themselves, and rebellious to nature' (*ibid.*, p. 8).

issimo can be so uncircumscribed in power, but that if he should turne his Canons upon his owne Souldiers, they were *ipso facto* absolved of all obedience, and all oathes and ties of allegiance whatsoever for that time, and bound by higher dutie, to seek their owne preservation by resistance and defence.' Reason of state included the right of resistance.[28]

What constituted a crisis or emergency? Who was to judge whether or not a specific course of action served the public interest? According to what criteria? According to Parker, these questions fell within the competence of Parliament and Parliament alone. It was the 'essence' of the kingdom, 'the very people itself artificially congregated, or reduced by an orderly election, and representation, into . . . [a] proportionable body'. The king, by contrast, 'does not represent the people' except in those cases 'wherein he can have no particular ends' – as in a legal contest between two subjects – or at such times 'when there is not a more full and neer representation by the Parliament'.[29]

According to Tuck, Parker's 'manner of dealing with the constitutional issue . . . was *pragmatic* . . . the public interest had to be secured, and it was most plausibly secured by a body of "the nobility and gentry"'.[30] Some of Parker's arguments appear to support this interpretation. For example, in response to the claim that the Militia Ordinance had usurped the king's powers, Parker defended Parliament in the following way: 'First we say they must in probabilitie be more knowing . . . Secondly, in regard of their publike interest, they are more responsible then any other . . . Thirdly, they have no private interest to deprave them, nothing can square with the Common Councell but the common good.'[31] While it is true that this argument is comparative and contextual, to describe it as 'pragmatic' is to invoke an artificially sharp and potentially quite misleading distinction between 'practical' and 'principled' justifications for parliamentary independence. The link between consent, representation and elections was historically contingent – it had arisen in the course of time, as a result of human invention – but it was, for men living in the seventeenth century, inescapable. There could be no turning back; to live freely, to ensure that *salus populi* was *suprema lex*,

---

[28] *Ibid.*, pp. 3–4.
[29] *Ibid.*, p. 5; [Henry Parker], *Jus Populi* (1644), pp. 18–19.
[30] Tuck, *Philosophy and Government*, p. 229.
[31] [Henry Parker], *Some few observations upon his Majesties late Answer to the Declaration* (1642), p. 5.

representative bodies must be supreme. Were this not true, 'then all nations are equally slaves, and we in England are borne to no more by the law of England than the asinine peasants of France are there, whose wooden shoes and canvas breeches sufficiently proclaim, what a blessednesse it is to be borne under a meer divine prerogative'.[32]

Parker's fusion of prudence and representation, and of reason of state and natural law, was original and influential. It focused attention on the juridical standing of discretionary political power and on the individuals, institutions and agencies empowered to exercise it. But as a prudential argument it invited discussion of means and ends, causes and consequences, reasons and purposes. On what grounds could Parliament be trusted? What made it an effective defender of the nation's security and welfare? And were there no limits to what it might do? Parker's answer to these challenges was revealing: 'Every man has an absolute power over himself; but because no man can hate himself, this power is not dangerous, nor need to be restrayned: So every State has an Arbitrary power over itself, and there is no danger in it for the same reason.'[33] There was no danger, that is, so long as the relationship between that power and the state paralleled the relationship between a man's will and his body. The language of self-preservation mandated that the nation be conceived as a single actor, a body politic, with a coherent will and a unified public interest. As Parker realized, the plausibility of this claim rested on a strong set of assumptions concerning the relationship between Parliament and the structure of English society.[34]

By happy accident England had never experienced 'enmity' or 'antipathy . . . betwixt the Representatives, and the Body, of the kingdome represented'. This was due to the magic of representation. The 'composition of Parliaments . . . takes away all jealousies, for it is . . . equally, and geometrically proportionable' to the nation as a whole. This was not to say that 'the base people' should hold sway

---

[32] *Ibid.*, p. 15. 'In the infancy of the world, when man was not so artificiall and obdurate in cruelty and oppression as now, and when policy was more rude, most Nations did chuse . . . to submit themselves to the meer discretion of their Lords . . . and to be ruled by Arbitrary edicts.' The discovery of 'an Art and peaceable Order for Publique Assemblies, whereby the people may assume its owne power to do itself right', rendered 'arbitrary rule' unnecessary and immoral (Parker, *Observations*, pp. 14–15).

[33] Parker, *Observations*, p. 34.

[34] As Michael Mendle has recently emphasized, Parliament was the 'hub' of Parker's argument, the 'central term joining' all others (*Henry Parker and the English Civil War* (Cambridge, 1995), p. 183).

within the walls of Westminster, however. 'Mechanicks, bred up illiterately to hand crafts', should not be placed at the 'helme' of the state, above men of 'Learning and gentle extraction'. As Parliament checked the ambitions of kings, so too it restrained the unruly passions of the people. 'By vertue of election and representation, a few shall act for many, the wise shall consent for the simple . . . the prudence of some shall redound to all.'[35] It is important to note in this context that Parker's distinction between reason and passion was not simply a claim about the faculties of the mind, or the structure of the human psyche, but also a description of a set of social practices. The genius of Parliament lay in the deference of the people.

During the early 1640s Parker's arguments were met and rejected by moderates and royalists.[36] By the mid 1640s they were embraced by radicals who doubted Parliament's trustworthiness.[37] There are signs that Parker may even have shared their views.[38] After the Restoration Roger L'Estrange sought to have Parker's pamphlets suppressed.[39] But during the crises of 1679–83 Parker's core ideas – that government is a trust founded on the consent of the people, and that magistrates can be resisted when they threaten the survival of the nation – saw light once again, when they were deployed to meet the perceived threats of popery and arbitrary government. 'All just Government' is grounded in 'a general consent', argued Algernon Sidney. Magistrates are 'Sentinel[s] of the Publick', 'Servant[s] of the Commonwealth'. Like any employee 'entrusted' with power, they can 'be restrained or chastised, if they betray their Trust'.[40] This

---

[35] Parker, *Observations*, pp. 11, 23; [Henry Parker], *Maximes Unfolded* (1643), p. 2; [Henry Parker], *A Letter of Due Censure, and Redargution to Lieut. Coll. John Lilburne* (1650), p. 21; Parker, *Observations*, p. 15.

[36] Parker's *Observations* was immediately subjected to withering criticism; cf. Henry Ferne, *The Resolving of Conscience* (1642); Henry Ferne, *Conscience Satisfied* (1643); Dudley Digges, *An answer to a printed book, intituled, Observations* (1642); [Dudley Digges], *The Unlawfulnesse of Subjects taking up Armes* (1643); William Ball, *A caveat for subjects* (1642).

[37] Lilburne once remarked that his *Innocency and Truth Justified* (1646) was 'an abridgment of the marrow' of Parker's tracts ([John Lilburne], *Regall Tyrannie Discovered* [1647], p. 42).

[38] 'He could not now call the parliament either vox populi or vox dei . . . The voice of parliament, seemingly so clear and unified in 1641, had fractured into a cacophony of contrary trumpets' (Mendle, *Henry Parker*, p. 186).

[39] Roger L'Estrange, *Considerations and Proposals in Order to the Regulation of the Press* (1663), pp. 13, 18, 19–20.

[40] Sidney, *Discourses*, I:10, p. 23; II:1, p. 60; II:20, p. 151; III:390, p. 429; III:16, p. 318; III:22, p. 356; I:6, p. 15. Even Henry Neville – held by many to be a 'strict' Harringtonian – used of the language of natural jurisprudence to establish the boundaries of legitimate government: 'Every man by the first law of nature (which is common to us and brutes) had, like beasts in a pasture, right to everything; and there being no property, each individual, if he were the

argument circulated freely in radical tracts. 'Self-preservation and necessity' justify the attempt to exclude the duke of York, declared the author of *A Word without Doors*. Thomas Hunt agreed: 'I will hope there are very few in this Nation so ill instructed, That doth not think it in the Power of the People to depose a Prince, who . . . really acts the Destruction or the Universal Calamity of his People.' When laws 'cease to be a security unto men', argued Robert Ferguson, they will be 'justified in having recourse to the best means they can for their shelter and defence'.[41]

Tories sought to contain these arguments by suggesting that the appeal to necessity could be made only in the face of incontrovertible threats to the nation's survival.[42] They also reasserted the early-Stuart claim that the king alone had the power and authority to act in an emergency or crisis. Parliament was and ought to be his handmaiden.[43] Similar claims had been made in the 1640s in response to Henry Parker, and the thematic continuity of these two periods gives plausibility to the revisionist assertion that seventeenth-century English political discourse was stable and unchanging. The echoes are undeniable; in fact, they were intentional, the fruit of a clever rhetorical strategy used to discredit radicals. Royalists rejected the language of consent only to revive the politics of necessity in the form of scorched historical memories. Parallels with the 1640s were drawn to demonstrate that the perils of that decade – civil war,

---

stronger, might seize whatever any other had possessed himself or before, which made a state of perpetual war. To remedy which, and the fear that nothing should be long enjoyed by any particular person (neither was any man's life in safety), every man consented to be debarred of that universal right to all things; and confine himself to a quiet and secure enjoyment of such a part, as should be allotted him. Thence came in ownership, or property; to maintain which, it was necessary to consent to laws, and a government; to put them in execution . . . It seems very improbable, not to say impossible, that a vast number of people should ever be brought to consent to put themselves under the power of others, but for the ends above-said . . . And it is full as impossible that any person . . . should by force get an empire to themselves' (Henry Neville, *Plato Redivivus*, in *Two English Republican Tracts*, ed. Caroline Robbins (Cambridge, 1969), p. 85).

[41] J. D., *A Word without Doors Concerning the Bill for Succession* (1679), p. 1; [Thomas Hunt], *The Great and Weighty Considerations, Relating to the duke of York* (1680), p. 6; [Robert Ferguson], *The Second Part of No Protestant Plot* (1682), pp. 1–2. These arguments were frequently cemented by comparing 'the king's oppressive activities' to a foreign invasion (Richard Ashcraft, *Revolutionary Politics and Locke's 'Two Treatises of Government'* (Princeton, 1986), pp. 394–402.

[42] [Matthew Rider], *The Power of Parliaments in the Case of Succession* (1680), pp. 37, 39; [Robert Brady], *The Great Point of Succession Discussed* (1681), p. 37; William Sherlock, *The Case of Resistance of the Supreme Powers* (1684), p. 203.

[43] [John Dryden?], *His Majesties Declaration Defended* (1681), p. 12; [George Hickes], *Jovian, Or, An Answer to Julian the Apostate* (1683), pp. 203–7; William Sherlock, *The Case of Resistance of the Supreme Powers* (1684), pp. 203–4.

foreign invasion, religious innovation, domestic insurrection, fiscal chaos, agricultural collapse and the judicial murder of the king – awaited all who fell captive to radical arguments.[44]

Radicals possessed potent historical memories of their own, of course. If the royalist imagination was defined by the miseries of the 1640s and the horrors of regicide, the republican imagination was defined by the glories of the Commonwealth (1649–53) and the tragic betrayal of Oliver Cromwell. As a republic, Slingsby Bethel argued, England had 'arrived at the highest pitch of Trade, Wealth, and Honour, that it, in any Age, ever yet knew'. 'Neither the Grecians nor the Romans in the time of their Liberty', crowed Sidney, 'ever performed any actions more glorious.'[45] This belief – regardless of its factual basis – provided an emotional and political touchstone for Restoration republicans. No less important were the events of 20 April 1653. In 'one morning', Henry Neville bitterly recalled, Cromwell had 'made himself tyrant of his country'. The violent clash between Cromwell's will and power and the legal institutions of the nation shocked these men in ways that even the collective misdeeds of Charles I had not.[46]

Implicit in the politics of necessity was a radical possibility: that the constitution itself could be changed to accommodate new reasons of state. History revealed the diversity of governments in the world at large and within the life of a single nation. This was not necessarily a sign of decay or corruption, but rather a consequence of each nation's right and ability to adapt to changing needs and circumstances.[47] For many critics of the later Stuarts the observation that government was a human fabrication served at most to justify the

---

[44] 'This is the true reason of the mention of the late War, that we may forgo our Parliaments for fear of another' (Thomas Hunt, *Mr Hunt's Postscript for Rectifying some Mistakes in some of the Inferiour Clergy* (1682), p. 54); 'when [Tories] can say nothing more, they turn us over to *Forty two* for a parallel' (*A Seasonable Warning to the Commons of England* [1679], 3). See also: *An Impartial Account of the Nature and Tendency of the Late Addresses* (1681), in *State Trials* (1693), I, 432–3; Thomas Hunt, *A Defence of the Charter, and Municipal Rights of the City of London* (1683?), p. 17.

[45] [Slingsby Bethel], *The World's Mistake in Oliver Cromwell* (1668), p. 3; Sidney, *Discourses*, II:28, p. 220.

[46] Blair Worden, 'Harrington's "Oceana": Origins and Aftermath, 1651–1660', in David Wootton (ed.), *Republicanism, Liberty, and Commercial Society 1649–1776* (Stanford, 1994), p. 117; Neville, *Plato Redivivus*, in *Tracts*, p. 180.

[47] [Sir John Somers], *A Brief History of the Succession* (1680), p. 16; J. D., *Word without Doors*, p. 1; [James Tyrrell], *Patriarcha non Monarcha* (1681), p. 243; Edmund Hickeringill, 'The History of Whiggism' (1682), in *The Works of Mr Edmund Hickeringill*, 2 vols. (London, 1716), I, 6; Thomas Hunt, *Mr Hunt's Postscript* (1682), p. 38.

reform of the prerogative and the regulation of the succession. But to
some it was part of a broader argument concerning the need for far-
reaching constitutional changes. As men like Bethel, Neville and
Sidney emphasized, the crises of 1679–83 had deep roots and were
not amenable to quick fixes. In order to see why, it is necessary to
turn from the language of natural jurisprudence to the logic of
interests and the history of England.

INTEREST AND SURVIVAL

'It is a Maxim among Politicians', wrote Marchamont Nedham in
1659, 'That *Interest will not lie*.'[48] The classic formulation of this
maxim was provided by Henri duc de Rohan in *De l'interest des princes
et des Estats*, first translated into English in 1641: 'The Prince may
deceive himselfe, his Counsell may be corrupted, but the Interest
alone can never faile. According as it is well or ill understood, it
maketh States to live or die.'[49] Interests were thought to be objective
facts about men and states, distinct from and not reducible to beliefs,
values, or psychic dispositions. Interests occupied the same terrain as
reason of state; both were concerned with the survival of the state.[50]

Interest will not lie, but interests can be misunderstood, ignored,
or rejected. The language of interest was intended to liberate
statesmen and politicians from the baleful influence of desire, passion
and superstition.[51] Nedham captured the normative dimension of
the language of interest in the following terms:

One sense of [the maxim 'interest will not lie'] may be this; That if you can
apprehend wherein a man's Interest . . . doth consist, you may surely know,
if the man be prudent . . . how to judge of his designe: For, which way
soever you foresee his Interest doth in prudence dispose him, that way

---

[48] Marchamont Nedham, *Interest will not Lie. Or, a View of England's True Interest* (1659), p. 3.

[49] Henri duc de Rohan, *A Treatise of the Interest of the Princes and States*, trans. Henry Hunt (1641),
    'Preface'.

[50] 'The prosperity, or adversity, if not the life and death of a State, is bound up in the observing
    or neglecting of its Interest' ([Slingsby Bethel], *The Present Interest of England Stated* (1671), sig.
    A2).

[51] 'In matters of State, one ought not to suffer himself to be led by inordinate desires, which
    carry us oftentimes to undertake things beyond our strength: nor by violent passions which
    doe diversly trouble us, according as we are possessed therewith: nor by superstitious
    opinions, whereby ill-conceived scruples are ministered unto us, but rather by our proper
    interest guided by reason alone, which ought to be the rule of our actions' (Rohan, *Interest*,
    preface to second part). This theme is explored in Albert Hirschman, *The Passions and the
    Interests* (Princeton, 1977); Stephen Holmes, 'The Secret History of Self-Interest', in Jane
    Mansbridge (ed.), *Beyond Self-Interest* (Chicago, 1990), pp. 267–86.

(provided he be so wise as to understand his own Concernment) he will be sure to go . . . The other sense of that Maxim [is], That if a man state his own Interest aright, and keep close to it, *it will not lie to him* or deceive him, in the prosecution of his Aims and ends of Good unto himself, nor suffer him to be misled or drawn aside by specious pretences; to serve the ends and purposes of other men.[52]

The language of interest cut through the confusing and hypocritical cant of political life, providing a clear and unambiguous guide to human conduct. Fluid and flexible, it captured the rapidly shifting conditions of European politics.[53] When well-understood – Nedham's repeated use of the qualifier 'provided' is decisive – it was capable of 'improving' and preserving men and states. During the second half of the seventeenth century a whole library of self-help books dedicated to mapping the 'true interests' of the states of Europe was produced.

The language of interest massively and deliberately simplified the intellectual horizons of political life. Cutting across traditional concepts and categories, it united public and private, national and international, material and ideological. In so doing it facilitated the reconsideration of a number of postulates or theorems that had long governed the conduct of states. Old necessities were dissolved, and new necessities were discovered.[54] Despite its modern association with conflict, discord and struggle, the language of interest was prized for its ability to illuminate new bases of political order and social cooperation. To theorists of interest, what was held in common or shared was at least as important as what was unique or distinctive.

The language of interest was neither inherently nor essentially republican; its *métier* was the preservation of national integrity. In the hands of men like Rohan *les intérêts publiques* provided the key to a rational foreign policy, free from dynastic considerations, and a blueprint for the construction of a strong and centralized French state. In the hands of republicans, however, it could be used for quite different purposes. England's preservation required a recalibration of

---

[52] Nedham, *Interest will not Lie*, p. 3.

[53] According to Bethel, princes 'ought to be exceeding carefull, of not being misled by former examples, which are to Politicians, as of old, the Stars to Navigators, rightly understood, the best guide, and mistaken, the most dangerous. For Interest in all Countryes is changeable, that which was in one Age, not being alwayes the same in the next' (*Present Interest*, sig. A2).

[54] The history of this process has yet to be written. Partial (and frequently problematic) accounts can be found in: Hirschman, *Passions and Interests*; J. A. W. Gunn, *Politics and the Public Interest in the Seventeenth Century* (London, 1969).

its interests and a reconstitution of its political institutions. As Bethel intoned, 'it is certain, that *Nations* will increase, or decline more or less, according as their *Interest* is pursued, and their Government suited to it'.[55] National survival required the construction and preservation of a political order that harmonized the interests of magistrates and people. It was precisely this harmony of interests that was lacking under the Stuarts.

THE GOTHIC BALANCE

According to English republicans, unprecedented and irreversible changes in the constitutional balance had rendered the royal prerogative uniquely hazardous. Where once king, lords and commons had lived in stable (if contentious) equipoise, they now confronted each other across an uneven playing field, locked in a contest that threatened to destroy them all. Were England to regain its strength and independence, its frame of government had to be altered.

The foundation for this argument was laid with unusual clarity by James Harrington. There are, he argued, three different forms of reason governing the conduct of men: 'private reason, which is the interest of a private man'; 'reason of state, which is the interest . . . of the ruler or rulers, that is to say of the prince, of the nobility, or of the people'; and 'that reason which is the interest of mankind or of the whole'. Different constitutions, with different rulers, had different reasons of state. Each realized – or threatened – the public good in a different way.[56]

Harrington added sophistication to this typology by emphasizing the degree to which an unbalanced or poorly designed constitution might itself contribute to conflict and discord. Necessity was relative to the actors involved, and the survival of the part was not necessarily the survival of the whole. 'Private reason', the passion of person or place, posed a permanent threat to the public good; institutionally based conflicts of interest could not be ignored. 'In [constitutions] that are mixed . . . there are so many reasons of state' running counter to each other that none have long endured intact.[57]

---

[55] Slingsby Bethel, *Observations on a Letter Written by the D. of Buckingham* (1673), in *The Interest of the Princes & States of Europe. To which is now Added, Observations on a Letter,* 4th edn, enlarged (1694), p. 12.

[56] Harrington, 'Oceana', in *Works*, p. 171.

[57] Harrington, 'A System of Politics', in *Works*, p. 853.

This multiplication of meanings made it possible to engage in a comparative science of politics, framed around the different reasons of state found in distinct constitutional orders. This science was particularly valuable because it permitted England to come to grips with its past.[58] Republicans debated the character of Anglo-Saxon England.[59] But they agreed that England's feudal monarchs ruled with the consent of the people. 'Tho the name of Conqueror be odiously given to *William* the *Norman* . . . he accepted the Crown upon the conditions offered.'[60] The cause of England's woes could be traced to the collapse of its constitutional balance during the centuries following that momentous event.

Sidney first described the feudal balance between the king and nobility in his *Court Maxims*, a manuscript treatise written during the early 1660s: 'Our boisterous fighting Kings of the Plantagenet Race were content with a limited power at home; they endeavour'd to increase the power of the nation by foreign conquests. For such designs it was necessary to have a Nobility great in power & credit, full of virtue and gallantry & exercised in arms that the people might follow them.' When he wrote the *Discourses* some sixteen years later he sharpened the focus of his argument:

[Our ancestors] knew that the kings of several Nations had bin kept within the limits of the Law, by the virtue and power of a great and brave Nobility; and that no other way of supporting a mix'd Monarchy had ever bin known in the world, than by putting the balance into the hands of those who had the greatest interest in Nations, and who by birth and estate enjoy'd greater advantages than Kings could confer upon them for rewards of betraying their Country.

Neville concurred: 'The barons' were 'such brisk assertors of their rights' that 'so long as the peers kept their greatness, there were no breaches [in the law] but what were immediately made up in parliament'. The Lords were 'the bulwarks of the government'.[61]

---

[58] A more detailed discussion of this aspect of Sidney's writings can be found in Houston, *Algernon Sidney*, pp. 181–91.

[59] Sidney argued that England's pre-Norman monarchs were elective; Neville rejected this claim (Sidney, *Discourses*, III:28, p. 381, III:10, p. 296, III:28, p. 383; Neville, *Plato Redivivus*, in *Tracts*, p. 113).

[60] Sidney, *Discourses*, II:5, p. 82; III:17, p. 327. 'Our ancestors . . . did not foresee or imagine, that any thought of invading their rights could enter into the prince's head. Nor do I read that it ever did, till the Norman line came to reign: which coming in by treaty, it was obvious there was no conquest' (Neville, *Plato Redivivus*, in *Tracts*, p. 121).

[61] Sidney, *Maxims*, pp. 56–7; Sidney, *Discourses*, III:37, p. 419; Neville, *Plato Redivivus*, in *Tracts*, pp. 122, 133.

This was the 'Gothic polity', a form of government that held sway until the sixteenth century.

Critics of Stuart policy frequently invoked the concept of a 'Balance . . . between the three Estates' when they felt that the king had exceeded his 'proper Chanel'. The theory of mixed government provided an ideal platform for reform. It was flexible enough to encompass a wide range of changes, yet conservative enough to leave undisturbed the basic institutions of the English government.[62]

Regardless of the virtues of the Gothic polity, republicans argued that it was no longer capable of meeting the needs of the English people. According to Sidney, England's 'ancient powerfull virtuous warlike Nobility' had been decimated by a process that began with the death of Henry V (1387–1422).[63] As that king's successors realized, the only way to increase their own power and independence was to decrease that of the nobility. Carefully devised incentives fractured the collective identity of the nobility and tied individual lords to the king. Court culture promoted base and corrupt values. Changes in land tenure undermined the material foundation of aristocratic armies. As a result, 'the Lords . . . [can] neither protect the weak, nor curb the insolent'. The tripartite balance of king, lords and commons that had given life to the 'Gothic polity' had been destroyed, and "tis as impossible to restore it, as for most of those who at this day go under the name of Noblemen, to perform the duties required from the antient Nobility of *England*'. As Neville observed, 'now that many of the lords . . . are merely grown titular . . . it cannot be wondered at if the king slight their addresses, and the court-parasites deride their honourable undertakings for the safety of their country'. The ancient constitution 'can no longer perform the functions of a political life; nor carry on the work of ordering and preserving mankind'.[64]

Under these conditions the royal prerogative assumed a menacing visage. In the Gothic polity royal authority had been checked by the power and position of the nobility. But the eclipse of feudalism unhinged the monarchy, rendering the prerogative erratic and

---

[62] Charles I, 'His Majesty's Answer to the Nineteen Propositions', 18 June 1642, reprinted in J. Rushworth, *Historical Collections* (1659–1701), v, 729–30. For example, in 1681 a Whig pamphleteer protested that the corruption of the House of Commons by placemen and pensioners was an attempt to overthrow England's 'mix'd or *Gothick*' form of government (C. B., *An Address to the Honourable City of London*, p. 4).

[63] Sidney, *Maxims*, pp. 57–8.

[64] Sidney, *Discourses*, iii:37, pp. 419–20; Neville, *Plato Redivivus*, in *Tracts*, pp. 145, 81.

untrustworthy. In this context the universal corruption of the human will was particularly significant. Every man is a slave of his passions. 'The question is only, Whether the Magistrate should depend upon the Judgment of the People, or the People on that of the Magistrate; and which is most to be suspected of injustice.' Given that even the best of kings 'are subject to mistakes and passions', and that the worst 'declare their contempt of all human and divine Laws', nothing could be more insane than to subject a nation to the unstable will of one man. 'No Liberty can subsist where there is such a Power.'[65]

Republicanism was founded on the eclipse of feudalism. But as Sidney explained, it was an eclipse of a unique and limited kind:

Our Ancestors may evidently appear, not only to have intended well, but to have taken a right course to accomplish what they intended. This had effect as long as the cause continued; and the only fault that can be ascribed to that which they established is, that it has not proved to be perpetual; which is no more than may be justly said of the best human Constitutions that ever have bin in the world. If we will be just to our Ancestors, it will become us in our time rather to pursue what we know they intended, and by new Constitutions to repair the breaches made upon the old, than to accuse them of the defects that will for ever attend the Actions of men.[66]

To prevent the English from becoming slaves, it was necessary to find 'new Constitutions to repair the breaches made upon the old'. As Neville compactly argued, 'no laws can be executed till our government be mended'. 'New experiments' in government had become a 'necessity'.[67]

THE RULE OF LAW (I)

Opponents of the Stuarts faced a difficult challenge: they could not deny the prerogative without seeming to deny the institution of monarchy itself, and yet the very presence of the prerogative made it difficult to guarantee that England's government would serve the common good. During the crises of 1679–83, many Whigs addressed this dilemma by means of an ingenious legal fiction: they acknowledged the king's prerogative, but simultaneously proclaimed that 'the king can do no wrong'. By this they did not mean that the king had the power to do as he wished, but rather that as king he could act

---

[65] Sidney, *Discourses*, II:24, pp. 178–9, III:21, pp. 348–9.
[66] *Ibid.*, III:37, p. 420. See also II:30, pp. 241–2, III:27, p. 379.
[67] Neville, *Plato Redivivus*, in *Tracts*, pp. 170, 182.

only in ways that cohered with the law and advanced the public interest. As James Tyrrell explained:

Putting it thus, that the supreme Power . . . must be limited by some Law, does not therefore place any coercive power above [the king] . . . But a Power that may remonstrate to him where he hath acted contrary to that Law, and may by that law punish, not the Monarch, but his Ministers that have dared to transgress those known laws. For as for the Monarch himself, it is still supposed that he in his own person can do no injury.[68]

The foundation for this argument lay in the fourteenth-century distinction between the king's 'personal' and 'political' identities. The king's 'person' could be ill-advised, misled or mistaken, but his sovereign powers could not.[69] Sometimes this argument seemed to reflect the genuine commitments of MPs; at other times – as in the attempted impeachment of Lord Chief Justice Scroggs in 1681 – it was a way of 'criticizing and embarrassing the king' that was acceptable to members who were 'reluctant to blame' him directly.[70]

The limitations of this strategy were manifest by the impeachment and pardon of the earl of Danby. As chief minister to Charles II during the 1670s, Danby asserted the prerogative, attempted to render the court financially independent, pursued a strict and intolerant Anglican agenda, and purchased parliamentary influence through placemen and pensioners. To many, his actions presaged 'an *Absolute* and *Arbitrary* Government' built on the twin rocks of church and crown.[71] On 19 December 1678 Danby was impeached by the

---

[68] James Tyrrell, *Patriarcha non Monarcha* (1681), second pagination, p. 129. See also: 'An Impartial Account of the Nature and Tendency of the Late Addresses' (1681), in *State Tracts* (1693), I, 429; [Henry Care], *English Liberties: Or, The Free-Born Subject's Inheritance* (1682), pp. 1–4; Hickeringill, 'History of Whiggism', in *Works*, I, 49, 84; *A Just and Modest Vindication of the proceedings of the Two last Parliaments* (1681), p. 2. See generally Janelle Greenberg, 'Our Grand Maxim of State, "The King Can Do No Wrong"', *History of Political Thought* 12 (1991), 209–28.

[69] This argument was used to justify parliamentary resistance during the early stages of the civil war. As Neville recalled, 'the war [our parliament] declared was undertaken to rescue the king's person out of those men's hands who led him from his parliament, and made use of his name to levy a war against them' (*Plato Redivivus*, in *Tracts*, p. 148). Tories understood the significance of this claim, and aggressively sought to undermine it: [Roger L'Estrange], *An Account of the Growth of Knavery* (1678), pp. 43, 48–9.

[70] Lois Schwoerer, 'The Attempted Impeachment of Sir William Scroggs, Lord Chief Justice of the Court of King's Bench, November 1680–March 1681', *Historical Journal* 38 (1995), 843–73. See also Greenberg, 'Our Grand Maxim of State'; Howard Nenner, 'The Later Stuart Age', in J. G. A. Pocock (ed.), *The Varieties of British Political Thought* (Cambridge, 1993), pp. 196–8.

[71] *Letter from a Person of Quality*, p. 29. See generally Mark Goldie, 'Danby, the Bishops, and the Whigs', in Tim Harris, Paul Seaward and Mark Goldie (eds.), *The Politics of Religion in Restoration England* (Oxford, 1990).

House of Commons. Faced with an increasingly strident opposition, Charles II dissolved Parliament in January 1679. In March, when a new Parliament proved even more inflexible than its predecessor, the king pardoned Danby. In a letter to Henry Savile, Sidney crisply summarized the constitutional question: could the king 'pardon a man impeached by Parliament upon a publick account'? If the answer were 'yes', then the doctrine of ministerial responsibility would be destroyed, and Parliament would lose one of its primary tools for influencing the crown.[72]

Henry Neville thought this problem soluble through 'an abatement of [the] royal prerogative'. In each of the 'four great *magnalia* of government' – 'peace and war, and treaties abroad; the management of the armies, militia, and the county force at home; the management of all the public moneys, and the election of all officers whatsoever' – councils 'named in parliament' were to supervise government policy. 'These men in their several councils . . . shall be answerable to Parliament, from time to time, for any malicious or advised misdemeanour.'[73] Without formally eliminating the monarchy, Neville stripped it of its discretionary power and authority in all 'matters of state'. To his critics, this marked a return to the 'antimonarchical principles' of 1642.[74]

Algernon Sidney recommended a root-and-branch strategy; rather than domesticate the prerogative, he sought to eliminate it altogether. 'The Laws of every place show what the Power of the respective Magistrate is, and by declaring how much is allowed to him, declare what is denied; for he has not that which he has not, and is to be accounted a Magistrate whilst he exercises that which he has.' This was true even of that supreme magistrate, the king: 'We in *England* know no other King than he who is so by Law, nor any power in that King except that which he has by Law.'[75]

Royalists countered these assaults on the prerogative by invoking the logic of sovereignty. In every stable government, they argued,

---

[72] Algernon Sidney to Henry Savile, 28 April 1679, in *Letters of the Honourable Algernon Sydney, to the Honourable Henry Savile* (London, 1742), p. 40. A contemporary argued that the king was precluded from pardoning an impeachment, 'which is the suite of all and for the safety of the king and all his people' (PRO SP 30/24/6B/425).

[73] Neville, *Plato Redivivus*, in *Tracts*, pp. 185–9.

[74] W. W., *Antidotum Britannicum, Or, a Counter-Pest Against the Destructive Principles of Plato Redivivus* (1681), p. 4.

[75] Sidney, *Discourses*, II:32, p. 248, III:21, p. 354. Contrast Locke: 'Many things there are, which the Law can by no means provide for, and those must necessarily be left to the discretion of him, that has the Executive Power in his hands' (*Two Treatises*, II:159–60).

there must exist 'one Person, from whose Definitive sentence there shall lye no appeal'. As Roger L'Estrange put it, 'wheresoever the *Last Appeal* lies, there rests the *Government*'. Henry Brady invoked the authority of Thomas Hobbes: without a sovereign, social order was not possible. Moreover, they argued, a sovereign Parliament was more dangerous than a sovereign king. Edmund Bohun, Sir Robert Filmer's seventeenth-century editor, put the point this way: 'Suppose we could set up a Parliament without a King, would not this be an Arbitrary Government? Are not the Gentlemen of Venice as Arbitrary in their way as the Grand Seigneur, and the People as much Slaves there as under the most Absolute Prince in the World?' Conjuring dark memories of the civil war, Bohun wondered out loud: what would prevent Parliament from attempting once again 'to make all the rest of the Nation truckle under them in Poverty and Slavery?'[76]

Republicans made no attempt to hide the fact that the legislative power was 'Arbitrary'. That did not mean that it was capricious or unrestrained, however; rather, it was discretionary. The content of the law was contingent and variable; apart from the condition that it be 'beneficial to the people', no 'general rule' had been established by God or nature. As Sidney proudly proclaimed of England, 'We know no Laws but our own Statutes, and those immemorial Customs established by the consent of the Nation; which may be, and often are changed by us. The Legislative Power therefore that is exercised by the Parliament . . . must be essentially and radically in the People, from whom their Delegates and Representatives have all that they have.'[77] The 'empire of laws' linked the sovereign power of the people with the institutions of representative government.

This argument drew on an insight made available by the new language of interest. 'Naturally and properly a man is the judge of his own concernments', and 'all men follow that which seems advantagious to themselves'.[78] It had long been a maxim in the law that no

---

[76] John Nalson, *The Common Interest of King and People* (1677), p. 97; [Roger L'Estrange], *The Freeborn Subject* (1679), p. 3; Brady, *Great Point*, pp. 37–8; [Edmund Bohun], *An Address to the Freemen and Free-Holders of the Nation* (1682), pp. iv–v. A sovereign Parliament might rule 'as Arbitrarily as the Senate of *Venice*, under which the People really are what we call Slaves' (Hickes, *Jovian*, p. 265).

[77] Sidney, *Discourses*, III:45, p. 455; III:44, p. 450. For an extended discussion of Sidney's theory of representation, see Houston, *Algernon Sidney*, pp. 179–219.

[78] Sidney, *Discourses*, III:41, p. 436, II:28, p. 218. 'Man naturally follows that which is good, or seems to him to be so' (II:25, p. 201).

man ought to be the judge of his own case. Without denying the importance of this principle, Sidney rejected its relevance to the determination of interests. 'If I find my self afflicted with hunger, thirst, weariness, cold, heat, or sickness, 'tis a folly to tell me, I ought not to seek meat, drink, rest, shelter, refreshment, or physick, because I must not be the judge of my own case. The like may be said in relation to my house, land, or estate.' In matters of private interest, the judgement of each man was sovereign; as an increasingly popular adage had it, only the wearer knows where the shoe pinches.[79] The same logic applied collectively: ''Tis ordinarily said in *France, Il faut que chacon soit servi a sa mode*; Every mans business must be done according to his own mind: and if this be true in particular Persons, 'tis more plainly so in whole Nations.'[80]

Given this premise, the genius of Parliament lay in the fact that it 'does ever participate in the present temper of the People'. Institutionally, this was ensured in three ways: by subjecting MPs to the laws they made, by calling Parliament annually, and by empowering electors to instruct their representatives. The practice of equal subjection to the law gave vital expression to the principle of equality embodied in the social contract.[81] It also provided a check on Parliamentary malfeasance by linking the interests of representatives with those of their constituents. As Sidney cynically put it, 'the hazard of being ruin'd by those who must perish with us, is not so much to be feared, as by one who may enrich and strengthen himself by our destruction'.[82]

For similar reasons, republicans insisted that Parliament meet annually.[83] Charles II had proven himself well-versed in the art of proroguing and dissolving Parliament, and during the crises of

---

[79] 'Who will wear a Shoe that hurts him, because the Shoe-maker tells him 'tis well made? or who will live in a House that yields no defence against the extremities of Weather, because the Mason or Carpenter assures him 'tis a very good House?' (Sidney, *Discourses*, I:3, p. 9).

[80] Sidney, *Discourses*, III:16, p. 318.

[81] 'The Laws that aim at the publick Good, make no distinction of persons . . . He that will not bend his mind to them, shakes off the equality of a Citizen, and usurps a Power above the Law, to which no man submits upon any other condition, than that none should be exempted from the power of it' (Sidney, *Discourses*, III:18, p. 141).

[82] Sidney, *Discourses*, III:45, p. 457. Neville used a similar strategy in thinking about the House of Lords: 'When this new constitution shall be admitted, the lords cannot have any interest or temptation to differ with the commons in anything wherein the public good is concerned; but are obliged . . . to run the same course and fortune with the commons; their interest being exactly the same' (Neville, *Plato Redivivus*, in *Tracts*, p. 193).

[83] Neville, *Plato Redivivus*, in *Tracts*, p. 144; Sidney, *Discourses*, II:21, p. 158, II:23, p. 167, II:24, p. 198, III:15, p. 315, III:27, p. 377.

1679–83 many came to view his actions as fundamental violations of the legislative power of the people.

Finally, as a matter of right, the English people 'always may, and often do give Instructions' to their representatives. This was a logical consequence of thinking of representatives as 'Servants we employ in our public Affairs'. At the same time representatives

> cannot foresee what will be proposed when they are altogether; much less resolve how to vote till they hear the reasons on both sides. The Electors must necessarily be in the same ignorance; and the Law which should oblige them to give particular orders to their Knights and Burgesses in relation to every vote, would make the decision of the most important Affairs to depend upon the judgement of those who know nothing of the matters in question, and by that means cast the Nation into the utmost danger of the most inextricable confusion.[84]

Strictly relying on instructions would frustrate the very purpose of representation. Although the public interest was grounded in the discrete judgement of individual men, it was articulated by means of a complex process of public discussion within and between the people and Parliament.

THE RULE OF LAW (II)

The rule of law was not defined by the legislative process. For law to rule, laws must be declared, interpreted and applied.[85] Even the best of laws can become instruments of oppression; as the marquis of Halifax observed in *The Character of a Trimmer*, 'if it is true that the wisest men generally make the Laws, it is as true that the strongest do too often interpret them'.[86] After the Restoration the judicial process provided fertile ground for arguments concerning the relationship between the politics of necessity and the rule of law.

Stuart monarchs repeatedly claimed that the interpretation and application of the law was an expression of their sovereign will. In 1608 James I maintained that he was the 'supreme judge', and that

---

[84] Sidney, *Discourses*, III:44, pp. 453–4.

[85] Cynthia Herrup, 'Law and Morality in Seventeenth-Century England', *Past and Present* 106 (February 1985), 102–23.

[86] George Savile, marquis of Halifax, 'The Character of a Trimmer' (1684), in *The Works of George Savile Marquis of Halifax*, ed. Mark N. Brown (Oxford, 1989), I, 182. 'In a commonplace book from the reign of Charles II an unknown compiler recorded a line attributed to Tacitus: "There is no Tiranne so bad as he that pretends much to observe the law" [BL Harley MS 4636, fol 27]' (Howard Nenner, *By Colour of Law* (Chicago, 1977), p. 65).

'inferior judges [were] his shadows and ministers . . . The king beinge the author of the Lawe is the interpreter of the Lawe'.[87] Lord Chief Justice Coke's defence of the superiority of the 'artificial reason' of judges notwithstanding, variations on James' claims were repeated throughout the seventeenth century. As John Byrdall put it in *A New-Years-Gift for the Anti-Prerogative Men* (1682), 'with the Soveraign Prince, resideth the prime and supreme Power of interpreting his own Laws'.[88] This claim was not without justification; the king's prerogative gave him the right to suspend laws and pardon criminals, as well as the power to appoint and remove judges and JPs.

During the crises of 1679–83 the political character of the legal process was exploited to the full. 'Charges given by judges at Assizes and by chairmen at Quarter Sessions, addresses of grand juries at Assizes and Quarter Sessions, sermons at Assizes and even cases heard at Assizes and Quarter Sessions: all were designed to advertise party principles.'[89] In the spring of 1679 Whigs demanded that all commissions of the peace be inspected, and that JPs deemed insufficiently protective of the English constitution and the Protestant religion be removed. Charles II sidestepped this manœuvre, only to copy it. He repeatedly purged the rolls of JPs between 1679 and 1681,[90] leading Whigs to complain that he was opening the nation's gates to 'slavery'.[91]

In this context many came to regard juries – particularly grand juries – as the moral foundation and institutional sanctuary of the rule of law.[92] 'The Trust and Power of Grand Juries is, and ought to be, accounted amongst the greatest, and of most concern, next to the Legislative', wrote John Somers in 1681. John Hawles agreed. Without juries Englishmen would be in 'the *miserable* condition of the poor people in most *other Nations*, where they are either *wholly subject* to the *despotick, arbitrary* lusts of their Rulers; or at best under such Laws as render their Lives, Liberties, and Estates, liable to be

---

[87] Quoted in Nenner, *Colour of Law*, p. 72.

[88] (John Byrdall), *A New-Years-Gift for the Anti-Prerogative Men* (1682), p. 12.

[89] Norma Landau, *The Justices of the Peace, 1679–1760* (Berkeley and Los Angeles, 1984), p. 46. Grand jury addresses were accorded special authority because they were thought to be 'the voice of the county speaking true' (*ibid.*, p. 51).

[90] *Ibid.*, pp. 73–5; Lionel Glassey, *Politics and the Appointment of Justices of the Peace 1675–1720* (Oxford, 1979), pp. 45–52; A. F. Havighurst, 'The Judiciary and Politics in the Reign of Charles II', *Law Quarterly Review* 66 (1950), 62–78, 229–52.

[91] [Elkanah Settle], *The Character of a Popish Successor* (1681), p. 13.

[92] Shannon Stimson, *The American Revolution in the Law* (Princeton, 1990), p. 26. See also Pettit, *Republicanism*, pp. 192–3.

disposed of at the *discretion* of strangers appointed their Judges, most times *mercinary*, and Creatures of Prerogative'. According to the author of the anonymous *Guide to English Juries*, 'you are England's *Ephori* and *Tribuni*, the Boundaries of *Prerogative* and *Privilege*'.[93] Juries provided an institutional check on the partisan abuse of the law. This was particularly important in treason trials, when the judicial process was explicitly used for political purposes.[94]

Radical arguments concerning the powers of the jury and the office of the juryman focused on the determination of both fact and law. As early as the sixteenth century the growth of social complexity and the rise of personal mobility meant that juries were dependent on the testimony of witnesses. Rules of evidence were devised to assist jurors in the process of weighing, sifting and balancing information that was previously unknown to them.[95] If judges disapproved of a jury's verdict, however, they retained the right to overturn its decision and to fine or imprison individual jurors. During the decade following the Restoration common law courts increasingly used this power 'to coerce juries into support for challenged political and legal authority'. It was not until Bushel's case in 1670 that jurors were insulated against judicial coercion. 'According to Chief Justice Vaughan, testimony and verdict were "very different things". A witness swears what he has seen or heard, while a juror swears "to what he can infer and conclude from the testimony . . . by the act and force of his understanding" '.[96]

During the crises of 1679–83 critics of the crown repeatedly invoked Bushel's Case to reassure prospective jurors of their legal independence.[97] As Vaughan himself had noted, 'the judge and jury might honestly differ in the result from the evidence as well as two judges may, which often happens'.[98] Radicals expressed hostility to

---

93 [John Somers], *The Security of English-mens Lives; Or The Trust, Power, and Duty of the Grand Jurys of England* (1681), p. 19; [John Hawles], *The English-mans Right. A Dialogue between a Barrister of Law, and a Jury-man* (1680), p. 7; *A Guide to English Juries* (1682), sig. A2.

94 In a recently identified manuscript, occasioned by Shaftesbury's arrest for treason in 1681, John Locke disputed the power of judges to 'reform' the panels from which grand juries were selected (J. R. Milton and Philip Milton, 'Selecting the Grand Jury: a Tract by John Locke', *Historical Journal* 40 (1997), 185–94).

95 Barbara Shapiro, *Probability and Certainty in Seventeenth-Century England* (Princeton, 1983), pp. 176–92.

96 Stimson, *American Revolution*, p. 26; Barbara Shapiro, *'Beyond Reasonable Doubt' and 'Probable Cause'* (Berkeley and Los Angeles, 1991), p. 13.

97 Hawles, *English-mans Right*, pp. 24–34; *Ignoramus Vindicated, In a Dialogue between Prejudice and Indifference* (1681), pp. 8–12; Care, *English Liberties*, pp. 223–8; *Guide to English Juries*, p. 37.

98 'Bushel's Case' (1670), in Kenyon, *Stuart Constitution*, p. 429.

emerging rules of evidence as well. In an attempt to render the legal system more pliant to the crown's wishes, royalists had claimed that grand jurors need only determine whether there was 'probable cause' to indict a suspect. 'This may be a very good ground, for betting in a Tennis Court, or at a Horse race,' observed John Somers, 'but he that would make the Administration of Justice to depend upon such Points, seems to put a very small value upon the Fortunes, liberties, and reputation of men.' A jury should 'swear, that the bill is true', only if 'they in their Consciences believe that it is so'. John Hawles agreed. Juries had serious obligations in the truth-finding process. They were to go over the evidence carefully, making notes if necessary. They were to judge when 'any Matter is sworn, Deed read, or offered, whether it shall be believed or not, or whether it be true or false in point of fact'. In the process, they were to consider whether there had been 'Subornation, foul practice, or Tampering' with witnesses. By 'apt questions', they were to 'sift out the Truth'. They were even to consider whether the judges had summed up the evidence 'truly, fully, and impartially'. In the end, it was they and they alone who must 'be fully satisfied in their Consciences'.[99]

The power and independence of juries was dramatically extended by the claim that they were judges of law as well as fact. John Lilburne first asserted this principle during his treason trials in 1649 and 1653, and William Penn invoked it in 1671 in an attempt to undermine the Conventicle Act. It saw life once again in 1679–83.[100] According to Sidney, 'grand and petit juries . . . are not only Judges of matters of fact, as whether a man be kill'd, but whether he be kill'd criminally'. Neville concurred: 'in all trials or causes which are criminal', juries 'have absolute power, both as to matter of law, and fact . . . They are to examine and judge, as well whether, and how far the fact committed is criminal, as whether the person charged has committed that fact.'[101] Slingsby Bethel demonstrated his support

---

[99] Somers, *Security of English-Mens Lives*, pp. 128–31; Hawles, *English-mans Right*. 'What therefore in Natural and Rational signification, Evidence is, and what that word means, is the question' (*The Power and Privilege of Juries Asserted* (1681), p. 9). See also: Shapiro, *Beyond Reasonable Doubt*, pp. 43–76.

[100] Thomas Green, 'The Jury, Seditious Libel, and the Criminal Law', in R. H. Helmholz and Thomas Green, *Juries, Libel, & Justice* (Los Angeles, 1984), pp. 37–90; Thomas Green, *Verdict According to Conscience* (Chicago, 1985).

[101] Sidney, *Discourses*, III:22, p. 354; Neville, *Plato Redivivus*, in *Tracts*, pp. 130–1. See also Hawles, *English-mans Right*, pp. 10–12; *Ignoramus Vindicated*, pp. 1–2; Somers, *Security of English-mens Lives*, pp. 9–10; Care, *English Liberties*, pp. 207, 220–3; Ferguson, *Second Part*, pp. 26–32; *Guide to English Juries*, pp. 21, 148.

for this principle through action and not words; it was his responsibility, as sheriff of London, to empanel grand juries willing and able to return 'Ignoramus' verdicts.

These claims were particularly important given the king's decision to use the law of seditious libel to crush his opponents. So long as juries remained independent, and were considered competent to judge matters of law as well as fact, they could prevent the courts from being used as instruments of oppression. The intellectual foundation of this claim was extraordinary. Each member of the jury, it was argued, had the capacity to judge the character of putatively criminal acts. In the case of a trial for treason, this meant that each juror was competent to judge whether or not an act constituted a threat to the survival of the government.[102] Royalists recognized the importance of this claim, and contended that 'these devilish Republicans' could not cite a single piece of legal or constitutional evidence to support their view.[103]

What kind of men were competent to perform the office of a juryman? According to Hawles, 'there needs no more than first *understanding* to know your duty, and in the next place *courage* and *resolution* to practice it with impartiality and integrity, free from accursed *bribery* and malice, or (what is full as bad in the end) base and servile *fear*'. Particularly dangerous were those that 'make a *Trade* of being Jury-men'. '*Standing*' juries, composed of 'people that made a *Trade* on't' or 'Fellows that were Indigent in Estates as Understandings', were to be avoided. Good jurors must be peers of the accused, 'presumed to be sensible of each others infirmity'.[104] Not surprisingly, these were also the qualities of good voters and good MPs. Mercenary behaviour in court, at the polls and in parliament was thought to threaten the very foundations of the polity.[105]

The limit to these claims is as important as their reach. Restoration republicans, like the Levellers before them, harshly criticized the complexity of the English law, and argued that a simplified legal

---

[102] 'If you are not satisfied, that . . . the *Act* he has committed was Treason . . . then what remains but that you are to acquit him? For the end of Juries is to preserve Men from *oppression*' (Hawles, *English-mans Right*, p. 17). See also *The Earl of Shaftsbury's Grand-Jury Vindicted* (1682), p. 2.

[103] Northleigh, *Remarks*, p. 552. See also [Laurence Womack], *Billa Vera, Or, The Arraignment of Ignoramus* (1682).

[104] Hawles, *English-mans Right*, pp. 2, 37; *Ignoramus Vindicated*, p. 3; Somers, *Security of English-mens Lives*, p. 11. See also *Guide to English Juries*, pp. 5–6; Ferguson, *Second Part*, pp. 22–4.

[105] Houston, *Algernon Sidney*, pp. 204–8.

system would be more just and less subject to corruption. They did not, however, argue that popular judgement could replace the law, either in part or as a whole. Indeed, a formalized and articulated legal system, independent of will and caprice, was the *sine qua non* of good government. Popular judgement, exercised through juries, 'functioned to mitigate a perceived lack of judicial independence'.[106] In so doing, it helped ensure the welfare and survival of the nation.

CODA

In his brilliantly mocking satire of European statecraft, *I Ragguagli di Parnasso* (1612–13), Traiano Boccalini announced the collapse of the Spanish empire. Though her monarchy was young and her rate of growth rapid, 'she will grow no greater'. The future of Europe did not lie with Spain, nor with any of the other monarchies that longed to dominate the continent. Instead, it lay with commonwealths, particularly 'those which . . . begin to rise between the Hollanders and Zealanders in the Low Countreys'. The revolt of the Netherlands had unleashed a new force in European politics – the trading republic – that threatened to spread 'like a contagious disease, or enraged cancer'.[107]

Boccalini also announced the demise of the language of reason of state. The rule of princes rested on their monopoly of politics; once their secrets – their *arcana imperii* – were made public, they would lose their power. In one telling tale from Parnassus, Machiavelli was charged with slander by the assembled princes of Europe. 'If my writings contain nothing, but such Politick precepts, such rules of State, as I have taken out of the actions of Princes', he protested, then 'I do not deserve to be punished.' Finding this challenge irrefutable, his prosecutors changed tactic. Machiavelli, they announced, had been 'found by night amongst a flock of sheep, whom he taught to put false teeth, dogs teeth in their mouthes, thereby endangering the utter ruine of all shepherds'. As all confessed, 'it was not the wool, cheese nor lambs which made men prise sheep so much, but their

---

[106] Stimson, *American Revolution*, p. 30.
[107] Traiano Boccalini, *I Ragguagli di Parnasso: Or, Advertisements from Parnassus*, trans. Henry earl of Monmouth (1656), pp. 400–1, 208–9, 205, 210. See also pp. 294, 407–8, 420–1, 428, 446–7.

great simplicity and meakness, and that it was impossible so great numbers of them should be governed by one lonely shepherd, unless they were totally deprived of horns, teeth, and wit'.[108]

We know, with the benefit of hindsight, that Boccalini was only half right in his predictions. The rise of trading republics transformed the balance of power in Europe, but it also imposed new constraints – new crises, new emergencies, new forms of necessity – on the conduct of politics. Seventeenth-century English republicanism was not originally equipped to deal with these challenges. Republicans assumed a natural congruence between self-government, trade and prosperity, on the one hand, and absolute monarchy, territorial domination and poverty, on the other hand. Freedom and slavery were polar opposites, between which lay no neutral ground. Where free men were independent, slaves were dependent on the capricious will of another; where freedom brought 'strength, glory, plenty, security and happiness', slavery brought 'misery, infamy, destruction, and desolation'.[109] As long as this matrix of ideas was preserved intact, republicans were able to view trade in essentially political and military terms. Economics was dependent on politics; the key to strength and prosperity lay in the preservation of free institutions. The growing trade war with the Dutch, and the intrusion of continental monarchies into international markets disrupted this equation. As Hume observed in the middle of the eighteenth century, the 'established opinion, that commerce can never flourish but in a free government' had been called into question by 'the great jealousy entertained of late, with regard to the commerce of France'. For the first time in European history, 'trade was . . . esteemed an affair of state'.[110]

The discovery of trade did not lead to a second English republic. It did, however, provide fertile ground for an insight central to the republican conception of 'the empire of laws': that the welfare and

---

[108] *Ibid.*, p. 176.

[109] Sidney, *Discourses*, III:21, p. 351. Poverty under monarchy was attributed to conflicts of interest between rulers and subjects, the instability of property rights, and the anti-commercial instincts of Catholicism (Sidney, *Maxims*, p. 64; Slingsby Bethel, *The Interest of Princes and States* (1680), p. 85; Bethel, *Observations on a Letter*, p. 16; Bethel, *Present Interest*, p. 21).

[110] David Hume, 'Of Civil Liberty', in *Essays, Moral, Political, and Literary*, ed. E. F. Miller (Indianapolis, 1985), pp. 92, 88. The impact of trade on English republicanism is brilliantly explored in Istvan Hont, 'Free Trade and the Economic Limits to National Politics: Neo-Machiavellian Political Economy Reconsidered', in John Dunn (ed.), *The Economic Limits to Modern Politics* (Cambridge, 1990), pp. 41–120.

survival of the nation rested on complex networks of social, political and economic cooperation. Necessities could not be resolved in secret; they required public discussion and public justification. It was this, ironically, that cemented the connection between power and representation, reason of state and the rule of law.

CHAPTER 10

From holy cause to economic interest: the study of population and the invention of the state[1]

Steve Pincus

'Trade was never esteemed an affair of state till the last century', observed David Hume in the 1740s, 'and there scarcely is any ancient writer on politics, who has made mention of it. Even the Italians have kept a profound silence with regard to it, though it has now engaged the chief attention, as well of ministers of state, as of speculative reasoners.' This new object of study, Hume thought, was directly attributable to the 'great opulence, grandeur, and military achievements' of the English and the Dutch who 'instructed mankind in the importance of an extensive commerce'. This change in the object of statecraft was readily apparent to later-seventeenth-century English observers. 'Trade is now become the Lady, which in this present age is more courted and celebrated than in any former by all the Princes and Potentates of the world', argued the nonconformist merchant Roger Coke. This was because commerce accorded 'the pleasant aspect of wealth and plenty of all things conducing to the benefit of humane life and society'.[2]

More recently scholars have been a good deal more reticent in highlighting the innovative nature of early-modern English political culture. Jonathan Clark, for example, has insisted that England remained an 'ancien regime' until at least the 1820s. The 'political values' of eighteenth-century England 'were those appropriate to a society Christian, monarchical, aristocratic, rural, traditional and

---

[1] I am grateful for the comments and criticisms of Bernard Bailyn, Jim Chandler, Tracy Davis, Sheila Fitzpatrick, Cornell Fleischer, Adam Fox, Peter Miller, Michael Murrin, Ben Polak, Sue Stokes and Frank Trentmann. Early versions of this chapter have been presented to the North American Conference of British Studies in Washington (October 1995), the Chicago History of Political Theory Workshop, Northwestern University and Princeton University.
[2] Roger Coke, *A Discourse of Trade*. Dedicated to Sir Charles Harbord (1670), sig. B1v. I will suggest that central to the new statecraft was not only the addition of economics but an historicist consciousness, a realization that the world was now a very different place and that new practices, arguments and cultures of politics were now appropriate.

poor'.[3] 'Political legitimacy', Clark suggests, was 'conceived in personal and theological' not economic terms.[4] 'The period between the Restoration and the Reform Bill', Clark concludes, 'is obviously marked by its conservatism.'[5] Jonathan Scott, whose work focuses on seventeenth- rather than eighteenth-century developments, has reached similar conclusions. There were no revolutionary shifts in the objects of state interest, no alterations in the subject of public discourse. Scott insists that the 'issues in the reign of Charles II' 'are almost xerox copies of events, structures and issues of the early Stuart period'.[6] The English, Scott suggests, were concerned 'about religion, not about politics or economics'; it was exclusively religion 'which drove seventeenth-century English people to compromise their political allegiances and mire themselves in one another's blood'.[7] John Morrill, writing from his perspective as a specialist on the early seventeenth century, has also emphasized 'the basic continuity of seventeenth-century English politics'.[8]

British historians have found a surprising interpretative ally in the French philosopher Michel Foucault. In his later work Foucault came to study the art of government. While Foucault suggests that a notion of 'the art of government' emerged in the sixteenth century, it was only in the eighteenth that it found its proper object: economy. The term 'in the sixteenth century signified a form of government', whereas Foucault claims that it 'comes in the eighteenth century to designate a level of reality, a field of intervention'. This is because, in Foucault's formulation, the object of governance shifts from 'territory' to 'things'.[9] So, 'in the late sixteenth and early seventeenth centuries, the art of government finds its first form of crystallization, organized around the theme of reason of state' meaning that 'the state is governed according to rational principles which are intrinsic to it and which cannot be derived solely from natural or divine laws

[3] J. C. D. Clark, *English Society 1688–1832* (Cambridge, 1985), p. 9.

[4] *Ibid.*, p. 51.

[5] *Ibid.*, p. 278.

[6] Jonathan Scott, *Algernon Sidney and the Restoration Crisis, 1677–1683* (Cambridge, 1991), p. 6.

[7] Jonathan Scott, 'England's Troubles: Exhuming the popish plot', in Tim Harris, Paul Seaward and Mark Goldie (eds.), *The Politics of Religion in Restoration England* (Oxford, 1990), p. 110. This despite Scott's important discussion of interest language in mid- and later-seventeenth-century thinkers: Jonathan Scott, *Algernon Sidney and the English Republic 1623–1677* (Cambridge, 1988), pp. 201–21.

[8] John Morrill, *The Nature of the English Revolution* (London, 1993), p. 392.

[9] Michel Foucault, 'Governmentality', in Graham Burchell, Colin Gordon and Peter Miller (eds.), *The Foucault Effect: Studies in Governmentality* (Chicago, 1991), pp. 92–3.

or the principles of wisdom and prudence'.[10] But it was only in the eighteenth century that the state focused on population, its proper modern object. 'Prior to the emergence of population', Foucault suggests, 'it was impossible to conceive the art of government except on the model of the family, in terms of economy conceived as the management of a family.'[11] The eighteenth-century government focused on population 'has as its purpose not the act of government itself, but the welfare of the population, the improvement of its condition, the increase of its wealth, longevity, health, etc.; and the means that the government uses to attain these ends are themselves all in some sense immanent to the population'.[12] For Foucault these changes could not have come in the seventeenth century because 'the art of government could only spread and develop in subtlety in an age of expansion, free from the great military, political and economic tensions which afflicted the seventeenth century from beginning to end. Massive and elementary historical causes thus blocked the propagation of the art of government.'[13]

Against these views I will argue that over the course of the seventeenth century the notion of economics[14] or, more properly political economy, does in fact become a central and publicly acknowledged object of the English state. This transformation by and about the state can be clearly seen in shifting English attitudes towards the Dutch. While the Dutch polity always had a controversial place in the English imagination, the nature of the controversy

---

[10] *Ibid.*, p. 97.   [11] *Ibid.*, p. 99.   [12] *Ibid.*, p. 100.

[13] *Ibid.*, p. 97. Despite his careful caveats, Keith Baker has accepted this periodization in 'A Foucauldian French Revolution?', in Jan Goldstein (ed.), *Foucault and the Writing of History* (Oxford, 1994), pp. 197–8. It is instructive to note in this regard that Gerhard Oestreich, who discussed similar problems, came to exactly opposite conclusions with respect to timing and causation, and unsurprisingly emphasized the importance of the Netherlands in this transformation. 'The spiritual conflicts and mental contortions of contemporary theology', Oestreich writes, 'the military confrontations and the cost in human lives on all sides, the permanent state of inhumanity, insecurity and misery, of flight and exile, created the basic conditions for the widespread adoption of the ideal of humanity, an appeal for humane attitudes and conduct in all those who felt themselves threatened by the religious wars and their consequences. The claim to human dignity and the aspiration for freedom seemed to be guaranteed and satisfied by the demands for the controlling of the passions and the urge for power, for self-inspection and discipline, tolerance and moderation.' Gerhard Oestreich, *Neostoicism and the Early Modern State*, trans. David McLintock (Cambridge, 1982), p. 9.

[14] By 'economics' here I do mean it in the sense of 'population' used by Foucault, not as an analytically distinct category which Tim Mitchell has shown is uniquely characteristic of twentieth-century statecraft. See Timothy Mitchell, 'Society, Economy, and the State Effect', unpublished paper presented to State/Culture Conference at the University of Chicago, pp. 26–9.

changed over the course of the century. In the early seventeenth century the English evaluated the Dutch based on their propensity to advance the cause of true religion; whereas in the later-seventeenth century Anglo-Dutch relations were analysed with respect to the national interest. Economics had indeed become a reason of state. This was because the economic and political dislocations of the mid seventeenth century – the Thirty Years War and the English Revolution – had compelled a reconceptualization of politics, both a retreat from universalism (religious and political) and a realization that wars were won by economic preponderance rather than martial virtue. The new scepticism resulting from the failure to conclude wars of religion had opened the ideological space necessary to import notions of population as a central object of statecraft. The sociological implications of both the English civil wars and the Thirty Years War convinced the majority of observers that economic supply was vital to military success. While an emphasis on the (later) eighteenth century might make sense from a French historical perspective, by reconceptualizing and relocating the emergence of modern governance in the seventeenth century, I have replaced England, and implicitly the Netherlands, as the central loci for the study of the emergence of a new kind of early-modern statecraft – a statecraft in which the study of political economy played a central role – and have suggested that we once again focus centrally on politics and economics as the causes of seismic shifts in European ideology.

I

The English in the Elizabethan and early-Stuart periods by and large understood their world in universalist terms. For these men and women – whether Catholics, Puritans, or moderate Protestants – the paths to truth and virtue were clearly defined. Individuals sought their own salvation; princes and commonwealths were responsible for the spiritual as well as the physical well-being of their subjects. Aspiring universal monarchs – those who hoped to impose an erroneous universalism upon the world – were the greatest threats faced by Elizabeth and her Stuart successors. Princes and potentates needed to pay attention to material and worldly concerns, but this was only in order to promote virtue and spiritual happiness. Politics and religion were inextricably intertwined.

Naturally the English were not unaware that some – especially some Italians – sought material and worldly ends for their own sake. However this practice, the English were repeatedly reminded in sermons, pamphlets, plays and ballads, could only lead to disaster. The Puritan pamphleteer John Stubbs castigated 'the example of Turkish and Italian practices', the example of those who neglected 'the holy and sure wisdom of God in His word, wherein are the only honorable instructions for politics, and honestest rules for governing our houses and our persons'.[15] Thomas Scott, for all of his appreciation of the subtleties of early-modern politics, for all of his criticisms of early Stuart and Dutch republican practices, vilified the reason of state thinking of Machiavelli.[16] 'The exalting of Reason of State', Thomas Scott claimed in his translation of the writings of Traiano Boccalini, was possibly 'a more detestable and execrable idolatry than worshipping Nebuchadnezzar's image, or the golden calf.'[17] Giovanni Botero, whose pamphlets came to England from Counter-Reformation Milan rather than Calvinist Utrecht, rehearsed the same themes.[18] Botero insisted that 'the profession of State-Rulers', the supposition that 'to retain subjects in obedience of their Prince, more may humane reason, than Divine Power avail', was 'the ruin of

---

[15] John Stubbs, 'The Discoverie of a Gaping Gulf Whereunto England is like to be Swallowed . . .' (1579), in *John Stubbs's Gaping Gulf*, ed. Lloyd E. Berry (Charlottesville, 1968), p. 3. For a discussion of Stubbs and the significance of this pamphlet in Elizabethan political culture see Wallace T. MacCaffrey, *Queen Elizabeth and the Making of Policy, 1572–1588* (Princeton, 1981), pp. 255–62. It is instructive that Stubbs makes no distinction between familial and political government.

[16] For a discussion of Scott's political and religious views, and an analysis that suggests that the touchstone of Scott's ideology was his complex notion of popery, see P. G. Lake, 'Constitutional Consensus and Puritan Opposition in the 1620s: Thomas Scott and the Spanish Match', *Historical Journal* 25: 4 (1982), 805–25. For Scott's criticism of Machiavellian reason of state thinking see Thomas Scott, *The Projector* (1623), sig. A4r.

[17] Thomas Scott, *Newes from Parnassus* (1622), p. 52. John Chamberlain knew and approved of Boccalini's work long before its translation. See John Chamberlain to Sir Dudley Carleton, 10 June 1613, in Norman Egbert McClure (ed.), *The Letters of John Chamberlain* (Philadelphia, 1939), I, 457; Chamberlain to Carleton, 23 December 1613, *Chamberlain Letters*, I, 492.

[18] Here I am suggesting that while Botero might be 'recognizably an inhabitant of Machiavelli's moral universe' as Quentin Skinner has claimed, this was not necessarily how he was read in early-modern England. See Quentin Skinner, *The Foundations of Modern Political Thought*, vol. I *The Renaissance* (Cambridge, 1978), p. 249. I am in accord with Peter Donaldson who claims that 'the reason of state authors' Botero, Frachetta, Ribadeneyra, Zuccolo, Campanella and Albergatti among others 'though they recognize Machiavelli as a writer on the same subject . . . almost always reject Machiavelli's amoralism and, at some point in their discourse, accept the more traditional subordination of political theory to moral or religious principles'. Peter Donaldson, *Machiavelli and Mystery of State* (Cambridge, 1988), p. 112. Johann Sommerville has also claimed that 'most theorists who wrote in favour of "reason of state" were careful to stress that the sovereign's power was limited by his Christian duties'. Johann Sommerville, 'Absolutism and Royalism', in J. H. Burns and Mark Goldie (eds.), *The Cambridge History of Political Thought 1450–1700* (Cambridge, 1991), p. 370.

Kings, plague of Empires, scandal of Christianity'.[19] In his famous *Ragione di Stato*, Botero warned princes 'not to put hand to anything but such as they are assured as to be warranted by God's law'. He castigated 'Ideas of State' which pretended as if 'there were one law of state another of conscience', because 'such as take away conscience's jurisdiction more in public than in private things have neither soul nor God'.[20] Ben Jonson ridiculed Sir Politic Would-Be in his play *Volpone* – a play which I read as a critique of worldly behaviour in either individuals or states – for advising Peregrine to 'protest, were there no other / But simply the laws o' the land, you would content you: / Nick Machiavel, and Monsieur Bodin, both, / Were of this mind.'[21] Reason of state, in the view of most Englishmen and women, was a mode of behaviour best avoided – or at least left to Italians.

Since the outset of the Dutch war of independence in the 1560s, then, many in England saw the Dutch as potential brethren in a struggle against papal and Habsburg universalist pretensions. The English and Dutch were struggling to preserve the true religion in the face of grasping popery, not simply to promote their material well-being. The war against Spain was not publicly justified on reason of state grounds.

Sermons, pamphlets and broadsides in the later sixteenth and early seventeenth centuries consistently explained Spanish and papal actions as part and parcel of a strategy to achieve the universal monarchy. Philip II, claimed one pamphleteer, 'will never think he hath a sufficient part of the earth, till his mouth be full of earth'.[22] His aim, most agreed, was 'to become monarch of the world', to obtain 'the whole empire of Christendom'.[23] The war against Spain and the pope, it was well known, was not like the wars of 'your

---

[19] [Giovanni] Botero, *Causes of the Greatness of Cities* (1635), trans. Sir T. H., pp. 66–7. This pamphlet had been available in a number of editions in England since the turn of the century.

[20] Richard Etherington (trans.), 'An Abstract of Boterus *Della Ragione di Stato*', Dedicated to Sir Henry Hobart, BL, Sloane MSS 1065, ff. 4r, 16r. See the similar views propounded by Pont, 'Of the Union' (1604), in Brian Levack and Bruce Galloway (eds.), *The Jacobean Union: Six Tracts of 1604* (Edinburgh, 1985), pp. 4–5.

[21] Ben Jonson, *Volpone*, ed. Philip Brockbank (London, 1968), Act IV, sc. i, p. 96. It is surely interesting for my concerns that Sir Politic recorded in his diary 'a discourse . . . 'bout *ragion del stato*' with a Dutch merchant (p. 100).

[22] *An Apologie of Essex* (1598), sig. C4r.

[23] John Fregueville, *The Reformed Politicke* (1589), p. 64; 'A Short View Taken of Great Britain and Spain', temp. James I, BL, Add 39254, ff. 47–8.

forefathers, against some one particular prince in France, in Spain, or in Scotland', it was not a fight 'for lands, for honor or conquest' but a great battle 'against that horrible beast, who hath received power from the dragon'.[24] Pamphlet after pamphlet, sermon after sermon, emphasized the eschatological nature of the struggle.[25] Papal and Spanish fury was not aimed exclusively against England, but 'against all such as do not or will not acknowledge the omnipotency of [the Papal] Bulls'.[26] In this context the Dutch were England's natural allies. Whereas the English and Dutch had many natural affinities, one commentator insisted that papist pretensions 'hath drawn both of us into one and the same cause in quarrel as well of policy as religion'.[27]

Although the Anglo-Spanish peace and the Twelve Years Truce between the United Provinces and Spain lowered the ideological temperature in the first two decades of the seventeenth century, English warnings against Spanish and papal universalist pretensions revived with a vengeance with the outbreak of the Thirty Years War. The successes of the Habsburgs in Bohemia and the Palatinate, the revival of the Spanish war against the United Provinces, and the proposed marriage of the Prince of Wales to the Spanish Infanta, convinced many in England of the imminence of the threat of universal monarchy and therefore of the need to take action.[28]

From the moment James I's son-in-law Frederick lost the Bohemian throne in November 1620, many in England were sure that

---

[24] Martin, *An Exhortation* (1588), sig. A2v.

[25] *The Copie of a Letter Sent out of England to Don Bernardin Mendoza* (1588), pp. 1–2; *An Oration Militarie* (1588), sigs. A2–A3; James Aske, *Elizabetha Triumphans* (1588), p. 11; Oliver Pigge, *Meditations* (1589), p. 33; Robert Greene, *The Spanish Masquerado* (1589), sigs. B2–B3; Thomas Tymme, *A Preparation against the Prognosticall Dangers of this year, 1588* (1588), sig. B6r; Thomas Bell, *Anatomie of Popish Tyrannie* (1603), p. 3; *Northern Poems* (1604), p. 8; H. S., *Queen Elizabeth's Losse and King James his Welcome* (1603), sig. B1r; Anthony Nixon, *Elizas Memoriall* (1603), sigs. D2v–D3; Robert Pricket, *A Soldier's Wish unto his Soveraigne Lord King James* (1603), sig. C2v; Richard Mulcaster, *The Translation of Certain Latin Verses written upon her Majesties Death* (1603), sig. B2; *Englands Wedding Garment* (1603), sigs. A4v, B1r; John Gordon, *A Panegyricke of Congratulation for the Concord of the Realmes of Great Britain* (1603), pp. 5–6.

[26] *An Apologie of Essex*, sigs. F1–F2.

[27] 'A Short View', BL, Add 39254, f. 45. See also *An Oration Militarye* (1588), sigs. A3–A4.

[28] For discussions of the revival of the Protestant cause see Simon Adams, 'Spain or the Netherlands? The Dilemmas of Early Stuart Foreign Policy', in Howard Tomlinson (ed.), *Before the English Civil War* (London, 1983), pp. 79–101; Simon Adams, 'Foreign Policy and the Parliaments of 1621 and 1624', in Kevin Sharpe (ed.), *Faction and Parliament* (London, 1978), pp. 139–71.

only a superhuman effort could prevent a Habsburg and popish universal dominion. Spain's 'principal end', wrote Thomas Scott in his wildly popular *Vox Populi*, was 'to get the whole possession of the world, and to reduce all to unity, under one temporal head' so that the Spanish king 'may truly be what he is styled, the Catholic and Universal King'.[29] Scott tirelessly repeated this claim in pamphlet after pamphlet in the 1620s. Spain's growth rate was such, he claimed, 'that she will arrive to that unmeasurable height of the Universal Monarchies, whereunto the Roman monarchy attained'.[30] Spain could depend upon the pope to use 'his ecclesiastical keys . . . for the enlargement of that quintessential monarchy'.[31]

Neither Scott nor his imitators understood the struggle against Spain to be for worldly ends. Failure to join in the Protestant cause, warned Thomas Gataker, would bring down 'the curse of Meroz'.[32] The prince of Wales's chaplain Thomas Winiffe compared the Habsburg general Spinola 'to the devil, that as he warreth and fighteth against the soul, so the other like a greedy wolf seeketh to devour the innocent lamb the Palatinate'.[33] 'The world hath cried out', claimed one pamphleteer, that Spain allied with the Jesuits 'would be the Monarch of the West'.[34] 'The religion and policies' of the Spanish and papists 'were all one', agreed another polemicist, and their aim was 'an ambitious superiority and sole monarchy of all Europe'.[35] No wonder the English, even in an era of economic hardship, were so 'ready to assist' the German Protestants 'not only with our prayers but with our purse'.[36]

Those who understood European politics in this way, those who feared and loathed a Spanish universal monarchy, insisted that the Dutch needed to be embraced as Protestant brethren. 'The vulgar multitude here in England . . . hate the Spaniards and love the

---

[29] Thomas Scott, *Vox Populi* (1620), p. 6. For the wild popularity of the pamphlet, see John Rous, 'Diary' (1620), BL, Add 28640, f. 100r.

[30] Thomas Scott, *Newes from Parnassus* (1622), p. 9. See also Thomas Scott, *The Belgick Souldier* (1624), sig. C1r; Thomas Scott, *Sir Walter Rawleigh's Ghost* (Utrecht, 1626), pp. 2, 14.

[31] Thomas Scott, *Symmachia: or A True-Lovers Knot* [1623], p. 11.

[32] Thomas Gataker, *A Sparke toward the Kindling of Sorrow for Sion* (1621), pp. 37–8.

[33] Chamberlain to Carleton, 13 April 1622, *Chamberlain Letters*, ii, 432.

[34] *Two Letters or Embassies* (Amsterdam, 1620), sig. E1r.

[35] 'A Private Consideration of the feared sequel of the intended marriage' (1622), BL, Egerton MSS 783, f. 1v.

[36] Chamberlain to Carleton, 13 November 1619, *Chamberlain Letters*, ii, 272. See also Chamberlain to Carleton, 10 November 1621, *Chamberlain Letters*, ii, 405.

Hollander', observed Thomas Scott.[37] It was because of Anglo-Dutch religious affinity, it was for 'religion's sake principally' that the English were 'ready to drop their money and their blood freely' for the United Provinces.[38] Should the Spanish conquer the Dutch, should the king of Spain become 'absolute master of this wise and diligent people, he would soon be master of all Europe besides'. 'We being for Christ, and he for Antichrist', the English, in Scott's view, had no choice but to aid their Protestant brethren.[39] It was this logic which made it 'the fervent desire' of 'the major part of the kingdom' to have a 'strong and hearty confederacy with that people'.[40]

Naturally not everyone understood European politics in this way. Not everyone was convinced of Habsburg universalist aspirations; not everyone was certain that the Dutch should be embraced as Protestant brethren. But those who dissented, dissented in their interpretation of events, not in their worldview. Confessional politics was not contrasted, at least in public discussion,[41] with a politics of reason of state. Dutch atrocities in the Indies, for example, and especially the spectacular massacre at Amboyna, demonstrated Dutch perfidy and lack of virtue. The massacre at Amboyna formed the basis of a mythology to set against the Black Legend of Spain; it was not seen as a battle in a modern trade war.[42] Significantly, the proponents of the Protestant cause responded to the massacre by blaming it on the republicans, the friends of Spain in the United Provinces. Thomas Scott hinted darkly 'that the disgust betwixt the

---

[37] Thomas Scott, *A Tongue-Combat* (1623), p. 52. Of course the same sentiments were expressed in the Parliament of 1621: see Chamberlain to Carleton, 1 December 1621, *Chamberlain Letters*, ii, 412.

[38] Scott, *Symmachia*, pp. 1, 31.

[39] Scott, *The Belgick Pismire* (1622), pp. 60–1.

[40] 'Some Reasons why England should Continue the protection of the United Provinces', *c.* 1620s, BL, Egerton MSS 783, f. 14r.

[41] I am well aware that both opponents and proponents of alliance with the Dutch did advance reason of state, even economic, arguments. But these were arguments reserved for the Privy Council, or at least addressed to the Privy Council. This was undoubtedly because of the strictures against the public discussion of *arcana imperii*. The most famous economic argument against alliance with the Dutch was written by Thomas Mun. It is telling that it did not appear in print until 1664. See also 'A Discourse Concerning Peace with Spain' (1602), Huntington Library, EL 7976(3). Most prominent among the proponents of alliance who employed secular as opposed to confessional language were the advocates of 'common cause' ably described by Tom Cogswell: see Thomas Cogswell, *The Blessed Revolution* (Cambridge, 1989), especially, pp. 74–5.

[42] Chamberlain to Carleton, 27 May 1620, *Chamberlain Letters*, ii, 305; Chamberlain to Carleton, 24 July 1624, *Chamberlain Letters*, ii, 569; Chamberlain to Carleton, 26 February 1625, *Chamberlain Letters*, ii, 602.

two nations in the East-Indies, was not sent without a Romish practice'.[43] 'The injuries and abuses offered to our nation in Moscovy, Greenland, and the East-Indies, were not the acts of the [Dutch state], but of wicked persons', persons who would 'gladly have the king of Spain their master'.[44] To the English mind, it was the republican faction, the faction of Oldenbarnevelt, 'the Arminian faction' so 'cunningly cherished by the Spaniard' which had treated the English so perfidiously.[45] The atrocities in the East Indies were not to be set against the Spanish Black Legend but in fact formed part of it. No wonder one popular ditty scattered on the streets of London warned that 'While for their shares / of Indian wares / English and Dutch do brawl, / The Spaniard watcheth / advantage catcheth / To seize on them and all.'[46]

The main thrust of the public critique of the Protestant cause, however, was an alternative battle cry, a call for a crusade against the Infidel.[47] In March 1621 James enthusiastically received the Polish ambassador and reassured him that the English and Scots could be counted on 'to resist the Turk'. The ideological stakes were immediately clear to John Chamberlain who wryly noted that the Poles had aided the Holy Roman Emperor in Bohemia, making them deserving of 'no great favour nor assistance'.[48] Nevertheless the ambassador's Latin oration was published at James's behest, initiating a flurry of

---

[43] Scott, *Belgick Pismire*, p. 67.

[44] Scott, *Tongue-Combat*, p. 69. Significantly the speaker in this dialogue is called 'Tawny-Scarf' indicating his Orangism and his opposition to the Dutch republican faction.

[45] 'A Private Consideration of the feared sequel of the intended marriage' (1622), BL Egerton MSS 783, f. 13v; Chamberlain to Carleton, 31 May 1619, *Chamberlain Letters*, ii, 239; Scott, *Vox Populi*, sig. B4v.

[46] David Underdown (ed.), *William Whiteway of Dorchester his diary 1618 to 1635* (Dorchester, 1991), October 1621, pp. 40–1. The same poem appears in the pages of John Rous's 'Diary' with the claim that 'these verses were said to be a caveat left by the States in London 1622'. BL, Add 28640, f. 103v.

[47] Despite James's epithet of *Beati Pacifici*, he and his propagandists made it clear that he was no pacifist. God bids princes to 'strike sometimes, and they must do it', reasoned Sir John Stradling: *Beati Pacifici*. Perused by His majesty and printed with authority (London, 1623), p. 11. It is interesting in this context to wonder why James sought such a militant self-image if he was really primarily concerned with functional breakdown. Surely a pacifist position would have better served his turn. F. L. Baumer long ago discussed the persistence of the idea of the common corps of Christendom. He has shown that 'during the sixteenth and early seventeenth centuries . . . the idea of "the common corps of Christendom" continued to hold its ground to an astonishing degree in official as in other circles'. See his 'England, the Turk, and the Common Corps of Christendom', *American Historical Review* 50: 1 (October 1944), 27–8. Baumer discusses the situation in early Stuart England, and shows that war against the Turk was long one of James's aims, see pp. 32, 36–9, 44–7.

[48] Chamberlain to Carleton, 10 March 1621, *Chamberlain Letters*, ii, 352; Chamberlain to Carleton, 24 March 1621, *Chamberlain Letters*, ii, 353.

anti-Ottoman literature.[49] The Turks seek 'wars after wars', the Polish ambassador warned, and not being 'satisfied with the Empire of Asia, Africa, and greater part of Europe, design what ever remains for prey, and according to their religion imagine it is not lawful for them to do otherwise'.[50] The Turks, chimed in one officially sanctioned pamphleteer, 'are indeed transported with an insulting bravery that they are a people designed by God to be the principal nation of the earth, and a scourge to whip the sinners of the world'.[51] Sir John Stradling belittled the differences between papists and Protestants, insisting that 'if learned men of temp'rate disposition, / Would reason mildly, rancor laid aside: / They might draw points of faith to composition' for it was 'known, as well one side, as th'other, / Call and esteem the holy Church their Mother'.[52] Instead of alliance with the Dutch in support of the Protestant cause, Stradling urged the unification of Christendom to fight the Turk, which was 'a blessed work indeed, and better far, / Than be the works wherein we stand engaged.'[53] 'He that will fight or maintain wars, wants not an enemy against whom he may show his valor', argued Botero, whose work was circulating in some court circles in the 1620s. 'The Turk', Botero concluded, 'we have at the door on each side'; there could be no 'more just and honored wars than against him, which hath so many forts, cities, kingdoms, empires which commands Asia and Africa and hath more countries in Europe than all the states of Princes Catholic, who by our discord is so increased that by land for 300 years last past he has been master of the field'.[54] So powerful was the claim, so large did Ottoman pretensions to the universal monarchy loom in the imagination of some in England, that the Lord Chancellor Francis Bacon also called for a holy war against the Infidel.[55]

---

[49] Tom Cogswell has discussed this theme with regard to the Spanish match in 'England and the Spanish Match', in Richard Cust and Ann Hughes (eds.), *Conflict in Early Stuart England* (London, 1989), pp. 120–1.

[50] *A True Copy of the Latine Oration of the Excellent Lord George Ossolinski*, 11 March 1621. Commanded by His Majesty to be published in print [1621], p. 14.

[51] *Newes from Poland*. Published by authority (1622), pp. 1–2.

[52] Stradling, *Beati Pacifici*, pp. 17–19.

[53] *Ibid.*, pp. 23–4, 35.

[54] Richard Etherington (trans.), 'An Abstract of Boterus', BL Sloane MSS 1065, ff. 43–4.

[55] Francis Bacon, 'Of an Holy War', in *The Works of Francis Bacon* (London, 1824), III, 478. Significantly, the proponents of the Protestant cause felt compelled to deny the seriousness of the Ottoman threat. See *Newes from Turkie and Poland* (1622), pp. 31, 39; Thomas Scott, *Sir Walter Rawleighs Ghost* (1626), p. 20; Scott, *Newes from Parnassus*, p. 31.

In the Elizabethan and early Stuart periods, then, discussion of European politics and in particular debates about a Dutch alliance were not conducted in the idiom of reason of state. The arguments were universalist not particularist, confessional not economic. While the Privy Council might have entertained arguments advanced using interest language, the public and popular conception of England's proper role was configured in terms of the Protestant cause or the reunification of Christendom. Economics was clearly not yet conceived to be the proper object of states.

II

The upheavals of the 1640s and 1650s in England produced a new social and cultural landscape. Political, social and religious experiments had generated a taste for popular political discussion. The notion that pamphlets and news were only suitable for the Privy Council or the privy,[56] that 'regal ruling is no common art, / King's councils upon secrecy are grounded'[57] was no longer widely held. The 'present humor of the nation' was such that 'not a fop or simpleton, but is a statesman'.[58] By the time of the Glorious Revolution it was a commonplace that everyone would 'dogmatically presume to censure and judge of transactions of state'.[59]

The failure to establish a constitution based on inspiration in the Nominated Parliament coupled with the inability of the interregnum regimes to conclude a religious war with the Dutch forced a reconceptualization of politics.[60] The language and style of politics underwent a dramatic shift. Englishmen and women now appealed to reason rather than inspiration, moderation rather than enthusiasm.

Naturally this transformation did not happen immediately or without resistance. The conflict between an older vision of politics

---

[56] Sir William Cornwallis, *Essayes* (1606), sig. H6v.

[57] Stradling, *Beati Pacifici*, p. 26.

[58] Henry Stubbe, *A Further Justification of the Present War Against the United Netherlands* (1673), p. 11.

[59] William Westby, Memorandum Book, August 1688, Folger Library, MSS v. a. 469, f. 34r. I have discussed the emergence and development of the early-modern English public sphere at greater length in 'Coffee Politicians do Create', *Journal of Modern History* 67: 4 (1995), 807–34.

[60] These themes are discussed at greater length in part III of my book *Protestantism and Patriotism: Ideologies and the Making of English Foreign Policy 1650–1668* (Cambridge, 1996) and in my 'England and the World in the 1650s', in John Morrill (ed.), *Revolution and Restoration* (London, 1992), pp. 129–47.

based on universalist concerns and one based on economic interest came into clear focus when the restored Rump Parliament debated whether and in what fashion to become involved in the impending conflict between Sweden and Denmark in the Sound. There Lutheran Sweden had attacked Lutheran Denmark in order to dominate the Baltic trade, drawing the Protestant United Provinces into the conflict on the Danish side. The situation seemed to confirm the existence of an amoral world of international relations – a world described forcefully by the French Huguenot military theorist, Henri duc de Rohan. Rohan had argued that all political actions were determined by interest, and that interest had nothing to do with 'the diversity of religion'. Princes and states, Rohan insisted, succeeded or failed based on whether they discerned and followed their true interest, not on zeal to promote the true faith.[61] So powerful was the draw of Rohan's analysis, so ostensibly relevant to the crisis in the Baltic, that it demanded a response from no less an intellectual figure than the Scottish virtuoso John Dury. Dury had no difficulty with Rohan's policy conclusions. Indeed he praised Rohan as 'rational and clear' for condemning the Spanish aspirations for universal monarchy. However, Dury found Rohan's lack of confessional analysis extremely disturbing. Rohan had ignored 'matters of far greater weight', Dury proclaimed. 'The Protestant cause (if rightly understood) doth not rely upon such state transactions', he thundered, it 'is not so much upheld and propagated by the balance of power and policy as of righteousness and of truth manifest'. The interest of England and the Protestant cause, Dury thought, should 'aim at nothing properly but at the greatness of Jesus Christ, that his kingdome of truth, of righteousness, of peace, and of joy in the world may be exalted and set up in the hearts of all men, above all other advantages of might, of honour, or of riches'.[62]

While some took Dury's brief to heart when the restored Rump Parliament discussed England's policy in the Baltic, most did not. The fierce debate raged over what policy to support, not over what were the terms of debate. Some argued for intervention on the

---

[61] Henri duc de Rohan, *A Treatise of the Interest of the Princes and States of Christendome* (1641), sig. A7, p. 44. Rohan's thinking, I am saying, was extremely important in England. However, Rohan did not systematically analyse the interest of states in economic terms. It is perhaps telling that only England and the Netherlands are said by him to have commerce as their true interest. The centrality of economics to public political analysis, then, was truly an English and Dutch invention.

[62] John Dury, *The Interest of England in the Protestant Cause* (1659), pp. 2–3.

Danish side on the grounds that King Charles X of Sweden was determined to achieve a Swedish universal monarchy. Others plumped for Sweden because the Dutch and the Danes have 'in all our troubles' sought to 'undermine the interest of England'.[63] All sides agreed, however, that the question at hand was about the interest of England not about universalist conflict. 'I will not judge whether this be a Protestant war or no', insisted Major-General John Lambert, 'the interest of England is, or ought to be, the great care in this business.'[64] Tom Challoner, who opposed war with the Dutch and Danes, chimed in that the debate was about 'the interest of England and preservation of your trade'.[65] Thomas Scott and John Maynard, who supported a war against the Dutch and Danes, also framed the debate in terms of 'the fairest mistress in all Christendom, trade'.[66] Sir Arthur Haselrigg explained just how irrelevant a confessional foreign policy, a foreign policy directed against the Antichrist, had become. 'I do not know who the Antichrist is', he exclaimed, 'I do not think that Antichrist must come down by the fleshly sword; it must be by another kind of weapon . . . Antichrist must not fall but by the spirit.'[67] Since governments are not founded in grace, since their purview is only of this world, the promotion of the true religion could not be their concern, could not be England's interest. Henry Neville eloquently summarized the situation. The age of wars for 'the Protestant religion' – wars fought on confessional grounds – was over. Now wars might be fought for the 'Protestant interest or cause', wars which had nothing to do with promoting religious truth but occurred 'when several particulars agree and league together for maintaining their respective dominions'. England's particular interest, he observed, was 'trade' and in the pursuit of that 'interests of state may, peradventure, far engage us'.[68]

The restored Rump collapsed without having done much to resolve the Baltic conflict. However, the lasting significance of the conflict lay in the mode of political analysis which the Rumpers finally adopted. Issues of national interest not universal truth domi-

[63] *A Reply to the Danish Papers*, 2 March 1659 [1659], p. 3.
[64] John Lambert's Speech, 21 February 1659, in John Towill Rutt (ed.), *Diary of Thomas Burton*, 4 vols. (London, 1828), III, 400.
[65] Tom Challoner, 24 February 1659, in Rutt, III, 464.
[66] Thomas Scott, 21 February 1659, in Rutt, III, p. 394; John Maynard, 24 February 1659, in Rutt, III, p. 462. The quote is from Scott.
[67] Sir Arthur Haselrigg, 24 February 1659, in Rutt, III, p. 458.
[68] Henry Neville, 21 February 1659, in Rutt, III, 387–8.

nated the vital and vitriolic debate over the proper constitutional form for England. The future bishop of Oxford and monarchist, John Fell, framed that debate in terms of 'the real good of the nation [which] consists not in the private benefit of single men, but the advantage of the public', a notion which he termed 'the common national interest'. Central to Fell's conception was the revival of England's 'languishing and almost dead trade'. While Fell was a deeply religious man, he felt that an interest analysis of politics was sufficient because in matters of secular government 'men do not use to be importuned to leave their torment or disease, or want rhetorical inducements, after the pleadings of interest and profit'.[69] In his vitriolic reply to Fell entitled *Interest will not Lie*, the republican Marchamont Nedham conceded only two things to his opponent: that the debate was about the interest of England, and that trade needed to be considered a reason of state.[70] The public debate about governments and their duties was clearly in the process of shifting into the idiom of reason of state – an idiom which they had subtly transformed to include the economy as one of its central objects.

Sceptical of their ability to discern the best course to promote the true religion, then, the English after the Restoration sought instead to further the national interest. Now 'the genius and disposition of the times' was 'to study more the interest and improvement of the nation than usually heretofore', observed Samuel Fortrey just after the Restoration.[71] 'Joint interests have often secured the peace of differing religions', that epitome of Restoration loyalism Sir Heneage Finch lectured the House of Commons, 'but agreeing professions hath no example of preserving the peace of different interests. Religion never united those whose interests were divided.'[72] Slingsby Bethel, who was more likely to speak a popular than a courtly language, agreed that 'the prosperity or adversity, if not the life and death of a State, is bound up in the observing or neglecting of its interest'.[73]

After the Restoration English people of all ideological stripes publicly argued that commerce lay at the heart of the national

---

[69] John Fell, *The Interest of England*, 22 July 1659 (1659), pp. 3–4, 8, 16.

[70] Marchamont Nedham, *Interest will not Lie*, 27 August 1659 (1659), pp. 4, 46.

[71] Jacob H. Hollander (ed.), *Samuel Fortrey on England's Interest and Improvement 1663* (Baltimore, 1907), p. 9.

[72] Sir Heneage Finch, 'Speech for Supply', 31 October 1673, Leicestershire Record Office, D.G.7/Box4957/pp.33.

[73] Slingsby Bethel, *The Present Interest of England Stated* (1671), sig. A2r.

interest.[74] Economy had become the central object of governance; population not land held the key to national prosperity. 'Trade and commerce', argued the Anglican Royalist Charles Molloy, 'are now become the only object and care of all Princes and potentates'. This was because 'the return of commerce is riches and plenty of all things conducing to the benefit of humane life, and fortifying their countries with reputation and strength'.[75] 'The undoubted interest of England is trade, since it is that only which can make us either rich or safe', agreed the religiously tolerant duke of Buckingham.[76] Unsurprisingly the merchant adventurer and future Whig sheriff Slingsby Bethel thought that 'trade is the true and intrinsic interest of England, without which it cannot subsist: from trade there doth not only arise riches to subjects, rendering a nation considerable, but also increase of revenue, and therein power and strength to the sovereign'.[77]

This new conception of the national interest was necessarily conceptually distinct from, though not politically antagonistic to, the sovereign's interest. While few argued that the national interest was comprised of the sum total of individual interests in the nation, most did believe that the national interest was best revealed by popular sentiment. 'Since interest will not lie', asked one Whig pamphleteer, 'how is it morally possible that the major part of a nation . . . should act contrary to the true and proper interest of their country?' 'For tho' particular men may be imposed upon by artifice, or deluded with pretenses, or biased by private advantages', concluded this polemicist, ''tis not imaginable that the whole body should either be so infatuated as not to see or so stupidly tame as not to oppose, as far

---

[74] Albert O. Hirschman has noticed this shift in interest language in later-seventeenth-century England without offering an account of its causes. 'It was thereafter [the Restoration]', Hirschman observes, 'toward the end of the century with political stability reestablished and a measure of religious toleration ensured that the interests of groups and individuals were increasingly discussed in terms of economic aspirations.' *The Passions and the Interests* (Princeton, 1977), p. 37. Hirschman, I think, overplays the similarity of thinking between England and France. Hirschman, of course, is interested to explain the emergence of a capitalist culture, not to identify a new form of the state. Anthony Pagden has recently reached similar conclusions for the entirety of Europe, also without explaining why such a transformation in the art of governance might have occurred: 'In one sense the growing recognition of the place of economics in the organization of states had, by the mid-seventeenth century, demonstrated to all but the most determinedly self-destructive that power could no longer be detached from what Diego Saavedra Fajardo in 1640 called "economic prudence"'. Anthony Pagden *Lords of all the World* (New Haven, 1995), p. 115.

[75] Charles Molloy, *De Jure Maritimo et Navali* (1676), sig. A3r,

[76] George Villiers, duke of Buckingham, *A Letter to Sir Thomas Osborne* (1672), p. 11.

[77] Slingsby Bethel, *An Account of the French Usurpation Upon the Trade of England* (1679), p. 4. See also John Smith, *England's Improvement Reviv'd* (1673), p. 258.

as lawfully they may what tends their universal ruin.'[78] Because
political power was now conceived in terms of the national interest,
the moderate Sir William Temple could uncontroversially assert that
'in running on Councils contrary to the general humor and spirit of
the people, the king indeed may make his ministers great subjects,
but they can never make him a great prince'.[79] Another Restoration
moderate or Trimmer, Sir Thomas Meres, made the point more
forcefully in criticizing Charles II's foreign policy. 'The interest of the
nation is in this House, and the ministers are of another interest', he
thundered to the Commons, 'we can never live happily without the
king's favour, nor he without our advice; and I will die in this
opinion'.[80] Significantly the Tory supporter of James II, Edmund
Warcup, explained his king's success in terms of the national interest.
'Never king more pursued the true interest of England', Warcup
explained to his Oxfordshire friend Hugh Jones, 'he will make this a
more glorious nation than ever we have been'.[81]

Unsurprisingly, then, the Restoration debate about England's
proper relations with the Netherlands was conducted in terms very
different from the pre-civil war discussion. The national interest
rather than religious virtue had become the measure of desirability.

Many of the most enthusiastic supporters of the newly Restored
monarchy were convinced that Charles II should immediately
initiate a war against the perfidious Netherlanders. This was because
the Dutch were on the brink of monopolizing the world's commerce;
they were on the brink of establishing a universal monarchy of trade.
The Dutch East and West India Companies might seem to be modest
trading concerns, but in reality they were the tools of empire-
builders. 'The Netherlanders', one pamphleteer pointed out during
the second Anglo-Dutch War, 'from the beginning of their trade in
the Indies, not contented with the ordinary course of a fair and free
commerce, invaded diverse islands, took some forts, built others, and
labored nothing more than the conquest of countries and the

---

[78] *Vox Patriae* (1681), sig. A1v. For Bethel this observation implied an obligation upon each
    Englishman to examine whether the government's 'counsels and actions are prusuant of,
    and consonant to, their interests'. Bethel, *Present Interest of England Stated*, sigs. A2v–A3r.
[79] William Temple, *Miscellanea* (1680), p. 166.
[80] Sir Thomas Meres, 7 May 1678, in Anchitell Grey (ed.), *Debates of the House of Commons From
    the Year 1667 to the Year 1694* (London, 1763), V, 357.
[81] Edmund Warcup (Northmore) to Hugh Jones, 14 September 1685, Bodleian Library, Rawl.
    Lett. 48, f. 11v.

acquiring of new dominion.'[82] The East India Company, whose 'Governor-General of the Indies' kept a 'royal court', had 'kings and kingdoms tributary to it'. 'Scarce any subject occurs more frequent[lie] in the discourses of ingenious men', William Aglionby reported, 'than that of the marvelous progress of this little state which in the space of about one hundred years . . . hath grown to a height, not only infinitely transcending all the ancient Republics of Greece, but not much inferior in some respects even to the greatest monarchies of these latter ages.'[83] No wonder the English Secretary of State Henry Coventry referred to the United Provinces as 'that sea-monarchy'.[84]

Perfidious Dutch activity in the Indies was no longer understood, as it had been in the earlier period, as a manifest failure to partake in the promotion of religious truth. Instead, Restoration Englishmen and women were well aware that the Dutch were promoting an economic universalism. They knew that the Dutch had made trade an object of state. The Dutch, it was argued, were not merely eager and aggressive merchants seeking to trade in new territories, they were grasping for a monopoly of all the world's trade. 'Who would have thought that our old petitioners should ever become our new controllers?' asked Charles II's chaplain Francis Gregory, 'that they, who were not able to secure to themselves a small spot of land, should now claim the vast dominion of the seas, and the main trade of the world?'[85] One Tory was convinced that the United Provinces aimed at 'the dominion of both the Indies'.[86] Another was certain that William III's invasion in 1688 had nothing to do with religion, but was rather an attempt to subdue 'us to the Dutch, and by the conjunction of our strength under their command, to make themselves masters of the sea and traffic'.[87]

---

[82] William Aglionby, *The Present State of the United Provinces of the Low-Countries* (1671), sig. A4v.

[83] *Ibid.*, sig. A4, pp. 163–4, 236; see also *Europae Modernae Speculum: Or, A View of the Empires, Kingdoms, Principalities and Common-Wealths of Europe* (1665), pp. 66–7. It is important to note that Dr Aglionby was a close friend of, and tutor for, the 'rabidly Anglican' Robert Paston, earl of Yarmouth. See William Aglionby to Mr Arundel, 26 May 1671, Cambridge University Library, MSS Dd.11.57, f. 67v. On Yarmouth see John Miller, *Charles II* (London, 1991), p. 249.

[84] Henry Coventry, 7 February 1673, Grey, *Debates*, II, 10–11.

[85] Francis Gregory, Rector of Hambleton, chaplain to Charles II, *The Right Way to Victory*. Preached at the Guildhall 22 June 1673 (1673), p. 13.

[86] 'An Essay on the Interest of the Crown in American Plantations and Trade' (1685), BL, Add 47131, f. 231.

[87] *The Dutch Design Anatomized* (1688), p. 18.

Anglican Royalist opinion at court, on the London exchange, in the provinces, even in Persia was unanimous in this interpretation of Dutch economic strategy. The court poet John Dryden expressed the sentiment most eloquently: 'Trade, which like blood should circularly flow, / Stop'd in their Channels, found its freedom lost: / Thither the wealth of all the world did go, / And seem's but shipwreck'd on so base a coast.'[88] It had become a commonplace that the Dutch 'thought to grasp a pow'r great as old Rome, / Striving to carry all commerce away, / And make the universe their only prey'.[89] Although 'no nation can be rich that abounds not in some part of his dominions in shipping, or who neglects trade', the moderate Anglican Royalist Sir Philip Warwick insisted, 'yet it is no policy to think to engross it, or be monarchs of it, as Holland hath for a time affected, & pursued that Sea-Monarchy as eagerly as Charles the Fifth or Francis the First did the Land Monarchy'.[90]

Those who advocated alliance with the Dutch after the Restoration did so not in the hopes of a Protestant compact which would finally extirpate the forces of the Antichrist, but because they thought it was in the national interest. Instead of attempting to explain away Dutch economic expansionism as a manifestation of Jesuit influence, most argued that there were enough economic resources to satisfy the appetites of both maritime powers. 'The world affords matter enough to satisfy both nations', testified Slingsby Bethel.[91] Joseph Hill derided the 'senseless clamor of men' for a war, men who insisted 'we are competitors for trade! It's our interest! Our interest! Down with the Dutch! Down with the English!' He was sure 'the world is wide enough, and the sea large enough for both nations to exercise their skill and industry'.[92]

---

[88] John Dryden, 'Annus Mirabilis', in Edward Niles Hooker and H. T. Swedenberg, Jr (eds.), *The Works of John Dryden*, vol. 1: *Poems 1649–1689* (Berkeley, 1956), pp. 59–60, lines 5–9. Similar points are made in *Hogan-Moganides: Or, The Dutch Hudibras* (1674), p. 112; *Dutch Design Anatomiz'd*, p. 18.

[89] Robert Wild, *A Panegyricke Humbly Addresst to the king's Most Excellent Majesty*. On meeting of the Parliament 4–5 February 1673 (1673), p. 3. Similar points were made by Edmund Waller in 'Instructions to a Painter' (1665), in George DeF. Lord, *Poems on Affairs of State*, vol. 1: *1660–1678* (New Haven, 1963), p. 25, lines 69–70; John Crouch, *The Dutch Imbergo, Upon the State Fleet* (1665), p. 7; and the author of *The Frog, or The Low-Countrey Nightingale, Sweet Singer of Amsterdam* [1672], pp. 1–2.

[90] Sir Philip Warwick, 'Of Government', 28 August 1679, Huntington Library, MSS HM 41956, p. 182. Warwick did not believe, in 1679, that the Dutch were still pursuing that policy. I owe this reference to the kindness and generosity of Professor Blair Worden.

[91] Bethel, *Present Interest of England*, pp. 32–3.

[92] Joseph Hill, *The Interest of these United Provinces*, 30 November 1672 (1673), sig. G2.

In this view the real threat to the English national interest, the most serious aspirant to universal monarchy, was not the United Provinces but France. Louis XIV sought through his mercantilist policies to monopolize the world's trade, and thereby establish the universal monarchy. The 'great duties and customs' with which all imports into France 'are clogg'd and encumbered' was the means by which Louis XIV built up 'such an inexhaustible fund of treasure to carry on his designs to the oppression of all Europe'.[93] Louis XIV, thought another polemicist, was 'endeavoring to make his subjects sole merchants of all trades'.[94] Marchamont Nedham was sure that the policies of Louvois and Colbert aimed to make France 'the only emporium or market in the world'.[95] Pamphlet after pamphlet, parliamentary speaker after parliamentary speaker, concurred that Louis XIV sought 'to become master of the commerce of Europe',[96] coveted 'the universal trade, all the world over',[97] was setting up 'an universal monarchy of commerce'.[98] 'It is agreed at all hands', summarized Slingsby Bethel, 'that the French set up for an universal commerce as well as for an universal monarchy. And in effect, the one is but a necessary consequent upon the other.'[99]

Only an Anglo-Dutch alliance could prevent the impending French universal monarchy of commerce. An Anglo-Dutch alliance, in this view, was clearly in the national interest. '"Tis the interest of Holland to be ready to join with us and we with them', thought William Sacheverell, 'and, if joined, France can never come up to us, in number or force.'[100] Marchamont Nedham reported that the French were well aware that 'a durable friendship between us and the United Provinces' was 'that alone that can set bounds to their ambition, and redeem Europe from that yoke which they are framing, and devising how to put about our necks'.[101]

[93] *The French Intrigues Discovered* (1681), pp. 5–6.
[94] *Popery and Tyranny: Or, The Present State of France* (1679), p. 13.
[95] Marchamont Nedham, *The Pacquet-Boat Advice* (1678), p. 4.
[96] *A Free Conference Touching the Present State of England Both at Home and Abroad: In Order to the Designs of France*, 21 January 1668 (1668), pp. 22–3.
[97] Sir William Coventry, 29 January 1678, in Grey, *Debates*, v, 20.
[98] *French Intrigues Discovered*, p. 5. See also Slingsby Bethel, *The French Usurpation* (1679), p. 4.
[99] Slingsby Bethel, *The Present State of Christendome and the Interest of England, With a Regard to France* (1677), p. 11.
[100] William Sacheverell, 21 May 1677, in Grey, *Debates*, IV, 356. See also Bethel, *Present State of Christendome*, pp. 27–8; *French Intrigues Discovered*, pp. 13–14.
[101] Marchamont Nedham, *Christianissimus Christianandus. Or, Reasons for the Reduction of France to a More Christian State in Europe* (1678), p. 34. See also Nedham, *Pacquet-Boat Advice*, p. 11; Temple, *Miscellany*, pp. 30–1; Sir Thomas Littleton, 31 January 1678, Grey, *Debates*, v, 44.

By the later-seventeenth century, then, political discussion was conducted in an idiom far different from that of the sixteenth and earlier seventeenth centuries. States were thought to act for their own ends; their aim was to promote the national interest. Political particularism had triumphed over confessional universalism, reason of state had replaced promotion of the true religion as the idiom of public political discourse. The Dutch were now vilified as economic universalists or embraced as commercial fellow travellers in the face of French mercantilism. In either scenario, interest rather than confessional affinity provided the guide to political action.

III

What had caused such a profound ideological transformation? Why was political debate now conducted in the language of interest and commerce rather than in the accents of the godly?

Early-modern Europeans were not at a loss for an explanation. The Thirty Years War and the various national upheavals of mid century had demonstrated beyond a reasonable doubt the impossibility of ever concluding wars of religion and the centrality of trade to political power. In England, the failure to achieve godly rule in the 1650s coupled with a series of wars against the Protestant Dutch convinced the vast majority of the political nation that governments had nothing to do with salvation, that politics was exclusively of this world.[102] 'Honor or gratitude', lamented the Marquis of Ormonde who very much longed for an older more traditional politics, 'are things now wholly lost in all nations'; the art of governance was now dominated by 'the notion of reason of state'.[103]

By the later-seventeenth century reason of state had come to dominate the analysis of international relations. While the Thirty Years War might have begun as an apocalyptic struggle between the forces of Reformation and Counter-Reformation, by the conclusion of the Treaty of Munster the ideological landscape had irreversibly changed. Some did ascribe the king of Sweden's entrance into the

---

[102] I have touched on these themes in previous work. For the 1650s, see my 'England and the World in the 1650s', in John Morrill (ed.), *Revolution and Restoration* (London, 1992), pp. 129–47; for a broader discussion see my *Protestantism and Patriotism: Ideologies and the Making of English Foreign Policy, 1650–1668* (Cambridge, 1996), especially pp. 441–52.

[103] Ormonde to Nicholas, 6 June 1651, BL, Egerton MS 2534, f. 90.

struggle 'to controversies in religion', Algernon Sidney recalled, but 'no man can continue in that opinion who considers that France, Venice and Savoy, three Popish states were the contrivers and advancers of it'.[104] No one understood the French pretensions to universal monarchy as part of a religious crusade. It was sheer lunacy to think that Louis XIV 'would trouble his conscience what religion was professed in England', remarked one pamphleteer, especially after the slaughters he had perpetrated 'in Lorraine, Burgundy, Alsatia, and the Spanish Netherlands, though peopled by Roman Catholics'.[105] It was clearly 'the true interest of his Holiness himself, and the Roman clergy, to curb the growing grandeur of such a haughty monarch', thought another polemicist.[106] Louis XIV was a Machiavellian imperialist, not a religious zealot. 'His ambition is that sail on which nothing can grow to advance the interest of another', averred John Yalden, 'he hates all superiors or equals; and with restless pains and labour covets and pursues universal monarchy'.[107] For that reason a war against him would not be a war of religion. 'Though the preservation of the Protestant religion be most the concernment of England and Holland', explained the author of the *Discourses Upon Modern Affairs*, 'yet the special and immediate end of the preservation of Flanders [against the French] and the general end of holding the balance of Europe is universal'.[108] To make the struggle against France into a war of religion rather than a war to protect national interest would prove nothing short of disastrous. 'If you make this a war of religion', argued Sir Thomas Lee drawing on decades of experience both domestic and foreign, 'you will never have done'.[109]

Not only had the Thirty Years War, the civil wars and the Anglo-Dutch wars (1652–4, 1665–7, 1672–4) taught the English the impossibility of ever concluding a war of religion, but these monumental struggles had also educated them in the centrality of political economy. The failure to conclude wars of religion created the ideological space necessary to reconceptualize the state; the effects of those wars, especially the Anglo-Dutch conflicts, determined the

[104] Algernon Sidney, 'Court Maxims', *c.* 1666, Warwickshire Record Office, pp. 153–4.
[105] *Europe a Slave, Unless England Break her Chains* (1681), pp. 62–3.
[106] T. de hay, *A Letter from Paris* (1681), p. 2. See also Nedham, *Christianissimus*, p. 72.
[107] John Yalden, *Machiavil Redivivus* (1681), sig. B3. See also *French Intrigues Discovered*, p. 9.
[108] *Discourses Upon the Modern Affairs of Europe* (1680), pp. 9–10.
[109] Sir Thomas Lee, 14 March 1678, in Grey, *Debates*, v, 242.

nature of that reconceptualization. After the Restoration, people no longer believed that wars were won by the most godly or the most virtuous soldiers. Trade and economic vitality had become the key to political power and military might as well as domestic tranquillity. 'Since the discovery of the Indies, and increase of trade', reported Peter du Moulin in his wildly popular *England's Appeal*, 'navigation and commerce [have been] the greatest (if not the only) supporters' of the power of states.[110] The decline in Spanish power, it was widely believed, could be explained by the failure of the Habsburgs to retain control of the Indies. 'Whoever commands the ocean, commands the trade of the world', remarked John Evelyn in his capacity as official historian of the Anglo-Dutch wars, 'and whoever commands the trade of the world, commands the riches of the world, and whoever is master of that, commands the world itself'.[111]

The events of mid century decisively transformed the English state. While it has traditionally been argued that England did not experience the upheavals associated with Europe's military revolution, this conclusion rests on untested assumptions.[112] Michael Mann's recent work on English state finances has shown that 'only after 1660 does the state's financial size increase substantially in real terms (in fact the jump probably occurred during the undocumented period of the Commonwealth in the 1650s)'. Mann suggests that wars, specifically England's naval wars with the Dutch, account for this rise. 'Only when England and Holland began to supplant parasitic private activity with their independent empire-building activities and encountered each other's naval power, did their state really take off', he observes, 'the three Anglo-Dutch naval wars date this precisely to the 1650s, 1660s and 1670s'.[113] This newly enlarged state needed new ways to raise money. Michael Braddick has shown

[110] Peter du Moulin, *Englands Appeal from the Private Cabal at White-Hall to the Great Council of the Nation* (1673), pp. 6–7.

[111] John Evelyn, *Navigation and Commerce* (1674), p. 15.

[112] For one recent restatement of this position, see Brian M. Downing, *The Military Revolution and Political Change* (Princeton, 1992): during the civil wars, Downing claims, 'Parliamentary forces underwent no military revolution' (p. 171); 'the Thirty Years War presented no challenge to the island nation and no military modernization came about' (p. 179). Downing's conclusions rest on his acceptance of a revisionist historiography which downplays the effects of 1640–60. Downing's conclusion also rest on his dismissal of the Dutch wars as 'brief wars' with no great significance (p. 177).

[113] Michael Mann, *States, War and Capitalism* (Oxford, 1988), pp. 98–9. Mann's claim that countries in which naval war, rather than land war, dominated tended towards nonabsolutist development paths strikes me as persuasive. Mann's financial analysis largely accords with Michael Braddick's conclusion that 'from the early years of the civil war

that 'from the 1640s onwards land-based taxes were complemented by the excise, a tax collected and paid by different and to some extent previously unaffected social groups'. There was increasingly, Braddick argues, a 'shift' in 'the burden of taxation' away from the land, a development which 'brought merchant wealth into close contact with government after the [R]estoration'.[114]

These developments led to a shift in the sociology of power. Already by the later 1650s one observer, perhaps the future Restoration moderate William Coventry, could observe that trade was 'the greatest security of the nation'. This was because 'the major part of the people of England have their best and chiefest dependence and subsistence by foreign and domestic trade'.[115] This new realization, predicated on the development through warfare of a much larger state, necessitated a transformation in the language of politics, necessitated a language which made economics a reason of state. 'Trade and negotiation has infected the whole kingdom', averred one Anglican supporter of James II, 'by this means the very genius of the people is alter'd, and it will in the end be the interest of the crown to proportion its maxims of power suitable to this new nature come among us'.[116] That such a new nature had indeed come to dominate English life is incontrovertible. David Sacks, for example, has shown how the worldview of Bristolians had come by the later seventeenth century to be dominated by one in which it was possible 'to think of political economy, if not economics itself, as an autonomous subject'.[117] Similarly Bernard Bailyn has described 1660 as a major 'turning point in the history of the New England merchants'. By the later seventeenth century the merchant community was decisively transforming the New England way of life, and the ways in which that life was understood. 'Though the merchants' influence did not

---

onwards the nation paid an enormously increased tax burden with little or no resistance'. M. J. Braddick, *Parliamentary Taxation in 17th-Century England* (Rochester, 1994), p. 292.

[114] Braddick, *Parliamentary Taxation*, pp. 297–8.

[115] W. C., *Trades Destruction is Englands Ruine* 28 May 1659 (1659), pp. 3–4. Nuala Zahedieh has demonstrated that much of the growth in London's economy in the later seventeenth century was directly related to the new and growing colonial trades: 'London and the Colonial Consumer in the Late Seventeenth Century', *Economic History Review* 47: 2 (1994), 239–61.

[116] 'An Essay on the Interest of the Crown in American Plantations' (1685), BL, Add 47131, ff. 24–25. 'Trade is much the over-balance of the wealth of the nation', concluded the same observer, consequently it 'must influence the power for good or ill'.

[117] David Harris Sacks, *The Widening Gate: Bristol and the Atlantic Economy, 1450–1700* (Berkeley, 1991), p. 343.

yet extend over the political system', Bailyn maintains, 'it reached into those subtle fundamental attitudes and assumptions which ultimately determine institutions.' The view of the Puritan old-guard that 'the purpose of New England had fallen from the perpetuation of God's word to the furtherance of trade' was largely correct.[118] This shift in political language confirms Charles Tilly's observation that the English polity gave its monarchs 'access to immense means of warmaking, but only at the price of large concessions to the country's merchants and bankers'.[119]

While medieval and Reformation aspirants to universal monarchy had sought to unite spiritual dominion with a monopoly of territorial sovereignty, after the 1650s English and Dutch commentators thought universal dominion could only be achieved through dominance of trade.[120] This was because the very universalism of the late sixteenth and early seventeenth centuries, given new emotional fillips by the Reformation and Counter-Reformation and their attendant eschatologies, demanded new wars. These wars, unlike the dynastic conflicts which dominated medieval Europe, could not be resolved in the first instance by mediation. There could be no compromise over universal truth. In England and Europe these much larger wars demanded greater financial commitments from the states fighting them. While initially the English state could turn to landed wealth, in the long run it had to depend on merchant capital. Once brought into contact with the state the merchants transformed the discussion of politics from one in which wars were demanded with no possibility of resolution, to ones in which wars could be conceived with limited and hence negotiable ends. Commerce and economics had become a reason of state.

Over the course of the seventeenth century the nature and object of statecraft had dramatically altered. Whereas conducting reason of state analysis in public was unconscionable in the later sixteenth and early seventeenth centuries, it had become the accepted norm after

[118] Bernard Bailyn, *The New England Merchants in the Seventeenth Century* (Cambridge, MA, 1955), pp. 112, 139–40.

[119] Charles Tilly, *Coercion, Capital and European States* (Oxford, 1990), p. 159. It should be noted that while I am sympathetic to Tilly's model, I disagree with his chronology. Tilly locates the fundamental developments in the later eighteenth century. This is a view he has set out at greater length in *Popular Contention in Great Britain, 1758–1834* (Cambridge, MA, 1995).

[120] See my discussion of this point in my 'The English Debate over Universal Monarchy', in John Robertson (ed.), *A Union for Empire: Political Thought and the Union of 1707* (Cambridge, 1995), pp. 37–62.

the Restoration. Whereas alliance or confrontation with the Dutch was evaluated on confessional grounds in the earlier period, after the Restoration national interest had become the measure of policy. This new realization that trade was the key to political power, that commerce was necessarily a reason of state,[121] was a significant advance on the earlier Italian discourse. For Machiavelli and his followers territory had remained the central object of statecraft; in England (and the Netherlands) in the mid and later seventeenth century political economy was vitally and centrally the object of governance.[122] In the 1680s John Locke claimed, for example, that for those who truly understood 'the great art of government . . . numbers of men are to be preferred to largeness of dominions'.[123] Locke, in the midst of a political crisis, had come to see that the proper object of governance was population not territory. This transformation was not blocked by the economic and political upheavals of the seventeenth century, but precipitated by them. Only by focusing on developments in England and the Netherlands in the seventeenth century, I have suggested, can one understand this transformation of statecraft which Michel Foucault[124] has seen as central to the emergence of the modern state. Only by shifting the locus of study away from eighteenth-century France[125] and towards

---

[121] This element of statecraft was trumpeted in a wide variety of genres. For advice literature, see Marquis of Newcastle, 'Treatise' (1660–1), Bodleian Library, Clar MSS 109, p. 7; for drama, see Roger Boyle, earl of Orrery, *Henry V* (1668), p. 40.

[122] Pagden has made this same observation: *Lords of All the World*, p. 116.

[123] John Locke, 'Second Treatise of Government', *c.* 1681, in David Wootton (ed.), *Political Writings of John Locke* (New York, 1993), p. 282.

[124] I share with Michael Walzer the sense that Foucault's 'account does appear to have conservative implications' but I suspect for somewhat different reasons. Michael Walzer *The Company of Critics* (New York, 1988), p. 196. While Walzer emphasizes the lack of existence of a 'focal point', a state, in Foucault's thought (a point which I have not considered here), I emphasize Foucault's refusal to ask questions about crisis and change. Richard Ashcraft has argued, persuasively I think, that Whig political thought not only emphasized the shift in the socioeconomic basis of government and consequently of the appropriate nature of government itself, but also insisted on a 'causal explanation' for the inappropriateness of absolute monarchy. Richard Ashcraft, *Revolutionary Politics and Locke's Two Treatises of Government* (Princeton, 1986), pp. 214–27 (quote from 217).

[125] Perhaps this is the place to note that there was a reason of state tradition in sixteenth- and seventeenth-century France. This tradition, however, never took the economic turn which I have noted took place in England and the Netherlands. Henri, duc de Rohan, for example, enunciated an extremely sophisticated interest theory in *A Treatise of the Interest of the Princes and States of Christendome* (1641), a theory which insisted that 'religion was the pretext' not the cause of political activity. However, his theory of interest of states was defined purely in terms of geopolitical security not in terms of economy. Populations never figure in his discussion. See the useful discussion in J. H. M. Salmon, 'Rohan and Interest of State', in his *Renaissance and Revolt: Essays in the Intellectual and Social History of Early Modern France*

the emerging commercial and naval societies of sixteenth- and seventeenth-century Europe can one locate and come to understand the emergence of modern statecraft.[126]

(Cambridge, 1987), pp. 98–116, especially, p. 101. Cardinal Richelieu, for all of his willingness to deploy interest language, insisted that 'there is not a single sovereign in the world who is not obliged by this principle to procure the conversion of those who, living within his kingdom, have deviated from the path to salvation' (*The Political Testament of Cardinal Richelieu*, trans. Henry Bertram Hill (Madison, WI, 1961), p. 69). For Richelieu, then, the end of government was still salvation of the souls of its subjects. I am well aware of Colbert's mercantilist innovations. However, they should not be seen as great innovations in early-modern statecraft, as the appropriation of economic interest to ideas of reason of state. First, they were arguably reactions to the successful appropriation of economic interest in the Netherlands and then in England. Second, there was no notion of improvement in Colbert's thought. He conceived of property as natural, not plastic, and hence finite. He was thus merely adding goods to land in the list of things to be conquered. Finally, the French historian James B. Collins has cogently argued that 'Colbert's tariff policy had less to do with economic than with financial interest: like his state finance system, it was a family, not a national affair' (*The State in Early Modern France* (Cambridge, 1995), p. 93).

[126] Roland Axtmann has seen a similar shift in mid-seventeenth-century German thought, perhaps spurred by the logic of the demands of the Thirty Years War. See his ' "Police" and the Formation of the Modern State', in *German History* 10: 1 (February 1992), especially pp. 44–5.

Natural philosophy and political periodization: interregnum, restoration and revolution[1]

Barbara Shapiro

INTRODUCTION

In order to characterize Restoration English natural philosophy, it will be necessary for us to examine the pre-1660, Restoration and the post-1688 periods. We will look for continuities and changes in scientific belief, practice and organization, and then ask if the traditional divisions of English political history are relevant to changes in scientific belief, practice and organization. Necessarily involved in this analysis are the connections of English science to government, the universities, religion and continental natural philosophy.

ENGLISH NATURAL PHILOSOPHY TO C. 1660

Prior to 1660 English scientific activity[2] was sparse and followed rather than led that of the continent. This is the period of William Gilbert and John Dee, the humanist attack on scholasticism and the creation of Gresham College devoted to the needs of practical mathematics and navigation.[3] Bacon offered a new programme of experimental philosophy beginning in 1605 but his pleas to King James for royal patronage of scientific research were ignored. The period witnesses creation of the Savilian chairs of astronomy and geometry at Oxford, a botanical garden for the medical faculty at

---

[1] I am grateful to Margaret Osler for comment and criticism on an earlier version of this chapter.

[2] I sometimes use the anachronistic words 'science', 'scientist' and 'scientific' although the second term did not yet exist and the first conveyed a very different meaning than current usage. 'Natural history' and 'natural philosophy' better convey contemporary meaning.

[3] Gresham College opened in 1597. For Gresham College and London science before 1640 see Mordecai Feingold, *The Mathematician's Apprenticeship: Science, Universities and Society in England 1560–1640* (Cambridge, 1984), pp. 166–89.

Oxford, as well as Bacon's frustrated effort to endow chairs of natural philosophy at both universities.[4] Comfortable coexistence between the new natural philosophy and traditional scholarship can be seen in the mathematics library for the Savilian professors contained within the Bodleian library and the library's painted frieze of portraits (1616) honouring Copernicus, Brahe, Paracelsus, Vesalius and Mercator along with more traditional scholars.[5]

The 1620s and 1630s brought the defence of Copernican hypothesis and Galilean astronomical findings, Harvey's biomedical research, and publication by Descartes, Bacon and Van Helmont. The natural philosophies of the time were often amalgams of old and new containing elements of Aristotelianism, hermeticism and alchemy.

English scientific activity increased substantially between 1640 and 1660 despite the disruptions of the English civil war and interregnum. There was further circulation of the Baconian programme for a natural philosophy built on the foundation of a new natural history that rejected the emblematic and etymological in favour of careful observation and experiment. Baconian experimentalists rejected Aristotelian scholasticism, eradicated the traditional distinction between art and knowledge and were unsympathetic to and unappreciative of hypothesis and mathematics. Bacon played a key role in the development of 'scientific fact' by adapting legal techniques of proof for matters of fact to the investigation of natural phenomena.[6] Although English science of the 1640–60 period cannot be wholly equated with Baconianism, to the extent that the optimistic and

---

[4] Bacon considered returning to Cambridge when he left public life. Collegiate structure allowed for introduction of new ideas. By 1610 Oxford had experienced disputations on the Copernican thesis, the infinity of the universe, the plurality of worlds and the earth as a magnet in formal university exercises. Much of the new interest was pursued outside the statutory limits of the curriculum. Sir Thomas Smith had provided for a readership in arithmetic and geometry at Queens College. A chair in natural philosophy and an anatomy lectureship were added in 1621 and 1624, respectively. See Barbara Shapiro, 'The Universities and Science in the Seventeenth Century', *Journal of British Studies* 10 (1971), 47–82; Nicholas Tyacke, 'Science and Religion at Oxford before the Civil War', in D. Pennington and K. Thomas (eds.), *Puritans and Revolutionaries: Essays in Seventeenth-Century History Presented to Christopher Hill* (Oxford, 1978), pp. 73–93; Feingold, *The Mathematician's Apprenticeship*.

[5] See J. N. L. Myres, 'The Painted Frieze in the Picture Gallery', *Bodleian Library Record* III, 87; J. N. L. Myres, 'Thomas James and the Painted Frieze', *ibid.* IV, 30–65. The first catalogue of the library in 1620 included publications of many continental and English mathematicians and natural philosophers working in non-scholastic modes. T. James, *Catalogus Universalis Librorum in Biblioteca Bodleiana* (Oxford, 1620).

[6] See Barbara Shapiro, *A Culture of Fact. England 1550–1720* (Ithaca, NY, 2000).

cooperative Baconian programme dominated the English scientific scene, we can perhaps speak of a characteristically 'English science'.

Scientific activity developed in a number of different, though somewhat overlapping, venues. First there was the Hartlib group which engaged in a number of Baconian and Comenian pansophic projects. Held together by the émigré 'intelligencer' Samuel Hartlib, it was oriented toward agricultural, medical and educational reform, and emphasized the utilitarian aspects of Baconianism.[7] Perhaps most closely allied with Puritan goals, it was not particularly involved with mathematics or astronomy. While it did not receive much in the way of government assistance, the government was associated with efforts to bring Comenius to England.

Royalist exiles formed another cluster, mostly congregating in Paris, and in contact with French virtuosi Descartes, Mersenne and Gassendi. Another cluster yet, sometimes called the 1645 group, met in London. It was primarily concerned with astronomy, pneumatics, the Torricellian experiment and falling bodies, though some attention was given to anatomy and physiology. Members convened weekly at first at Jonathan Goddard's lodgings, sometimes in taverns and during term time at Gresham College. The connection of English natural philosophy with Gresham college would be long-lasting. The group was self-sustaining, members making weekly contributions to defray the 'charge of Experiments'. It excluded discussion of the divisive discourses of 'Divinity' and 'state Affaires'.[8] Political disruptions of the late 1640s broke up the group.

The Royal College of Physicians, also located in London, became an active centre for scientific research in the 1650s – research not restricted to medical topics. The Harvean approach to medicine, with its emphasis on dissection and experiment, modified medical and anatomical instruction at the College and in the universities.[9] When Harvey came to Oxford with the king in 1642, he gathered a

---

[7] See Charles Webster, *The Great Instauration: Science, Medicine and Reform 1626–1660* (London, 1975). Hartlib was provided with modest support.

[8] We know of its activities and membership largely from John Wallis. Four of the nine mentioned by Wallis were physicians. John Wallis, *A Defense of the Royal Society* (London, 1678), p. 8.

[9] The number of experimentalists declined during the Restoration period as those with strong scientific interests shifted their investigations to the Royal Society. See Charles Webster, 'The College of Physicians: "Solomon's House" in Commonwealth England', *Bulletin of the History of Medicine* 41 (1967), 393–414; R. G. Frank, 'The Physician as Virtuoso in Seventeenth-century England', in Barbara Shapiro and R. G. Frank (eds.), *English Virtuosi in the Sixteenth and Seventeenth Centuries* (Los Angeles, 1979), pp. 55–114.

group of physician-experimenters who worked on a variety of medical, anatomical and chemical projects. This group was active in Oxford until the Restoration and beyond, interacting with the Wadham College circle of experimenters and later with the Royal Society.[10]

The Wadham group was composed of Oxford academicians, Harvean physicians and young virtuosi, most, but not all, associated with Wadham College. The Warden of Wadham, John Wilkins, a former '1645er' and a popularizer of Copernicus and Galileo, was the centre of this group. Philosophically eclectic, its range of interests was very wide, covering astronomy, mathematics, anatomy, transfusion experiments, mechanical devices and universal language. This group had some features of a formal organization – fairly regular meetings, dues to finance experiments and instrument purchases, and rules, such as the exclusion of religious and political topics. It was held together by Wilkins who provided a safe haven for those of differing religious persuasions.[11] The Wadham group had no patron and its activities, like that of the 1645 group, were self-financing. It could not undertake costly projects.

The Wadhamites began to disperse when Wilkins left to become Master of Trinity College, Cambridge, in 1659. Some returned to London, some continued to meet in Oxford. Henry Oldenburg wrote that the 'Oxonian Sparkles', might 'be called the Embryo or First Conception of the Royal Society'.[12] From about 1648 to 1670 Oxford was, as Robert Frank has written, as 'brilliant a center of the sciences as any place in Western Europe . . . In toto Oxford had a scientific community whose size, complexity, and longevity rivaled that of London before 1660.'[13]

Cambridge lacked the equivalent of the Savilian professorships. The Cambridge Platonists had some interests in natural philosophy, initially Cartesian. John Ray, Francis Glisson and Isaac Barrow worked on mathematical and natural philosophy topics.[14]

[10] See Frank, 'The Physician as Virtuoso', passim; R. G. Frank, *Harvey and the Oxford Physiologists* (Berkeley, 1980). Harvey was Warden of Merton College in 1645–6. The group included George Ent, Francis Glisson, John Greaves, Charles Scarborough and Daniel Whistler.

[11] Both Christopher Wren and Paul Neile came to Wadham because of Wilkins's presence. See Barbara Shapiro, *John Wilkins 1614–72: An Intellectual Biography* (Berkeley, 1968), pp. 118–47.

[12] *Philosophical Transactions*, IV, Dedicatory Letter.

[13] Frank, 'The Physician as Virtuoso', p. 92.

[14] Harvey hoped to endow a professorship of experimental philosophy at Cambridge but was deterred by the ascendancy of the Parliamentarians (*ibid.*, p. 80). Barrow reported that the

The civil war and interregnum interrupted careers, often to the benefit of scientific development. Young men were diverted from clerical careers or became involved in natural investigation as an escape from that 'dismal age'.[15] If these scientific groups received little outside support, neither did they face significant vocal criticism. Their activities, being private, were of low visibility, though some clerics considered such diversion from religion undesirable.

There was one major challenge. The rejection of a university-trained clergy on the part of some radical sects led to discussion of 'suppressing Universities and all Schools of Learning, as heathenish and unnecessary'. This attack was sometimes accompanied by suggestions for secularization and incorporation of the new natural philosophy, supposedly ignored by the universities, into the curriculum. The universities were defended by Wadhamites John Wilkins and Seth Ward, who defended their traditional functions, attacked the claim that they were devoid of mathematical studies and activity, and ridiculed the alchemical projects, 'enthusiasm', and mystical language of the sectarians.[16] Ward was later praised for publicly defending the universities 'in those rough times'.[17]

Instability was a characteristic feature of civil war and interregnum virtuosi groups, most relying on charismatic leaders whose loss or movement could lead to the group's decline or collapse. Although each group had a somewhat difference focus, there was also considerable overlap. Some 1645ers went to Oxford. Wadhamites Boyle and Petty had Hartlib connections. Exchange between Oxford and Gresham continued. In the organization of several of these groups and their regularly scheduled meetings that excluded religious and political topics, we can see foreshadowed the inclusive or compre-

---

conditions of natural philosophy and mathematics improved between 1651 and 1654. 'Oratio ad Academicos in Comitiis', *Theological Works*, 9 vols. (Cambridge, 1859), IX, 34–47.

[15] Walter Charleton, a Royalist physician, also suggested that the 'late Warrs and Schisms', while discouraging men from theology and civil law, encouraged 'young Schollers in our Universities' to 'addict themselves to Physick'. Isaac Barrow, a Cambridge scholar, was temporarily diverted into medicine and mathematics. Seth Ward turned to astronomy and mathematics. When he returned to a clerical career in 1660, he spent relatively little time on scientific matters. Wallis's interest shifted from divinity to mathematics. Jonathan Goddard reversed the process.

[16] See Shapiro, *Wilkins*, pp. 97–117; Shapiro, 'Universities and Science', pp. 63–7; John Webster, *Academiarum Examien* (London, 1654); [Joh]N. [Wilkin]S. and [Set]H. [War]D., *Vindiciae Academiarum* (Oxford, 1654). Although alchemy was also castigated in the *History of the Royal Society*, supervised by Wilkins, many virtuosi, including Boyle and Newton, were deeply interested in alchemy.

[17] *Philosophical Transactions*, IV, Dedicatory Letter. See also Royal Society, Early Letters, B. 1. 62.

hensive policy of the later Royal Society and its exclusion of religious and political topics.[18]

Although it has sometimes been suggested that the Puritans now in power especially fostered scientific work, the governments of these decades behaved little differently than their royal predecessors.[19] Colleges continued to be headed by prominent clergymen whose religious views corresponded to those of the government and universities continued to be governed largely by clerics. Appointments to the Savilian and other chairs associated with natural philosophy continued to be filled with well-qualified persons. Seth Ward, a staunch Anglican, though ousted from Cambridge, became Savilian professor of Astronomy. John Wallis, a Presbyterian advocate in 1643, remained the Savilian professor of geometry for decades.

The 1640–60 period, without doubt, witnessed a substantial increase in scientific activity, some inspired by Bacon, some by Descartes, Galileo, Harvey and others. Should the increased pace and participation be viewed as incremental development that characterized other locales, or was there something about these developments that was peculiarly English and especially indebted to the nature of civil war and interregnum regimes or to the attendant disruptions of traditional careers and intellectual institutions?

THE RESTORATION

Although the history of Restoration science is not coterminous with the history of Royal Society, our discussion of the Restoration will focus on the Society because so much scientific work was rightly or wrongly associated with it. The Royal Society was in many respects an amalgamation of the scientific groups of the interregnum.[20] Many

---

[18] The Wadham group's rules of 23 October 1651 required a majority vote, secret voting, all paying an equal share, two-thirds of moneys to go for instruments. Faithful attendance was expected at the weekly meetings (Bodleian Library, Ashmolean MSS, 1810). In 1652 Seth Ward estimated the group at about thirty. He also noted a smaller club of eight that engaged in chemical experiments. There were also efforts to build an observatory. Wilkins had plans for a college for experiments and mechanics. Christopher Wren was engaged in astronomical, anatomical and microscopic work. In 1659 Peter Steel came to Oxford to teach chemistry in his lodgings.

[19] Feingold, however, has pointed out royal interest in mathematical instruments from the time of Henry VIII. He notes James I's patronage of Fludd, the interests of Henry, prince of Wales, and of Charles I as well as those of several members of the government. See *The Mathematician's Apprenticeship*, pp. 190–213.

[20] See A. R. Hall and M. B. Hall, 'The Intellectual Origins of the Royal Society: London and Oxford', *Notes and Records of the Royal Society* 23 (1969), 157–68.

members had been at Oxford, though a crucial contingent were Royalist exiles. The Hartlib group was less well represented and its programme of social and educational reform was dropped.

Meetings of the virtuosi quickly resumed at Gresham College. We soon can observe an organization with officers, membership lists, dues and a clear sense of purpose. In November 1660 the group decided to found a college for promoting 'physico-mathematicall Experimentall Learning'. Wilkins was appointed to the chair and a list of prospective members drawn up. Soon they decided on weekly meetings, a more elaborate set of rules and regular debating procedures.

From the beginning the group was sensitive to the need to attract support from the Restoration elite. Although the original list of forty-one was vetted for those willing and 'fit' to join, the qualifications of those of the rank of baron or above were not scrutinized. The first list contained almost 30 per cent physicians, the most active subgroup, as well as a considerable number of crown servants and state officials.[21]

Returned Royalists Sir Robert Moray, a friend of the king, and Viscount Brouncker provided essential services. It was Moray who informed the king of the group's intentions and who reported back that he 'did well approve of it'. In 1661 Moray and John Evelyn discussed the group's petition for a royal grant of incorporation with the king, Moray reporting that Charles was 'Pleased to offer of himself to be enter'd one of the Society'. The charter of incorporation, which passed the Great Seal in July 1662, created the Royal Society of London.[22] It was given a mace and coat of arms by the king. Thanks were voted to the king, Clarendon, who had been supportive, and Moray. Brouncker, a Royalist mathematician who

---

[21] Among them were Sir William Coventry, secretary to the duke of York, Matthew Wren, a Wadhamite who was secretary to Lord Clarendon, and Thomas Henshaw, a privy councillor. Several were physicians to the king. Ralph Bathurst was chaplain to the king. Viscount Brounker was chancellor to the queen and the poet Abraham Cowley was secretary to the queen. There were fifteen physicians and sixteen who held significant government posts were state officials or servants of the crown. On the role of the physicians see Robert Frank, 'The Physician as Virtuoso'. For the social composition of the Royal Society see Michael Hunter, *The Royal Society and its Fellows 1660–1700: the Morphology of an Early Scientific Institution* (Preston, 1981); Lotte Mulligan and Glenn Mulligan, 'Reconstructing Restoration Science: Styles of Leadership and Social Composition of the Early Royal Society', *Social Studies of Science* 1 (1981), 327–64; R. G. Frank, 'Institutional Structure and Scientific Activity in the Early Royal Society', *XIVth International Congress of the History of Science: Proceedings*, no. 4 (1975), 82–101.

[22] The charter was revised in 1663.

worked indefatigably for the Society, became the first president at the nomination of the king.

The creation of the Royal Society gave English natural philosophy a clearly visible institutionalized presence as well as a symbol to admire or criticize. The Society rapidly became a clearing house for both foreign and domestic virtuosi. Only those who lived in London for considerable lengths of time, however, were able to participate in its activities.[23] Not all members were equally active, and only a small core carried most of the burden of experiments. Some were active for a time and then became less so for one reason or another. Even Boyle was inactive for a time. Barrow, Bathurst and Ward became preoccupied with clerical concerns. Christopher Wren and, to a lesser extent, Robert Hooke became engaged in rebuilding projects after the Fire. The Society was never the sole focus of its members.

An important feature of the Society was its correspondence and publication network which assisted its integration with European naturalists. The indefatigable efforts of Henry Oldenburg, who as Secretary handled Society correspondence and managed its relations with domestic and foreign members, were extremely important. If his work resembled that of earlier 'intellegencers', it now enjoyed the visibility of an institutional identification.[24] Oldenburg also created the *Philosophical Transactions* in 1665. Though a private venture not an official publication, it seemed like one and enhanced identification of English natural philosophy with the Society. Oldenburg's death in 1677 revealed the fragility of the enterprise, which floundered until the 1690s.

Many scientific publications were associated with the Royal Society though relatively few were officially their publications. Society virtuosi often underlined their association with the Society on title pages or dedications and nonmember publications frequently resulted in an invitation to join. The Society also was responsible for publication of the work of some foreigners, Malpighi in particular. Censorship does not appear to have been considered a problem.

---

[23] Philosophical societies were organized in Oxford (1684) and Dublin (1684) with the aim of replicating Society activities. There was a close connection between Trinity College, Dublin, and the Dublin Society. There was also a short-lived Philosophical Society in Boston. Raymond Stearns, *Science in the British Colonies of America* (Urbana, 1970), pp. 155–6.

[24] See M. B. Hall, 'The Royal Society's Role in the Diffusion of Information in the Seventeenth Century', *Notes and Records of the Royal Society*, 29 (1975), 173–92; Michael Hunter, 'Promoting the New Science: Henry Oldenburg and the Early Royal Society', *History of Science* 36 (1988), 165–81.

The Restoration era initiates the self-conscious promotion of the new natural philosophy. The promotional and apologetic works of Thomas Sprat and Joseph Glanvill and the vast correspondence of Henry Oldenburg did much to trumpet the Baconian message of the Royal Society which was a prominent feature of Restoration scientific ideology and practice. Sprat, a hired publicist working largely under the supervision of Wilkins, was to describe the Society's purpose, methods and accomplishments and disarm real and potential critics. Sprat's *History of the Royal Society*[25] and Glanvill's publications described a new natural philosophy based on the collection of natural history, that is on the collection of matters of fact in a wide range of subjects. The Society was represented by Sprat as being somewhat suspicious of and as avoiding authoritative and dogmatic pronouncements. Scholastic modes of argumentation were rejected in favour of polite discourse. Both authors combined an emphasis on human fallibility with an optimistic view of the progress of knowledge. Useful knowledge was emphasized, though 'usefulness' referred to religious as well as economic and technological benefit. Like several of the Society's leading members, they insisted that the new philosophy was a support for both religion in general and the established church in particular. The natural philosophy they defended was primarily observational, often aided by instruments, or based on experiments collectively pursued. Sprat announced the need for scientific practitioners to alter the language of science away from metaphor and rhetorical ornamentation. These propaganda efforts reinforced identification of English natural philosophy with the Royal Society at home and abroad.

Sprat and Glanvill tended to ignore or slight some aspects of Society practice. They do not tell us about how practice changed over time, for example, how cooperative experimentation gave way to the reporting of more individual efforts[26] or how the 'history of trades' project, so enthusiastically begun, declined. Although Sprat, Glanvill and Oldenburg may have somewhat overemphasized Baconian themes, Baconianism was a prominent feature of Restoration scientific ideology and practice.

There were continuing efforts to create a complete natural history.

---

[25] Thomas Sprat, *History of the Royal Society*, ed. Jackson I. Cope and H. W. Jones (St Louis, 1958).

[26] Frank, 'Institutional Structure', pp. 83–101.

Guidelines for travellers and seamen were developed. Reports on matters of fact on a vast range of geographical, topographical, climatic, biological, social and economic topics were sought and received by the Society. Witnessing of natural phenomena and experiments were crucial to Restoration scientific practice.[27] Matters of 'fact', observed, experimentally produced and reported, were evaluated very much as juries evaluated the testimony of witnesses.

This vast programme of data collection proceeded rapidly and enthusiastically and was perhaps the most visible part of the naturalists' efforts. Some members become dissatisfied with simply piling up the data of natural history and began to combine fact and hypothesis to produce some of the most remarkable work of the Restoration era. Hypotheses, which had been rejected by Bacon, were now ranked from merely possible to highly probable, depending on the extent to which they were supported by well-established 'facts'. The best were characterized as 'morally certain'.[28]

Although Baconian themes remained prominent, Baconianism itself was modified, and there was considerable diversity within the Restoration virtuosi community. Some advocated a mechanical philosophy, atomism, or had strong mathematical commitments. Others did not. Though Sprat criticized alchemy, alchemical interests were not uncommon. Some looked optimistically toward the future, others wished to recover ancient wisdom.

Although Sprat stressed the Society's social inclusiveness, it showed little inclination to include artisans or tradesmen.[29] Despite the many modern scholarly discussions about the relationship between class and natural philosophy, little consensus has emerged. Although some have emphasized the middle classes and bourgeois values, interest has recently shifted to the role of gentlemen and gentlemanly values.[30] There are problems, however, with identi-

---

[27] See Steven Shapin and Simon Schaffer, *Leviathan and the Air Pump: Hobbes, Boyle, and the Experimental Life* (Princeton, 1985); Shapiro, 'The Concept "Fact": Legal Origins and Cultural Diffusion', pp. 227–52. See also Steven Shapin, *The Social History of Truth* (Chicago, 1995).

[28] The Baconian emphasis on arriving at 'forms' enjoying complete certainty was, for the most part, replaced by a probabilistic natural philosophy. See Barbara Shapiro, *Probability and Certainty in Seventeenth Century England: a Study of the Relationships between Natural Science Religion, History, Law and Literature* (Princeton, 1983); Henry G. van Leeuwen, *The Problem of Certainty in English Thought 1630–1690* (The Hague, 1963).

[29] The expense of membership alone would have excluded most artisans and London's mathematical practitioners. See Hunter, *The Royal Society and its Fellows*, p. 8.

[30] See Shapin and Schaffer, *Leviathan and the Air Pump*; Shapin, *The Social History of Truth*.

fying Restoration science with the category gentleman. Michael Hunter's assessment that the Society exhibited a nexus between landed wealth, trade and government seems most accurate,[31] perhaps with the addition of greater emphasis on the participation of physicians and the apologetic role of the latitudinarian clergy. Despite Sprat's somewhat democratic language, there is no evidence of Society interest in undermining the social hierarchy. The activities of the Royal Society, however, did bring together many who in ordinary circumstances would not have been likely to interact socially. This intellectual community, like most others, did not include women.

Natural philosophy was largely a recreational activity. Only those who combined science with medicine, mathematics or astronomical teaching could integrate natural philosophy into their professional lives. Robert Hooke, a Society employee, was perhaps the sole 'professional scientist' of the time. The virtuosi had extremely wide interests. Sprat's model virtuoso, Christopher Wren, was involved in astronomy, microscopy, transfusions experiments, mathematics, physics and model building. Institutionalization, as Robert Frank has pointed out, did not require professionalization.[32]

Policies governing Restoration universities changed little. They continued to be governed by leading clerics, now high church Anglicans.[33] Appointments to chairs relating to natural philosophy, mathematics and medicine remained of high quality.[34] Ability counted for more than religious affiliation. The Oxford Philosophical Society, founded in 1683, met weekly.

Elias Ashmole, provided for a museum at Oxford to house antiquities and chemical laboratories with Robert Plot, secretary to the Royal Society, as its first keeper as well as professor of chemistry. Its library, the vice-chancellor wrote, would 'containe the most conspicuous parts of the great Booke of Nature', and rival the

---

[31] Hunter, *Debate over Science*, p. 111.

[32] See Frank, 'Institutional Structure'.

[33] Twenty-two per cent of masters became bishops 1660–1688. John Gascoigne, *Cambridge in the Age of the Enlightenment* (Cambridge, 1989), pp. 15, 21, 30.

[34] Wallis continued in his Savilian post. Wren replaced Seth Ward when Ward became bishop of Exeter. Willis, who became Sedleian professor at Oxford, was succeeded by Thomas Millington (1675–1704), physician to the king and president of the Royal College of Physicians. Ralph Bathurst FRS, president of Trinity College, Oxford, in 1663 and vice chancellor 1673–70, helped to insure that scientific and mathematical instruction continued. Robert Morison became professor of botany at Oxford in 1669.

Bodleian's manuscript and print collections.[35] Those 'delighted with
the new philosophy' were taken with the museum's contents, 'but
some, for the old', saw only 'baubles'.[36]

John Fell, dean of Christ Church and head of the Oxford University
Press, was not unsympathetic to some aspects of the new science. The
university press published Plot's *Natural History of Staffordshire* and
Robert Morison's botanical work. He promoted Francis Willughby's
History of Fishes (1686) and considered modifying Tom Tower at Christ
Church into an observatory (1681).[37] High churchmen such as Fell,
brother-in-law to Thomas Willis, did not utilize their new strength to
seriously undermine natural philosophy in the universities.

At Cambridge a mathematics chair was created in 1663, occupied
by Barrow and then Newton. Encouraged by high churchmen,
medicine and related studies were taught in the Harvean research
tradition.[38] Interchange between the universities and Gresham
College continued and now included the Royal Society which
continued to meet at Gresham until the Great Fire destroyed its
buildings.[39]

Religious issues were important during the Restoration. There
were not only disputes within the church concerning how inclusive it
should be but also questions about how to deal with Protestant
dissent and Roman Catholicism. Only the first affected the Society.
Several of its leaders were identified with latitudinarian comprehension efforts. The Royal Society itself was religiously comprehensive,
allowing 'themselves to differ in the weightiest matter, even in the

---

[35] Quoted in A. G. Macgregor and A. J. Turner, 'The Ashmolean Museum', in L. S. Sutherland and L. G. Mitchell (eds.), *The History of the University of Oxford: The Eighteenth Century* (Oxford, 1986) p. 643.

[36] Anthony Wood, *The Life and Times of Anthony Wood Antiquary* (Oxford, 1891–1900), ed. A. Clark, III, 56. See also A. V. Simcock, *The Ashmolean Museum and Oxford Science* (Oxford, 1984).

[37] The proceeds of Willughby's book were to pay salary arrears of Hooke and Halley.

[38] John Ray, Martin Lister and Francis Glisson were active researchers, though Ray gave up his fellowship in 1662. Charles Scarborough obtained the Lumleian lectureship in 1661. Chemical lectures were given by John Vigani during the 1680s. Efforts to establish a Cambridge equivalent of the Oxford Philosophical Society, however, failed. See Gascoigne, *Cambridge*, pp. 52–63. See also Robert Frank, *Harvey and the Oxford Physiologists* (Berkeley, 1980).

[39] Wren left Gresham to become a Savilian professor. Hooke combined a Gresham professor-ship and the curatorship of experiments for the Society. By the time Sprat's *History* appeared there had been or were ten Society members who were or had been Gresham professors. See also Mordechai Feingold, 'Tradition versus Novelty; Universities and Scientific Societies in the Early Modern Period', in Peter Baker and Roger Ariew (eds.), *Revolution and Continuity: Essays in the History and Philosophy of Early Modern Science* (Washington, DC, 1991), pp. 45–62.

way of Salvation itself'.[40] It explicitly excluded religious and political topics from discussion to enable participants with different views to work together and to minimize problems with religious and governmental authorities.

Many virtuosi insisted that natural philosophy provided support for religion. They countered the threats of atheism and 'Hobbism' by providing proofs for the existence of God and the immortality of the soul but opposed dogmatism and 'enthusiasm'. We saw the beginnings of the connections between a practical latitudinarianism and natural philosophy at interregnum Oxford. During the Restoration the latitudinarian desire for a more comprehensive church was often associated with the Society. Apologists and critics, with good reason, associated Boyle, Glanvill and Wilkins with the latitudinarians, in this period a small, rather beleaguered minority in the church.[41] It is sometimes suggested that high churchmen were hostile to the new philosophy and the Royal Society. Clerics like Fell were hostile to latitudinarianism rather than to natural philosophy itself. Several bishops were members of the Society, albeit not active ones.

There was no institution that seriously attempted to prevent or curtail scientific work.[42] Although the universities initially feared the Society that would initiate a rival teaching program, that fear subsided, and they continued to provide modest encouragement to mathematics, medicine and natural philosophy. Some churchmen made negative comments about the Royal Society but their antagonism was inspired more by distaste for religious comprehension and overemphasis on natural theology than its natural philosophy.

---

[40] Sprat, *History of the Royal Society*, p. 76. But see Michael Hunter, 'Latitudinarianism and the Ideology of the Early Royal Society: Thomas Sprat's "History of the Royal Society" Reconsidered', in R. Kroll et al. (eds.), *Philosophy. Science and Religion in England 1640–1700* (Cambridge, 1992), pp. 199–229.

[41] See Barbara Shapiro, 'Latitudinarianism and Science in Seventeenth Century England', in Charles Webster (ed.), *The Intellectual Revolution of the Seventeenth Century* (London, 1974), pp. 286–316; Barbara Shapiro, *Probability and Certainty in Seventeenth Century England* (Princeton, 1983). It may be useful to distinguish two types of latitudinarianism. The first consisted of a party within the established church favouring a more rational approach to religion and greater comprehension. The second, somewhat broader and overlapping the first, lauded a nondogmatic temperament. This second version encompassed both those like John Locke who abandoned comprehension for religious toleration and those like Christopher Wren and Thomas Willis who held high church views without wishing to impose them on others.

[42] For a different view, see Michael Hunter, 'The Debate over Science', in *Science and the Shape of Knowledge in Late Seventeenth Century Britain* (Woodbridge, UK, 1995), pp. 1–119. See also Margaret Espinasse, 'The Decline and Fall of Restoration Science', *The Intellectual Revolution of the Seventeenth Century*, pp. 347–68.

However much controversy there was among Baconians, Paracelsians and Cartesians, there was little if any scholarly defence of Aristotelian natural philosophy published in England during this period. Aristotelian textbooks, however, continued to appear.

Ridicule by 'wits' caused virtuosi annoyance and anxiety. But this teasing never constituted a substantial threat. There was plenty of humorous potential in many virtuosi activities. Telescopic descriptions of the moon and microscopic work on the anatomy of fleas and flies easily led to parodies like Samuel Butler's *Elephant on the Moon*, in which a mouse and gnats trapped in a telescope are misread as a lunar war.[43] Robert South's 1669 speech at the opening of the Sheldonian theatre contained 'satyrical invectives against Cromwell, fanaticks, the Royal Society and the New Philosophy'.[44] Shadwell's play *The Virtuoso* (1676), featured the foolish Sir Nicholas Gimcrack and satirized many Royal Society activities.[45] The Society's emphasis on useful knowledge led to ridicule of their seemingly 'useless' projects like weighing air.[46] Theatrical portrayals of physicians and lawyers were far more common than those of the virtuosi, and often more vicious. The virtuosi were certainly not exempt from the satirical pens of Restoration wits, but Evelyn was excessively worried by the 'Scoffs & Raillery, of the Bouffoones, & ignorant Fops'.[47] Addison in the early eighteenth century noted how easily it was to 'render a science ridiculous'. 'When a man spends his whole life among the Stars and Planets, or lays out a twelve-month on the spots in the Sun, however noble his speculations may be, they are very apt to fall into burlesque.' Evelyn thought it even 'more natural' to laugh

---

[43] Shadwell, like Butler, used the telescope for satiric purposes. Thus Sidrophe, looking through the telescope, seeing a boy flying a kite mistook it for a comet, or star 'that ne'r before appeared'. Quoted in Marjorie Nicolson, *Science and Imagination* (Ithaca, NY, 1956), p. 38. See also Marjorie Nicolson, *Pepys' Diary and the New Science* (Charlottesville, VA, 1965), pp. 114–58.

[44] Letter from John Wallis to Robert Boyle quoted in Gascoigne, *Cambridge*, p. 56. The last portion contained 'Execrations against fanaticks, Conventicles, comprehension, & New Philosophy', *ibid.*

[45] Gimcrack, mocking Boyle's experiments, collected air from different parts of the country so as to provide his guests with a choice of country and town airs. Nicolson, *Science and Imagination*, p. 148, see also pp. 172–3; Claude Lloyd, 'Shadwell and the Virtuoso,' *PMLA* 44 (1929), 472–94.

[46] The king was reported to have ridiculed the Society's weighing of air. R. H. Syfret, 'Some Early Critics of the Royal Society', *Notes and Records of the Royal Society* 8 (1950), 20–64.

[47] Quoted in Michael Hunter, *Science and Society in Restoration England* (Cambridge, 1981), p. 177. See also John Evelyn, *Sylva*, 3rd edn (London, 1679), Preface. Sprat suggests that the wits might do 'more injury than all the Arguments of our severe and frowning and dogmatical Adversaries', *History of the Royal Society*, p. 417.

at such studies as 'Spiders, Lobersteärs, and Sociklesheĺls: . . . the very naming of them is almost sufficient to turn them into raillery'.[48] For all sorts of reasons satire flourished during and after the Restoration. It is, after all, the function of satirists to mock the establishment and particularly that part of it that openly proclaims its own virtues.

The literary world was not fundamentally hostile. Abraham Cowley, a leading poet and early member of the society, provided the laudatory poem prefacing Sprat's *History* as well as a Baconian plan for scientific research. Dryden too was a member of the Society, albeit an nonparticipating one, who expressed enthusiasm for the progress of knowledge.[49]

Only a handful of serious critiques can be found, and they failed to provide any serious threat. Most appeared to be triggered by the public relations efforts of Sprat and Glanvill. Robert Crosse, an elderly Puritan divine with a personal grudge against Glanvill, praised Aristotelian science and accused the Royal Society of being a Jesuit conspiracy. Henry Stubbe, whose vitriolic pen admitted to having once been 'passionately addicted to the New Philosophy' before discovering the Society's antimonarchical and atheistic tendencies, was an idiosyncratic radical, who lambasted Sprat, Glanvill and the Society, defended Aristotle and scholastic logic and portrayed the Society as a popish plot to undermine Church, State and the universities.[50] Such conspiracy-oriented attacks did not prove successful and were largely deflected by the Society's association with the crown.

The most thoughtful critique was offered by Meric Causabon, a traditional scholar and respected clergyman who suggested that the new science ignored ethical issues, led to the neglect of scholarship,

---

[48] *Dialogues upon the Usefulness of Ancient Medals* (London, 1726), pp. 10–11. The same kind of criticism was made of antiquaries.

[49] See Robert Hinman, *Abraham Cowley's World of Order* (Cambridge, MA, 1960); James Anderson Winn, *John Dryden and His World* (New Haven, 1987), pp. 63, 129–30, 133, 173–4; Earl Miner, 'The Poets and Science in Seventeenth Century England', in John Burke (ed.), *The Uses of Science in the Age of Newton* (Berkeley, 1983), pp. 13–14. Poets Edmund Waller and John Denham were also members.

[50] See Jackson Cope, *Joseph Glanvill: Anglican Apologist* (St Louis, 1956), pp. 26–301. For a more sympathetic view of Stubbe see J. R. Jacob, *Henry Stubbe: Radical Protestantism and the Early Enlightenment* (Cambridge, 1983). Stubbe felt that an all-inclusive religious policy promoted popery and that the latitudinarian–Royal Society alliance was dangerous. See also Harold J. Cook, 'Physicians and the new Philosophy: Henry Stubbe and the Virtuosi-Physicians', in Roger French and Andrew Wear (eds.), *The Medical Revolution of the Seventeenth Century* (Cambridge, 1989) pp. 246–71. Stubbe contributed a report on Jamaica to the Royal Society in 1667.

particularly religious scholarship, and promoted a materialistic philosophy leading to atheism and Hobbism. The last charge was rejected by the virtuosi's continuing efforts to show how natural philosophy supported religion and served as an antidote to atheism. Casaubon felt experimental philosophy might be suitable for recreation but must not be allowed to replace more important scholarship. Although his modern interpreter, Michael Spiller, views Casaubon as a man of an earlier generation,[51] the 'Clatter' from Casaubon who had 'so great a Name amongst the Critics and Antiquaries' worried at least one anxious virtuoso.[52] Though discomforted by conspiratorial allegations and satiric treatment, Restoration virtuosi did not face a substantial intellectual or institutional threat.

The importance of natural philosophy in Restoration culture, however, must not be overstated. It was pursued by a relatively small circle of men in London, Oxford and Cambridge and did not dominate cultural life. Neither Aristotelian natural philosophy nor or its Restoration replacement penetrated deeply into the thought patterns of the English population.

The Society did, however, have problems – financing, patronage and relations with court and government. It was least successful in remedying its precarious financial condition and thus remained a royal but largely self-supporting institution constantly worried about poor attendance and the members failure to pay the dues that supported their experimental programme. There were periodic campaigns to gain greater financial security, all of them relatively unsuccessful. Moray worked tirelessly for more royal support and received several never-realized promises. In 1664 the Society was given a grant of the decaying Chelsea College and obtained possession in 1667. Chelsea, virtually unusable, was resold to the crown in 1682 for £1300. Charles ordered a grant to the Society out of Irish debentures but nothing came of it. John Evelyn was disappointed that the Society 'should have found so few Promoters, and so cold a welcome in a Nation whose eyes are so open'.[53]

The Plague and the Fire compounded the Society's difficulties, the former disrupting its meetings in London, the latter destroying its

---

[51] Michael Spiller, '*Concerning Natural Experimental Philosophie*'. *Meric Casaubon and the Royal Society* (The Hague, 1980). Spiller suggests that Casaubon had no personal knowledge of the Royal Society and was reacting to Sprat and Glanvill.

[52] Quoted in Hunter, *Science and Society in Restoration England*, p. 139.

[53] Evelyn, *Sylva*, Preface.

place, Gresham College. Though Lord Howard lent space in Arundel House, the Society lacked space of its own for meetings and experiments.

The Society sought patronage and support in part by making special membership provisions for those of high social status. There was a substantial cluster of elite members though relatively few were active or paid their dues. Meeting at Arundel House (1667–74), a great centre of noble cultural patronage, underlined the elite connections of Society-oriented natural philosophy. *The History of the Royal Society* had an important fund-raising component.[54] Another strategy was to dedicate issues of the *Philosophical Transactions* to highly placed persons such as the duke of Buckingham, Lord Howard of Norfolk and Lord Arlington.[55] The dedication to Sir Joseph Williamson, principal secretary of state, noted the 'steady inclinations, you do on all occasions express to advance the Ingenuous Arts'. Several dedicatees later served as president of the Royal Society. Presidents were consistently chosen from those with good connections in government and at court.[56] The willingness of the elite to lend their names to the Society even without financial support helped to legitimate the scientific enterprise.

Whenever possible the society emphasized its royal foundation. It frequently offered profuse thanks to Charles who was praised for propagating the philosophical arts and the advancement of knowledge.[57] The 'protection' and 'favour' of the king and royal family was characterized as 'the very life, and soul' of the Royal Society.[58]

---

[54] Sprat justified their self-financing. Had they asked for 'mighty Treasures' they would have been condemned as 'Projectors'. They did not require a 'prodigality,' had used their funds wisely and shown that the most 'profitable Tryals are not always the most costly'. But he also warned royal delay in supporting Columbus meant West Indian silver had gone to Seville rather than London. *History of the Royal Society*, pp. 77–80.

[55] Buckingham was the patron of Wilkins and Sprat.

[56] Diplomatic channels were made available for Oldenburg's foreign correspondents. English consuls were expected to write weekly to the secretary of state Williamson, who later became president of the Royal Society. Williamson also requested information on a large variety of topics from English travellers abroad. See Peter Fraser, *The Intelligence of the Secretaries of State and Their Monopoly of Licensed News 1660–1688* (Cambridge, 1956).

[57] *Philosophical Transactions*, no. 92. 25 March 1673.

[58] Sprat, *History of the Royal Society*, p. 133. Sprat suggested that Charles had 'assur'd them of all the kind influence of his Power, and Prerogative'. He 'frequently committed many things to their search; he has referr'd many foreign Rarities to their inspection; he has recommended many domestick improvements to their care; he has demanded the result of their trials, . . . he has been present and assisted with his own hands, at the performing of many of their Experiments, in his Gardens, his Parks, and on the River.' Sprat also suggested that the Charles had even 'sometimes reprov'd them for the slowness of their proceedings' (*ibid*, p. 133).

Letters Patent to the Society emphasized 'Princely affection to all kinds of Learning, and more particular favour to Philosophical Studies. Especially those which endeavour by solid Experiment either to reform or improve Philosophy.' It also proclaimed 'To the intent therefore that these kinds of study, which are no where yet sufficiently cultivated, may flourish in our Dominions; and that the Learned world may acknowledge us to be, not only the Defender of the Faith, but the Patron and Encourager of all sorts of useful Knowledge.'[59] Numerous book dedications and prefaces repeated the message. Efforts to associate experimental work with the king had some success. Lorenzo Maglalotti, visiting England in 1668, indicated that the Society was under the protection of the king. The continental astronomer Hevelius remarked how 'the learned world especially owes humble and eternal Thanks to the king of England . . . because he founded a unique Assembly of those philosophers who cultivate and advance the arts and sciences by following . . . observations and experiments alone'.[60]

The king was cultivated whenever the opportunity arose. We have noted the valuable services of Moray and Brouncker. Wren presented a model of the moon to the king, and several microscopic drawings were included in his 'Collection of Rarities'.[61] Sir Paul Neile, a mathematician with court connections, set up a telescope in the Whitehall Privy Gardens, which was at least on one occasion used by Neile, Evelyn, Brouncker and the king to make observations of Saturn. There were occasional experiments and anatomical dissections in the royal presence.[62] Oldenburg expressed regret that Wren

59 *Ibid.*, p. 134. Sprat's epitome of the Society's Letters Patent emphasized the royal commitment 'to promote the welfare of Arts and Sciences' (*ibid.*, p. 134).

60 See *Lorenzo Maglalotti at the Court of Charles II. Relazaione d'Inghilterra of 1668*, ed. and trans. W. E. Knowles Middleton (Waterloo, Ontario, 1980), p. 134; Oldenburg, *Correspondence*, II, 138. See also II, 14. Charles II was characterized as 'a second Apollo' for his patronage of learning as well as 'a great favourer of Learning' (*ibid.*, VII, 16). See also Birch, *History of the Royal Society*, I, 28, Sprat, *History of the Royal Society*, p. 133.

61 Robert Hooke, *Micrographia* (London, 1665), Preface. Moray and Neile told Wren that the king wanted him 'to delineate by the Help of the Microscope the Figures of all the Insects, and small living Creatures' like those he presented to the king. Stephen Wren (ed.), *Parentalia* (London, 1750), p. 210. Wren, however, was unable to finish the task and asked Hooke to complete it. The king also requested that rarities sent to the Royal Society by John Winthrop be brought to Whitehall. Moray steadily reported Royal Society activities to the king. Birch, *History of the Royal Society*, I, 320, 420; II, 5, 115, 375.

62 Sprat, *History*, p. 234. Hartley, *Royal Society*, pp. 42–3; Marjorie Nicolson, *Pepys' Diary and the New Science* (Charlottesville, VA, 1965), pp. 135–6. Several members were physicians to the king. Bathurst was chaplain to the king and Ward and Wilkins preached before him on several occasions.

had not submitted his model for rebuilding London to the Society before presenting it at court so that it might have the Royal Society name attached to it.

The king's personal interest in natural philosophy was intermittent and probably never serious. Charles pursued some experiments during his exile and brought the Helmontian physician Lefevre back to England. On returning to England the king had some kind of laboratory, with Moray in charge, and placed Robert Morison, a leading naturalist, in charge of the royal gardens. Although distinguished foreign visitors often visited the Society, the king's projected visit never materialized. Although Charles founded a mathematical school at Christ's Hospital in 1673 and the Royal Observatory in Greenwich (1675), they were created primarily for potential navigational benefits. Connections between navigation, astronomy and scientific instrumentation were important, as the continuing search for an accurate and practical method of determining longitude suggests.[63]

Like Bacon, Sprat had tried to show that the Society's work was 'so vast that it cannot be performed without the assistance of the Prince' and that experimental work coincided with the interest of the state.[64] Failure to gain substantial royal financial backing should not be particularly surprising. English governments, royal and otherwise, did not have a tradition of providing lavish outlays for intellectual activities. Plans for a Royal Academy also faltered. Indifference by the political establishment to its financial needs caused the Society hardship but it also permitted the pursuit of whatever relatively inexpensive scientific activities were desired without substantial external control.

The gift of the king's name was nevertheless of great importance. It provided respectability, legitimized the pursuit of natural philosophy and probably helped to limit criticism. Particularly in the early days of the Restoration, who would reject what the king sanctioned? Mere existence of the Royal Charter provided an assumption of royal support.

Institutionalization, however brought problems as well as advan-

---

[63] See Frances Willmoth, 'Mathematical Sciences and Military Technology: the Ordnance Office in the Reign of Charles II', in J. V. Field and Frank James (eds.), *Renaissance and Revolution: Humanists, Scholars, Craftsmen and Natural Philosophers in Early Modern Europe* (Cambridge, 1993), pp. 117–31.

[64] See Julius Martin, *Francis Bacon: the State and the Reform of Natural Philosophy* (Cambridge, 1992).

tages. Since active participation was largely limited to metropolitan residents, the success of the Society's experimental programme depended on relatively few regular participants. There were periodic crises associated with reduced attendance, reluctance to provide experiments and a poor record of dues payment. On the other hand, institutionalization meant that these ups and downs could be weathered more easily than in previous decades because the Society had a legal status and mechanisms for continued existence when participation flagged.

The creation of the Royal Society provided a visible representation of English science identifiable by Englishmen and foreigners alike. The 'invisible colleges' of earlier decades were now clearly visible. Such visibility on the whole proved desirable though it also provided critics a target on which to focus their attacks.[65]

To what extent did the Society embody the cultural goals of the restored monarchy? Given the limited nature of royal support and the absence of parliamentary interest, it does not seem reasonable to think of Restoration science as part of a socially conservative, monarchical, cultural programme. Scholarly efforts to show that everything not vigorously repressed should be seen as deeply implicated in the regime have produced some rather strange results, e.g. that the universal language schemes of Wilkins and Dalgarno should be seen as part of the Restoration's repressive programme.[66] The argument ignores earlier seventeenth-century interest, the fact that these language schemes were largely interregnum products and that they failed badly. Failure to give sufficient weight to continuities can lead to serious interpretive distortions.

My overview of Restoration natural philosophy suggests considerable continuity throughout the seventeenth century in the style, content and personnel and its relation to the universities. The Restoration does introduce a new institutionalization in the Royal Society, which rendered science more visible and legitimate and

---

[65] Institutionalism has also been fortunate for historians since much of what we know about Restoration natural philosophy comes from the archival records of the Royal Society, the *Philosophical Transactions* and Society-sponsored publications.

[66] See Joel Reed, 'Restoration and Repression: the Language Projects of the Royal Society', *Studies in Eighteenth Century Culture* 19 (1989), 379–412. Robert Stillman's 'Invitation and Engagement: Ideology and Wilkins's Philosophical Language', *Configurations* 1 (1995), 1–26 also treats Wilkins's *Essay Towards a Real Character and a Philosophical Language* as embodying Restoration political and economic ideology, despite the fact that most of work on the project was done during the interregnum and many Royal Society members were dubious about its value.

provided a centralized correspondence network, and the publication of the *Philosophical Transactions*. Yet the Society had clear antecedents in pre-Restoration scientific groups. The continued importance of Baconianism is one of the major continuities but one that did not prevent important changes in the conceptualization and practice of natural philosophy. I have noted the limited but nevertheless very important royal support that came with the Restoration and suggested that criticism of Restoration investigation of natural philosophy in that period was never a serious threat to scientific practice or its further development. If by 1688 English science did not dominate intellectual life, natural philosophy had gained a secure, legitimate position, and the Royal Society had become the visible symbol of scientific life in England.

1688–1714

We now turn to the 1688–1714 era, querying whether changes in natural philosophy should be attributed to the revolution of 1688 and its political and religious aftermath. The first change resulted from Newton's *Principia* of 1687, which combined the Copernican astronomy, Galilean physics and insights of Kepler into a single system described mathematically. Newton's mathematization of nature and natural laws altered the character and goals of natural philosophy. His work appeared to modify the tentative, modest approach associated with Boyle and Restoration science and to promise greater certainty in natural philosophy. Newton now replaced Boyle as the exemplar of English natural philosophy. Locke saw Newton as a great luminary whose laws of nature transformed natural philosophy. While previous 'systems of physics' afforded 'little encouragment to look for certainty or science . . . the incomparable Mr Newton has shown, how far mathematics, applied to some parts of nature, may, upon principles that matter of fact can justify, carry us in the knowledge of some . . . particular provinces of the incomprehensible universe.'[67] Newton's

---

[67] John Locke, *On Education*, ed. P. Gay (New York, 1964), p. 160. See G. A. J. Rogers, 'Locke's *Essay* and Newton's *Principia*', *Journal of the History of Ideas* 39 (1978), 217–37. Current views of Newton, the result of the research of R. S. Westfall and Betty Jo Dobbs, suggest a different and more complex figure who searched for boundaries between God and nature and seriously attempted to use alchemy and biblical prophecies to construct a unified system. His published works took a small portion of his intellectual energies.

difficult work required popularization in the form of public lectures, sermons and new textbooks.

The Royal Society continued to experience ups and downs.[68] The *Philosophical Transactions*, in abeyance between 1687 and 1691, revived under Sir Hans Sloane. Newton became president of the Royal Society in 1703, dominating it for twenty-five years.[69] Here Newtonianism coexisted with natural history, and the more hypotheses-oriented endeavours of earlier decades. Sloane, president prior to Newton, continued to insist that the 'Knowledge of Natural History, being Matter of fact, is more certain than [theories] . . . and less subject to Mistakes than Reasonings, Hypotheses and Deductions are.'[70]

The publication of John Locke's 1690 *Essay concerning Human Understanding*, which generalized a sense-based empirical epistemology had great impact. Locke's 1693 statement that a gentleman to be 'fit for Conversation' should look into modern systems of natural philosophy[71] suggests that at least a passing familiarity with science was now expected of the ruling elite, some of whom were attending public lectures designed to facilitate the spread of scientific knowledge to broader audiences.[72]

The Revolution resulted in a latitudinarian takeover of the higher echelons of university and church. At Oxford Newtonians David Gregory and John Keill occupied the Savilian chairs of astronomy and Edmund Halley the chair in geometry. A defensive and un-successful minority before 1688, latitudinarians now filled the ranks of the bishops. John Tillotson, son-in-law of John Wilkins and friend of Robert Hooke, became archbishop of Canterbury. The church, however, remained divided. Indeed recently it has been suggested that late Stuart Anglicanism can be more accurately characterized as a conflict between Tories and Whigs than as a support for an ancient regime based on deference.[73]

---

[68] It continued to have financial and attendance problems but was able to purchase a building in 1710. Hunter, *The Royal Society*, pp. 44, 48–9.

[69] By 1703 Newton was an experienced public servant who served as Master of the Mint.

[70] Hans Sloane, *A Voyage to the Islands* (London, 1701) quoted in Harold Cooke, 'The Cutting Edge of a Revolution: Medicine and Natural History on the Shore of the North Sea', in Field and James (eds.), *Renaissance and Revolution*, p. 49.

[71] John Locke, *Some Thoughts on Education* (London, 1693), p. 230.

[72] These combined entertainment and serious treatment and were directed at a mixed gentlemanly and merchant audience. See Larry Stewart, *The Rise of Public Science: Rhetoric, Technology and Natural Philosophy in Newtonian Britain* (Cambridge, 1992).

[73] The problem of how to characterize the English church in the post-1688 era has attracted

The alliance between natural philosophy and natural theology thrived in the new environment. Cambridge is said to have witnessed a 'holy alliance' between Newtonian natural philosophy and Anglican latitudinarianism and natural theology.[74] John Ray's *Wisdom of God Manifested in the Creation* (1691), which utilized natural knowledge to prove the existence of God, was extraordinarily successful and the Boyle lectures (1692–1714) provided a public exposition of Newtonianism and latitudinarianism.[75] Some post-Newtonian latitudinarians attempted to establish theories of the earth as an exact science controlled by fixed laws and divine providence. In 1696 the Deluge was said to be 'the Subject of most of the Philosophical Conversations of the Virtuosi about the Town'.[76]

Patronage patterns changed remarkably little. Neither late Stuart monarchs nor aristocrats provided significant financial support. Declaring that 'the Business and Studies of the Society' were for 'public not private Advantage', Newton sought royal financial aid to assist the Royal Society's move from Gresham to its own quarters[77] but had little more success than Bacon so many years earlier. The Hampton Court Gardens, under the patronage of Queen Mary, however, provided a rich botanical collection. Queen Anne was said to converse with Newton.[78] The archbishop of Canterbury and

the attention of Jonathan Clark and his critics. See J. C. D. Clark, *English Society, 1688–1832* (Cambridge, 1985); Gascoigne, *Cambridge*; William Watson, 'Rethinking the Late Stuart Church: the Extent of Liberal Anglicanism, 1688–1715', paper presented at the Pacific Coast Branch of the Conference on British Studies, 1996. For Oxford see G. V. Bennett, 'Loyalist Oxford and the Revolution', in *The History of the University of Oxford: the Eighteenth Century*, pp. 9–30; G. V. Bennett, 'Against the Tide: Oxford Under William III', in *Ibid.*, pp. 31–60; G. V. Bennett, 'The Era of Party Zeal', in *ibid.*, pp. 61–98; G. V. Bennett, 'University, Society and Church 1688–1714', in *ibid.*, pp. 359–400; Larry Stewart, 'Samuel Clarke, Newtonianism and the Factions of Post Revolutionary England', *Journal of the History of Ideas* 42 (1981), 53–71.

[74] Gascoigne, *Cambridge*, pp. 72, 73, 142–84. Gascoigne traces the reshaping of the natural philosophy curriculum. Changes were slowed by an initial lack of simplified textbooks.

[75] M. C. Jacob, *The Newtonians and the English Revolution 1689–1720* (Ithaca, NY, 1976).

[76] The theories of the 1690s would have been impossible without the work of earlier fieldworkers. Newton initially thought Burnet's theory 'the most plausible account' but later gave his approval to Whiston's. Roy Porter, *Making of Geology: Earth Science in Britain 1660–1815* (Cambridge, 1977), pp. 23, 34, 35, 51, 63, 79, 83. Newtonianism was also accepted by Tories and nonlatitudinarians. See Stewart, 'Samuel Clarke, Newtonianism, and the Factions of Post-Revolutionary England', pp. 53–72; Anita Guerrini, 'The Tory Newtonians: Gregory, Pitcairne and their Circle', *Journal of British Studies* 10 (1977), 288–311.

[77] Quoted in John Heilbrun, *Physics at the Royal Society under Newton's Presidency* (Los Angeles, 1983), p. 17. Newton and Sloane were able to raise some government funds (*ibid.*, p. 18). See also Michael Hunter, 'The Crown, the Public and the New Science 1689–1702', *Notes and Records of the Royal Society* 43 (1989), p. 116.

[78] Bernard de Fontenelle, *The Elogium of Sir Isaac Newton* (London, 1708), reproduced in I. B.

Henry Compton, the bishop of London, also supported the creation of the Society of Chemical Physicians.[79] Compton, a generous patron of botanical studies, was responsible for creating one of the most important botanical gardens of the late-seventeenth century.

English governments in all periods sought to increase information, especially relating to taxes and state resources, but few efforts in this direction by post-1688 governments can be directly linked to natural philosophy.[80] The government's 1713 order that ambassadors, admirals and officers going abroad should 'receive directions and instructions from the Royal Society for making enquiries relating to the improvement of natural philosophy'[81] only made official the long-standing practice of the Society. The application of Newtonian science to commercial and industrial life has, like that of Baconianism, been much discussed and debated. As of yet no consensus has emerged.

Natural philosophy still faced no dangerous enemies, though high churchmen sometimes grumbled and continued in their preference for biblical and patristic scholarship. The controversy between ancients and moderns, which had its origins in the Restoration, began in earnest in 1697 but focused more on moral and literary than scientific issues[82] because few supporters of the ancients were prepared to argue that ancient natural philosophy was the superior. It is sometimes difficult to know who should be classed as a critic or how seriously to take their critiques. Joseph Addison often praised natural philosophy, but on occasion he suggests that naturalists dealt with trivia.

The key changes of these years were the impact of Newtonian

Cohen, *Isaac Newton: Letters and Papers* (Cambridge, MA, 1978), p. 466. Newton was knighted in 1705, two years after becoming the president of the Royal Society. Fontenelle noted that Newton, like 'persons of the greatest quality and sometimes crowned heads', was buried in Westminster Abbey and that six peers were Newton's pall bearers (*ibid.*, p. 471).

[79] See Harold J. Cook, 'The Society of Chemical Physicians, the New Philosophy, and the Restoration Court', *Bulletin of the History of Medicine* 61 (1987), 61–77. The duke of Buckingham and twelve other peers were involved. Eleven were already or about to be fellows of the Royal Society.

[80] Political arithmetic, which originated during the Restoration, increased the ability to calculate state resources. The Inspector General of Imports and Exports, the first government department devoted to statistical compilation, was created in 1696. John Brewer, *War, Money and the English State, 1688–1783* (Cambridge, MA, 1990), pp. 121–6.

[81] Quoted in Heilbrun, *Physics at the Royal Society*, p. 25.

[82] The Battle of the Books was more about whether the ancients were superior to modern philological criticism. See Joseph M. Levine, *The Battle of the Book: History and Literature in the Augustan Age* (Ithaca, NY, 1991).

science and the alliance of natural philosophy with the latitudinarianism of the post-Revolutionary church.

ENGLAND AND FRANCE

But were the developments I have been describing peculiarly English? English historians have rightly focused on the Royal Society. But the institutionalization of science was not peculiarly English nor especially new. Italy led the way with the Academia dei Lincei and the Academia del Cimento. The French Academy of Sciences was founded at approximately the same time as the Royal Society. In France, however, institutionalization was fostered by the monarchy which attempted to bring existing academies and private scientific groups under its control.[83] Academicians were coopted into a governmental structure that expected loyalty to the regime. In France science was part of a large-scale cultural programme assigned to a crown minister. The crown provided salaries and support that made long-term and large-scale projects possible but also exercised supervision. Although science remained an avocation for some, the Academy created a cadre of full-time salaried scientific professionals.[84] The Royal Society, less well supported, with a more eclectic membership, experienced greater independence.

Like its English counterpart, the Academy changed over time. Fontenelle's 1699 description of Academy ideology was remarkably similar to Sprat and Glanvill's earlier apologias. Fontenelle distinguished fact and conjecture, emphasized experimentation and rejected dogmatism and the domination of any single system. Like the Royal Society the Academy adopted an anti-authoritarian stance and rejected dogmatic systems. The Academy too insisted it would not encroach on teaching institutions and excluded religious topics.

---

[83] Marin Mersenne had operated a complex European-wide correspondence network roughly analogous to that of Hartlib and Oldenburg.

[84] See Roger Hahn, *The Anatomy of a Scientific Institution: the Paris Academy of Sciences, 1666–1803* (Berkeley, 1971). See also see Roger Hahn, 'The Age of Academies', in T. Frangsmyr (ed.), *Solomon's House Revisited: the Organization and Institutionalization of Science* (Canton, MA, 1990). Colbert's plan was modified by pressure from the guilds, the faculties of medicine, law and theology and the Académie Française. David Lux, 'The Reorganization of Science 1450–1700', *Patronage and Institutions: Science, Technology, and Medicine at the European Court: 1500–1750* (New York, 1991). See also David Lux, *Patronage of Royal Science in Seventeenth Century France: the Académie de physique in Caen* (Ithaca, NY, 1989); David Lux, 'Societies, Circles, Academies: a Historiographical Essay on Seventeenth Century Science', in Barker and Ariew (eds.), *Revolution and Continuity* pp. 23–43.

The influence of Bacon and Newton was stronger in England, in part because Newton was felt by many in France to have reintroduced occult causes.[85]

The Academy too cultivated the acquisition of information from distant locales though greater French resources allowed it to organize expeditions and to build an observatory housing both meetings and research activities. Contrast the hand-to-mouth existence of the Royal Society in constant search for permanent quarters. Continental natural philosophy was not solely dependent on princely support. The church and especially the Jesuits were responsible for many important contributions to modern physics.

Looking at the English scene, one is immediately struck by the importance of the *Philosophical Transactions*. But the scientific journal was not a peculiarly English development. The *Journal des Savans* (1665) began the same year. Serial publication on intellectual topics was a characteristic feature of the 1660–90 cultural landscape.

French virtuosi found a less congenial home in the universities and had to face, at least for a time, the hostility of the Sorbonne. Although several important early French natural philosophers, e.g. Mersenne and Gassendi, were associated with religious orders, natural philosophy in France encountered more hostility from the clerical establishment than in England. Early-eighteenth-century *philosophes* thus preached a virulent anticlericalism largely, though not completely, absent from England. If both English and French naturalists emphasized national pride and national interest, they also expressed universalist and cosmopolitan goals associated with the 'Republic of Letters'.[86] Natural philosophers, like Renaissance humanists and their scholarly successors, participated in a European as well a national intellectual life.

CONCLUSION

We have examined several facets of English science employing traditional English political periodization and have taken a glance at France. If what we have described for England suggests more

---

[85] Newton was invited to become a member of the Academy in 1699.

[86] See Lorraine Daston, 'The Idea and Reality of the Republic of Letters in the Enlightenment', *Science in Context* 2 (1991) 367–86; and Anne Goldgar, *Impolite Learning: Conduct and Commentary on the Republic of Letters 1680–1750* (New Haven, 1995). Christiaan Huyghens was invited to head the new French academy and the Italian Cassini headed its observatory.

continuity than periodic change, we might erase the political markers and tell the story of English natural philosophy as a narrative characterized by continuity and incremental change. Such a narrative need not adopt an internalist or a Whiggish stance. We can place scientific development and activity amidst an ever-changing social and political context without assuming, in advance, that particular political regimes were responsible for particular modifications in the nature and practice of natural philosophy.

My cursory survey of English developments suggests a good deal of continuity with respect to governmental support, the absence of major threats and the relationship between science and the universities. Organized religion was neither a formidable obstacle nor a constant ally. The alliance with latitudinarianism was sometimes an asset and sometimes a liability. There were critics to be sure, but none so destructive as to undermine or prevent continued growth. From the 1630s and 1640s onward we can begin to see the coexistence and sometimes combination of a Baconian-style natural history and experimentalism, Harvean medical and physiological research and a mathematical–physical tradition. The only major development that appears to correspond to changes of political regimes is the founding of the Royal Society. On the one hand that event constituted only the institutionalization of previous scientific groups and came at the initiative of members of those groups rather than the crown. On the other, the institutionalization constituted a major step in the legitimization and visibility of English science. So the story may be told as either one of continuity of scientific development or a discontinuity linked to political discontinuity.

If it is not particularly useful to speak of Restoration science, we should also question whether we can usefully speak of English science. My all too brief glance at the continent suggests the desirability of a more European perspective. I think the case can be made for viewing English science as a distinct regional variant of a European cultural movement. This would allow us to recognize the role of Baconianism and the Harvean medical tradition as well as a European-wide mathematically oriented physics. It would allow us to recognize the immense importance of the Royal Society and the *Philosophical Transactions*, keeping in mind that institutionalization and serial scientific publication were not uniquely English. A more comparative approach would place us in a better position to assess whether or not the aristocratic courtesy tradition, stronger in France than England, played a critical role in English natural philosophy. It would also shed light on the role and extent of university participation in the development of natural philosophy. Placing English natural philosophy in a more European context might provide a better sense of how and why England, something of a scientific backwater early in the seventeenth century, moved to the forefront so rapidly, resulting in foreign emulation of English accomplishments. We could more easily determine whether the quickening pace of English scientific work was replicated elsewhere and whether the quickening owed something to religious and political disruption.

Viewing England as a national variant of a European-wide movement would almost certainly lead to a reduced concentration on changes in English politics. An England viewed in relation to France, Italy and the Netherlands would emphasize England's participation in a European cultural development, but it would simultaneously help us see the unique features of English scientific culture. We might fruitfully adopt the model of historians of humanism, who have described a European movement with significant chronological, national and regional variations. Yet given our continuing propensity to focus on nation states we should recognize that it is very likely that narratives of English science will continue to be produced.[87]

I would like to end with a speculation about what kinds of narratives of English science might be produced employing some current interpretations of English history and how other contemporary interpretive concerns might affect the treatment of English science. There are a number of political chronologies that currently shape thinking about English life. One places great emphasis on dynasties – the Tudors or the Stuarts; another utilizes the notion of the long eighteenth century, a century that acquires half of another and tends to view the Restoration as either a new beginning or a prelude to something else. Such a history may safely ignore early- and mid-seventeenth-century developments in natural philosophy. For others the Restoration and 1688 are viewed as codas to the religious and constitutional conflicts of the seventeenth century with natural philosophy likely to be ignored or slighted. Some see the 1640–60 era as an aberrant interruption, while for others it represents a highpoint that expressed progressive values that would not be

---

[87] See R. Porter and M. Teich (eds.), *The Scientific Revolution in National Context* (Cambridge, 1992).

embodied again until much later or were driven underground. The latter characterization typically treats the Restoration as an unfortunate return to a repressive political regime and the Royal Society and Restoration science either as supports for an undesirable political regime or subversive of it. Still others see the seventeenth and eighteenth centuries together as harbingers of the liberal state or as an *ancien regime* characterized by deference and domination of the church. My point is that each of these large visions of English political history carries a good deal of baggage with it that affects how the story of English science is to be characterized. Moreover as literary scholars return to cultural history their periodizations and concepts such as the 'Augustan Age' too influence proclivities to see Restoration natural philosophy in a positive or negative light. If few cultural historians are now likely to tell a simple Whiggish narrative of the advancement of learning and enlightenment, some are tempted to replace it with an equally simple account of class and gendered oppression or as the harbinger of a despised Enlightenment whose rationalist values should be rejected.

My focus here has been primarily on England though I believe it will be more fruitful to consider English natural philosophy as one of several regional variants in a Europe-wide movement. I have reviewed some of the characteristics of seventeenth-century English natural philosophy using the most traditional political chronology in the hope of assessing the value of political divisions in understanding the development of English scientific practice. My conclusion is that such divisions tend to obscure a rather continuous development and that the role of governments, royal or nonroyal, as helpmate or hindrance changed relatively little. No English ruler or government exhibited a desire to provide support comparable to that of Louis XIV and Colbert. Against this conclusion must be set the institutionalization of English science in the Royal Society, a development surely linked to regime change. Yet I remain inclined to count the continuities of scientific personnel, endeavours and informal social organization more heavily than the one-time, largely symbolic, government intervention.

Index

We thank Ryan Frace for helping make this index.